Double Award

Level

for OCR

el &

sm

Sue Stewart

www.heinemann.co.uk
✓ Free online support
✓ Useful weblinks
✓ 24 hour online ordering

01865 888058

Heinemann Educational Publishers
Halley Court, Jordan Hill, Oxford OX2 8EJ
Part of Harcourt Education

Heinemann is the registered trademark of
Harcourt Education Limited

© Hilary Blackman, Ann Rowe, John D. Smith, Sue Stewart, 2005

First published 2005

10 09 08 07 06 05
10 9 8 7 6 5 4 3 2 1

British Library Cataloguing in Publication Data is available
from the British Library on request.

ISBN 0 435 44641 X

Designed by Lorraine Inglis
Typeset by 🅃 Tek-Art, Croydon, Surrey
Original illustrations © Harcourt Education Limited, 2005

Cover design by Wooden Ark Studio
Printed in the UK by Bath Press Ltd
Cover photo: © Alamy
Picture research by Bea Thomas

Acknowledgements
Every effort has been made to contact copyright holders of material reproduced
in this book. Any omissions will be rectified in subsequent printings if notice is
given to the publishers.

Websites
Please note that the examples of websites suggested in this book were up to
date at the time of writing. It is essential for tutors to preview each site before
using it to ensure that the URL is still accurate and the content is appropriate.
We suggest that tutors bookmark useful sites and consider enabling students to
access them through the school or college intranet.

Tel: 01865 888058 www.heinemann.co.uk

Contents

Acknowledgements

The author and publisher would like to thank all who have given permission to reproduce material.

Alton Towers – page 261
Amadeus – page 234
Association of British Tour Operators (ABTA) – page 316
Aston Business School, Aston University – page 85
Barcelona City Council Tourist Information – pages 111–12
Billing Aquadrome – page 7
Blencathra Field Centre, the Field Studies Council, www.field-studies-council.org – pages 117–9
Cambridge Internal Examinations – page 215
Cambridge University Press – page 77
Civil Aviation Authority – pages 132, 210
Columbus Travel – page 97
Co-op Travelcare – page 25
Council for National Parks – pages 172, 173
Creativity Travel, www.CreativityTravel.com – page 295
Cresta Holidays Ltd – page 85
Crowne Plaza Hotel (Centre Island Hotels) – page 151
Daily Mail – page 63
Department of Culture Media and Sport – page 201
Department of Trade and Industry, www.dti.gov.uk – page 317
Department of Transport – pages 139, 141
Diggerland – page 30
Eden Project – page 181
European Tourism Conference – page 202
Eurostar page 308
Expedia and Lastminute – page 222
Falcon's Nest Hotel – page 44
Fast Track 100 Ltd – page 26
First Choice – page 297
Fylde Travel Services Ltd – page 211
Government of Dubai Department of Tourism and Commerce Marketing – pages 103, 107
Great North Eastern Railway (GNER) – page 80
Gulf Air – page 144
Holiday Inn – page 33
Holidaybreak – page 310
Horizons for Success (Horizons FS Ltd) – pages 269, 270
Huntingdon Marriott Hotel – pages 275, 275, 277, 279
Huntingdon Racecourse – page 273
Isle of Man Government – page 49
Isle of Man Transport – page 48
Lake District National Park Authority – page 195
Lily Publications – pages 41, 45, 47
Liverpool Culture Co – page 177
Liverpool Tourist Information – page 149
London Eye – page 188
Madame Tussauds – page 191
Manchester Airport Group plc – pages 89–90, 134, 135
Manx National Heritage – pages 42–3
National Trust – pages 28, 61, 184, 198
Northampton Borough Council – page 27
Norwich Area Tourism Agency – page 32
Old Rectory Hotel, Chris & Sally Entwistle – page 24
Ordnance Survey, map reproduced from Ordnance Survey mapping on behalf of Her Majesty's Stationery Office © Crown Copyright 100000230/2005

Oxford Illustrators – page 239
P&O Cruises – pages 78, 243
Peak Village – pages 178
Port Aventura – page 113
Port of Dover – pages 137, 138
Premier Holidays Limited – page 46
Queen Adelaide public house – page 258
Ramblers' Association – page 171
Ramsgate Costumed Walks, Ramsgate Tourist Information Centre – page 35
Rheged – pages 187, 262, 269
Ryanair – page 60
Saga – page 80
Salmon Picture Company, Postcard copyright The Salmon Picture Company © – page 3
Sandringham, By Gracious Permission of Her Majesty the Queen – page 30
Sefton Council, www.visitsouthport.com – page 115
Solo Syndication – pages 189, 313
South Lakes Wild Animal Park – page 179
Springboard UK – pages 56, 58, 80
Star UK, www.staruk.org.uk – pages 9, 10, 12
Sunday Times © NI Syndication, London, 5 September 2004 – page 99
Sycamore Inn – page 252
The Deep – page 180
The Times © NI Syndication, London, 4 August 2001 – page 297
Tourism South East (Welcome Host) – pages 52–3
Tourisma for All – page 200
Tradewinds – page 157
Travel Bag (ebookers plc) – page 163
TUI UK (Thomson/Lunn Poly) – pages 216, 220, 223, 232, 241
Virgin Trains – page 87
VisitBritain – pages 27, 201, 202, 205
Waddesdon Manor – page 28
Which? – pages 313, 318
World Tourism Organisation – page 4
World Trade Organisation – page 11
York Hospitality Association – page 65

Photo Acknowledgements

Alamy – pages 14, 30, 38, 101 (top), 102 (top), 105, 117, 138, 153, 172, 175, 181, 188, 226, 258, 259, 260, 267, 281
British Airways – page 2
British Waterways – page 38
Corbis – pages 252, 282
Corbis/Harcourt Education – pages 179, 304
CrystalSki – page 310
The Deep – page 180
Empics – page 133
Getty – pages 136, 198, 254
Dubailand – page 102 (bottom)
Getty/Robert Harding – page 109
Getty News and Sport – pages 78, 101
Huntingdon Racecourse Holdings Trust Ltd – page 271
Milepost 92½ page 76
P&O Stena Line – page 16
The Palm/Nakheel – page 102 (middle)
John D. Smith – pages 105, 108
Sycamore Inn – page 252
TravelCare – page 231

Introduction

Travel and tourism is a very exciting industry. You might be surprised at the range of opportunities for employment within the industry, or for further study if you proceed to the A2 level. As the industry is also growing rapidly, there is likely to be an increase in the employment opportunities open to you.

About the OCR qualification

By studying for this qualification, you will gain an understanding of the skills employers in the travel and tourism industry are looking for, and you will have an opportunity to develop skills in information technology, communication and application of number – as well as working as part of a team and developing your own performance. If you are working towards Key Skills, many of the tasks you undertake will help you develop those skills. The OCR qualification itself may also complement your work for other AS levels, such as Geography, and if you are studying languages you will find that these are very relevant within the travel and tourism industry.

The AS course should help you to:

* develop your interest in travel and tourism, the issues affecting the industry and their potential effects on employment opportunities

* assess the scale and importance of the industry, and of the interrelationships between its components

* appreciate the huge importance of customers to the industry

* develop the relevant practical and technical skills

* observe the global and dynamic nature of the industry, how people, environments and issues change, and how the industry responds to these changes

* gain an understanding of the impact of information and communication technology (ICT) on the future development of the industry

* appreciate the significance of the values and attitudes of key stakeholders

* develop your own values and attitudes in relation to travel and tourism issues

* use skills of research, evaluation and problem-solving.

As the course leading to the OCR qualification is vocational, it is very important that you actually have an opportunity to participate in the industry. This may be through a work placement, a part-time job, or by participating in visits to travel and tourism organisations and destinations. At the end of the course the knowledge, understanding and skills you have developed should assist you in gaining employment at operational level in direct contact with customers. You might decide to progress to the Advanced GCE course after successful completion of the AS.

Understanding the marking scheme

You will notice that the assessment evidence grids in the specification have three mark bands for each Assessment Objective (AO). These are all progressive, so to reach the second mark band you need to make sure you have addressed all the points in the first mark band and used the specification to guide you as to the content. Marks are awarded for each Assessment Objective according to your level of performance, then the totals for each assessment objective are added together to give a final marks score for that unit. You may achieve quite high marks for one of the objectives, but fewer marks for another, but it is your total marks for the unit that will be used to decide your final grade for the whole qualification.

As an example of this scoring, consider the assessment evidence grid for unit 5 on Tourist Attractions.

* If your work for AO1 shows ability to compare and contrast two UK visitor attractions, one from the private sector and one from the public or voluntary sector, which gives details of ownership, funding and the way each manages its operations according to the varying values and attitudes of each organisation, then this would lead to work within Mark Band 3. If you also demonstrate good understanding, knowledge of tourist attractions and their function in the travel and tourism industry, and there are no omissions, this confirms Mark Band 3. The presentation of your work should be coherent and clear as well as being well organised and include a

bibliography or list of source data, then this might achieve 15 marks for AO1.

* In AO2, you might also manage to compare and contrast the technological features of each of your chosen attractions. You might give some details of the success and suitability of these features which enhance the customer and staff experiences at the attractions. Again, if the work shows clarity and coherence and is presented logically with good use of appropriate terminology, this could be awarded 12 marks (as your coverage of the successes and suitability of the features is not comprehensive) for AO2.

* Looking at AO3, your research might be from limited sources which did not fully reflect an understanding of the importance of visitor and traffic management at the two attractions, and the research might not be very relevant to the task nor the findings appropriately analysed, this would only fall within Mark Band 1, possibly meriting 3 marks for AO3.

* Then for AO4 you may have made some use of the research data to compare the two visitor attractions in terms of target markets and how these affect the popularity of your two chosen organisations but there may be some omissions in your comparison, though these are relatively minor. This could reflect work within Mark Band 2, and might only be awarded 6 marks for AO4.

Your total marks for this unit would therefore be 15 + 12 + 3 + 6, making 36 out of a possible 50 marks.

About this book

This book has been prepared to help you understand the units of the OCR qualification. There is a chapter for each of the units covered within the qualification, written by senior examiners and moderators who have been involved with the development of the units. Each chapter will give you the relevant knowledge required for that unit, with lots of activities and discussion points to help you develop this understanding and apply it to various situations. There is also guidance given as to what is required for the assessment of the unit.

Each unit links very closely to the OCR syllabus. The 'What You Need to Learn' section of the specification is mirrored in the presentation of the units, so it will be easy for you to ensure you have covered all the knowledge elements. It is advisable to work through each unit thoroughly, rather than 'dropping into' a section – you might not then see the whole picture and your understanding will not be as thorough. To gain higher marks in the assessment (whether it is examination or portfolio) you will need to demonstrate a thorough understanding of that particular unit in the evidence you present to examiners or moderators.

Special features of this book

* **Think it over** is designed to provoke discussion on issues arising as you study.

* **Case studies** will give you an insight into real events and people you may encounter and provide opportunities for discussion in your class groups.

* **Theory into practice** activities are opportunities to work with others and implement the knowledge you will gain as you work through each unit.

* **Assessment guidance** tells you more specifically how you can meet the evidence requirements for the unit.

* **Knowledge check** is there to aid your revision.

Keep up to date!

At the time of writing this book, all the information was current and relevant. However, travel and tourism is a very dynamic industry and subject to many changes. Hotel groups may be taken over, organisations may change their names or logos, governments may pass new regulations which affect the industry, and so on. It is important that you not only use the information within this book but also keep up to date with developments. You will need to discuss issues with employers in the industry, as well as reading relevant articles in the daily, weekend and trade press to ensure that you are aware of these developments and how they affect the industry as a whole.

Enjoy your studies!

UNIT 1

Introducing travel and tourism

Introduction

This unit sets the scene for your programme of study for the GCE Travel and Tourism qualification. It is an important unit as it lays the foundation for study in many of the other units for the qualification.

This unit will provide an overarching understanding of one of the world's fastest-growing industries. You will investigate the reasons for the rapid growth in the modern travel and tourism industry and understand why it is commonly referred to as 'the world's biggest industry'. You will learn that the UK travel and tourism industry is made up of a wide variety of commercial and non-commercial organisations that interact to supply products and services to tourists. You will develop appreciation of the different values and attitudes of these organisations in travel and tourism. You will learn about the present significance of the industry to the UK economy.

Within this unit you will be able to develop vocational skills related to the travel and tourism industry – in particular, selecting and interpreting appropriate data, problem-solving and understanding and applying industry-related terminology.

How you will be assessed

The unit is assessed by an external examination of two hours' duration. Before the exam you will receive case study materials, which you can use to prepare thoroughly for the test.

What you need to learn

* the nature of travel and tourism
* the scale of the travel and tourism industry
* the development of the modern travel and tourism industry
* the structure of the travel and tourism industry.

The nature of travel and tourism

'Travel and tourism' covers the whole picture of people travelling away from home, whether for business or for leisure, as well as the industry that supports these activities. Right at the beginning you need to understand basic definitions of 'travel' and 'tourism'.

Tourism is defined by the Tourism Society as *'the temporary short-term movement of people to destinations outside the place where they normally live and work, and activities during their stay at these destinations; it includes movement for all purposes, as well as day visits and excursions'*.

Think it over ...

Use as many different sources as possible to find definitions for 'travel' and for 'tourism'. One obvious source is this book, but also use a dictionary and other sources. On the basis of all those definitions, devise *your own* definition of the two terms.

Think it over ...

Discuss these statements, to decide whether they are true or false. Answers are given on page 11.

- The majority of travel and tourism in the world is international.
- The most common method of travel for leisure purposes is by air.
- Tourism is only about leisure holidays.
- Getting a job in the travel and tourism industry means that you will have the chance to see the world.

In 1879, Robert Louis Stevenson wrote in *Travels with a Donkey*: 'For my part, I travel not to go anywhere, but to go. I travel for travel's sake. The great affair is to move.' Some people today still travel for the enjoyment of the travelling, but mostly travel is considered to be how people get to their chosen destination and how they move around the area once they are there.

There are many methods of travelling, including by aircraft, private car, coach, train and boat. We shall be looking at these methods of transportation later in the unit.

Think it over ...

Think about your own experiences:

- Where did you go on holiday last?
- Was it in the UK or abroad?
- How did you travel?
- What type of accommodation did you stay in?
- What did you eat and drink?
- What activities did you do on holiday?
- How was the holiday organised/booked?

Thinking about these things will help you to learn travel and tourism terminology.

You must remember that the travel and tourism industry is dynamic, so you must keep up to date with changes, both locally and nationally. Businesses change hands as well as their names, which can easily lead to confusion. New legislation comes into force that affects the industry, and industry statistics need updating each year. The resources section on page 49 should assist you in understanding the travel and tourism industry at the time of your studies.

Main types of tourism

Tourists can be classified according to where they come from. They can be domestic, inbound or outbound.

Domestic tourism

Domestic tourism involves residents of a country travelling only within their own country. This is generally an easy form of tourism, as there are no language, currency or documentation barriers. Domestic tourism in the United Kingdom was traditionally based at seaside destinations such as Blackpool and Great Yarmouth.

In 2002, expenditure in the United Kingdom on domestic tourism was estimated to be nearly £61 billion. In that year, UK residents took:

* 101.7 million holidays of one night or more, spending £17.4 billion

* 23.3 million overnight business trips, spending £5.6 billion

* 39.6 million overnight trips, spending £3.4 billion.

Key term

Many domestic tourists in the UK now favour the **short break**. This is usually a weekend or mid-week break of three nights or less.

CASE STUDY

Domestic tourism

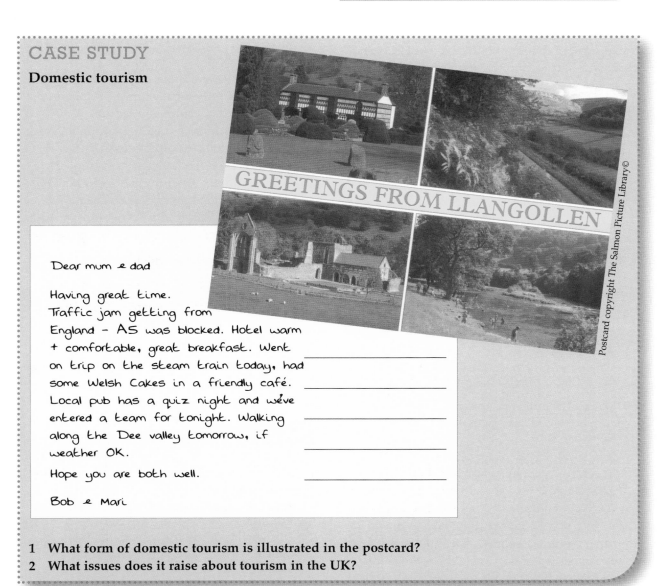

GREETINGS FROM LLANGOLLEN

Postcard copyright The Salmon Picture Library©

Dear mum & dad

Having great time.
Traffic jam getting from
England – A5 was blocked. Hotel warm
+ comfortable, great breakfast. Went
on trip on the steam train today, had
some Welsh Cakes in a friendly café.
Local pub has a quiz night and we've
entered a team for tonight. Walking
along the Dee valley tomorrow, if
weather OK.

Hope you are both well.

Bob & Mari

1 **What form of domestic tourism is illustrated in the postcard?**
2 **What issues does it raise about tourism in the UK?**

Inbound tourism

Inbound tourism involves overseas residents visiting the UK. In 2003, the UK ranked sixth in the international tourism earnings league, behind the USA, Spain, France, Italy and Germany.

The 24.7 million overseas visitors who came to the UK in 2003 spent £11.9 billion. Figure 1.1 shows the number of inbound tourists to the UK from various countries, and the amount of money they spent here.

COUNTRY	VISITS (000)	COUNTRY	SPEND (£M)
USA	3 346	USA	2 315
France	3 073	Germany	820
Germany	2 611	France	694
Irish Republic	2 488	Irish Republic	681
Netherlands	1 549	Australia	535

Source: World Tourism Organisation

Figure 1.1 The top five overseas markets for the UK in 2003

Think it over ...

1 Why do you think inbound tourists come to the UK from the USA and the Irish Republic?

2 Do you think the reasons are different for visitors from France, Germany and the Netherlands?

3 Why do you think inbound tourists from Australia make the top five in terms of expenditure?

4 Why should the UK encourage inbound tourism from these countries, especially the USA? (You may wish to work out the average spend per visitor.)

Theory into practice

You are an incoming tour operator serving the needs of the US market. You have been approached by a specialist tour operator, George Busch, of Busch Tours, Fort Lauderdale, Florida. He is interested in bringing groups to your area of the country, and has written to you to ask which local towns may be of interest to the older Florida residents.

Select one town you consider might be suitable. Undertake an evaluation of its attractions, amenities and accessibility for this customer. Write a business letter explaining the attractiveness of the destination, and its suitability for the market.

CASE STUDY

UKinbound

UKinbound (www.ukinbound.co.uk) is the official trade body representing UK inbound tourism. The association represents over 250 major companies and organisations in all areas of travel and tourism. Each month the association produces a Business Barometer which compares visitor numbers and booking forecasts with the previous year. The figures for August 2004 showed a 3.8 per cent increase in *inbound* visitor numbers.

Visit the UKinbound website to get up-to-date figures on inbound visitors.

Outbound tourism

Outbound tourism refers to UK residents taking holidays outside the UK.

Think it over ...

In 1870, the Reverend F. Kilvert wrote in his diary: 'Of all noxious animals, too, the most noxious is a tourist. And of all tourists the most vulgar, ill-bred, offensive and loathsome is the British tourist.'

Discuss whether British tourists are still considered to be badly behaved while on holiday abroad.

Outbound tourism can be classified in the following ways (the terms are explained below):

* inclusive tours or independent tours
* method of transport to leave the UK (air, sea or Channel Tunnel)
* length of holiday – short break of less than four nights or longer holidays
* short haul or long haul
* season of departure – summer or winter.

Visits abroad are classified as visits for a period of less than 12 months by people permanently resident in the UK (who may be of foreign nationality).

Since the 1970s the most popular type of holiday abroad has been the inclusive tour by air – the package holiday – lasting more than four nights, taken in the summer to short-haul Mediterranean destinations.

Main reasons why people travel

From all the many reasons why people travel, we shall be looking at leisure travel, visiting friends and relatives (VFR) and business travel. It is important to observe the differences between these, as the characteristics of each purpose of travel will be different.

Leisure travel

Leisure travel is the most common type and covers holidays, short breaks and day visits to tourist attractions – it therefore includes all 'recreational travel'. Leisure travellers are usually concerned about price. Lower prices will lead to an increase in the number of travellers, and may encourage others to change to destinations they consider are better value for money.

Business travel

Business travel includes all travel for business purposes. This may be a meeting, conference, exhibition or trade fair. Business travellers will have little choice in their destination or timing of the trip. Business trips frequently have to be arranged at short notice and are for specific and brief periods. Business travellers will need the convenience of frequent, regular transport, efficient service and good facilities at their destination. Because the company will be paying for all the travel arrangements, rather than the individual, the business traveller will be less concerned about the cost of travelling.

Visiting friends and relatives

Visiting friends and relatives includes such travel as visiting grandparents for a day, or staying with friends for a week. Although people usually stay free of charge when doing this, they do spend money on goods and services in the area they are visiting, such as on food, entertainment and local transport.

Unique characteristics of the travel and tourism industry

The main characteristics of the travel and tourism industry today are varied. It is dominated by small and medium-sized businesses. The industry is dynamic and entrepreneurial in nature. The travel and tourism industry is primarily a 'people business'. This is covered fully in unit 2.

The industry is also characterised by:

* seasonality
* intangibility
* perishability.

Seasonality

Seasonality is often the result of changes in climate over the year, so a destination that is attractive because of its beaches and hot summers is likely to have a highly seasonal demand. Seasonality also applies to a ski resort that has suitable snow for only part of the year. There are other factors besides climate that influence seasonality, such as the timing of school and work holidays, or regular special events held at a destination.

Seasonality causes major problems for the travel and tourism industry. As it is a service industry the product cannot be stored, so a hotel room that remains unbooked, an empty seat on a flight or an unsold theatre ticket are all lost income to the organisation.

Attempts can be made to reduce the impact of seasonality. One way is to create or move demand to the 'shoulder' or 'trough' months (times of reduced demand), either through reducing prices at these times or by providing all-year facilities. Those who are able to travel at that time of year, such as the retired, may be specifically targeted.

Seasonality also affects travel and tourism organisations over a single week. For example, hotels often experience differences in room bookings at weekends compared with weekdays. This is especially the case when the hotel is filled with business travellers during the week at high rates and achieves a lesser level of room occupancy at the weekend with short-break special offers. Visitor attractions often attract more visitors at weekends than on weekdays.

Look at Figure 1.2, a leaflet advertising Billing Aquadrome.

1 What was the duration of the 2004 season?

2 When is high season and when is low season?

3 At what times of the year are a greater number of bookings expected? How does the leaflet illustrate this?

4 When are cars and motorbikes charged for entry on a daily rate?

5 Why do you think facilities such as Billing Aquadrome operate on a seasonal basis?

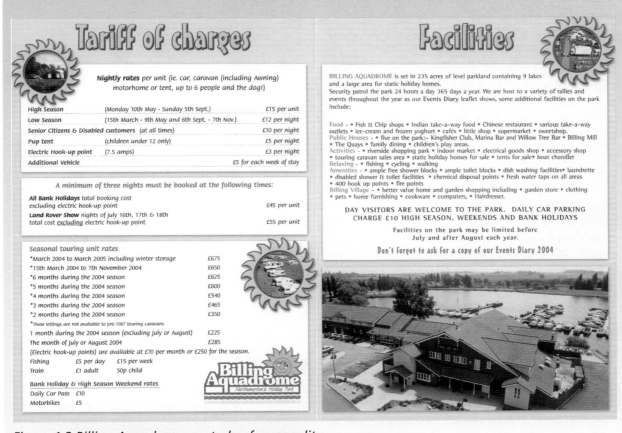

Figure 1.2 Billing Aquadrome: a study of seasonality

Collect a selection of holiday brochures. Look at the pricing panels for the holidays. How does the change in pricing reflect seasonality?

Intangibility

It has often been said that selling holidays is like selling dreams. Travel and tourism is a service rather than a tangible good. 'Tangible' means that you can touch it, but travel and tourism is intangible – you cannot feel a holiday!

This intangibility produces problems for people whose job it is to sell travel and tourism. You cannot, for example, inspect a holiday before you buy it, unlike a car that you can take for a test drive. As a purchaser of a package holiday you can only take on trust what is said or printed about the holiday. This can be a problem as holidays are one of the most expensive purchases made throughout a year. When you buy a package holiday abroad, you are buying more than a simple collection of services, such as an airline seat, hotel room, meals and the opportunity to sit on a sunny beach. You are also buying the temporary use of a different environment, plus the culture and heritage of the region as well as other intangible benefits such as service, atmosphere and hospitality. The planning and anticipation of such a holiday may be as much a part of its enjoyment as the trip itself. Recalling the experience later and looking at photos and videos are a continuation of the experience.

The challenge in travel and tourism is to make the dream equal to the reality. This is difficult as the travel and tourism product tends to vary in standard and quality over time and under different circumstances. A package tour in which you experience bad weather can change an enjoyable experience into a nightmare.

Think it over ...

How has new technology, such as DVDs and the Internet, attempted to overcome the intangibility of travel and tourism? Think about virtual tours and interactive holiday brochures.

Perishability

Perishability is a feature of all travel and tourism products. This means that service products such as tourism, unlike goods, cannot be stored for sale on a future occasion.

For example, a hotel bed or an airline seat unsold, or a conference centre left empty, means lost revenue. This demonstrates the high-risk nature of the travel and tourism industry. Complex pricing and promotion policies need to be devised in an attempt to sell 'off-season' periods.

Weak demand is not the only problem, as travel and tourism is characterised by hotels, airlines, attractions, museums etc., all of which have fixed capacity with a maximum upper level. In peak periods the industry often has difficulty in coping with demand and so charges premium prices or uses queuing as a control mechanism. It is a skill to try to smooth out demand by offering, for example, off-peak prices at theme parks. Airlines try to sell surplus seats by offering a *standby fare*. This is a discounted rate offered to travellers who are prepared to turn up without booking in advance, in the hope that there will be a spare seat.

CASE STUDY

Hotels

Hotels use two statistics to measure their success, and these illustrate perishability. These statistics are (a) the level of occupancy and (b) the average achieved room rate. The latter is the price achieved on rooms sold, and bears little resemblance to the full advertised price or 'rack rate'. Typically most rooms are sold at a discount to rack rate.

1 **Find out rack rates and actual room rates for hotels belonging to chains in your locality.**
2 **At what time of the week are these discounted rates?**
3 **Can you offer an explanation as to why the rooms are reduced at these times?**

The scale of the travel and tourism industry

This part of the unit investigates the scale of the industry at local and national levels. You will be developing skills in order to analyse the most commonly used statistics in travel and tourism.

Consumer spending in the UK on travel and tourism

When you are on holiday or on a day trip you spend money. This may be on food and drink, entrance fees, shopping for souvenirs or fuel to get you there.

The balance of payments

Travel and tourism makes an important contribution to the UK's balance of payments –

that is, the difference between what is imported to the UK and what is exported. It is difficult to assess the true contribution that travel and tourism makes, owing to the intangible nature of the industry, and the fact that people pay for a service rather than a tangible product.

Generally, the money received from visitors to the UK can be considered as an export because it earns foreign currency and brings money into the UK economy. The money spent overseas by outgoing tourists from the UK can be considered as an import because money is taken out of the UK economy. If the value of exports is greater than imports there is a surplus on the balance of payments. If the imports are greater than the exports there is a deficit on the balance of payments.

Currently the amount of tourism export earnings is in deficit – there is more outgoing tourism than incoming tourism. In 2002, there was a record deficit of £15.2 billion, which was £1.2 billion more than in 2001. In 2002, for every £1 spent in the UK by other Europeans, UK residents spent £3 in other parts of Europe. This compares with a £1 to £2 ratio in 1982.

Spending on domestic tourism

Domestic tourists in the UK spend money – not as much per head as overseas visitors, but a substantial amount (see Figure 1.3).

	UK	ENGLAND	SCOTLAND	WALES
1995	20 072	14 630	2 793	1 573
1996	22 041	15 763	3 276	1 781
1997	24 137	17 264	3 724	1 626
1998	22 814	16 383	3 490	1 674
1999	25 635	19 106	3 600	1 723
2000	26 133	19 890	3 699	1 654
2001	26 094	20 278	3 412	1 664
2002	26 699	20 787	3 682	1 543

Source: Star UK

Figure 1.3 All domestic tourism spending (£m), 1995 to 2002

Spending in the UK by overseas residents

In 2002, overseas residents spent £11.7 billion in the UK, nearly four times the amount spent in 1982, but £1.1 billion lower than in 2000. As we have seen, this is important for the UK's overall balance of payments. Incoming visitors to an area help to create or sustain jobs. The government benefits as overseas visitors pay VAT and other taxes on a range of products and services. Overseas visitors are likely to use public transport and so help ensure that routes will continue to run. British theatres and the arts benefit especially – the majority of the audiences of West End shows are incoming tourists.

Employment in the industry

Numbers of people employed in travel and tourism

The travel and tourism industry employs a vast number of people, in a wide range of jobs. Employment in the industry in the UK is, in government figures, measured at 2.1 million, which is some 7.4 per cent of all people in employment. Approximately 163 000 of these jobs are in self-employment.

Around 50 000 new jobs are created in travel and tourism each year. There are employment opportunities in travel agencies, tour operators, hospitality providers, airlines, coach companies and tourist attractions.

The dynamic nature of the industry means that permanent, full-time positions are not the norm in travel and tourism employment. Much employment is part-time or short-term contractual, and many jobs operate during unsociable hours (evenings and night-shifts or weekends). The seasonality of the industry means that there are peak times when more people will be employed.

The ability of the travel and tourism industry to create jobs is one of its main economic benefits and is often the main reason why public sector bodies invest in UK tourism. It is estimated that for every one direct job created in travel and tourism, one-half of an indirect job is created elsewhere in the economy.

Employment by category of tourism-related industries

The following Standard Industrial Classification (SIC) codes are used when measuring employment in tourism-related industries:

* 551/552 – hotels and other tourist accommodation

* 553 – restaurants, cafés etc.

* 554 – bars, public houses and nightclubs

* 633 – travel agencies and tour operators

* 925 – libraries/museums and other cultural activities

* 926/927 – sport and other recreation.

Think it over ...

Look at Figure 1.4 relating to employment in travel and tourism in the UK in 2001. Why do you think this might not be a full and accurate picture of employment in travel and tourism in the whole of the UK?

	551/552	553	554	633	925	926/927	Total
ENGLAND	269 617	455 810	464 309	113 189	64 490	229 148	1 696 563
Cumbria	6 843	4 409	4 192	549	720	3 013	19 726
Northumbria	9 387	16 618	24 278	3 016	2 637	15 097	71 033
North West	27 858	51 491	64 376	15 814	6 957	38 540	205 036
Yorkshire	23 217	38 094	48 403	6 223	8 373	33 492	157 802
Heart of England	44 272	72 079	102 993	13 532	10 692	61 217	304 785
East of England	25 566	45 383	45 492	12 359	5 172	36 541	170 513
London	48 050	121 630	58 364	34 156	14 689	54 108	330 997
South East	19 538	37 134	36 063	14 454	4 847	27 727	139 764
Southern	26 555	36 650	39 527	7 308	5 119	38 107	153 266
South West	38 330	32 322	40 620	5 778	5 285	21 304	143 639
SCOTLAND	51 330	49 824	40 755	8 855	8 350	38 284	197 398
WALES	17 837	20 730	27 244	3 146	3 908	16 597	89 461
GB	338 783	526 364	532 307	125 190	76 748	384 029	1 983 421

Figures exclude Northern Ireland, and self-employment jobs are excluded.   *Source:* Star UK

Figure 1.4 Employment in tourism-related industries in 2001

Key terms

Direct employment is jobs that are in hotels, tourist accommodation, travel agencies, tour operators, tourist attractions etc.
Indirect employment is in, for example, the decor of a hotel, the printer supplying the brochures for a tour operator, and the web designer of the website for an airline.

Tourists coming into the UK

The number of visits by overseas residents to the UK more than doubled from 11.6 million visits in 1982 to a peak of 25.7 million in 1998, before falling each year to 22.8 million in 2001. The largest fall of 9.4 per cent occurred in 2001 when there was foot and mouth disease between February and September, and the terrorist attacks in the USA on 11 September.

Think it over ...

The UK is ranked sixth in the world in terms of the number of inbound tourists (see Figure 1.5).

1 Discuss why you think France is the number one destination in the world.

2 Why do you think there was a 6.7 per cent reduction in international visitors to the USA?

3 Which country has the greatest growth in international visitors? Think of reasons why.

RANK		2002	CHANGE 2002/2001	SHARE
1	France	77.0	2.4%	11.0%
2	Spain	51.7	3.3%	7.4%
3	USA	41.9	–6.7%	6.0%
4	Italy	39.8	0.6%	5.7%
5	China	36.8	11.0%	5.2%
6	UK	24.2	5.9%	3.4%
7	Canada	20.1	1.9%	2.9%
8	Mexico	19.7	–0.7%	2.8%
9	Austria	18.6	2.4%	2.6%
10	Germany	18.0	0.6%	2.6%
	World	703	2.7%	100%

Figure 1.5 International tourist arrivals (millions)

Source: World Trade Organisation

Think it over ...

These are suggested answers to the questions asked in the second 'Think it over' box on page 2:
(1) Tourism in the world is mainly domestic travel, accounting for about 80 per cent of tourism trips. (2) The majority of transport is by surface methods, mainly by car. (3) Tourism includes all types of purposes for a visit, including business and visiting family and friends. (4) Most employment in tourism is in the hospitality sector and involves little travel.

Domestic tourism

Figure 1.6 shows the number of UK residents taking holidays within the UK in 1996 and 2002, and their spending.

TOURIST BOARD REGIONS	1996		2002	
	Number of trips (millions)	Expenditure (£m)	Number of trips (millions)	Expenditure (£m)
United Kingdom	154.2	22 041	167.3	26 699
Northumbria	3.7	402	4.8	868
Cumbria	3.7	503	4.3	728
North West	11.9	1 632	14.5	2 316
Yorkshire	11.9	1 713	12.2	1 595
East of England	15.8	1 860	14.5	1 704
Heart of England	18.9	2 164	24.6	3 166
London	12.9	1 633	16.1	2 818
Southern	11.5	1 586	14.6	2 065
South East England	11.9	1 240	10.9	1 355
South West	17.5	3 029	21.0	3 901
England	117.3	15 763	134.9	20 787
Wales	13.6	1 781	11.9	1 543
Scotland	19.6	3 276	18.5	3 683
Northern Ireland	3.8	698	2.8	525

Source: Star UK

Figure 1.6 UK residents taking holidays in the UK in 1996 and 2002

Theory into practice

1 Locate each of the regional tourist boards represented in Figure 1.6 on a map of the United Kingdom.

2 Which regional tourist board area had the greatest number of domestic trips to it in 1996 and 2002? Research this tourist board area to find out the attractions visitors would want to see.

3 Which regional tourist board area had the greatest domestic spending in 1996 and 2002? Research this tourist board region to find out what domestic visitors might be spending their money on.

4 Why do you think the regional tourist board with the most trips is different from that with the most spending?

Domestic tourism trends

The travel and tourism market has been unstable in recent years with a number of unforeseen events having an impact on the domestic market. These include:

* fuel blockades at UK petrol stations
* the restrictions imposed on the rail network after the Hatfield disaster
* the events of 11 September 2001
* the foot-and-mouth outbreak.

Despite the instability caused by these events, the underlying trend in the demand for domestic tourism continues to grow. The increasing interest in travel as a leisure activity, the fall in the real cost of travelling, and the change in modern lifestyles are all factors that are driving demand for holidays. The growth in multi-holidaymaking has stimulated the market for short holidays in the UK, while long holidays in the UK have remained more or less constant.

Theory into practice

1 Visit www.staruk.org.uk and locate the section on domestic tourism trends.

2 Analyse these statistics. Look specifically at the different trends in holiday tourism, business tourism and VFR.

3 Try to explain the patterns in the trends.

Outbound tourists

UK residents taking holidays outside the UK

A record 59.4 million visits were made abroad in 2002, nearly three times the number in 1982. The amount of spending was also a record in 2002, at £27.0 billion.

Of all the visits in 2002, 39.9 million were holiday visits (that is, two-thirds of the total). Over half of these were package holidays.

Continental Europe was the most popular region for UK residents to visit, accounting for 74 per cent of all visits but only 57 per cent of total spending. For the first time, Spain became the most popular country visited with 12.5 million trips – beating France as a destination by just 0.4 million visits.

Why the big increase in outbound tourism?

The growth in the value of sterling compared with other currencies has had a positive effect on outbound holidays, which are growing at a faster rate than domestic holidays.

UK consumers expect more choice, variety and individuality than ever before. Although mass-market sun and sea holidays are still the majority of the outbound holiday market, it is specialist holidays targeted at particular market segments that are the key to profitability. Many of the major outbound tour operators offer a range of different product brands targeted at different markets.

The main reason for the underlying growth in the UK holiday market is the increasing level of repeat purchases or multi-holidaymaking in any year. However, since 1999, the percentage of UK adults taking an annual holiday has not changed significantly.

Outbound holiday growth has been much more dynamic than domestic holiday growth, with long and short holidays each showing increases. Much of the growth in short holidays abroad has been stimulated by the establishment and expansion of low-cost airline services. These services are characterised by direct independent booking facilities via the Internet. Their operation has encouraged a growth in the use of the Internet for seeking information on travel and for booking transport and accommodation.

Travel arrangements of outbound tourists

Travelling by air was the most popular mode of transport and accounted for 74 per cent of all visits. Travelling by sea was the next most popular mode, accounting for 17 per cent of visits. The Channel Tunnel was used for the remaining visits (9 per cent).

Spending of outbound tourists

On average, air travellers spent the most money per visit (£519), while those travelling by sea or the Channel Tunnel spent far lower amounts (£339 and £277 respectively). These differences were due to a number of factors, including variations in the reason for the visit, the length of stay and the region of the world visited.

The average spending per visit ranged from £348 for VFR, to £528 for business trips. The average spending on holidays was £465.

Why do UK residents travel abroad?

As you have already read, two-thirds of visits made by UK residents were to go on holiday, making this the most popular reason for travelling abroad. More than half (52 per cent) of these holidays were taken as an inclusive tour. Business trips and VFR were the next most popular reasons for travelling abroad.

Think it over ...

What are the implications for the UK economy of the continued increase in outbound tourism? Think about the balance of payments.

The development of the modern travel and tourism industry

The growth in international and domestic travel and tourism has been dramatic. Figures from the World Tourism Organisation (WTO – www.world-tourism.org) stated there were 703 million international tourist arrivals in 2002, climbing from 25 million in 1950 and 592 million in 1996. To understand today's travel and tourism industry, you need to know about the major developments in recent times. You have to show you understand the dynamic nature of travel and tourism. This section is about the key factors that have contributed to the dramatic growth in the travel and tourism industry.

Changing socio-economic factors

These factors include:

* changes in car ownership
* increasing leisure time
* an increase in disposable income
* the impact of the national economy.

Car ownership

Car ownership has increased dramatically in the last 50 years. This is because the income of people has risen and cars are more affordable to buy and run. In 1970 there were approximately 11 million cars on UK roads, compared with 2.3 million in 1950. Figures from the Department for Transport (www.dft.gov.uk) show that in 2002 there were over 25.5 million private cars in the UK.

This means that car owners have an additional travel option, and can reach destinations that are inaccessible or difficult to reach by public transport. Car owners can also choose *when* to travel without timetable restrictions and the speed of travel – car ownership offers flexibility of travel.

The rise in car ownership has led to a drop in demand for traditional types of public transport, such as trains and coaches for holiday travel. This leads to cuts in services. Another effect of the increase in car ownership in the UK has been the rise in associated environmental problems, such as pollution, congestion and the loss of land to road building programmes.

Think it over ...

How many cars are owned by people in your household? What are the cars mainly used for? Try to find out the answers to these questions also for your parents' and grandparents' generations when they were your age. What do these differences show you about increases in car ownership?

Increasing leisure time

The increase in leisure time has come about primarily due to paid holiday entitlement. In the UK we have a number of one-day Bank Holidays

as well as annual leave. Holiday entitlement is partly responsible for the seasonality of travel and tourism, as parents take holidays in the summer to coincide with school holidays.

The 'working week' has also been made shorter, to an average of 37 hours. This has to be compared with the 1950s when a 50-hour working week was normal, including at least half a day on Saturday. Many employers now operate flexitime (flexible working hours), which is of great benefit to the travel and tourism industry, allowing employees to have long weekends and hence take short breaks.

Labour-saving household equipment, such as dishwashers, washing machines and microwaves, mean that household chores can be carried out more quickly, so leading to greater leisure time.

People are on average also living longer and retiring earlier. This so-called 'grey' market is important in travel and tourism, as retired people frequently have the time and money to spend on holidays and other activities.

CASE STUDY

Saga

The Saga group (www.saga.co.uk) has its origins in the 1950s, when the founder of the company, Sidney De Haan, bought his first seaside hotel in Folkestone, Kent. In 1951 he organised a package holiday exclusively for retired people, realising that many would appreciate a quieter off-season break by the sea.

The Saga organisation now aims to serve the 50+ market. It aims to offer excellent value for money and direct booking, fully focusing on and responding to the changing demands of the older target market, which is the fastest growing demographic group in the UK. The product range of Saga covers virtually every holiday type, including those with an historic and/or cultural dimension in the UK and beyond, city breaks, as well as exotic long–haul destinations, adventure holidays and cruises.

Discuss the differences in requirements of the 50+ age group compared with other age groups of holidaymakers.

Disposable income

There has been a general trend for UK disposable income to rise, so leading to increased expenditure on leisure activities, including travel and tourism.

The impact of the national economy

The national economic situation affects the travel and tourism industry significantly. When there is enough disposable income in the economy due to high levels of employment, people have on average more money to spend on travel and tourism products and services. This can be measured by the gross national product.

The reverse is also true. When there are high levels of unemployment and little growth, people have on average less disposable income to spend money on travel and tourism.

Technological developments

The travel and tourism industry has developed as a direct result of technological developments. These developments have been in transport technology, such as jet aircraft, improved trains and luxury coaches. There have also been developments in information and communications technology such as the Internet, computer reservation systems (CRS) and global distribution systems (GDS), as well as credit and debit cards which allow customers to pay in more convenient ways.

Developments in transport technology

The most significant development for air travel was the introduction of jet aircraft in the 1950s, particularly the Boeing 707 in 1958. Air travel became fast, safe, comfortable and – relative to previous decades – cheap. The 'jumbo jet' (Boeing 747) introduced in 1969 had several impacts on the travel and tourism industry. It was possible to fly further in less time, so making long-haul destinations more accessible, and the price of air travel was reduced due to the increased capacity of the jumbo jet (400 seats).

It is not just air transport that has been revolutionised by new technology. The Channel Tunnel was opened to passengers in 1995 and led to competition for cross-channel ferry services.

Theory into practice

Using brochures or the Internet, complete the table below to compare the range of methods of travelling across the English Channel. Try to include at least *two* operators for each method.

Method of travel	Operator	Departure point	Arrival point	Journey time	Return fare
Rail					
Sea with own car					
Sea as foot passenger					
Air					

Technological developments in booking systems

Ten years ago travel agents had almost complete control of travel bookings. Customers liked the convenience of a package holiday, and bargain priced beach breaks could often be found displayed in the travel agency window. Using viewdata systems, travel agencies could make direct bookings with tour operators.

Key term

Viewdata consisted of a screen that displayed information transmitted by phone lines. By 1987, 85 per cent of all package holidays were booked through this system.

Then there was the development of CRS technology. Using their computers, travel agents could find out information on destinations that would take you, the customer, dozens of phone calls to uncover. The market leader in the UK for computer reservation systems is Galileo. Other systems are Sabre, Worldspan and Amadeus. Global distribution systems now link up several CRS and present information to the user.

Teletext turned the TV in your sitting room into a shop window, offering late deals at the touch of a remote control and one phone call. The tour operators set up call centres and encouraged you to ring them directly, often at times when high street travel agencies were closed. The explosion of the Internet and of no-frills airlines selling direct to the public meant that travel agents and tour operators no longer had the monopoly on holiday bookings, and everyone thought that they could save time and money by cutting out the travel agent.

The Big Four tour operators (TUI, Thomas Cook, First Choice and MyTravel) bought up dozens of smaller operators and built up huge chains of high street travel agencies, all with the intention of selling as many of their own-brand holidays as possible. The media started forecasting the demise of travel agents, so travel agencies had to *add value* to their sales – either by offering bargains not available elsewhere or by finding ways to provide a superior service.

Changing consumer needs and expectations

Alongside the huge growth in travel and tourism, as outlined in an earlier section, there have been significant changes due to a variety of cultural and social factors. We also now demand higher standards of quality and customer service, a subject covered in detail in unit 2.

The simple sun-and-sea holidays of the 1960s seem to appeal to fewer people today, and more flexibility is demanded. Customers today prefer to choose the type of accommodation, the board basis, the type of transport and the length of the holiday. Package holidays now need to offer this choice.

Special-interest holidays in particular have been developed to cater for a range of interests. Activity and adventure holidays have become increasingly important, especially those that include activities such as white-water rafting or scuba diving.

As leisure time increases and disposable incomes rise, the 'second holiday' has developed. Skiing became popular as a second (winter) holiday from the 1970s, and in the 1980s the short-break market developed. This has benefited the domestic travel and tourism industry. Also, due to low-price air fares and other quick transport methods, the overseas city break is now very popular.

Protecting the environment

The travelling public is becoming more environmentally aware, as we see the damage that can be done to popular holiday destinations. Tour operators have responded to this and many brochures will make a statement about what they are doing to support local communities.

The Travel Foundation (www.thetravelfoundation.org.uk) is a charity that develops practical solutions to help protect and improve holiday destinations. It works in partnership with the UK tourism industry to encourage action to spread the *benefits* of tourism to local communities. First Choice is among the travel companies that asks in its brochure for every customer to make a small voluntary contribution of 10p per adult and 5p per child to the charity when booking a holiday.

Product development and innovation

Package holidays

The origin of the package holiday is credited to a man called Thomas Cook, who took his passengers by train from Loughborough to Leicester in 1841. The modern package, or inclusive tour, was created by Vladimir Raitz, who in 1950 carried a party of thirty-two holidaymakers to Corsica. That package included return flights, transfers, tented accommodation and full board. By chartering a flight and filling every seat he managed to keep the price low. He then established Horizon Holidays and chartered planes to Palma, Malaga and other Mediterranean resorts, carrying 300 passengers in the first year of operation.

Package holidays have since grown with Thomson, Airtours and First Choice being the biggest outgoing tour operators in terms of the number of package holidays sold. Mediterranean destinations are still the most popular with the British, but long-haul destinations including the Caribbean, the USA, the Far East and Australia are becoming increasingly important package holiday destinations as travel costs fall. More information on package holidays can be found later in this chapter.

All-inclusive holidays

'All-inclusives' were introduced by Club Med in the 1950s. All-inclusives can now include all meals, drinks, sports and entertainment, for example, but what is covered in the package does vary between operators. As an example, an all-inclusive package with First Choice at the Occidental Grand Fuerteventura four-star hotel in Jandia included the following:

* Food – buffets for breakfast, lunch and dinner; unlimited snacks 10 a.m. to midnight; afternoon tea and cakes; picnics available on request; unlimited ice cream between 3 p.m. and 6 p.m.

* Drink – unlimited locally produced alcoholic drinks between 10.30 a.m. and midnight for adults; unlimited soft drinks, tea, coffee and mineral water between 10 a.m. and midnight.

Theory into practice

Collect a number of brochures, or use the Internet, to find five all-inclusive packages. Compare the packages to find out exactly what is on offer as part of the deal. Which package do you think offers the best deal?

Holiday camps

Holiday camps are purpose-built complexes providing family accommodation and a range of entertainment facilities on site for a relatively low, all-inclusive price. They were pioneered by Billy Butlin in the 1930s, who opened his first camp at Skegness on the Lincolnshire coast in 1936. Holiday camps worked on the principle that if children were happy on holiday, then the parents would be too. Butlin's, Pontin's and Warner's became market leaders in this type of holiday.

In recent years they have modified these camps to meet changing consumer needs and expectations. New types of holiday centre, such as Center Parcs, have evolved.

Theory into practice

Research changes that have occurred in the holiday camp and holiday centre sector of the industry in the past 50 years. Why did these changes happen? Do you foresee further changes in the next few years?

External factors

Legislation

Key term

Legislation consists principally of Acts of Parliament passed by central government. Local authorities can introduce by-laws that apply only locally.

The Holidays with Pay Act 1938

This encouraged voluntary agreements by employers on paid holidays and generated the idea of a two-week paid holiday for all workers. Although this ambition was not fulfilled until several years after the end of the Second World War, by 1939 some 11 million of the UK's 19 million workforce were entitled to paid holidays, a key factor in generating mass travel and tourism.

Countryside and Rights of Way Act 2000

This Act (referred to as 'CROW') made it lawful for the public to enter areas that were previously restricted to the landowners. In England, the public will have 'open access' to around one million hectares (4000 square miles, 8 per cent of the country). The right does not include cycling, horse riding, driving a vehicle or camping, and there are various other rules to protect the land and the interests of the landowners, such as farmers.

Theory into practice

The Countryside Agency provides details of the new legislation on its website (www.countryside.gov.uk). Use the website to attempt to answer the following questions.

1 When was the major new right of access introduced?

2 What activities are people permitted, and not permitted, to do on all land?

3 What type of land is being opened up due to CROW?

4 What discretion do landowners have?

5 What are the main points of the Countryside Code?

Development of Tourism Act 1968

This established the British Tourist Authority (BTA), which was set up to encourage incoming tourism from overseas visitors, as well as the four national tourist boards (NTB) of England, Scotland, Wales and Northern Ireland which oversee tourism in their own areas. The BTA and the NTBs were given the power and authority to act in the name of the government and to promote British tourism. Since 2004 the BTA and the English Tourism Council have been merged into VisitBritain.

Each NTB works within its own country to encourage and improve amenities for travel and tourism. They offer information services, undertake research and provide grants for tourism-related projects. In order to extend their influence within their countries, each NTB sets up Regional Tourist Boards. You can find more information on NTBs and regional tourist boards later in this chapter (see page 35).

EU Directive on Package Travel 1995

This ensures that customers of package holiday providers have financial protection. If a company fails, customers who have not yet travelled can get their money back. Those on holiday at the time do not have to pay additional costs.

The Directive places a number of duties on the organisers of package holidays, including providing clear contract terms, giving emergency telephone numbers, providing a variety of compensation options if the agreed services are not supplied, producing accurate promotional materials including brochures, as well as providing proof that the organiser has security against insolvency.

Disability Discrimination Act 1995

This came about through public pressure to persuade people and businesses to remove the barriers facing people with disabilities.

Key term

In terms of this Act, **disability** means a physical or mental impairment that has a substantial and long-term adverse effect on a person's ability to carry out normal day-to-day activities.

Travel and tourism organisations such as visitor attractions have to be accessible to those with restricted mobility or in wheelchairs. Public transport providers have been encouraged to adapt their vehicles with facilities to make it easier for people with disabilities to use their service, for example by fitting low steps on to buses. Commercially, all adaptations can be seen as a positive move, as there are 10 million disabled people in the UK with a spending power of £48 million.

The Act came fully into force in October 2004. It requires travel agents to make 'reasonable' adjustments to their shops to ensure that disabled people can have access to their facilities and services. If adjustments to the premises are not made, the travel agency can be sued and required to pay compensation.

Health and Safety at Work Act 1974

This applies to workers in all areas of travel and tourism. It can be summarised as follows.

* Employers have a general duty to provide for the health, safety and welfare of those they employ. Employers are also required to consult employees about health and safety arrangements and prepare a written health and safety policy statement.

* Employers need to ensure that their operations do not put non-employees (such as customers) at risk.

* Adequate information about any work-related hazards and the precautions needed to contain them must be made available.

* All employees have to take reasonable care to ensure their own health and safety at work and that of other people who might be affected by their actions.

Other relevant legislation

Other legislation that applies to travel and tourism includes:

* Control of Substances Hazardous to Health Regulations 1999 (COSHH)

* Health and Safety (First Aid) Regulations 1981

* Data Protection Act 1998

* Food Safety Act 1990
* Adventure Activities Licensing Regulations 1996
* Trade Description Act 1968
* Consumer Protection Act 1987
* Sale of Goods Act 1979 and the Sale and Supply of Goods Act 1994.

This is not a complete list. Much of this legislation specifically applies to the travel and tourism industry, and you will be studying many of these in other areas of your course.

CASE STUDY

Lost bags

From September 2004, travellers are entitled to far higher levels of compensation if an airline loses, delays or damages their luggage. The UK is now bound by the terms of the 1999 Montreal Convention, which bases claims on the value of a bag's contents. Previously passengers relied on the Warsaw Convention, which based claims on luggage weight, regardless of contents. Now, if a 20kg bag is lost on a flight to New York, the maximum compensation travellers are entitled to is £807, compared with £276 beforehand.

1 **Collect newspaper articles on legislation relating to travel and tourism.**
2 **For each one, summarise how it benefits travellers.**

The role of local authorities and government

Local government has a part to play in providing tourism facilities for both local people and visitors to the area.

Local councils are also responsible for providing services such as litter bins, toilets, car and coach parking. Primarily these services are provided for local people who have elected the council but, particularly in tourist centres and seaside resorts, the council will take into account the needs of visitors. Local government also works in collaboration with the private sector, as

planning permission will need to be sought for any building or development in the area.

Fluctuations in currency

Exchange rates have always been an important factor in the rise, or fall, of the travel and tourism industry. If there is a rise in the value of sterling compared with other currencies, outbound tourism tends to increase as travellers know they will receive more for their money abroad. Exchange rates obviously depend on the strength or weakness of sterling, but they are also affected by the internal strengths of currencies in the main destination countries.

Theory into practice

You can find up-to-date exchange rates from many sources – TV text, the Internet, foreign exchange bureaux and newspapers. Keep a record of the sterling exchange rates for the euro, the US dollar and the Australian dollar over a period of a few weeks. What changes have happened in the exchange rates over the period? What does this mean for outbound UK travellers?

Climatic change

Climate plays a crucial role in how people use their leisure time. In the UK there are marked differences in climate, with the west and south generally experiencing warmer summers and less severe winters than the north. You will probably be aware of the debate over global warming and climate change.

Natural disasters

In 2004, three major hurricanes affected the Caribbean and Florida, Japan was lashed by typhoons, and China coped with mud slides and floods. There was an ice storm in Sydney and enough torrential rain in New York to disrupt the US Open Tennis. The summer in the UK was the wettest since 1912, with some rivers bursting their banks. There was severe flooding in the Cornish village of Boscastle, leading to considerable damage to property, and the midlands, northern and eastern England suffered twice their average August rainfall. These are the types of natural disaster that can disrupt the travel and tourism industry.

CASE STUDY

Ivan the Terrible

In early September 2004, the third hurricane in a month affected the Caribbean and Florida in the USA. Hurricanes Charley and Frances had already rampaged through Florida, killing 50 people and creating £5 billion of storm damage. Theme parks were shut and coastal areas evacuated.

Ivan was a category 5 hurricane (the top of the scale). It generated 156mph winds. It devastated 90 per cent of buildings on its rampage across Grenada, an island supposedly outside the hurricane belt.

Jamaica's southern shore was affected by waves as high as houses, howling winds and horizontal rain. Power lines were torn down, large trees crashed to the ground and rivers running through the capital city, Kingston, overflowed and flooded the streets. Looters went on the prowl. About 2500 British holidaymakers were airlifted from Jamaica to hotels in the Dominican Republic.

The hurricane also left a path of destruction affecting resorts in Cuba, the Cayman Islands, Mexico and Florida. The Federation of Tour Operators estimated that around 10 000 UK holidaymakers in total were caught up in the hurricane.

Additionally, thousands of UK travellers faced disruption or the cancellation of their holidays to the Caribbean and Florida. The Association of British Travel Agents (ABTA) advised anyone travelling to the region to contact their tour operator and airline before leaving for the airport. People whose holiday plans are disrupted have three options: defer their trip; change to an alternative destination; or take a refund. It was the tour operators that covered the substantial cost of repatriating passengers.

Sandals, which has 14 resort hotels in Jamaica, estimated that Hurricane Ivan cost it £3 million in replacement holidays. Its Blue Chip Guarantee means that if a customer's holiday is hit at any time by a hurricane – even on the last day – the operator will provide another completely free of charge.

A technological advancement that was used during the hurricane was text messages on mobile phones. The charter airline Britannia and First Choice Airways kept duty managers informed of hurricane conditions by text messages. Staff on the ground in Florida and the Caribbean received regular updates about the path of the hurricane, plus news of flight cancellations, aircraft swaps and airport closures which they could then pass on to reps and customers. This innovative system replaced pagers, and allowed staff in the UK to send text messages from a computer to numerous phones at once at low cost.

1 **Imagine you are on holiday when a natural disaster affects the area. What would be your main concerns?**
2 **What information would you expect to receive from the organiser of your holiday?**
3 **What information would you expect to receive from the authorities in the area affected?**
4 **How does the case study demonstrate the impact of technological developments in travel and tourism?**

War, civil unrest, terrorism and crime

The travel and tourism industry is vulnerable to war, civil unrest, terrorism and crime. Examples are the war in Iraq, terrorism attacks such as on 11 September 2001, and the nightclub bombs in Bali. Most of these have only a short-term effect on the numbers who travel, but that effect can still result in a huge amount of business lost, and some companies failing.

The Foreign and Commonwealth Office (www.fco.gov.uk) has a section on its website that informs visitors of potential danger areas around the world.

The future

The World Tourism Organisation (WTO) (www.world-tourism.org) produces a report each year on the long-term prospects for tourism. The WTO forecasts that worldwide international arrivals are expected to reach over 1.56 billion by the year 2020. Of these, 1.18 billion will be between regions and 377 million will be long-haul travel. It is predicted that by 2020 the top three tourist receiving regions will be Europe (717 million tourists), East Asia and the Pacific (379 million) and the Americas (282 million), followed by Africa, the Middle East and South Asia.

It is impossible to make precise predictions of the future developments in travel and tourism. The following examples may or may not happen.

Space tourism is a development that is likely to take place over the next few years. The world's first privately financed spacecraft was launched in 2004, and in future space tourists will have the opportunity to travel 62 miles above the earth and stay in a hotel while they are up there. The price charged for such flights is likely to be considerable.

Other developments in transport technology include Airbus's A380 'superjumbo', with 555 seats compared with the 'regular' Boeing 747 jumbo's 415 seats. The first commercial flight, with Singapore Airlines, is scheduled for 2006. Inside the airplane could be fountains, cocktail bars, showers and beds. It will have extra fuel capacity so it has a longer range, making it possible for the first time for a full plane to fly for 14 hours, for example from Melbourne to Los Angeles. Air travel is growing at a rate of 5 per cent each year, so it is likely to double in 15 years and treble in 23 years. The superjumbo will be quieter than the Boeing 747, carry 35 per cent more passengers and burn 12 per cent less fuel per seat.

The Chinese and Russian markets, with a population of 1.3 billion, are likely to produce many new tourists. VisitBritain is expecting the number of visitors from China to the UK to double in the next five years to 130 000, and the number of visitors from Russia to increase by 50 per cent in the same period to more than 200 000. Travel companies are targeting these upcoming markets. The UK is seen as a desirable destination by Russians. Chinese consumers are cost and quality conscious and are less likely to buy on-line as they do not have credit cards.

According to the WTO, China itself is expected to become the world's leading tourism destination by 2020, with some 100 million outbound tourists and 130 million international arrivals each year.

The structure of the travel and tourism industry

The structure of the travel and tourism industry is complex because it is made up of a wide variety of interrelated commercial and non-commercial organisations. The travel and tourism industry is predominantly led by the private sector, with the majority of enterprises being small and medium-sized. You need to know how these organisations work together and interact to provide the tourist 'experience', and you need to show appreciation of the different values and attitudes of these organisations. The structure of the industry includes:

* commercial organisations
* non-commercial organisations (including public and voluntary sectors)
* agencies delivering travel and tourism products and services.

Figure 1.7 shows that the needs of the visitor are met by a variety of components at a destination. Attractions are often the stimulus for a visit. Transportation both to and from the destination and whilst there ensures accessibility. Accommodation and catering provides places to stay and receive hospitality whilst at the destination. Tourism development and promotion will provide the visitor with information about the destination and activities such as guided tours.

Figure 1.7 Components of a destination area

1 Select a UK tourist destination you are interested in. It may be a city, seaside resort, countryside area or major attraction. Collect information on the destination, such as promotional leaflets and brochures.

2 Produce a display that illustrates the components that make up the destination.

Commercial organisations

This section looks at the range of *private sector organisations* that make up the travel and tourism industry.

The commercial or private sector of the travel and tourism industry involves business organisations owned by individuals or groups of people. Business organisations in this sector tend to operate for profit. This means that the money the businesses receive from trading (i.e. from selling their goods or services to customers or clients) must be more than is spent on buying stock or providing services.

Profit maximisation may be an overriding priority for some organisations. Survival may also be a distinct aim – for example to survive a downturn in trade in the hope of a better future in the next few years.

More aggressive private sector organisations may aim to increase their market share in direct competition with similar business organisations offering products or services. For example, a travel agency may aim to progress from being a local organisation based in one town to a regional or national company with many branches, by competing with, taking over or merging with other travel agencies.

Another aim might be to maintain a constant cash flow, to keep money flowing into and out of the organisation, and not allowing debts to pile up.

There are five different legal forms of business operating in the private sector in the travel and tourism industry. These are now looked at in greater depth.

Sole trader

This business is owned and controlled by one person. This person takes the risks, provides the capital (perhaps from savings or a loan), keeps the profits or bears the losses. This is known as 'unlimited liability'.

The sole trader is able to employ additional workers if necessary, but is restricted as the business is usually small and cash flow needs to be controlled carefully. Examples of sole trader enterprises in travel and tourism are independent travel agents and owner proprietors of hospitality businesses (e.g. bed and breakfast establishments or fish and chip shops).

1 Examine Figure 1.8. What evidence can you find to show that this is an example of a sole trader?

2 Collect a selection of leaflets and advertisements on travel and tourism organisations in your local area that are sole traders. What areas of travel and tourism are covered by these organisations?

The Old Rectory   map 2 G4

103 Yarmouth Rd, Thorpe St Andrew, NORWICH NR7 0HF
Tel: 01603 700772 Fax: 01603 300772
email: enquiries@oldrectorynorwich.com
www.oldrectorynorwich.com   ★ ★ ❀

STANDARD RATE BED & BREAKFAST
Single: £68 Twin/double: £85 - £110

Enjoy traditional hospitality in Chris and Sally Entwistle's charming Georgian home, overlooking the Yare Valley just 2 miles from Norwich city centre. Stylish, spacious guest rooms offer every comfort and our gardens, sun terrace and heated swimming pool (summer months) are available for your pleasure. Elegant dining room with award-winning cuisine, private meeting/dining facilities. Self-contained garden cottage, also available for weekly let (see Dowagers Cottage under self-catering). Johansens Most Excellent Service Award 2001, AA 81% Quality Score, Which? Hotel Guide, AA Top 200.

- 8 bedrooms: 1 twin, 7 double
- Bathrooms: 8 en-suite

COURTESY BREAKS
Per person, per night sharing twin/double room for a minimum of two nights

DINNER, BED & BREAKFAST

	Nov	Apr-Oct
	£53	£58

Thurs/Fri/Sat/Mon nights. Dinner not available Sun.

Figure 1.8 The Old Rectory

Public limited companies

Public limited companies operate within the UK only, or in several countries as *multinationals*. Examples of public limited companies involved in the travel and tourism industry and listed on the Stock Exchange include Hilton Group, Whitbread, Carnival, Stagecoach, British Airways, Avis Europe, MyTravel, First Choice and Euro Disney. All of these companies are public limited companies and must include 'plc' as part of their name.

1 For each of the public limited companies listed above, research what its main activity is within travel and tourism.

2 The Footsie 100 lists the highest valued public limited companies in the UK. Using a quality national newspaper or the Internet, list the companies that are involved in travel and tourism.

Because the share prices of these companies are 'quoted' and the shares are sold openly on the Stock Exchange, you or any member of the public can invest in them.

Ownership control is divided between the shareholders who technically own the company (because they have invested the capital) and the controllers who are the board of directors.

Co-operatives

A co-operative is based on shareholders who own the company. However, the principles involved are more democratic – in a co-operative there is only one vote per shareholder, rather than one vote per share owned.

Partnerships

A partnership means that the ownership of the business is undertaken by several individuals – between two and twenty people.

Since a partnership involves more than one person, there is usually more capital available, so the business is likely to be larger than for a sole trader. Profits have to be shared and so does the decision-making process. All partners of a business are subject to unlimited liability. The exception to this is a 'sleeping partner' who invests in the partnership but has no active role in running the business, and whose liability to debt

CASE STUDY

Co-op Travelcare

Travelcare is part of the Co-operative Group. Travelcare is not owned by a tour operator but is the UK's largest independent travel agent. Travelcare prides itself on being able to offer impartial advice and a wide range of holidays and impartial pricing. The travel agents in high street agencies of Travelcare are not instructed to sell the holidays of one particular tour operator. This is summed up in the 'right to know' policy launched in 1998, which is unique in the travel industry. Travelcare is based on the co-operative values of openness, honesty and responsibility.

Travelcare has 390 branches nationwide and has nearly 2000 employees. Customers can also book online and over the telephone.

The Co-operative Group is a co-operative society, not a company. It has shares but their value doesn't fluctuate and they cannot be traded. All Co-ops have members and the customers become the members. The members own and democratically control what the Co-operative Group does.

See Figure 1.9, and visit www.co-op.co.uk for more information about the history, development and philosophy of the Co-operative society.

1 **In what ways does Travelcare differ from other high street travel agencies?**

2 **Explain the ways in which Travelcare has used technology.**

Figure 1.9 Leaflets from Travelcare

is limited to the amount of capital that person has invested. Each of the partners is bound by the actions of the others, which may cause a problem. For instance one partner might be unreliable and may cause the demise of the business, landing the other partner(s) in debt too.

Private limited companies

Any business organisation with the word 'limited' in its name implies that investors in the business (or shareholders) are liable only for the company's debts up to the amount of money they have invested.

CASE STUDY
Private limited companies
Sir Richard Branson's Virgin Atlantic has begun negotiations to buy 30 more aircraft by 2010, which would double the size of Virgin's fleet and employ 1400 new staff. The airline hopes to be flying to Sydney via Hong Kong by the end of 2004, and will launch new routes to Havana and Nassau in July 2005. Virgin Atlantic reported annual sales of £1503 million in the year ending April 2004 and increased operating profits on its 22 routes to £13 million. The company's audacious bid to take over Concorde came to nothing, but Branson remains keen on a merger with private airline BMI.

Another private limited company, Trailfinders, expects its staff to have travelled independently for several months on several continents. Their knowledge is one of the reasons why the company has become one of Britain's most popular independent travel agencies. It was founded in 1970 by Mike Gooley after he left the Army, and initially depended on postal bookings, almost failing to get off the ground when its launch coincided with a postal strike. Now most of Trailfinders' sales, which totalled £465 million in 2004, come through telephone bookings.

Source: The Sunday Times Top Track 100 league table

Find out about these other private limited companies in travel and tourism, and prepare your own brief case study of each: (a) Travelex (foreign exchange), (b) Welcome Break (motorway service operator), and (c) Hogg Robinson (business travel management).

Competition in the private sector

Business organisations operating in the commercial private sector have to compete in order to survive. Competition affects all types of business, from the market stall selling travel goods to the prestigious hotel in the neighbourhood. In order to compete, businesses must find out who their customers and clients are, and who is demanding their goods or services. They must also keep up to date with who their competitors are and how they market their products and services. Failure to keep up with trends and fashions will have severe repercussions on the business – it will lose customers and incur financial losses.

Theory into practice

Research the private sector businesses involved in travel and tourism in your locality. You might do this by looking in Yellow Pages or using www.yell.co.uk. Try to classify them under the different types of private sector businesses.

Non-commercial organisations

This section looks at the range of non-commercial organisations that are part of the travel and tourism industry. These include public and voluntary sector organisations. We shall look at how they define and meet objectives, their funding and generation of revenue, and how they meet stakeholder expectations.

Key term

A **stakeholder** is an interested party in a non-commercial organisation, such as a member of a charity or a taxpayer.

The public sector

The state (central or local government) provides travel and tourism activities and facilities in the public sector. In theory the public sector facilities exist to provide a service to the community – a service in this context means something that benefits or is useful to the members of the public in the area.

CASE STUDY

VisitBritain

The government department which oversees travel and tourism in the UK is the Department for Culture, Media and Sport (DCMS). The DCMS funds VisitBritain, whose website is www.visitbritain.com.

VisitBritain was created on 1 April 2003 to market Britain to the rest of the world and England to the British. It was formed by the merger of the British Tourist Authority and the English Tourism Council, with a mission to build the value of tourism by creating world-class destination brands and marketing campaigns. It will also build partnerships with other organisations that have a stake in British and English tourism.

VisitBritain has a range of goals:

- to promote Britain overseas as a tourist destination, generating additional tourism revenue throughout Britain and throughout the year

- to grow the value of the domestic market by encouraging UK residents to take additional and/or longer breaks in England

- to provide advice to government on matters affecting tourism and contribute to wider government objectives

- to work in partnership with the national tourist boards in England, Scotland, Wales and Northern Ireland and the regional tourist boards to build the British tourism industry and to promote an attractive image of Britain.

VisitBritain is funded by the DCMS to promote Britain overseas as a tourist destination and to lead and coordinate England marketing. The net Grant-in-Aid to promote Britain overseas for 2003/04 was £35.5 million. Additionally VisitBritain raises around £15 million in non-governmental funding from partners. The total resources available for England marketing is £14.1 million. VisitBritain operates a network of 25 offices covering 31 key markets – new markets for 2003/04 were Poland, Russia, China and Korea. VisitBritain employs 450 staff, 60 per cent of whom are employed overseas.

Why is it important that countries have national tourist boards funded by central government?

Aims of public sector travel and tourism organisations

The aims of a travel and tourism organisation in the public sector (e.g. a museum which is a visitor attraction) might be:

✳ to provide a service for the population in the surrounding area, such as a major event in the summer holidays

✳ to keep within the local authority budget and to make an adequate return on the local authority capital invested in the organisation.

✳ to provide jobs for people in the locality.

Think it over ...

Why do you think a local council provides and promotes events such as St Crispin's Fair, as illustrated in Figure 1.10?

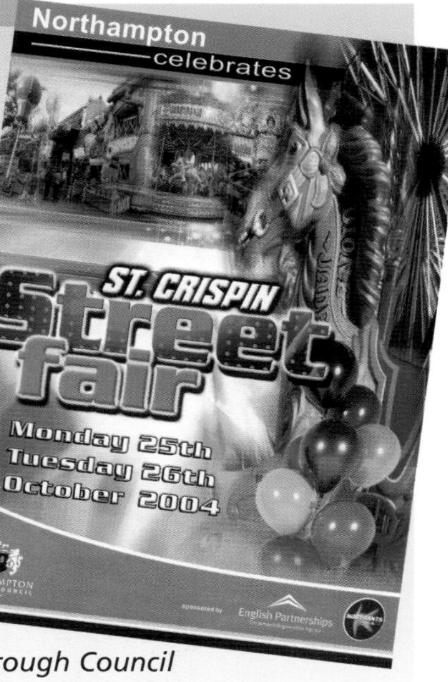

Figure 1.10
Northampton Borough Council advertises the St Crispin Street Fair

The voluntary sector

Falling between the public sector and the private sector is the voluntary sector, which embraces all kinds of organisations, such as clubs, societies and charities. These are not controlled by the state nor do they operate solely for profit. They have been formed because of some interest or need in the community.

The aims of travel and tourism organisations in the voluntary sector could include the following broad issues:

✳ to provide facilities that are not otherwise provided

✳ to strictly observe a non-profit making rule, ensuring that any surplus income that the organisation makes goes back to its members or is invested in the organisation's future (the National Trust operates in this way)

✳ to bring to the public's attention some issue in society, such as conservation or environmental protection (e.g. Friends of the Earth and Greenpeace).

There might be some political or social aim or reason for the organisation's existence, such as to encourage sustainable tourism. An example is the charity Tourism Concern (www.tourismconcern.org.uk).

In the voluntary sector an objective may be to recruit a certain number of members per year, or to hold a number of social functions in a month, or to raise a sum of money for a specific purpose.

CASE STUDY

The National Trust (NT)

The National Trust (www.nationaltrust.org.uk) is a registered charity founded in 1895 to look after places of historic interest or natural beauty permanently for the benefit of the nation across England, Wales and Northern Ireland. It is independent of government and receives no direct state grant or subsidy for its general work. The NT is one of England's leading conservation bodies, protecting through ownership and covenants 251 223 hectares of land of special importance and 965 kilometres of outstanding coastline. The Trust is dependent on the support of its 3 million members, visitors, partners and benefactors. The NT is responsible for historic buildings dating from the Middle Ages to modern times, ancient monuments, gardens, landscape parks and farmland leased to over 1500 tenant farmers.

Figure 1.11 One of the National Trust's many properties

Over the summer of 2003 the NT gained members faster than babies were born in the UK: one recruit every 42 seconds. This record membership (3.3 million) and increase in visitor figures (13 million visitors in pay-for-entry properties and an estimated 50 million to coastline and countryside owned by the NT) reflects the need of visitors for enjoying natural attractions and visiting places of historical and cultural significance.

The price of such success is high. The assets of the NT, the buildings and estates (such as Waddesdon Manor in Buckinghamshire – see Figure 1.11), are also great liabilities. Four out of five historic properties still run at a loss because the costs of looking after them outstrip any income they generate.

1 Explain why the NT is part of the voluntary sector.
2 Which type of people do you think become members of the NT? Why do you think they join?

Voluntary organisations are extremely varied in the range of activities they cover. For example, youth organisations are formed specifically for 'young people' in order to provide them with certain facilities. There is some discrepancy over what constitutes a young person – some organisations allow teenagers (those aged between 13 and 19 years) to join, while others state that a person is still 'young' up to the age of 30!

The Youth Hostel Association (www.yha.org.uk) is a registered charity. It was founded in 1930 to 'help all, especially young people of limited means, to a greater knowledge, love and care of the countryside, particularly by providing Youth Hostels or other simple accommodation for them in their travels, and thus to promote their health, rest and education'. People of all ages (including families) can join the YHA.

Adventure organisations are not for the faint-hearted. These are for outdoor recreation in the UK and abroad. Examples are the Duke of Edinburgh's Award Scheme, Outward Bound, and Operation Raleigh.

Agencies delivering products and services

Key term

A **visitor** (or **tourist**) **attraction** can be defined as a permanently established excursion destination, a primary purpose of which is to allow public access for entertainment, interest or education, rather than being a primary retail outlet or venue for sporting, theatrical or film performances. It must be open to the public, without prior booking, for published periods each year, and should be capable of attracting day visitors or tourists as well as local residents.

There are many different types of attraction, which can be broadly split into three categories: built attractions, natural attractions, and events as attractions.

Built attractions

Built attractions can be divided into:

* leisure and theme parks
* museums and art galleries
* places of worship

* historic properties
* wildlife attractions
* visitor/heritage centres
* steam/heritage railways
* country parks
* farms
* gardens
* workplaces
* other attractions.

Theory into practice

The list below names a range of built attractions in the UK with the estimated number of visitors in 2002.

York Minster (1.6 million)
London Zoo (891 000)
The Deep (750 000)
Tate Modern (4.6 million)
Blackpool Pleasure Beach (6.2 million)
Tower of London (2 million)
Westminster Abbey (1 million)
North York Moors Railway (290 000)
Eastbourne Pier (2 million)
British Airways London Eye (4 million)
Roman Baths, Bath (850 000)
Giant's Causeway Visitor Centre (400 000)
Eden Project (1.8 million)
Cheddar Gorge Cheese Company (300 000)
British Museum (4.6 million)
Cannon Hall Open Farm (350 000)
Strathclyde Country Park (5.1 million)
Edinburgh Castle (1.1 million)
Hatton Farm Village (190 000)
The Lowry, Salford (810 000)
Glasgow Botanic Gardens (400 000),
Legoland Windsor (1.4 million)
Stonehenge (760 000)
Drayton Manor Family Theme Park (1.4 million)
Carsington Water Visitor Centre (800 000)

1 Classify the tourist attractions into the categories listed above.

2 Try to explain the differences in the number of visitors to the attractions.

3 Find out the location of each of the tourist attractions. Is there any pattern to their location?

4 Find out which attractions are free to enter and those you have to pay to get in. Does this make any difference to visitor numbers?

Theory into practice

Figure 1.12 shows the fronts of two leaflets for very different visitor attractions. One is for Diggerland (www.diggerland.com), where children and adults can, among other things, drive a JCB. The other is for Sandringham (www.sandringhamestate.co.uk), the country retreat of Queen Elizabeth. Visit the websites to obtain further information, and then compare and contrast the products and services available at the two visitor attractions. If you prefer, carry out this activity using other contrasting attractions, possibly using leaflets that you collect.

Figure 1.12 Two very contrasting visitor attractions: Sandringham and Diggerland

Natural attractions

The range and variety of natural attractions in the UK is vast. There is beautiful coastline, rugged mountain scenery, picturesque lakes and plentiful countryside. Many of these areas are of national and international significance, such as Snowdonia, the Lake District and the Scottish Highlands and Islands.

Natural attractions are a major factor in motivating visitors to travel to an area, and

around these other tourist facilities, services and amenities will develop. For example, tourists may be attracted to Cornwall by the beauty of its beaches and inland scenery, but will want other tourism services such as accommodation, transportation and built attractions to provide a total holiday experience.

Many areas of the UK have been granted special status to help protect the environment and provide facilities for the public to enjoy. These include national parks, areas of outstanding natural beauty (AONBs) and heritage coasts.

The most dramatic and relatively wild expanses of countryside in England, Wales and Scotland have been designated as national parks. The purpose of national parks is to preserve and enhance the natural beauty of each area and promote its enjoyment by the public. In England and Wales, the National Parks and Access to the Countryside Act 1949 paved the way for the designation of areas to national park status. National parks provide some of the finest natural resources for tourism related to sport and active recreation. For example they provide many internationally important sites for climbing, mountaineering, hill walking, canoeing and caving. They are also the location of many outdoor adventure and environmental education centres.

Events as attractions

Why do events take place? Every organiser of every event will have a different answer for this question. Raising money is frequently a top priority, whether for a particular attraction, a society or a charity. Often raising the profile of an organisation is equally important. Sometimes events are organised as essentially private affairs to say 'thank you' to a specific group of people.

An example is English Heritage (www.english-heritage.org.uk) which has three branches of its organisation running events. The Special Events Unit organises events intended to entertain and educate existing members, raise revenue, and raise the profile of EH to recruit new members. The Concerts Unit organises concerts that are intended to raise both the profile of, and revenue for, EH and to provide entertainment for EH

members and for the general public. The Education Service organises a small number of events for groups within formal education that are intended to supplement and extend aspects of particular curriculum areas.

Accommodation and catering

Accommodation and catering are extremely important aspects of travel and tourism. When coming back from holiday the two most common questions asked of the holidaymaker are 'what was the accommodation like?' and 'what was the food like?' Tourists usually have high expectations of eating well. The catering component of the travel and tourism industry has grown rapidly in the UK. This is looked at in more depth in option unit 7.

Accommodation can be described as either *serviced* or *unserviced* (self-catering). In serviced accommodation, meals and housekeeping are provided. The meals provided can range from simply breakfast only to breakfast plus two main meals a day.

> ### Key term
>
> **Housekeeping** means that the guests' rooms are cleaned, beds made and towels changed.

With self-catering or unserviced accommodation there are no meals or housekeeping provided. This type of accommodation is often less expensive than the serviced type. Houses, cottages and apartments can be rented for self-catering purposes. Camping and caravanning sites have developed extensive facilities to make visitors comfortable in their stay. The sites are often luxurious, providing a whole range of facilities such as restaurants, pubs, sports and leisure centres, shops and all kinds of entertainment from play leaders for children to nightclubs. These sites are often called 'holiday parks' as they offer much more than simply a place to camp or site the caravan.

*Holiday centre*s are another form of accommodation that provide entertainment and leisure facilities. In the UK these used to be called 'holiday camps' – more information on these was given earlier in the chapter (see page 18).

Hotels are serviced accommodation ranging from luxury to basic, and from those with hundreds of bedrooms to those with a handful. A small hotel or *guest house* may be run by only one or two people, often the owners, while larger hotels employ hundreds. The standards of facilities provided by hotels vary widely too.

Visitors need an easy way of knowing the standard of facilities they can expect in a hotel. For this reason *classification systems* have been developed. In Britain classification is voluntary, so accommodation establishments can choose whether or not they wish to become classified. The AA, the English Tourism Council (ETC), now called VisitBritain, and the RAC joined together to create one overall rating scheme for hotels and guest accommodation. When you see one of the signs showing stars or diamonds, you know that the place has been visited anonymously by qualified inspectors, who all work to the same high standards. The establishment is allowed to display the classification it is given on a plaque near the entrance, and to use the classification in advertising material.

For more information about these hotel and guest accommodation ratings, contact the AA (www.theaa.co.uk), the RAC (www.rac.org.uk) or VisitBritain. A summary of the classification is shown in Figure 1.13.

Accommodation establishments can call themselves hotels, guest houses or bed & breakfasts (B&Bs). What they are called often depends on the size of the establishment and the facilities offered. Large hotels are operated by hotel groups, such as Hilton or Holiday Inn. These companies own a number of hotels and run them as a recognisable chain. However, just because hotels belong to a group does not mean they are all identical.

ratings you can trust

The VisitBritain, AA and RAC ratings are your sign of quality assurance, so you can have the confidence that your accommodation has been thoroughly checked and rated for quality before you make a booking.

HOTEL

Hotels are given a rating of from one to five Stars - the more Stars, the higher the quality and the greater the range of facilities and level of services provided.

⭐ Red stars denote an establishment within the Top 200 as graded by the AA

GOLD & SILVER

Awarded to those establishments that exceed the overall quality required for their rating

GUEST ACCOMMODATION

Guest Accommodation, which includes guesthouses, bed and breakfasts, inns and farmhouses, is rated one to five Diamonds. Progressively higher levels of quality and customer care must be provided for each of the Diamonds.

◆ Red diamonds denote an establishment within the Top 200 as graded by the AA

Awarded to AA appointed establishments serving food distinctly above the standard encountered throughout most of the restaurant industry

HOLIDAY PARK

Holiday Parks, Touring Parks and Camping Parks are also assessed using Stars. You will find progressively higher standards of quality for One Star (acceptable) to a Five Star (exceptional) park.

▶ ▶ ▶

AA equivalent grading (on a scale of 1-5).

Awarded by the RAC to guest accommodation for excellent standards of hospitality & service.

SELF-CATERING

All properties have to meet an extensive list of minimum requirements. The more Stars, the higher the overall level of quality you can expect to find. Establishments at higher rating levels also have to meet some additional requirements for facilities.

Raᴄ Awarded only to RAC accredited establishments. the RAC Dining Award recognises excellence in the overall dining experience, encompassing quality of cooking, service, ambience and comfort.

Accessibility for Serviced & Self-Catering Accommodation

Accommodation that displays one of the signs shown below are committed to accessibility. When you see one of the symbols, you can be sure that the accommodation has been thoroughly assessed against demanding criteria.

Mobility Impairment

 Level 1 – Typically suitable for a person with sufficient mobility to climb a flight of steps but would benefit from points of fixtures and fittings to aid balance.

 Level 2 – Typically suitable for a person with restricted walking ability and for those that may need to use a wheelchair some of the time.

 Level 3 – Typically suitable for a person who depends on the use of a wheelchair and transfers unaided to and from the wheelchair some of the time.

 Level 4 – Typically suitable for a person who depends on the use of a wheelchair in a seated position. They can require personal/mechanical assistance to aid transfer (eg carer, hoist).

Hearing Impairment

 Level 2 – Recommended (Best Practice) additional requirements to meet the National Accessible Standards for guests with hearing impairment, from mild hearing loss to profoundly deaf.

Visual Impairment

 Level 2 – Recommended (Best Practice) additional requirements to meet the National Accessible Standards for visually impaired guests.

Figure 1.13 Accommodation ratings

Figure 1.14 is part of a brochure for a Holiday Inn hotel.

1 Why do you think there are different tariffs for weekdays and weekends?

2 What do you consider to be the advantages and disadvantages of the hotel's location?

3 The hotel is advertised as 'great value for business or leisure'. What facilities are particularly for business travellers? What could a leisure visitor find of interest in the area?

Express by Holiday Inn

Northampton M1, Jct15

Tariff	£69.95*
Weekends	£49.00*

- 126 en-suite bedrooms
- Power shower and hairdryer
- Colour TV with Sky channels in all rooms
- In-room pay movies
- Tea/coffee making facilities
- Direct-dial telephones
- In-room computer points
- Complimentary buffet-style continental breakfast

meet smart

- Laundry and dry cleaning service
- Vending area for drinks and snacks
- Meet Smart business centre with 2 large air-conditioned meeting rooms seating up to 60 theatre-style and 6 syndicate rooms
- Photocopying, facsimile and e-mail services
- Licensed Bar

Children up to 19 years old can stay free in parents' bedroom.
*Prices based on 2 adults per room - extra adult charge £15.00.

These prices include VAT and are subject to change without notice.

Express by Holiday Inn

Northampton M1, Jct15

Express by Holiday Inn Northampton
Junction 15, M1
Cheaney Drive
Grange Park
Northampton
NN4 5FB

Tel: +44 (0) 1604 432800 Fax: +44 (0) 1604 432832
Email: northampton@expressbyholidayinn.net
Website: www.hiexpressnorthampton.co.uk

Located at junction 15 of the M1: at the motorway access roundabout, follow signs for Northampton and Grange Park. At the traffic lights, take the dedicated road into Grange Park and follow signs to the hotel entrance.

In the county of spires, squires, Silverstone and Althorp House, Northampton is a quintessentially English town with a wonderful mix of traditional craft heritage, modern industries, sport, leisure pursuits and rural history. The hotel offers a great launchpad for exploring the Midlands and undiscovered Eastern England.

Great Value for Business or Leisure and
Easy to Book
Just call
0800 434040

Figure 1.14 One of Holiday Inn's hotels

1 Where do visitors stay when they come to your area for business or pleasure? Where do they go to eat and drink?

2 Conduct a survey of local newspapers to find out various examples of each kind of accommodation and catering mentioned in this section.

Tourism development and promotion

Tourist destinations and attractions can be successful only if they attract enough tourists. People need to be told of a destination and encouraged to visit. Tourism promotion is concerned with making potential visitors aware of a destination and persuading them to choose to visit there rather than anywhere else.

Key term

Tourism promotion is the name given to the business of persuading tourists to visit a particular area.

Promotion is so important in tourism that most destinations have established official organisations that are responsible for encouraging people to visit them.

Local tourism development and promotion

A local Tourist Information Centre (TIC) informs you about accommodation, transportation, visitor attractions and events in the area it serves. When arriving at a holiday area, many tourists make the TIC their first stop. TICs in the UK offer a free, nationwide service. Most of them are run by the local authority. TICs can be found in a variety of locations – railway stations, airports and ports, town halls or libraries, and at major tourist attractions. TICs can be managed by the national or regional tourist board, or by the local authority. They are almost always paid for out of public funds, and you rarely have to pay for any information provided.

Most TICs provide accommodation services. The TIC will make a reservation for you at a local hotel or guest house. The TIC will check availability of accommodation in your price range and will contact the hotel or guest house to make a booking. Alternatively, the TIC may run a book-a-bed-ahead service, which is useful if you are travelling from place to place. By going to a TIC in one location, a room can be booked in the next town you are planning to visit. A small charge will be made for these services.

Theory into practice

Visit your local TIC and complete the research sheet in Figure 1.15.

LOCATION OF TIC: ______________________ OPENING TIMES: ______________________

WHAT INFORMATION IS AVAILABLE AT THE TIC?
e.g. special event product information, leaflets

WHAT PRODUCTS ARE AVAILABLE FOR SALE AT THE TIC?
e.g. guide books, maps, souvenirs, postcards

WHAT SERVICES DOES THE TIC PROVIDE?
e.g. car hire, excursions, coach, rail and theatre tickets, hotel bookings

Figure 1.15 Tourist Information Centre research

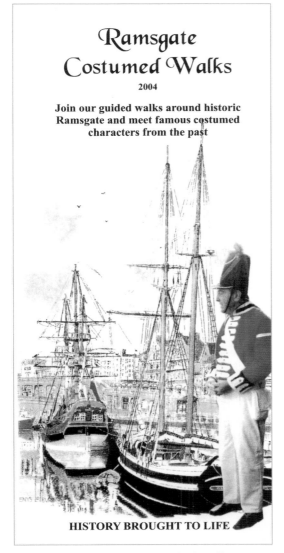

Ramsgate Costumed Walks

2004

Join our guided walks around historic Ramsgate and meet famous costumed characters from the past

HISTORY BROUGHT TO LIFE

"If there should be no human being that you can love enough, love the town in which you dwell... I love Paris and London, though I am a child of the pine woods and the beach in Ramsgate"

Vincent Van Gogh in a letter to his brother, Theo. Autumn 1876

***

"To Ramsgate we used to go frequently in the summer and I remember living in Townley House (near town), and going there by steamer."

From the manuscript of Queen Victoria's reminiscences of her early childhood. 1872

***

"Besides, my whole soul is devoted to building this church here. I have got the site and am collecting the materials. I have a delightful plan of a <u>flint</u> seaside church, and everything gives way to that"

A W N Pugin, writing to his patron, the Earl of Shrewsbury. 1846

There is no set charge for these walks as we are all volunteers but donations to help meet the cost of the walks and the upkeep of the costumes are welcome. We suggest £2 per person. All those taking part in the walks do so at their own risk. No specific liability insurance is held.

Special thanks go to Denys Le Fevre for his illustrations and to all those who have helped in so many ways, especially those providing refreshments and to Thanet District Council.

Special walks for parties can be arranged with notice. For further information contact: Tourist Information Centre on 01843 583333.

Figure 1.16 Ramsgate's guided walks

Guiding services are also part of tourism information services, as demonstrated in Figure 1.16.

Theory into practice

1 Draw a simple street map of your town centre, the centre of a town you know well, or part of the city in which you live.

2 On this, mark places of interest to the day visitor – museums, special buildings, theatres, sports or leisure facilities etc.

3 Write down instructions for a one-hour walking tour, and give details of the places of interest to be seen on the walk.

Regional tourism development and promotion

In England there are ten regional tourist boards (look back at Figure 1.6 on page 12). They are essentially membership organisations that provide a range of services for their private and public sector members. Members of a tourist board come from many areas of travel and tourism – hoteliers, restaurant owners and tourist attractions, as well as local councils, educational establishments and guest houses. Many of the regional tourist boards operate as private limited companies, so are commercial organisations.

The main responsibilities of the English regional tourist boards are to:

* have a thorough knowledge of tourism within the region, the facilities and organisations involved in the tourism industry
* advise the national board on the regional aspects of major policy issues and to supply management information
* service enquiries attributable to nationally developed promotions and to provide literature
* coordinate regional tourist information services as part of the national TIC network
* maintain close liaison with planning authorities on policies affecting tourism
* carry out a continuing domestic public relations campaign with the local authorities, the travel trade and the public within the region, with a view to ensuring that issues are understood and the regional and national objectives are known: to create awareness of the need for tourism to be managed for the benefit of residents as well as tourists
* promote tourism to the regions both from other parts of the country and from overseas.

In Wales, the Wales Tourist Board has established associated companies – North Wales Tourism, Mid Wales Tourism and Tourism South Wales.

National tourism development and promotion

The UK national tourist boards (Northern Ireland Tourist Board, Wales Tourist Board, Scottish Tourist Board and the English Tourism Council) were established in 1969 with the Development of Tourism Act.

These NTBs want to maximise the economic benefits of tourism to their particular country by stimulating the development and marketing of high-quality travel and tourism products. These national tourist boards do not get involved in the day-to-day running or tourist facilities, but set out the ways in which such organisations should operate.

Besides the four main tourist boards stated above, there are separate NTBs for the Isle of Man, Guernsey and Jersey. All have the same broad aims:

* advising the government and public sector organisations on all matters concerning tourism
* maximising tourism's contribution to the economy by creating wealth and jobs
* enhancing the image of their countries as tourist destinations
* encouraging sustainable tourism development
* researching trends in tourism and consumer requirements.

Transportation

Air transport

Air travel is attractive because it is quick and has a great distance range. In fact, no part of the world is now more than 24 hours flying time from any other part.

Scheduled flights offer a safe, convenient, reliable and frequent method of transportation. Scheduled flights are so called because they operate regularly, according to published schedules (or timetables) that are fixed in advance. This is especially attractive to business travellers, who appreciate the speed and flexibility and the routes available, but also to leisure travellers who enjoy being able to reach their destination quickly. Ground services and terminal facilities are more advanced and sophisticated than for other forms of transportation, and so the travelling experience is enhanced. The quality of service and comfort offered on board is high. These flights operate whether or not there are enough passengers to make a profit for the airline company. Most airlines offering scheduled services are national airlines – British Airways, Air France, Qantas for example.

Charter flights are used principally to move holidaymakers on package holidays and operate only when they have been hired for a specific purpose. Sometimes charter airlines belong to tour operators (e.g. Britannia Airways is part of Thomson). Charter flights fly direct to their final destination, often at less busy times for airports (which may be inconvenient times for the traveller). The space in the aircraft is reduced in comparison with scheduled flights and only basic services are offered. Most charter flights are to holiday destinations, such as the Mediterranean, and the cost of a charter flight is usually less than a scheduled flight to the same destination as charter flights have fewer empty seats on them.

Theory into practice

Locate UK airports on a map. Research your closest airport that offers international flights.

Land transport by road or rail

Road transport is dominated by the motor car and coaches. Road transport can even offer accommodation, in the case of recreational vehicles (RVs), caravans and trailer tents.

Coaches that are chartered are again exclusive for visitor purposes, but scheduled services provide for commuters and shoppers as well as visitors. Coaches represent a relatively cheap form of transport to and around tourist destinations. Express services run between most of Britain's cities on well-equipped coaches, with toilet facilities and refreshments served.

Local bus services are also used by visitors to a town or city. In London about 20 per cent of passengers on the buses are tourists.

Journeys by motorway are faster than on other roads because they are planned for efficiency and enable drivers to travel at higher speeds. Motorways do not pass through towns, and there are no traffic lights, crossroads or roundabouts to slow down traffic.

Car hire is popular, among those travelling for business as well as leisure. Cars can be hired at one location and returned to an office of the same car hire company at another location.

Key term

Hiring a car as a pre-paid part of a holiday package is known as a **fly/drive** holiday. The car is frequently picked up at the airport at the destination.

Trains are perceived to be safe and inexpensive, and sometimes also travel through attractive scenery. Railway terminals are often in the centre of the destination, which is not always the case with airports.

The traditional train traveller is the independent holidaymaker, particularly in the VFR category, as well as the traveller with a fear of flying. Most trains offer passengers a choice of service and facilities, which may include sleeping accommodation, restaurant cars serving snacks and meals, sockets for charging mobile phones and laptops, and on-board entertainment.

Water transport

Water transport can be divided into short sea ferry transport and ocean-going cruises. Other categories of water transport also exist, such as inland waterway craft and small pleasure boats.

Ferries

Britain is linked by regular ferry services to all European countries with North Sea and channel coasts, and to Ireland. These ferry services are usually used by passengers in combination with some form of land transport such as coach, train or car that will carry them to the ferry port from their place of origin and on to their final destination after the sea crossing.

Theory into practice

Use these websites of ferry companies to discover the UK departure ports and the continental ferry ports they sail to. Plot these ports and routes on a map.

- www.brittany-ferries.co.uk
- www.condorferries.co.uk
- www.dfds.co.uk
- www.fjordline.co.uk
- www.hoverspeed.com
- www.norfolkline.com
- www.poferries.com
- www.seafrance.com
- www.speedferries.com
- www.stenaline.co.uk
- www.transmancheferries.com.

Cruise ships

For tourists on ocean-going cruise ships, it is the ship that is a major feature of the holiday. The cruise ship is their means of transport, their accommodation and the source of their meals and entertainment. The tourists may disembark at various points along the route to explore the ports and possibly sample the local fare, but they always return to the ship to spend the night.

Inland waterways

Inland waterways consist of navigable rivers and canals along which holidaymakers travel at a leisurely pace on various types of boat. They move from place to place, disembarking to explore when they wish.

The canals of the UK have their own style of boats – 'narrowboats'. These are long and narrow and often painted in bright colours. Cabin cruisers are shorter and wider boats and more often found on rivers.

The boats used for canal or river travel are usually rented by the week and can be handled by people who have no previous experience of sailing. The most popular cruising areas in the UK are the Norfolk Broads, central England and Wales, the River Thames and the Caledonian Canal.

Travel agencies

Retail travel agencies are found in every high street, but also on dedicated TV channels, TV text and the Internet. All travel agencies have the main aim of selling holidays and associated products like insurance, car hire and currency exchange.

Travel agents provide information and advice to their clients. Much of the information presented to clients is by means of brochures, and the staff should possess all the necessary travel skills to interpret these. They should understand timetables, know the system of fare pricing and how to obtain tickets for all forms of transportation. Travel agents can also put together an itinerary and arrange a round-the-world tour.

The retail travel industry in the UK is dominated by national multiples. Multiples are agencies that have branches throughout the country, such as Lunn Poly and Thomas Cook. There are also independent travel agencies who do not form part of a national chain. These may be 'miniples', having a number of shops in a particular geographical location (e.g. Yorks Travel located in Northamptonshire) or just one retail outlet, perhaps providing a specialist service.

There are other travel agencies that concentrate solely on business travel. Many large commercial organisations are longstanding clients of these specialist agencies and require speed and flexibility. Business travel agencies deal almost exclusively with scheduled flights on major airlines and accommodation in large international hotel chains.

Many travel agents and tour operators are members of the Association of British Travel Agents (ABTA). Members are entitled to display the ABTA logo. Customers know they have a firm guarantee that if the travel agent or tour operator goes out of business before the customer goes on holiday, or while he or she is overseas, the special emergency fund created from travel agents' and tour operators' subscriptions to ABTA is used to provide a refund or to bring the person back to the UK at the end of the holiday. ABTA travel agents sell holidays only by tour operators who are members of ABTA.

Travel agents who wish to earn commission from sales of international airline tickets must obtain a licence from IATA, the International Air Transport Association.

Theory into practice

You should ask the permission of the retail travel agent before you carry out this activity.

Visit a local travel agency. Make rough sketches of the window, highlighting any late availability displays and special offers. Which countries or resorts are being advertised? Is the travel agency a member of ABTA or any other organisation? Is the travel agency owned by a tour operator?

Tour operators

A tour operator puts together holiday packages – by pre-booking travel with national and international carriers, chartering aircraft, organising transfers from ports and airports, buying space in all types of accommodation, devising a variety of excursions, and providing overseas representation. The tour operator then arranges all these elements in various combinations, presents them as ready-made holidays in a brochure, in newspapers and possibly on its website. The packages are offered to

travel agents to sell for a commission, as well as directly to customers.

Components of a package holiday

Package holidays are made up of three components:

* accommodation
* transportation
* other travel services and ancillaries.

The accommodation component of a package can be serviced or self-catering (unserviced). Serviced accommodation is usually in a hotel that can offer a range of meal arrangements, including:

* all-inclusive
* full board (three meals a day are provided)
* half board (breakfast plus either a midday or evening meal)
* bed and breakfast
* European plan (no meals included).

Customers can usually request a certain type of room – perhaps with a sea view or a balcony – for the payment of a *supplementary charge*.

The transportation element of a package holiday can be travel by air, coach, rail, ship or self-drive car. Seventy-five per cent of all package holidays sold in the UK include air travel.

Ancillary services may include:

* the services of a representative
* transfers to and from accommodation and the point of entry
* car hire
* excursions
* equipment hire (skis, bicycles etc.)
* insurance.

Theory into practice

1 Collect a holiday brochure from each of the 'Big Four' tour operators – TUI, Thomas Cook, First Choice and MyTravel. Ensure they are for similar products (for example, all summer-sun).

2 Compare and contrast a similar holiday in each brochure.

Integration

Key term

Integration is the combination of two or more companies under the same control for mutual benefit.

A feature of tour operators is integration, which reduces competition, saves costs by reducing overheads, captures a larger market share, and pools technical or financial resources. There is also the opportunity to co-operate on research and development of new products. This can be illustrated by the case of one of the 'Big Four' operators, TUI (see Figure 1.17).

AVIATION

Britannia Airways
Thomson Flights
Thomsonfly

BRANDS – TOUR OPERATORS

Thomson Holidays
Freestyle
Just
Skytours
Crystal Holidays
Jetsave
Jersey Travel Service
Airtravel
Headway Holidays
Magic Travel Group
OSL
Simply Travel
Something Special Holidays
Spanish Harbour Holidays
Tropical Places

RETAIL TRAVEL AGENCIES

Lunn Poly
Budget Travel Shops
Callers – Pegasus
Sibbald Travel
Team Lincoln
Travel House

Figure 1.17 The world of TUI

Theory into practice

Collect a variety of newspapers and magazines, especially the weekend papers that have travel sections. Divide these up between the class. Working individually, cut out several travel or transportation-related advertisements. Classify these advertisements into those paid for by tour operators, by tourism promotion bodies and by principals. Group these together and make a classroom display of the advertisements.

Destination case study: Isle of Man

The Isle of Man (IoM) is situated in the Irish Sea, surrounded by Northern Ireland, Scotland, England and Wales. It is easily reached by sea or air, and is 33 miles long and 13 miles wide (see Figure 1.18).

The IoM is a unique self-governing kingdom – a Crown dependency. It has its own parliament, laws, traditions, culture, postage stamps, currency and language, though everyone uses the English language and all UK currencies are accepted.

The capital is Douglas, a thriving port on the east coast. It is the hub of much island activity and has a great variety of accommodation, holiday attractions and amenities such as first-class shopping, pubs and restaurants. Other popular holiday towns and resorts are Port Erin, Port St Mary, Castletown, Peel, Ramsey and Laxey, plus many rural villages. A visitor's needs can be met comfortably, from four-star hotels and idyllic country cottages, to quality B&B accommodation and self-catering apartments.

Built tourist attractions on the IoM

The IoM is rich in history; the Vikings, Celts and other peoples having left their marks on the island. These features are captured in the Manx National Heritage 'Story of Mann' (see Figure 1.19 for part of the leaflet advertising this).

The Great Laxey Wheel (known as 'Lady Isabella') celebrated its 150th anniversary in 2004. It was built to pump water from the Laxey mines, and is now the largest surviving water-wheel of its kind in the world. A climb to the top is

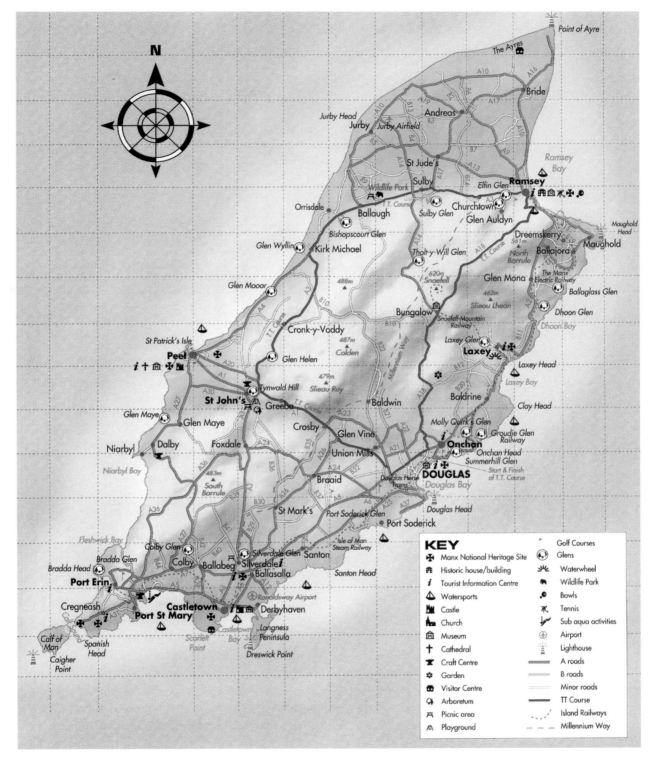

Figure 1.18 The Isle of Man

rewarded with breathtaking views across the valley. The 'Mines Trail' displays the remains of a once thriving industrial complex and offers a pleasant walk through Glen Mooar.

The Laxey Wheel has a long history of tourism. In the middle of the nineteenth century the

Figure 1.19 The Manx Museum and the house of Manannan

island's tourist industry was in its infancy, but the coming of a statutory week's holiday meant that workers from the manufacturing towns of Lancashire and Yorkshire came to Douglas and made a trip out to climb the wheel. The wives living in the miners' houses close to the wheel found it profitable to turn their front rooms into small cafés, and the road is now known as 'Ham and Egg Terrace'. The site is now managed by Manx National Heritage and National Trust.

Natural tourist attractions on the IoM

The island has 26 miles of uncrowded beaches and 100 miles of spectacular coastline. Raad ny Fiollen (Road of the Gull) is an around-the-island coastal walk with magnificent views. The walk is approximately 90 miles and has been marked by a sign incorporating the silhouette of a gull. The walk can be split into sections, as the complete route takes about four days to complete. Bayr ny Skeddan (Herring Road) is the second of the long-distance footpaths, clearly marked with a sign incorporating the herring. It is approximately 14 miles long and based on the route taken by Manx fishermen in the past as they went between Castletown and Peel.

The IoM has seventeen national glens all with their natural beauty maintained and preserved by the Forestry Department. There are no admission charges. There are two types of glen, coastal and

Story of Mann TEN THOUSAND YEARS OF UNIQUE MANX HERITAGE

the HOUSE OF MANANNAN

Audio-visual presentations and walk-through displays present vivid ilustrations from the age when fishing and trade were the life blood of the Island. Explore the busy quayside of 19th century Peel town, see the famous Manx kipper in production and listen to the people whose fascinating stories describe the rich maritime heritage of Mann.

The mythological sea god, Manannan, guides you through the Island's rich Celtic, Viking and Maritime past, over 2000 years of unique Manx heritage. Step inside splendid reconstructions of a Manx Celtic roundhouse and a Viking longhouse. Discover the stories of Celtic Christianity and Viking mythology which are carved into the magnificent Manx stone crosses. The specially built 'Odin's Raven' Viking longship was actually sailed from Norway to Mann as part of our Millennium of Tynwald celebrations, and this impressive display emphasises the importance of seafarers and the sea in the Story of Mann.

mountain. The coastal glens often lead down to a beach, while the mountain glens are spectacular with their streams, waterfalls and pools. Many glens include picnic facilities.

IoM events

The island is known as the 'road-racing capital of the world' because it hosts some of the most exciting motor sports events on two and four wheels. Road-racing on the IoM began with the 1904 Gordon Bennett Cup Eliminating Trials comprising a hill climb, speed trials on Douglas promenade and a high-speed reliability trial over five laps of a 51-mile course. From late May through to September, road-racing frequently

takes place on the island, the fastest being the legendary TT (Tourist Trophy) Festival Fortnight held in the first two weeks of June.

Accommodation and catering on the IoM

The IoM is one of the few destinations in the British Isles which operates compulsory registration of accommodation, classification and grading of all its tourist accommodation. Every year all tourist accommodation receives an independent assessment and is awarded a rating. Visitors can therefore be confident that their accommodation has been thoroughly checked and quality rated accordingly. Figure 1.20 shows an example of what is on offer.

FALCON'S NEST

★★   AA ★★

This family run hotel can offer you more than you might think...

There are spectacular views from many of the bedrooms, the seaward bar and restaurant. The Falcon's Nest is a friendly, traditional hotel committed to a straightforward, value-for-money policy; providing you with quality service and the opportunity to relax in comfortable surroundings. Only two minutes walk from the sheltered, sandy and idyllic Port Erin Bay – an ideal base from which to explore the sights of our magnificent island.

Superb cuisine is professionally prepared and served in the à la carte restaurant, carvery and bars – table d'hôte and children's menus are available.

All the bedrooms are ensuite, comfortable and attractively furnished, with tea and coffee making facilities, satellite TV and direct-dial phones. Baby listening and cots can be provided. Non smoking rooms available.

The hotel's lounge bar is in the true spirit of the public house. You can relax in front of a traditional open fire to enjoy the magnificent views and the local ales. The saloon bar, meanwhile, has a pool table, juke box and a lively, convivial atmosphere. The hotel also has business conference facilities and private function suites.

We look forward to making your stay an enjoyable one.

Prices per person, including VAT	High season: May – September	Low season: all other months.	
Bed & breakfast	Seven days high £245.00	Seven days low £199.50	Daily £42.50

Weekend B and B special – £60.00 per couple per night – min. stay 2 nights (max. 4 nights) only available low season. Ref: AW1 must be quoted when booking to ensure this price.

No single-room supplement. TT and inclusive travel prices on request. Children under 12 £5.00 B and B daily. Children 12–16 sharing £12.50 B and B daily. Reduced rates for groups. Dogs welcome. FREE transfers from Douglas sea terminal and Ronaldsway airport by prior arrangement, whenever possible. Prices correct at time of printing.

Freephone: 0500 121275 ext 2

Falcon's Nest Hotel, Port Erin, Isle of Man. IM9 6AF

Telephone: 01624 834077   Fax: 01624 835370   email: falconsnest@enterprise.net
www.falconsnesthotel.co.uk

Phone, fax or write for a free brochure and quote for your inclusive holiday.
Please use BLOCK CAPITALS:

Name ....

Address ....

....

....

Postcode ....   Tel. No. ....

Figure 1.20 The Falcon's Nest Hotel

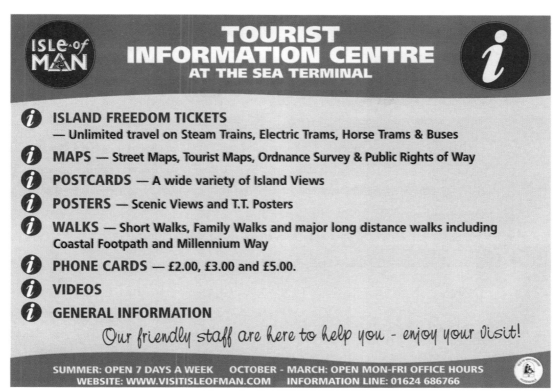

Figure 1.21 Isle of Man's Tourist Information Centre

Tourism development and promotion for the IoM

The Tourist Information Centre is based at the sea terminal in Douglas and is open throughout the year (see Figure 1.21). Leaflets, books and maps, some of which are free, are available from the TIC – some have been produced also in French and German. There are other tourist information points at various places on the island.

The IoM is making a name for itself as a film location – since 1995 more than 50 feature films and TV drama series have been made on location on the island. The Isle of Man Film Commission, part of the Department of Trade and Industry, was set up to promote the island to film-makers, to whom it offers incentive packages to shoot at least part of their movie on the island. More information is available by visiting www.gov.im/dti/iomfilm.

The Department of Tourism and Leisure operates a consumer website under the name www.visitisleofman.com. The site receives between 40 and 60 thousand visits per month and provides comprehensive information on most of the island's accommodation as well as airlines and

ferry details. It also contains a wealth of information on activities and special interests such as golf, walking, fishing, cycling and motor sport, to help plan programmes and itineraries.

The media strategy by the Department of Tourism and Leisure for 2004 was based on raising awareness. The colour press was used to generate extra response using three major titles – *Telegraph Magazine*, *Sunday Express Magazine* and the *Mail on Sunday's You* magazine.

Radio also featured on the schedule with a Classic FM mini-campaign which comprised airtime, a presenter promotion, website activity and advertorials in the radio station's publication.

The most exciting change to 2004's schedule was the use of TV, back on the schedule for the first time in over seven years. A 60-second commercial was produced focusing on the beauty of the IoM, brought alive through the people that live and work there. The commercial was highly targeted towards delivering brochure requests, and interactive TV has been used as the main mechanism for this. The commercial ran on a number of Sky channels targeted towards the key audience.

Isle of Man Direct

It's as easy as 1, 2, 3...

1 Choose to **travel** by air from 15 regional airports or by sea from Liverpool, Heysham, Belfast or Dublin - you can even take your own car!

2 Call your chosen accommodation from this guide and ask them to book your travel arrangements with **Isle of Man Direct Faresavers** and take advantage of our superb rates.

3 **Or call us direct and we can arrange the whole package.**

Travel by sea and the
Kids go FREE
if booked by 29 February 2004

Sea travel from £38 per person

Travel by sea from only £38 per person. Departures are available from Liverpool, Heysham, Belfast or Dublin. Why not take your own car on the ferry too! - prices start from £29 return.

Price Pledge - We are confident that you will find the sea prices within our brochure competitive. However, should you find sea prices offered at a lower rate **we guarantee to beat that price**. Our price pledge is only applicable at the time of booking and cannot be requested once your sailing has been confirmed.

Air travel from £85 per person

Flights are offered from 15 regional airports. Prices are constantly fluctuating so we may well be able to quote a cheaper price than offered here, so please call today for the **most competitive fares.**

Whatever you want...
Whatever your requirements may be in the Isle of Man

call 7 days a week on...

0870 889 0819 Please quote reference **XV**

or email: specials@everymann.co.uk

Our Prices include...
- Air passenger duty
- **Financial security** - we are an ABTA & ATOL bonded operator
- We can also arrange low cost **car hire** and **holiday insurance**

ABTA V0762

www.everymann.co.uk
Select 'travel information' for travel fares

Everymann & Isle of Man Direct are trading names of **Premier Holidays Limited**.

Figure 1.22 Some package holidays to the Isle of Man

Tour operators

Some tour operators specialise in packages to the IoM. With most of these you can book direct over the telephone, by fax or through a travel agent. Most have on-line details available and produce brochures of the packages they have on offer (see Figure 1.22).

Transportation

The map and route information in Figure 1.23 show the IoM's uniquely convenient position between England, Northern Ireland, Scotland and Wales, and how well it is served by air and by sea from locations all over the British Isles. There are also connecting flights to the rest of the world.

Flights touch down at Ronaldsway Airport and ferries dock at the Douglas Sea Terminal. Flights from UK airports can take as little time as 40 minutes.

Transport by road on the island

The IoM has 688 miles of roads. Driving is on the left and road signs are in English. Cars can be transported on the ferries, or can be rented on the island.

There are frequent bus services on routes all over the island. Money-saving Explorer Tickets can be used on buses, trains and horse trams (see Figure 1.24). Coach tours of the island run throughout the summer.

The island has a remarkable Victorian transport system. The Steam Railway originated in 1873 and at 15 miles is the longest narrow-gauge steam line in the British Isles. It travels between Douglas and Port Erin.

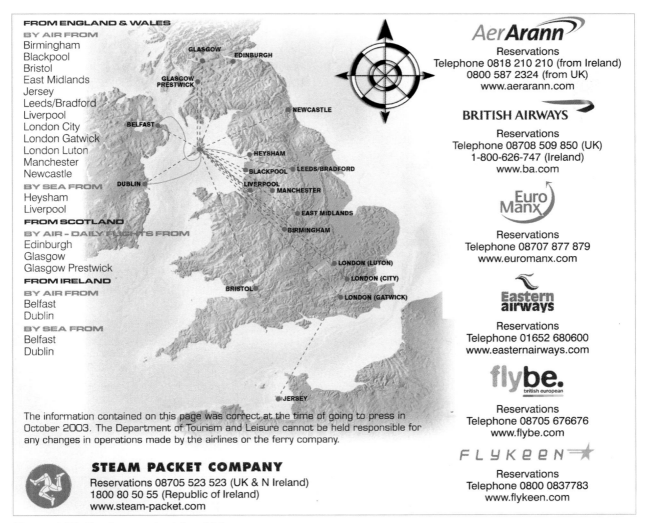

Figure 1.23 Getting to the Isle of Man

Figure 1.24 The IoM Explorer ticket

The Manx Electric Railway has been in operation since 1893 and runs for 18 miles between Douglas and Ramsey, much of the route along the coastline.

Snaefell Mountain Railway is the only electric mountain railway in the British Isles, and is a 5-mile journey from Laxey to the summit of Snaefell, up gradients as steep as 1 in 12.

Douglas horse trams date from 1876 and are the oldest in the world. They run in the summer along the 2-mile promenade at Douglas.

The Isle of Man Passenger Survey

The report of the IoM Passenger Survey contains details of various aspects of passenger traffic in 2002 and a review of some of the major trends to have emerged. The survey is conducted by staff of the Economic Affairs Division of the IoM Government Treasury, who interview departing passengers at Douglas Harbour and Ronaldsway Airport. In the survey, interviewees are classified under the various definitions of passenger type (see Figure 1.25). What follows below is a summary of the survey's findings.

The structure of passenger traffic

✳ Total scheduled passenger departures increased by 9.2 per cent on its 2001 level to stand at 673 279. Total scheduled air passenger traffic rose by 4.0 per cent on the previous year, whilst the figure for sea traffic increased by 15.9 per cent.

✳ The PVPA category (regarded as the main tourist category) rose by 16.9 per cent to 113 978, and at 117 165 the number of PVVFRs was up 17.4 per cent. Non-resident business traffic increased by 13.0 per cent to 87 536.

PASSENGER TYPE	DEFINITION
Period visitors in paid accommodation (PVPA)	Passengers visiting the IoM and staying in paid accommodation for at least one night (excluding business people)
Period visitors visiting friends and relatives (PVVFR)	Passengers visiting the IoM and staying with friends or relatives for at least one night (excluding business people)
IoM residents (RES)	IoM residents leaving the IoM
Business people (BP)	Passengers visiting the IoM for business
Day-trippers (DT)	Passengers visiting the IoM who do not spend a night on the island (excluding business people)

Figure 1.25 Classifications in the IoM Passenger Survey

* Resident traffic reached a new record level, rising by 5.2 per cent to 346 519.

Special events

The survey found that, within the PVPA category, the number of visitors whose arrival was connected with a special (organised) event represented 22.8 per cent of total PVPAs.

Number of bed-nights

* The average number of nights spent on the island by PVPAs rose from 4.8 in 2001 to 5.2 in 2002, bringing the total number of bed-nights for this category to 596 228.

* The average stay by PVVFRs was 6.1 nights.

* Of those PVPAs questioned, 58 per cent said that their trip to the island was a short break, rather than their longest or second longest holiday of the year. Of the 93 per cent who said they would be returning to the island, 66 per cent said that it would be for a short break.

Area of residence

As always, the largest number of PVPAs came from the North West of England (39.4 per cent). Other regions that provide a substantial share of this category of visitor include South East England (15.5 per cent), and the Midlands (10.1 per cent). Just 2.3 per cent of those questioned came from outside the UK/Eire.

Opinion analysis

The Passenger Survey gathers opinions from all respondents on aspects of their journey and stay. The results for 2002 continued to show that the clear majority of passengers were satisfied with the air and sea transport services to the island, with the air services generally obtaining more favourable ratings than the sea services.

A clear majority of visitors were also more than satisfied with the entertainment and facilities on the island.

Expenditure

* Average expenditure by PVPAs was estimated at £352 in 2002, around £68 per day.

* The figure for VFRs was £191, which equates to £31 per day.

* Estimated expenditure of business visitors in 2002 was £333, or £159 per day.

Knowledge check

1 Explain what is meant by the travel and tourism terms: (a) seasonality, (b) perishability, and (c) intangibility. Illustrate your answer with examples from the Isle of Man.

2 Explain the terms: (a) domestic tourists, (b) incoming tourists, (c) outgoing tourists, (d) VFR, (e) leisure tourism, and (f) business tourism.

3 Draw conclusions about consumer spending and types of tourism on the Isle of Man.

4 How have changes in socio-economic factors led to increased tourism to the Isle of Man?

5 How have technological developments and changing consumer needs and expectations affected domestic holidays?

6 What is the role of the public sector in relation to the travel and tourism industry on the Isle of Man?

7 Describe two services provided by the Isle of Man's TIC.

8 Explain, using examples from the IoM, the components that make up a package holiday.

9 Evaluate the issues facing transport to and from and within the Isle of Man.

Resources

Data tables from the IPS (International Passenger Survey) and other statistics relating to travel and tourism are available from National Statistics Online, the government's web-based statistical service. The information can be found under the Transport, Travel and Tourism section of the website at www.statistics.gov.uk. There are a great number of tables and associated activities in this section. Practise your number skills using these tables, as you will find similar ones in the examination for this unit.

There are many websites referred to in this unit, but you must be familiar with Star UK (www.staruk.org.uk) and the statistics relating to travel and tourism in the UK available there.

The main source of information should be visits to travel and tourism organisations. Experiencing the industry first-hand is vitally important.

Customer service in travel and tourism

Introduction

This unit will introduce you to customer service as provided by travel and tourism organisations. You will study the principles of customer service and why it is so important to the survival of these organisations, and the necessity of individuals working in travel and tourism to provide good quality customer service to meet the needs of all types of customers.

Different people have different expectations of a facility, but all want to be treated fairly, honestly and by someone who can answer their questions or deal with any problems. You will learn about these customer needs and how they can be addressed, how to undertake effective customer service through role plays and simulations. Some of you may have part-time jobs or undertake work experience to help you develop good customer service skills, and this can be valuable in developing these skills. Your assessment of this part of the unit will be through the performance of customer service to a variety of customers in a variety of ways, such as face-to-face, on the telephone or in writing.

You will also study why organisations have mission statements and customer service policies in order to ensure consistency of service by all people within the organisation. These policies will set down practices and procedures which employees should follow, but they will need to be checked regularly to ensure all staff meet the requirements and identify any training needs, and be updated where necessary. The ways in which organisations check the quality of customer service vary, but this is often done through the use of questionnaires, mystery shopper customer feedback and internal quality checks. You will undertake research into one travel and tourism organisation's practices and procedures and present an analysis of your findings after acting as a mystery shopper, then evaluate these procedures, identifying areas for improvement or development.

How you will be assessed

Your portfolio will probably be in two parts. You have to study one organisation to address Assessment Objectives 1, 3 and 4. This will be a comparison of how needs of the internal and external customers are met by one travel and tourism organisation (for AO1). You will then research and analyse the ways in which that organisation measures the effectiveness of the customer service it provides (for AO3), and extend this by evaluating the customer service provision, giving reasons for improvement. These must match the values and attitudes of that organisation (for AO4). The second part of your portfolio evidence will be your customer service performance (for AO2). This must cover at least two different types of customer and a minimum of two different situations, which will include the handling of a complaint or problem.

What you need to learn

* principles of customer service
* personal presentation
* needs of external and internal customers
* customer service skills
* assessing the quality of customer service in travel and tourism.

Principles of customer service

Why is customer service so important?

Organisations within the travel and tourism industry offer the public similar products and services, and the quality of customer care may be the deciding factor as to whether customers use one organisation or another. It is therefore important that customer service is seen by owners and managers as necessary to the survival and development of the organisation. The quality of customer service is what distinguishes one organisation from another.

The need to increase sales

Why are customers important to organisations within the travel and tourism industry? Any organisation needs to sell its product or service, and the first contact a customer has with the organisation can be the deciding factor as to whether the customer uses that product or service, or goes elsewhere to obtain it. Both commercial and non-commercial organisations share the same customer focus – the aim to provide products and services that potential customers need or want.

The positive aspects

Satisfied customers

If customers feel 'cared for' and welcome, then they are more likely to use the service or buy the product. As the products or services on offer by different organisations are somewhat similar, it is very often the quality of the customer service provided that influences potential customers, leading to customer satisfaction and increased sales. Also, a satisfied customer is more likely to recommend an organisation to friends and colleagues if a problem has been dealt with fairly and competently. Customers today expect more from organisations than just a basic product, and will stay with a particular organisation only if they feel confident in the quality of service provided.

The need for repeat business

Customer satisfaction will tend to lead to repeat business. Personal recommendations to other people may increase sales still further. This chapter will look at the real importance of excellent customer care and how this can be achieved within the organisation, so that the organisation can achieve its aims and develop working practices to meet or exceed its sales and productivity targets.

The need to attract more customers

Every organisation tries to attract new customers, in addition to repeat business, so it might want to target its products to appeal to a wide customer base or offer additional services. A hotel may offer conference facilities in addition to its core business, or it may attract other events such as receptions or be a venue for groups which meet regularly, such as members of the Rotary Club or social groups. The visitors who attend these meetings and enjoy the facilities in the hotel could easily choose to use them for their personal events such as weddings or parties. However, they will be attracted to the facility only if it provides good customer support and advice on arrangements – so it is the quality of customer service at all times which can attract more customers.

Airlines, too, are in a very competitive market, and most people make a small number of journeys by air. Airlines must offer their product at the right price in order to attract customers to fill the seats on the plane. Customers will choose the airline which offers the services to their chosen location at a fair price. But they will also choose one which can cater for their specific needs. The services provided by the airline could be the factor which persuades a customer to choose that airline over others on the same route.

A better public image

> **Key term**
>
> **Public image** is the perception customers have of an organisation.

When an organisation's public image is positive, customers have more confidence that they will be dealt with fairly. So if the organisation can improve and develop its public image so as to acquire a highly reputable status, then it should be able to increase its sales and attract customers as more people become aware of what the organisation has to offer. This is very important in an industry where there is fierce competition between organisations.

An edge over the competition

Organisations should try to provide that 'little extra service' which gives them an edge over competitors. This could be by anticipating what customers need and offering them extra services – such as the hotel which provides guest toiletries in the bathroom for those customers who have forgotten to pack them. It could be by providing transport to and from the airport free of charge, which might be important for those customers who have heavy luggage and value highly the convenience of easily accessible transport. You will often see advertisements for airport hotels which offer free car parking for up to 15 days, or provide minibus transport for clients at regular intervals to the airport departure and arrival terminals.

Happier and more efficient employees

Another feature of good customer service is that staff are usually happier working in an organisation that provides the facilities and equipment to enable them to do their jobs efficiently. The organisation should take the time to study the best working methods and include the staff in development of the systems to help them do their jobs better. It should also undertake training to ensure the best use of equipment.

If an employee feels that the services he or she provides are appreciated by both the organisation and the customers, that staff member will be better motivated to work well. If employees look happy and pleased to be working in that organisation, then they will work harder as a way of ensuring their jobs are safe and secure.

Many organisations undertake the Welcome to Excellence training programmes offered by Regional Tourist Board Partnerships Ltd as part of their staff development, and some schools and colleges incorporate the day's training package into their travel and tourism courses. It is a recognised customer service qualification within the industry. The aims of Welcome Host are set out in Figure 2.1.

Welcome Host

What is Welcome Host?   The Benefits   Course Content   Taking Part

What is Welcome Host?

Welcome Host is a one-day training programme which concentrates on improving customer care skills. It is part of a high-profile national initiative that can help your organisation to:

- increase sales and profitability
- build repeat business
- provide higher standards of service for visitors and local residents
- enhance customer satisfaction
- reduce complaint levels
- improve staff understanding of customer value

The training is aligned to the NVQ Level 2 in Customer Service and provides valuable underpinning knowledge. (Please contact your Regional Tourist Board for more information on the NVQ qualification.)

Figure 2.1 Extract from the Welcome to Excellence website www.welcometoexcellence.co.uk

Think it over ...

Think of somewhere you have been or visited when you considered the customer service to be good. Write down why you thought it was good. What gave you that impression?

Compare your example with that of a colleague, or discuss in a group, to see whether there are any features which are similar between your examples.

The results of providing excellent customer service can be seen clearly in Figure 2.2.

Figure 2.2 Benefits of good service

Consequences of poor customer service

Think it over ...

Now that you have looked at the reasons why organisations must try to offer good customer service, think of the effects on that organisation of poor customer service. Attempt to list at least four. You may find it helps to focus on a specific organisation for this exercise.

Having thought about some of the consequences for an organisation of poor customer service, see how your list matches the ideas presented in this section.

Poor communication systems

If the customer service is poor, or if the systems of the organisation do not help staff to perform effective customer service, then the consequence could be failure of that business. If you were carrying out a web search for hotels in a particular foreign destination, and the site took a long time to load to your browser, and then was in the language of that country, you would probably not proceed with your enquiry but rather find another website that could help you better. If then you were able to locate a suitable hotel's details but could not book it on-line, you might feel even more frustrated. Poor communications would have resulted in that hotel not attracting your business, even though it might otherwise have suited your needs ideally. This is just one example of less than adequate customer support.

Unable to get information

If you ring to make initial enquiries at a tourist attraction and the voice at the other end of the line sounds bored or disinterested, to the extent that you are not able to get all the information you want, you will probably lose interest in that attraction. This will result in a lost sale, but not only that. You may well relate the story to others, meaning they will also hear the negative side and may also decide not to visit or contact that attraction. It is said that 'bad news travels fast' and, in the case of poor customer service, this is usually true.

Loss of income

Not only does an uncaring organisation lose sales, it also fails to attract new customers, leading to further loss of income. This loss of income means that the organisation is not able to carry out basic maintenance and repairs. The environment can then appear uncared for, but there is not enough revenue to pay for refurbishment. There is also no money for improved facilities, so the organisation continues to lose customers and potential income.

High staff turnover

If systems and procedures at an organisation do not perform their functions effectively, then the employees will become frustrated with them. They will lose enthusiasm for their jobs and may well decide to leave. Staff turnover can be high, which results in increased expenditure for the organisation as it has to advertise for and interview new recruits, then train them for the specific jobs. During this process, other employees may have to do more than one job, so they become frustrated too. Their job satisfaction is virtually non-existent, and this can become apparent to customers very quickly.

Fewer customers could also mean that staff are no longer required and they are made redundant. This in turn can lead to an unhappy workforce, who may be doing jobs in the organisation for which they are not properly trained or carrying out the work of two people, and therefore they are less efficient. It also means that the organisation may have difficulty recruiting staff in the future if potential employees do not feel their jobs will be secure.

Inefficient telephone systems

Some organisations set up telephone call-transfer systems whereby a caller is given various recorded options when the call is received, and asked to choose one. Some systems go even further, so that when the caller is switched to his or her first choice, the person is then given further options to respond to. It is possible to be transferred in this way several times without speaking to a customer service adviser, which can be time-consuming for the customer, and frustrating when it is found that the correct advisory service has not been reached after all this time – and the customer is often the one paying for the telephone call. So it is important that when such systems are set up with the intention of helping customers they are fully tested to ensure they really achieve what they set out to do.

Loss of customers

Customers can be fickle and move from one organisation to another easily, so unless an organisation effectively responds to customers' enquiries and needs, it is unlikely to maintain customer loyalty. This means it has to work harder to obtain new customers to replace the ones it has lost, so it is in a vicious circle without gaining any benefits.

Poor public image

The image can be affected by negative publicity. For example, if an attraction receives negative publicity as the result of an accident on one of its fun rides, or shows little consideration to local residents because of inadequate parking arrangements, then the publicity generated from complaints and possible court cases will have a negative impact for that organisation. Potential customers may read negative publicity and prefer to visit other attractions that have a more favourable public image.

News of redundancies might also affect the public image of an organisation in the travel and tourism industry. If it is having to make staff redundant, it is probably not getting enough customers. Potential new customers then start to wonder whether there might be something seriously wrong with the organisation.

Lack of repeat business

There can be various outcomes of poor customer service, and organisations that fail to deliver satisfactory products or services to their customers will not achieve their aims. The outcome could be fewer customers, or lack of repeat business – customers do not come back to that organisation because they were not satisfied on a previous occasion.

Lack of customer loyalty

Customers can usually easily switch to another organisation to see whether it meets their needs better. If receiving a poor quality of service, these customers will be dissatisfied customers and they will, in turn, tell others of their experiences, which can lead to fewer customers and decreased sales.

Loss of competitive edge

If an organisation is not attracting the numbers of customers it hoped to get, then the sales of products and services will be reduced and the organisation itself will lose some of its competitive edge. Competitors may be offering new products or better services and could attract customers away. The organisation needs to be aware of what the competition is offering in order to keep its competitive edge.

Personal presentation

Personal presentation is very important when dealing with any type of customer. The manner in which individuals present themselves has a direct influence on their own job satisfaction and on the future success of the organisation that employs them.

Dress code

Many organisations have a dress code for employees, or even a uniform that helps to identify employees as members of staff and makes them easily identifiable to customers.

The dress code may include restrictions on the amount of jewellery or make-up an individual can use, or acceptable hair length or style. This is very relevant within the hospitality sector of the industry where employees could be in contravention of health and safety or food standards regulations.

Some organisations provide uniforms for certain employees, such as hotel receptionists, airline crew and travel agency consultants. The use of uniforms helps to distinguish staff from customers, and also presents a 'corporate image' (see Figure 2.3). Employees will feel they belong to a caring organisation and will take pride in their work. They are usually responsible for maintaining the uniform which is provided and ensuring it is clean

Uniforms must be worn at all times whilst on duty.

Clothing must be maintained in a clean and sound condition.

Failure to comply with this is taken very seriously by the management.

More specifically:

- Long hair should be tied back.
- Make-up should be discreet and simple.
- Earrings can be worn, but no other piercing or jewellery is allowed except for religious purposes.
- Shoes should be blue or black and sturdy. For reasons of safety, high heels must not be worn.

Source: Springboard UK Customer Service training pack

Figure 2.4 Extract from a training pack

and tidy at all times. Figure 2.4 shows an extract from one organisation's approach to staff presentation.

Other organisations may not have specific uniforms but instead have dress codes for particular types of job. A conference organiser in a hotel might have to wear a dark or light suit. Such people are usually dealing with business visitors and need to represent their employer with an appropriate style of dress to convey efficiency and responsibility.

Many organisations provide employees with name badges, or a badge showing the person's role within the organisation. This helps customers to identify specific employees they might wish to praise for their customer service (through employee awards programmes), or to identify the level of seniority if raising a complaint.

Personal hygiene

People who take care with their own appearance are generally considered to take more care of their surroundings and their work. As it is often considered that 'first impressions count', it is the customer's initial contact with an individual that can affect his or her relationship with the organisation as a whole.

Figure 2.3 Presenting a corporate image

So it is considered essential that employees attend to the cleanliness of their bodies (including hair, hands and nails), making effective use of deodorants and avoiding overuse of perfume or scented products. Uniforms, if worn, should be clean at all times. Few people want to eat in a restaurant where the waiters or chef look dirty, even in the middle of a shift of duty – it could be interpreted that the kitchens are just as dirty and unhygienic. Those who smoke should also be aware that their breath and clothes can hold the smell of tobacco for some time, and many people now find this offensive.

> *** REMEMBER!**
>
> Personal hygiene is important and should not be overlooked in customer service situations.

Personality

An outgoing person is usually more comfortable dealing with customers, because he or she has the confidence to meet people and usually the friendly personality to accompany it. If you have a generally cheerful nature, this comes across in your attitude and voice, and customers tend to feel more reassured when dealing with someone who appears to care. If you are a quiet, shy person you might find customer service situations rather daunting at first, and you may not speak clearly enough for customers to hear.

Imagine you are on holiday and the representative who greets you at the airport is miserable, attempts little communication with customers and does not give much information on the way to the accommodation. This representative is the agent of the tour operator and your views of the tour operator could be affected immediately and you feel less confident about the rest of your holiday. But if the representative is bubbly and has a good sense of humour, you are likely to feel more assured about the rest of the arrangements for the holiday.

Personality is something that can be developed through gaining self-confidence, knowledge of the product or service you are offering, and experience of dealing with customers.

Needs of external and internal customers

It is important to appreciate that organisations have internal as well as external customers.

> **Key terms**
>
> **External customers** are those we normally consider to be 'the customers', and these are the people who buy the products or services of the organisation and come from outside the organisation itself. **Internal customers** are other employees within the organisation. They might be colleagues with whom you work closely, or other employees in a different department or in other branches. They might be regular suppliers of goods and services who deal with the organisation perhaps on a contract basis.

It is important to treat the internal customers with the same level of care that you offer to external customers. In other words, you should treat everyone, whether internal or external, as you would wish to be treated yourself. Managements usually include dealings with any type of customer within their customer care policy or mission statement. We shall be looking at these later in this chapter.

External customers

There are various types of external customer and they all have differing needs. But they all expect to have these needs recognised and dealt with, and to be treated well by members of the organisation. Of the many possible ways of categorising customers, we shall look at those used most frequently within the travel and tourism industry.

Individuals

Individuals are those customers who are making enquiries or bookings on their own behalf. They may be independent travellers who contact a variety of organisations in order to obtain information to make up their own package. They could be individuals who are travelling alone, say on business, who need to arrange transport or accommodation for themselves only. Anyone who makes a booking for one person is obviously an individual, and the needs of an individual should be considered by organisations.

A business traveller may require additional facilities in his or her accommodation, such as a telephone/modem link, wake-up calls and newspapers, express checkout facilities, and perhaps car parking.

A male traveller might not be quite as concerned about security as a female traveller, who may not wish to be in a ground floor room, may prefer to eat in a busy restaurant rather than a deserted one (or have room service), and wants a secure lock on the door of the room.

So, there are differences in expectations of individuals, even though they are classed as a single customer category. An individual customer can be of any age, who wishes to be treated as an individual, not as part of a larger group. Each individual's needs are different and each person should be considered according to the circumstances or situation, and their specific requests. The responses given must relate to these requests.

Groups

Groups of customers could be families, parties of young people going on holiday together, students on a residential break, or clubs and societies going to events for example. Their needs might include seating together on a train or in a restaurant. They will expect a discount for the size of the group, or possibly one free place for every ten people in the group booking. A class on an educational break – such as a cookery holiday – may expect to be taught as a group but treated as individuals at other times.

Dealing with groups of customers can be more difficult than dealing with individual customers, and you need to appreciate this when we look at customer service skills later in this chapter. If you are dealing with a group of customers on a guided tour, the chances are they will have come voluntarily and are eager to learn what you have to say. However, if you are dealing with irate customers whose plane is

delayed, then there is obviously going to be more aggression in their attitude.

> **✷ REMEMBER!**
>
> Skills in dealing with groups are necessary within the travel and tourism industry. You will need to develop and demonstrate this ability not only in this unit but also in other units of the qualification.

CASE STUDY

London Aquarium – Employee profile

'The hardest part of being an Information Assistant within the Education Department at the Aquarium is to understand the mechanics of group interaction and behaviour. No two groups are the same, and being able to engage with the various customer types is the key to being an effective member of the team.

'Staff are trained to meet the needs of a range of customers. In terms of dealing with schoolchildren aged between 5 and 10, staff undertaking the tours in particular need to:

- focus on the visual elements of the displays, shapes and colours
- use simple language and easy-to-understand facts
- appeal to the children's sense of danger (e.g. with food-chain examples)
- appeal to their sense of humour (e.g. funny stories which maybe stretch the truth)!

Older children up to the age of 16/17 will need a different approach. Staff will need to:

- use clear signals to maintain interest and grab attention at key points of the tour
- relay 'cool' facts about the marine life (e.g. feeding habits, mating rituals)
- ask for opinions on more controversial issues such as marine conservation.'

Source: Springboard UK

Consider these two client groups and analyse why the London Aquarium needs to identify different approaches to the two age groups.

Different age groups

The groups discussed above were all of a similar age or interest, but often groups can be made up of customers of widely differing ages. This may be seen on a package holiday, where the overseas representative is welcoming new arrivals and the audience is made up of a variety of people who have just reached the destination – some may be individuals, some couples, some family groups, some young teenagers, others more elderly.

When dealing with customers in this category, it is important not to offend any age group. Speak to all in general terms, but highlight various features of the resort which might appeal to different age groups. If a venue is trying to appeal to different age groups, then there needs to be a variety of activities and facilities which would interest those age groups.

Different cultural groups

Customers can be from widely differing cultural groups, and therefore from a culture that is different from your own. They do not necessarily have to be visitors from another country. They could be visitors from within the UK who have a different cultural background from yourself. This cultural diversity can be in terms of food (Indian, Chinese or Kosher, for example), or beliefs (Hindu, Muslim, Judaism or Shinto, for example), or style and mode of dress. You need to be aware that these differences must be respected and considered. Avoid offence through inappropriate language, attitude and moral behaviour.

> **✱ REMEMBER!**
>
> You will study more about cultural diversity on the A2 programme, but it is also relevant for this unit, and for unit 7 (Hospitality), particularly on the AS level programme.

Non-English speakers or those with limited understanding of English

These customers have to be considered in terms of their specific needs. If you have to give directions, for example, it is often simpler to draw a diagram that can be easily followed. The international display signage for such things as fire exits, baggage collection points or any particular facility within the organisation can be used, as these are

Figure 2.5 International signage

well-recognised and can be clearly understood. Three examples are shown in Figure 2.5.

When communicating with these customers it is also useful to try to make use of a third language you can both understand a little – possibly French or German. Alternatively, try to locate a colleague who has a wider language base than yourself. For those with limited understanding of English it may be necessary to speak very slowly and clearly, using simple words and phrases.

Many organisations produce information in a variety of languages to cater for this group of customers, or websites that can be accessed in different languages. An example can be seen on some of the newer North West trains, where signage within the carriages can be seen in Welsh, Urdu, Hindi and English to reflect the multi-ethnicity of the area. A good example to research is the ryanair.com website, where customers for whom English is not their natural language can access information from the site and make flight bookings through translated webpages (see Figure 2.6).

Figure 2.6 A website banner showing the languages available to visitors

Customers with specific needs

There are many types of specific needs that organisations should consider. Here are some examples:

* families with young children
* customers with impaired mobility (e.g. wheelchair users, those on crutches)
* those with hearing problems, including the deaf
* those with sight problems, including the blind
* the elderly
* customers with special dietary requirements (e.g. gluten free, vegetarian, kosher).

As you can see above, there is a wide variety of specific needs for organisations to consider. It may be a question of wheelchair accessibility, special rooms in hotels designed to accommodate those with impaired mobility, handrails on stairs or in toilets, avoidance of hazards which may not be noticed by those with impaired vision, assistance on transport services, baby changing rooms, and so on.

Customers with a hearing impairment can be difficult to identify as there is often no outward visible sign of their specific problem. Communication may be difficult with someone who has a speech impairment. Many organisations have hearing loop systems to aid communication with these groups of customers.

Customers with young children often require access for prams, baby changing facilities, cots in accommodation outlets, highchairs in restaurants, and lifts or moving ramps to enable access to other floors of a building.

Those with sight problems may hope to receive information in braille but this is seldom provided. However, organisations often have audio communication which can assist these customers, or braille impressions on key pads such as in lifts. Many museums provide audio guides to assist

these customers and enable them to enjoy the attraction.

People who cannot stand for long periods at an exhibition may need additional seating or rest areas. Many tourist attractions provide benches or chairs for people to rest for a while, but these are not always available for customers at all attractions or venues, particularly check-in areas at busy airports.

Organisations that provide catering need to consider dietary requirements and identify specific meal types available, or take requests at the booking stage for special needs.

Guidebooks and brochures sometimes include symbols to identify facilities suited to those with special needs, as you will see from the example in Figure 2.7. These symbols are then displayed according to the facilities provided for each attraction or facility.

The law has recently changed in relation to groups with special needs. All organisations – not just those in the travel and tourism industry – now have to comply with the Disability Discrimination Act and the most recent equal access laws (October 2004) supported by the Disability Rights Commission's Open4All campaign. Anyone who provides a service to the public needs to remove any physical barriers to ensure disabled people receive a fair service, and services had to be reasonably accessible by 1 October 2004. A Code of Practice was produced jointly by the government and the Disability Rights Commission which gave guidance on the 2004 duties and the government's proposals for regulations to underpin them.

Think it over ...

You can find out more about this through using the www.drc-gb.org or www.disability.gov.uk websites.

🏛 Historic house	🐾 Nature reserve	🛍 Shop
🏰 Castle	★ Points to note	☕ Refreshments
🏠 Other buildings	ℹ Contact details	🏔 Suitable for picnics
✝ Church, chapel etc	£ Admission details	👪 Facilities for families
⌧ Mill	🎭 Guided tours	Learning
🏛 Prehistoric/Roman site	😊 Events	🐕 Dogs welcome
⬆ Industrial heritage	🚶 Country walk	🚲 Facilities for cyclists
🐄 Farm/farm animals	♿ Access for visitors with disabilities	→ How to find the property
❄ Garden		⇌ Railway station
🌳 Park	👁 For visually impaired visitors	P Parking
⛰ Countryside		🔔 Licensed for civil weddings
🏖 Coast	👂 For hearing impaired visitors	T Available for functions

Figure 2.7 Symbols used by the National Trust

Members of certain clubs and groups

Some customers are members of travel or tourism clubs. This could be an organisation such as Resort Condominiums International (RCI), a timeshare group whose members have specific priorities over non-members as regards access. Other examples are the Cycling Tourist Club (CTC) and the Caravanners' Club, whose members receive publicity related to their needs and interests. This publicity may include promotion from travel and tourism organisations and offers may be specific to members of the group. The National Trust offers special events for members only and allows reduced admission prices for members to the various facilities it manages (see Figure 2.8).

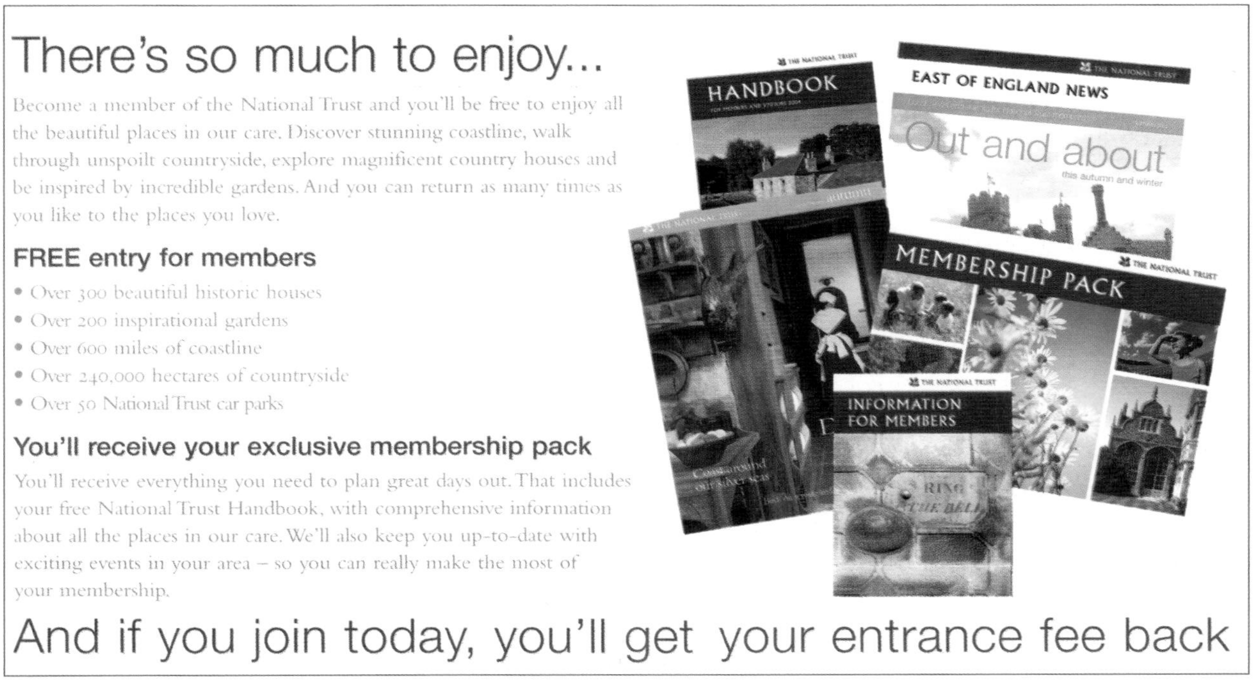

There's so much to enjoy...

Become a member of the National Trust and you'll be free to enjoy all the beautiful places in our care. Discover stunning coastline, walk through unspoilt countryside, explore magnificent country houses and be inspired by incredible gardens. And you can return as many times as you like to the places you love.

FREE entry for members

- Over 300 beautiful historic houses
- Over 200 inspirational gardens
- Over 600 miles of coastline
- Over 240,000 hectares of countryside
- Over 50 National Trust car parks

You'll receive your exclusive membership pack

You'll receive everything you need to plan great days out. That includes your free National Trust Handbook, with comprehensive information about all the places in our care. We'll also keep you up-to-date with exciting events in your area – so you can really make the most of your membership.

And if you join today, you'll get your entrance fee back

Figure 2.8 Membership details for the National Trust

Also included in this category are loyalty programmes such as Airmiles, Hilton Hotels group membership, or other frequent-user reward programmes. Customers may have preferential rates or treatment through these schemes, so obviously it is important to retain this custom through continued good customer service.

Conclusion

Having considered a wide range of customer types, you may now appreciate the vast range of customer needs which must be considered within facilities or by providers of services in order to meet the requirements or expectations of customers.

When you are undertaking simulations or role plays of customer service situations, you will need to reflect on this important section about customer needs in order to adapt your responses suitably and meet the expectations of your 'customers'. If you are in part-time employment or have been on work experience you may have dealt with a variety of customer needs, and this will give you valuable insight into dealing with various customer types.

Think it over ...

A family of four (two adults, a six-year-old child and a baby) are departing from Manchester Airport for a holiday flight within the European Union but they have limited use of the English language. Identify at least *ten* needs for this group, from arrival at the airport to departure on their flight. Exchange your list with a colleague and discuss the possible ways the airport management could meet these needs.

Internal customers

Who are the internal customers?

As you read earlier, internal customers are those who belong to the organisation, or suppliers of products and services to that organisation.

When you visit an attraction or facility, the people you see while buying tickets and then touring the attraction and using the facilities are not the only ones providing customer service. These are just the people who are 'front of house'.

More activity will be going on behind the scenes to ensure the customers' experience is a good one.

When you were thinking about the activity you have just completed above, about Manchester Airport, you probably thought mainly of things such as signs showing the check-in desk, checking-in processes, toilets with baby changing facilities, catering with seating areas, shops, visual flight departure screens, security, and so on. But far more people or services than these are involved with delivering the customer service at the airport.

Think it over ...

Think more carefully now about other services provided at Manchester Airport that are intended to help customers. List as many as you can and compare your own list with those of colleagues. Discuss the impact of one of these internal customers failing to provide the service they are contracted to provide.

There are several airline companies, baggage handlers, technical support staff, medical and emergency support staff, special assistance support and provision, HM Custom and Excise personnel, immigration, left luggage/lost and found luggage, business centre personnel, conference and banqueting providers, prayer room, telephone and meeting points. And this list is not complete.

Some of these personnel are not always dealing with customers face-to-face, but the services they provide all form part of the customer service provision of the airport itself. These are all internal customers of the airport and contribute to the provision of customer service there.

So internal customers are not only the members of staff within the organisation (in this case those directly employed by the airport) but also outside suppliers (such as shop staff, contracted check-in staff or baggage handlers, airline as well as front-of-house catering staff). They all need to work together to support the customer service provision at the airport, and there must be good working relationships between not only direct colleagues but also these other suppliers.

Threat of holiday nightmare as BA staff vote to strike

Daily Mail headline, 14 August 2004

The following is based on part of the *Daily Mail* article:

The August bank holiday weekend looks set to become a nightmare for holidaymakers after British Airways staff voted to strike over pay. Check-in staff and baggage handlers voted in favour of action in the dispute. Heathrow, Gatwick, Birmingham, Manchester, Glasgow and Edinburgh airports will all be affected for 24 hours. It will also cause massive delays for days, with knock-on effects for other airlines. Strike action is something BA can ill afford as it struggles to get to grips with costs and fierce competition. It has already warned that a stoppage would 'seriously damage' the company and possibly put its future at risk, damaging business and its reputation.

The headline identifies a possible strike of BA staff at various airports around the country. This includes BA flight crew, check-in staff, and other BA ground staff.

1   **Consider the effects of this strike for the following groups of internal customers: (a) contracted catering staff, (b) retail outlet staff at terminals, (c) baggage handlers, and (d) other airline companies flying to similar destinations.**
2   **Consider also the effect if the strike went ahead on the reputation of British Airways.**

Dealings with colleagues

Within a smaller organisation, such as an independent travel agency, you could be working closely with colleagues. It is necessary that standards of customer service be maintained between each other. You should address a colleague as you would hope to be addressed yourself. Even if you are not happy with something or someone within the organisation, you cannot let these feelings be apparent to external customers. If one colleague does not follow through an external enquiry, you should not make any personal comments about that colleague to the customer but undertake the work yourself as efficiently as possible.

The organisation should have systems in place which enable you to do your job effectively and maintain high levels of customer satisfaction, and there should be good communication between all departments of an organisation. The operation of the organisation should appear to be smooth and trouble-free to the external customer as well as to the internal customer, if they are providers of ancillary services.

Needs of internal customers

Developing new systems

Internal customers need to be kept informed of any changes to procedures or practices operated by the organisation so that they can carry out their duties effectively. This may involve discussions with the internal customers about the current operation of systems and procedures in order to develop or improve them. If internal customers feel involved with the process they are more likely to be willing and co-operative when new systems are put into action.

Training with new systems and procedures

Employees also need to be trained to use new systems and procedures in order to enable smooth and efficient operation of these. If employees have been involved with the discussions and their views have been heard and considered, they will feel more valued by the organisation and therefore be happier in their jobs and more efficient.

Good communication between departments

There must be good communication between various departments within an organisation so that one set of internal customers is listening to another and is aware of changes or developments. So if, for example, a hotel is considering extending its conference facilities, then other departments will need to be aware of the proposals.

Your answers to the above activity should have included other departments such as housekeeping, restaurant and catering, marketing, finance, personnel. They would all be involved at some stage with any expansion and the relevant costing and staffing needs. Other internal customers include suppliers of conference support materials, food and provisions, cleaners if these are sub-contracted, florists or other interior design contractors, to name just a few.

The external customer using the extended facilities should not be offered reduced customer service facilities because of lack of internal communication and planning. It is therefore important that all these contractors and providers be consulted at all stages of the development to ensure consistency of service to any external customer.

Involvement with other administrative departments

Some departments within an organisation may not see or come into contact with external customers at all, but they still need to consider customer needs. For example, if a tour operator is producing a new brochure, the production department will probably deal with the sales department, photographers, local representatives or agents, but not with the actual purchasers of package holidays. They still need to be aware of the types of information the customers will need to have and the overall aims of the tour operator with regard to profit margins and presentation styles. So they must always bear in mind the users of the final product in order to respond to their needs.

Departmental priorities coming before external customer needs

Departments within organisations will also have their own priorities and may tend to forget that they still need to communicate effectively within the organisation. On occasions they need to put their own priorities in a lesser position in order to respond to the needs of the whole organisation or another department.

For example, the catering department of a large hotel may have set priorities which include updating the kitchen equipment in order to improve efficiency of providing the meals service. But if they have agreed dates for this to happen without consulting the conference or accommodation section, this could occur at a very busy time in the hotel, and customers would not receive the service they expect in the restaurant.

Links must be recognised between the service provided by one department with others in the organisation in order to provide an overall experience for the external customer. A lack of awareness of the importance of external customers could lead to a 'them and us' attitude between front-line and support staff, which will have consequences for the overall viability of the organisation.

Benefits for internal customers

Internal customers may be provided with different benefits from external customers. They could receive discounts on the use of particular services, such as a gym or spa, or receive 'benefits in kind', such as free meals or overnight accommodation for reception staff on late shifts. They might also be offered incentives to improve customer service, such as 'employee of the month' awards or financial rewards in terms of bonuses or shares if the company is a public limited company (see Figure 2.9). These are incentives that are intended to lead to company loyalty.

Employees also need to have a healthy and safe environment in which to work and it is the employer's duty to provide this.

The Awards for Excellence

Award Categories:

■ **Employees of the Year 2004**

The Awards are open to all tourism-based businesses in the York area. Nominations can be made by employers.

Reward your employees, highlight quality and offer a chance of promoting your business not only within the community but also to potential recruits. The 8 Awards open to all staff are:

Receptionist
Housekeeping
Restaurant/Bar
Chef/Kitchen Assistant
Person Friday
Tourism Employee
Sales, Administration and Reservations
  (New this year)
Supervisor/Dept Manager

■ **Trainee of the Year Award** – open to anyone doing an NVQ in the tourism and hospitality industry – nominations are made by tutors or employer.

■ **The Customer Care Award** – is the most recent addition to the Awards and is also open to and suitable for the retail sector of tourism and hospitality.

Figure 2.9 York Tourism Awards for Excellence supported by York Hospitality Association

Theory into practice

Arrange a visit to a travel and tourism facility to meet employees. Discuss with them how the organisation meets their needs. This could be through the form of a pre-prepared questionnaire produced by the class as a whole, but used in a variety of organisations or with a variety of employees in an organisation. Compare the results from the questionnaires to identify any common trends or needs.

Customer service skills

Customers today *expect* to receive high standards of service, so it is necessary to ensure that the employees of the organisation are aware of the part they play in meeting these expected standards. There are skills involved in dealing with customers which employees need to be aware of. We will start by looking at some of these skills and how you can develop your confidence in dealing with various types of customer.

The customer may feel that his or her view is correct, but it might be necessary to explain the circumstances which make the customer realise that there are two sides to the story. How this is dealt with by the customer service personnel can influence that customer's view of the organisation and can change a dissatisfied customer into a satisfied one.

Appropriate language

✱ REMEMBER!

In their personal lives many people tend to be lazy about the type of language they use. When you are dealing with customers, remember that you are also representing your organisation or employer, so your language should be appropriate to the situation.

It is very easy to be careless about the language used, and many people can be offended by unsuitable language. The language should be appropriate for the audience. If you are speaking to a child, or someone whose first language is not English, you will probably use simple phrases and expressions. When dealing with adults, your level of language may be more involved with longer sentences. But you still want to try to ensure that what you are saying is clear and meets the needs of the situation.

The way we actually express ourselves can influence the message we are trying to convey. Try the next exercise, and you will notice how the meaning of the sentence is changed according to how certain words are emphasised.

Repeat this sentence several times: 'I did not say you stole the book.' Each time, put emphasis on the word or words underlined. As you do this, think about how this changed the meaning of the sentence.

I did not say you stole the book.
I did not say you stole the book.
I did not say you stole the book.
I did not say you stole the book.
I did not say you stole the book.
I did not say you stole the book.
I did not say you stole the book.

Get your colleagues to write down how they interpreted each of the statements above. Did they match the meanings below?

Statement	Meaning
I did not say you stole the book.	Someone else said you stole it.
I did not say you stole the book.	I firmly deny saying that.
I did not say you stole the book.	I implied you stole it.
I did not say you stole the book.	Someone else stole it.
I did not say you stole the book.	You possibly borrowed it.
I did not say you stole the book.	You stole a cheaper book.
I did not say you stole the book.	You stole something else.

You need to think carefully about how you stress words in order to make the message clear to the listener. Emphasis on the wrong word or at the wrong time can change the meaning and can lead to friction or misunderstanding between yourself and the listener.

It is also necessary to avoid being hesitant, using words such as 'like', 'um', 'you know' to fill gaps or because you cannot think of a way of expressing yourself more clearly. Often we pick up these bad habits in expression and don't always realise we are using phrases over and over again – but they can be annoying and distract the listener. It is a useful exercise to tape-record yourself talking to others, so that you can look out for expressions you should try to avoid using when communicating in a business environment.

Bad language offends many people, so it is unfortunate that some young people do not realise that the type of language they use between themselves can be very offensive to others. If you are in a front-of-house situation and are annoyed with a colleague, for example, any passing customer must not hear bad language being used. It reflects negatively on the organisation as well as yourself and can influence the experience of that customer in the organisation.

Positive body language

There are many aspects to body language, just a few of which are illustrated in Figure 2.10. For example, the way you sit, stand or walk can convey messages to other people. If a person is slouching at a desk, he or she gives the impression of being bored or not really caring about what is happening. If that person is sitting upright, looking towards the listener, then the impression given is that he or she is interested in what the speaker has to say, and will try to respond to any requests. The listener is involved in the discussion without being intrusive.

On the other hand, if someone speaking is sitting at a desk and leaning forwards with hands pointed towards the listener, this could be seen as threatening to the listener, who could react negatively to the conversation. This is almost as though the speaker is 'invading someone else's space'. This can also apply when you are standing to discuss an issue. If someone comes too close to

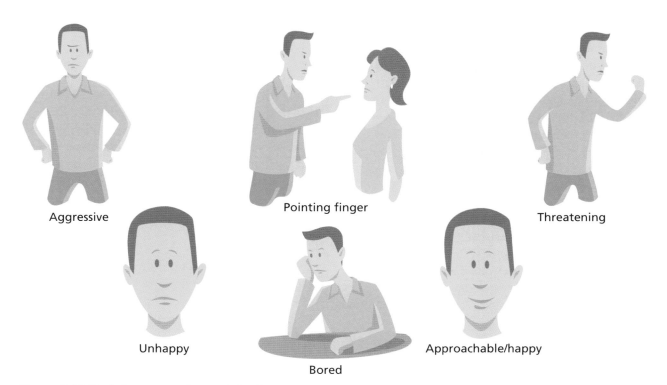

Aggressive

Pointing finger

Threatening

Unhappy

Bored

Approachable/happy

Figure 2.10 Body language dos and don'ts

you, you feel threatened and back away – your personal environment has been invaded and you feel under pressure.

Another aspect of body language which is very important is facial features. A frown usually means you don't want to be interrupted, or are angry, whereas a smile means you are contented, welcoming and approachable. Eyes can also reveal a lot about our attitude to others. Staring can appear threatening or rude, and usually comes with the frown. If you try to frown and smile at the same time, your face cannot cope with that – so if you smile, immediately your eyes become more friendly and softened.

Think it over ...

Look at yourself in a mirror or watch other people communicating, and note the body language they are using. What messages are they giving you, and how comfortable would you feel in their company?

Listening skills

We all think we listen to other people, but often we hear them but are not really listening to them. So much can be gathered from the tone of voice,

the way sentences are spoken, what is not actually said, and you need to develop the skill of listening carefully to the speaker.

Sometimes we are not concentrating on what another person is saying because in the back of our mind are other thoughts. This means we do not really hear the full conversation and pick up only part of a message. However, what is heard in customer service situations is very important, so you will need to develop good listening skills.

Using other senses to 'hear' the message

You need to use more of your senses than just your ears to hear the message. Use your eyes as well to spot the body language of the speaker, so that you can deal with the situation effectively. If someone is complaining to you, it is very easy to take the defensive action, but what you need to do is communicate with that person in order to establish the real reason for the complaint – then you know what action needs to be taken to try to solve the problem.

You may have other things on your mind when someone is speaking to you so you do not hear the full message, but pick up key words here and there and jump to a conclusion. If you are in a face-to-face situation, you have body language to guide you as to the intentions of the speaker, but if you are on the telephone, this is a different matter – you cannot see the body language of the speaker, so it is even more important to listen carefully to what is being said. It could be an important message that needs to be passed on to another person accurately, so you need to ensure you have got all the facts right.

When listening, bear in mind the following:

C	Calm your emotions
L	Listen actively
E	Empathise with your customers
A	Apologise/acknowledge the situation
R	Resolve the problem or refer it to a superior

While listening actively, you should ask questions to establish the concern of the customer and make sure you have all the relevant and correct facts. Rather than jumping in with your answer, decide what you need to say to answer the query, and use simple, direct language to put your point across. If you have to give an explanation, put the simplest areas first which the customer will find easiest to understand before going into a lot of detail. You must then check that the customer has understood by asking confirming questions, and then check that your explanation answers the query.

Theory into practice

An elderly couple come into a travel agency where you are the consultant. They want a holiday in a quiet resort in Europe, for a week, at a cheaper time of the year. What questions do you need to ask to ensure you provide a suitable location for their holiday?

You could act out this scenario with a colleague, completing a customer enquiry form to ensure you have all the relevant details before you start your search. You will need to establish when the person wants to travel, how far he or she wishes to travel, what method of transport is preferred, the type of accommodation required, any special needs the person has, and his or her budget. Only by listening carefully to the responses and checking you have the right information can you obtain the relevant information to meet the individual's needs.

Good clear telephone manner

How many times have you rung an organisation, where the telephonist has given the name of the firm so quickly you are not sure you have the right number? It is essential when dealing with customers on the telephone that you speak clearly and use language that is easily understood. An explanation with a lot of jargon will not often help the customer, so keep explanations simple and clear.

Clear response

Many organisations set out procedures for responding to telephone calls. These usually involve a welcoming greeting, the name of the company and the telephonist's name followed by 'Can I help you?' An example could be

> *Good morning/afternoon, Ultimate Travel.*
> *Hazel speaking. Can I help you?*

This immediately confirms to the caller that he or she has the right number and a contact name, and that you want to help in some way. This makes the caller feel reassured. However, if your voice sounds bored or disinterested, this is immediately conveyed to the caller, who wonders whether you will give the service hoped for. If the voice is bright, cheerful and warm, then the caller will feel more confident of getting the help needed.

You should avoid eating or drinking when answering a telephone call, as this again can convey the image of an organisation that does not care about its public image.

✳ REMEMBER!

When answering the telephone, smile or put a smile in your voice. This lightens the voice and makes it sound fresh and welcoming.

Use listening skills

You will need to use your listening skills very carefully when taking telephone calls. If you do not hear something clearly, you must ask the caller to repeat the sentence so that you have appropriate information. You should also check with the caller regularly that you have heard and understood the message correctly. A good tip is always to have pen and paper to hand when answering the telephone – then you can write down the important information, such as the caller's name and telephone number, the main points of the conversation, who the caller wishes to speak to, and the date and time of the call. Many organisations use telephone message forms to assist this process, and it does save having to write things down twice (once in note form and once on the official message form). An example of a telephone message form is given in Figure 2.11.

Telephone Message

Date: _____ Time: _____

Name of caller: _____

Telephone number: _____

Message for: _____

Message: _____

_____

_____

_____

_____

_____

Taken by: _____

☐ Urgent ☐ Please ring back

Figure 2.11 A telephone message form

Careful use of language

When responding to callers, it is important that you do not use language which could be considered too informal, or slang, because this can give the impression that the organisation is so informal that it is lazy and doesn't care about its customers. Examples of this are given below:

Don't say	Say this instead
Hang on a minute	Please hold the line for a moment
OK, yeah	Yes, fine
Well, I'll see what I can do	I will do what I can
You what?	I'm sorry, could you please repeat that

Theory into practice

Create a table, putting other expressions used in the left-hand column, and what you should say in the right as in the above example.

Do not keep a caller waiting while you find an elusive colleague. Rather than keeping him or her on hold for a long time, take a message and advise the caller that you will get the colleague to ring back as soon as possible.

✷ REMEMBER!

Don't forget to ensure that the message is passed on as a priority.

It may not be as necessary to avoid informal language when you are speaking to an *internal customer*. However, that internal customer could be a manager from another department, so it is better to maintain a standard telephone technique for all calls. You may not be aware you are using slang terms or informal language, but you will need to develop your telephone skills before you undertake your assessments in customer service.

Theory into practice

Practise making and receiving telephone calls with a colleague and, if possible, tape-record your conversations. Having listened to the tape, identify the slang or informal language used, then try the same type of telephone calls again with more careful use of language.

Good written communication skills

You may be involved in communicating with customers through letters, fax, email, or memos (for internal customers) and your written communication skills are just as important as your spoken communication skills. You need to sustain the image of the organisation and respond effectively. The organisation may have a 'house style' for the production of letters, with some standard paragraphs or expressions, and you need to be aware of these and use them appropriately. It is also necessary to put yourself in the customer's shoes and think how the recipient will feel on receiving your communication.

Think what you want to say

Prepare what you want to say, and think about how you are going to write this to maintain the image of the organisation but still respond to the customer's concerns or questions. Use simple language which can convey the message clearly. Avoid long complicated sentences – these can become too wordy and the message itself is lost or open to misinterpretation. You must also avoid jargon or complicated words, and in most cases keep your response to four or five paragraphs at the most.

Preparing your letter or written communication

There are some standard techniques you need to know about. For example, if you start a letter with 'Dear Sir/Madam' then end with 'Yours faithfully', but if you start with 'Dear Mr Smith' then end with 'Yours sincerely'. The first approach is very formal and tends to be used when writing to an organisation when you don't have a contact name, possibly when writing for the first time, or wishing to register a complaint. The second approach is more informal and friendly, and tends to be used when responding to an initial letter or complaint. However, avoid being over-friendly and addressing Mr Smith as 'Dear John' – this can be seen as too personal and intrusive and many people of the older generation or those of different cultures dislike this very informal approach.

It is best to plan a letter by sorting out the information into some sort of logical order. The first section should make clear your reason for writing. The middle section can give the details and any relevant information. The final section should give some indication of what happens next, or a brief sentence to end the letter.

There are some standard phrases used in business letters, so if you become familiar with these it may help you start and end a letter appropriately. Some of these are given in Figure 2.12.

Starting letters:

Thank you for your enquiry dated 20 July 2005 regarding …

Your letter dated 20 July 2005 has been passed to this department for attention, and …

Further to the telephone conversation yesterday concerning …

With reference to the booking made by you …

Ending letters:

We look forward to hearing from you.

I will contact you again within the next few days to discuss the matter further.

Thank you for your help in this matter.

If we can be of any further help, please do not hesitate to contact us.

We look forward to receiving your reply.

Figure 2.12 Useful phrases to start and end letters

Some organisations set timescales within which letters must be responded to. If a full response cannot be given on the first occasion, it may be necessary to send an acknowledgement letter first, but this should state the time within which a fuller reply will be given. An example is given in Figure 2.13. You will note that this letter displays the sender's address and contact details, the address of the recipient, a friendly opening greeting and a heading. There are only four paragraphs, which keeps the letter concise but provides sufficient information to the customer of the actions being taken, and a named signatory is given at the end.

XYZ Trains
Main Station
HIGHTOWN HT1 2XZ
Tel: 0123-456789
29 July 2005

Mr J Smith
24 Andale Road
HIGHTOWN HT2 3AB

Dear Mr Smith

COMMENTS RE JOURNEY ON 24 JULY 2005

Thank you for your letter of 25 July 2005 regarding your recent rail
journey between Manchester and Hightown.

We regret to read that you consider we did not provide the service
you should have received on this occasion and we are investigating
the matter fully. When we have further information about the
problems you experienced we will contact you again.

You should expect to hear further from us within the next two weeks,
when we hope that the matter can be fully explained.

Thank you for bringing this problem to our attention and you can be
assured that we will try to achieve a satisfactory outcome for you.

Yours sincerely

J Bloggs
Regional Manager

Figure 2.13 A sample letter

Theory into practice

You have received a letter from Mrs A Jones about the poor service received when enquiring about booking a room for a conference at a local hotel. Draft a reply to this customer pointing out that the matter will be investigated and a reply made in detail within a week. Think carefully about how you should phrase the letter.

Compare your letter with those of others in the class to see whether you could have expressed yourself better. You could then go on to develop this with a follow-up letter explaining the circumstances and offering some sort of compensation or apology.

When communicating via email or fax, the message is usually kept fairly short and to the point, but it is still important to maintain the organisation's image and avoid the use of slang or informal phrases. There is not quite the same formality in layout for this type of communication, but it is still necessary to plan what you want to say and keep the message clear and concise.

Theory into practice

Prepare a suitable email communication which could be sent from yourself in Customer Services to a colleague in the Education Department at a local visitor attraction (e.g. Cadbury World), informing him or her that there will be a school visit in two weeks' time. The students want a presentation on customer services and a tour of the attraction.

Include details such as date, time, numbers of students and teachers, and what they want a presentation about. Don't forget to mention the tour of the attraction.

You need to make sure you include all the facts that the Education Department would need in order to organise this visit.

Selling skills

'Selling skills' is a term used whether or not you are actually selling a product. You may be offering a service to a customer, such as providing information at a Tourist Information Centre, but you are 'selling' your organisation or a service offered by your organisation. How you deal with customers is very important because it influences whether or not they accept your product or service.

If you visit a local TIC, for example to enquire about an attraction in the area, then you want as much information as someone who is purchasing an admission ticket. You need to know where the attraction is, what it offers, any other facilities or services provided at that attraction (such as wheelchair access, catering facilities), and prices. The way in which this information is given to you could be what persuades you to visit that attraction, so the employee at the TIC is to that extent 'selling' the facility to you.

Identifying reactions to persuade customers to buy

With selling skills, you need to observe the customer's reaction to any statements you make, to assess whether the customer looks fully persuaded to buy, is still considering, or is perhaps wavering as to whether to buy. Your development of these statements may act as a catalyst and finally lead to a sale.

For example, a travel agency consultant advising a customer on possible holidays needs first to get basic information as to the requirements. Then this position is developed with the use of brochures guiding the customer to possible hotels or accommodation that meets the needs. It might be necessary to describe a resort or location. First-hand knowledge of resorts can help in the persuasion process, otherwise there is usually information within the brochures that can be used to highlight features. If the consultant looks interested, gets involved in the discussion and can interpret the customer's body language appropriately, this could lead to a sale of a holiday package. If the customer looks unsure, then the consultant might need to discuss alternative locations or accommodation, without appearing to pressurise the customer.

The customer needs to feel confident in the points being made and in the accuracy of the information being given. The more useful information the consultant has, or can obtain (such as colleagues' opinions if they have visited that location), the more likely it is that the outcome is a satisfactory sale.

Theory into practice

Arrange to visit a local travel agency to observe a consultant advising a customer on a suitable holiday. Note the consultant's and customer's body language. Note the consultant's listening skills and questioning techniques. Decide whether these affected the sale of the product.

Using customer service skills effectively while selling

Skills you have read about earlier in this unit, such as communication, the use of good body language and listening skills, are all used in a selling situation. Even in a restaurant, if the waiter or waitress can describe the components of a dish or menu, that could lead to the customers being more satisfied with a meal they enjoyed, leading to repeat business.

Product knowledge

You will not be able to use your selling skills effectively unless you also have knowledge of the products you are selling. In a restaurant, the person who promotes the sweet dishes might be asked to sample all the sweets on offer so as to be able to accurately describe them to customers. This might also apply to all the main dishes too, during induction or interim employment.

A travel agent who has actually visited locations offered to customers can speak with more authority and conviction than one who has just read about them in books, or seen them on the television. This is a type of 'insider knowledge' and can be invaluable in the travel and tourism industry.

Gaining customer confidence

Customers want to feel confident in the product or service they are buying – that it is the most appropriate product or service for them. This type of information can be offered only if you have first established the customer's needs, and then identified the product from your organisation that best meets those requirements.

For example, if a customer who has to use a wheelchair wishes to book a room in a hotel with adequate facilities for the disabled, preferably on the ground floor, offering the customer a room on a higher floor would not meet the requirements, especially if the hotel did not have a lift, or there were flights of stairs on corridors that had to be negotiated. Whoever responds to that customer's

enquiry, whether on the telephone or face-to-face, needs to have the right product knowledge to respond effectively.

Use of colleagues' knowledge

If you do not know the organisation's products well yourself, then you need to be aware of who in the organisation does have that information. You can then refer any queries to them quickly and efficiently. Therefore you need to know about the roles and responsibilities of colleagues in the organisation.

Necessary personal skills

A range of personal skills are required of those providing customer service, whether face-to-face or behind the scenes, when dealing with customers in a variety of situations. Though there is a common belief that 'the customer is always right', this is not strictly true, and often it will be necessary to use tact and diplomacy when dealing with a customer appropriately.

Self-confidence

When you are dealing with customers, they expect to find someone who appears knowledgeable and approachable. You will need to develop confidence in your ability to deal with customers. However, there is a difference between self-confidence and over-confidence.

Self-confidence means that you give the impression you know what you are doing and why, and your body language and attitude demonstrate this. A person who is shy and retiring will not feel able to deal with all types of customers. A shy person may not speak clearly and face the customer but look down and mumble or speak so quietly the customer cannot hear. A confident approach is an important skill to develop because it relates not only to dealing with customers but also to any other situation when you are dealing with people you do not know well – such as an interview.

Over-confidence on the other hand tends to result in brash statements or exaggerating the truth and the facts. It can also lead to a customer being directed inappropriately to another colleague if you have not checked responsibilities, and this will lead to customer dissatisfaction and displeasure. The body language of an over-confident person gives the impression of boastfulness or 'I know best', and this is not appropriate particularly when dealing with a customer who is not satisfied with something. It can lead to confrontation and difficult situations which can reflect badly on the employer.

Diplomacy and sensitivity

This skill often takes some time to acquire, because it comes with experience in customer dealings. It represents the skill of dealing tactfully with situations without betraying the organisation.

If a large customer complains, for example, that the chairs are too small in the restaurant, you would not turn round and say

'Well, you should lose some weight'. You should offer to find a more comfortable seat for the customer without causing offence. Or you might offer to serve the meal in an area that has alternative seating but explain that it would be less convenient for the waiting staff. It is not a question that the customer is always right, but what you can do to help the customer be more comfortable and therefore more satisfied with the outcome.

Respect for the feelings of others

With sensitivity, one should respect the feelings of others and not say something that could upset or offend them. A holiday representative who has to convey bad news to a client should consider how best to inform the client of the situation, because this reflects on the tour operator. The representative would need to consider carefully the words to use and how to open the conversation. The use of words and tone is very important to maintain good customer relations.

Even if you do not entirely support the opinion of a customer, you must be sensitive to his or her needs and try to respond accordingly. You need to think 'If I were in that situation, how would I want to be told?'.

You need to use diplomacy and sensitivity, too, when dealing with people from other countries, as they often have different approaches to situations and different values. What is acceptable in one country is not always acceptable in another. Each nation has its own cultural principles. Although you will have an opportunity to study this more at A2 level in Cultural Tourism, everyone dealing with customers needs to be aware of different acceptable international approaches, body language and communication styles.

Effective IT skills and awareness of developments in IT

Many organisations use information technology (IT) systems to prepare documentation and keep records. An induction programme should introduce you to the systems used in the organisation employing you. Most hotels now have integrated systems, whereby a customer enquiry will lead to that customer's details being on a database for future marketing approaches.

When a booking is confirmed, this should trigger not only a room reservation but also inform housekeeping of occupancy. If the customer takes a meal in the restaurant, the details of the meal may be automatically transferred to the customer's account at reception and be added to the account (see Figure 2.14).

Information technology is used also *within* organisations. For example, paging systems are often in place to call for assistance from maintenance, security, senior management or departmental supervisors.

Some hotels near airports display flight departure and arrival timetables, similar to those displayed within the airport itself. This is a service to customers who are likely to be staying there because of the proximity to the airport. At airports and railway stations you will see examples of IT being used to display information, make announcements, and process flight and train schedules.

The latest trains used by Virgin – the Pendolino and Voyager class for example – have display panels on or by the carriage doors with details of the final destination of the train, its next station stop and the identity of the carriage for those with pre-booked seats (see Figure 2.15). Inside the carriages there are display panels over

THE CITY HOTEL

Ms Siobhan O'Reilly

Arrival: 23 October 2004 14:56
Departure: 25 October 2004 09:52
Checked in by: Karen
Checked out by: Tony

Invoice No: 10045
Date: 25 October 2004
Room No: 106
No. of persons: 1

Date	Particulars	Debit	Credit
23 October 2004	Room Charges	95.00	
23 October 2004	Restaurant	32.45	
24 October 2004	Room Charges	95.00	
24 October 2004	Room Service	12.60	
24 October 2004	Bar	9.50	
25 October 2004	Deposit (Credit Card)		−95.00
	Total	244.55	−95.00

Figure 2.14 Example of a hotel account

Figure 2.15 An electronic door panel on a train and a booking ticket

the seats to identify those that are pre-booked and for how long, and those free for other passengers to use. These systems are controlled by programmes used by the train managers and drivers and are designed for each train journey from passenger booking details.

Call centres use information technology a great deal, with redirections through the use of numbered keys on a telephone pad until you reach the department you hope will deal with your query or problem.

These are just a few examples of how information technology has developed within the travel and tourism industry. It is essential that you have effective and current IT skills so that you can cope with a variety of computer programs and systems and adapt to developing technology.

Think it over ...

Does your school or college have an automated system? If so, after how many rings is the call answered initially and how many options are you given? Do these options offer you sufficient choice to get to the person or department you want? Are there any other options you think should be offered?

Can you think of any other information technology system used within your school or college designed to help management decision-making – electronic registration, for example, automated class lists and attendance figures? You could discuss this with the Head of IT or the Bursar to give you a fuller understanding of systems used and the reasons for these.

Dealing with complaints

Every organisation aims to achieve complete customer satisfaction. In reality the likelihood of this is very remote, particularly in the travel and tourism industry where customers tend to have high expectations and the value of individual customer spending is high. Staff who deal with customers regularly on a face-to-face basis or over the telephone – such as those in direct sales, in restaurants, on hotel reception desks, at airport check-in counters – are more likely to have to deal with customer complaints from time to time.

The customer care policy will include procedures and practices to be followed in order to help staff deal effectively with customer complaints. The skills of employees need to be developed so that they can suitably pacify a complainant yet deal with the complaint appropriately, and avoid being subjected to abuse, aggression or offensive behaviour often displayed by dissatisfied customers – yet still maintain a good company image and high reputation. If the customer leaves feeling disgruntled, then that is a dissatisfied customer. If the complaint is handled effectively and discreetly, even if not fully responding to the complaints, then that customer is more likely to feel reassured and therefore more satisfied.

Key term

Complaints procedures are usually made known to the customer, so that the customer understands the types of processes to be followed and the structure for expressing dissatisfaction.

If an organisation has considered methods of dealing with customer complaints, it is demonstrating that customer satisfaction is the ultimate goal and that customer needs are important. The four most common types of complaint in the travel and tourism industry are:

* poor quality of service

* delays in receiving products and services

* being given incorrect information

* standards not meeting customer expectations.

These types of complaint lead to varying responses and remedial actions, and staff need to know how to react in any situation in order to minimise the chances of customer dissatisfaction.

Checklist for dealing with dissatisfied customers face-to-face or on the telephone

1 Listen carefully to everything the customer has to say – do not interrupt or argue.

2 Apologise in general terms for the inconvenience, to convey sympathy for the problem.

3 Inform the customer that the problem will be investigated and steps will be taken to put things right.

4 Remain calm and do not take the complaint personally. Even if the customer appears to be critical of you personally, remember that it is the organisation against which the complaint is really being made.

5 Find a solution to the problem and agree this with the customer. If this is not possible, refer the customer to a supervisor or manager, who will be able to deal with the problem.

6 Make sure that action is taken to ensure promises made to the customer are kept.

7 Record details of the complaint and what action was taken.

Source: Career Award Travel & Tourism Standard Level, Rowe, Borein, Smith

Legal considerations

You are representing your organisation when you undertake customer service, but other considerations need to be remembered. You have to be aware of various legal requirements when giving information to customers or helping customers in any way, though you are not expected at this stage to know about all the laws and all the details of these laws.

Health and Safety

> ### * REMEMBER!
> Health and safety regulations relate not just to customers but also to yourself and all your colleagues.

Care must be taken when using equipment that you are not causing a danger to anyone else. There should be no trailing wires which could trip people up. This is especially relevant if you are setting up a conference room where a power supply is needed for laptops or slide projectors. Unless the room has power cables at various points inside the room, most power points are on exterior walls and cables have to be laid to the equipment. These should be suitably covered to ensure that no one falls over them.

If liquid is spilt on tiled floors, where customers could slip, there should be suitable signs warning of the hazard.

Most organisations have a health and safety officer who would be consulted when setting up procedures to deal with issues. However, as an employee you have a *duty of care* to both customers and colleagues, and you need to be aware of health and safety legislation as it concerns you at work.

Security

This is a very important issue, particularly in the current climate of terrorist threats and violent attacks. Customers want to be reassured that their safety is foremost in the minds of the organisation. Many organisations make use of closed-circuit television (CCTV) to monitor activity in the vicinity of the business. This could be the car park

Figure 2.16 A security notice

What not to pack

The Aviation & Maritime Security Act prohibits the carrying of certain items on board ship. For reasons of security and passenger safety the following items of property will *not* be allowed on board ship without authorisation from P&O Cruises:

- All firearms and ammunition, sporting weapons, replica firearms and explosives of any kind

- Knives and all other sharp-bladed weapons

- Flammable substances (petrol, methylated spirits, paint thinners, etc.)

- Items containing incapacitating substances that could be used to maim or disable, such as gas cylinders, unless they are part of a ladies hairdressing kit

If you are thinking of taking plants, seeds, bulbs, cuttings, fruit, vegetables, flowers, etc., please do ask us for details, as there are restrictions on the import and export of such items in many countries.
We regret that there are no facilities for carrying animals on board.

Source: Things You Need to Know About Your P&O Cruises Holiday, *K765, April 2004*

Figure 2.17 An example of customer information

areas, access routes and nearby roadways, and possibly inside the building at strategic points. One of the duties of reception staff may be to monitor these CCTV images and be aware of intruders, so that the relevant security services can be called.

Luggage deposited by customers for safe-keeping, for example while visiting a conference or attraction, must be kept in a secure location. At some attractions, only small bags are allowed to be carried by visitors, and security staff at reception will identify any bags that must be handed over to their left luggage department (see Figure 2.16).

Some attractions and facilities use body scanners to check for dangerous objects carried on persons. Airports are an obvious example of this, but they are used at other facilities too. Though this may seem time-consuming when queuing to pass through, the majority of customers feel reassured that their safety and security is of importance to the organisation. Customers are advised about what cannot be packed in hand luggage, such as scissors or sharp instruments, flammable substances and matches, and often tour operators give advice as to what cannot be taken on board under any circumstances (see Figure 2.17).

Consumer protection legislation
Trade Descriptions Act 1968
When you are giving information to consumers you need to be aware of the Trade Descriptions Act, which requires that information be accurate and reliable. This means that organisations cannot state something as being a fact when it is not accurate. A good example is a hotel that advertises itself as being 'five minutes from the beach' – is that five minutes on foot, or by car? It would be safer to give the actual distance to the beach so that the potential customer has a more accurate impression. So, when you are describing facilities to a customer, the description must be as accurate as possible.

Consumer Credit Act 1974
Another form of consumer protection is given by the Consumer Credit Act. If you are responsible for taking payments from customers you need to be aware of the regulations which relate to payment by credit or debit card, and the need to

check the customer's details carefully when processing payments. Customers should also be informed if there are additional charges made by the organisation for payment by credit card, in case they prefer to pay by another method. Some organisations add a percentage (say one or two per cent) to payments made by credit card.

EU Directive on Package Travel 1995

The EU Package Travel Directive may affect dealings with customers, especially if you are working within a travel agency or for a tour operator. The components that make up a holiday package should be provided as described originally to the customer at the time of booking. So, for example, if transfers are included in the price then they should be made available to the holidaymaker.

✱ REMEMBER!

Although you do not need to study all the finer details of the relevant legislation, you do need to be aware of these issues when dealing with customers and apply them in your role play or simulation exercises.

Theory into practice

Study the brochures of various tour operators and identify several situations where legal requirements have been considered. You may find it useful to look also at the section on 'booking conditions' at the back or front of many brochures to identify legislation or regulations that are in place to protect the operator and the consumer.

Assessment guidance

You will have to undertake activities involving customer service situations for your assessment, and these should be as realistic as possible. Whether you are an extrovert or an introvert, you need to *convey* a happy, confident image, performing to a reasonable standard in order to achieve good marks for the practical performance of customer service. Remember all the pointers you have been given about communication, body language and personal skills. Practise these as often as you can.

Assessing the quality of customer service

Because organisations in the travel and tourism industry offer products and services that are similar to those of their competitors, they need to continually monitor and assess their provision of customer service. This will also help them to set and maintain standards of customer service, and to identify areas where it could be improved in order to exceed their customers' needs and expectations. Various methods are used to assess the current provision of customer service and we shall be looking at some of these.

Before it can set out customer service practices and procedures, an organisation needs to identify clearly its *aims* and *objectives*. This might be in the form of a 'mission statement'.

Mission statements

The use of mission statements (or customer charters) has increased in recent times, following government initiatives to promote customer service. They set out the main aims of the organisation to the public and its staff. Other organisations may have a strategy which is not necessarily written down but can be summed up by simple statements of objectives. The staff employed by the organisation are therefore aware of what they are working towards, and the public may be influenced to use that organisation. Some examples of mission statements or strategies of well-known travel and tourism organisations are set out in this section.

A mission or vision statement may be quite brief, but it should be clear, be easily understood by employees, reflect the values, beliefs, philosophies and culture of the organisation, and be broad enough to allow flexibility. Two examples are given below:

> *The Ritz–Carlton is a place where the genuine care and comfort of our guests is our highest mission*
>
> [Ritz–Carlton]

> *Exceptional service from exceptional people*
>
> [Thomas Cook]

A charter, on the other hand, may express broader aims and intentions of the organisation but should still emphasise the main issues that the organisation can monitor and control. Three examples are given below:

We take your comfort and safety very seriously. We want you to be able to relax, enjoy yourself and get to your destination on time and unruffled. Our staff are trained to look after your every need – be sure to ask them if you need any help, or have any comments. The National Rail Conditions of Carriage sets out the service standards that all train companies must meet and also explains the legal contract you have with us when you buy a ticket and travel. You can pick up a copy of this leaflet at any ticket office. Our charter builds upon those standards. It explains clearly the high performance standards we have set ourselves, and how we will make it up to you if things go wrong. In many cases, we are more generous than we are required to be under the National Rail Conditions of Carriage.

[GNER Passenger's Charter: www.gner.co.uk/pages/pcharter/html]

Saga is committed to providing the highest standards of service from the moment you book direct with us, right through every aspect of your holiday. We take care of all the details, leaving you free to relax and enjoy yourself on your well-earned holiday. Saga has more than 50 years' experience of organising holidays for discerning travellers. We believe our success is based on our personal service, attention to detail and our continual response to the suggestions of our holidaymakers.

[Saga Holidays: Winter Escapes brochure 2004–2005]

As a company – profitability will be achieved through quality investment and training, excellent relationship marketing and a unique commitment to service.

As a hotel – we will be the best and most successful hotel in Wales and the South West of England, customer driven and delivering constant service and value.

As an employer – we will be an employer of excellence, who invests in its people.

As a neighbour – we will be active within our local community and the wider community of Cardiff and Wales

[St David's Hotel and Spa, Cardiff: RF Hotels, www.springboarduk.org.uk]

Theory into practice

Many schools and colleges have mission statements or students' charters. Obtain a copy of the one for your centre. As a group, discuss its main clauses. Decide whether it is what you as a customer expected, and what changes you would want to make to it that would meet your expectations more fully.

Quality criteria

Having set out the mission statement and standards the organisation is working towards, it needs then to set out the *quality criteria* to help it achieve these aims. If the quality criteria are clearly laid out, then it is possible for the performance of the organisation to be assessed against them. The quality criteria usually used by travel and tourism organisations are discussed below.

Price or value for money

Most customers are concerned with the price they pay for goods and services, so organisations consider the price they are charging and how this compares with other providers of similar services. You may have seen features in national newspapers, for example, which compare various theme parks in the UK for price and value for money. These articles will have covered the range of rides or attractions available at the theme park and the prices charged, either for each ride or for a day ticket. Customers can then study the article and consider the views expressed in order to form judgements as to whether X park is cheaper than Y park. But if customers consider that the price charged at Y park offers better *value for money* than that for X park, they may be more persuaded to visit that park.

Key term

Value for money is a concept that is difficult to describe, and it is something that individuals will define differently. One might ask 'Does the park offer us more for our money at a better quality?' Another might ask 'If our family spends a day there, will there be enough for us to do and enjoy to make the initial expense worth while?' Each is asking about value for money in different terms.

So when an organisation is setting its prices it needs to consider not only what price the competition is offering, but what other features may be included in that price to give the impression of better value to the customer.

Consistency and accuracy

Is the customer service provided by the organisation consistent? Is there the same quality provided whoever is on duty, in all departments, at all times? It may be excellent at reception, for example, in a hotel, but the restaurant is not providing excellent customer service which matches reception. Or a customer making an enquiry at a travel agency may find that one of the consultants works hard to meet the customer's needs whereas another takes a more laid-back approach and does not ask the appropriate questions to really ascertain the needs of the customer. The quality of service is not consistent between these two employees and there is obviously a need for training to ensure that this provision is more reliable and uniform.

Accuracy also needs to be monitored to ensure that information produced or provided by the organisation is always appropriate. If you receive inaccurate travel details for a planned journey, that will frustrate you and make you feel that the organisation providing the information is not 'on the ball'. You might even miss your flight or connections! So there needs to be some section in the measurement of quality criteria that considers accuracy of detail.

Reliability

If something is promised to a customer, is that promise kept or a good reason given for it not being fulfilled? A customer asking for a morning wake-up call at 6.30 is not going to be very pleased, particularly if there is a plane to catch, if that call does not come through until 6.45. A train arriving late causes problems for those with on-going connections to catch or those needing to attend a meeting at a set time. A visit to a theme park will be disappointing if one of the main rides the customer wishes to visit has broken down and no notification was given at the ticket office or anywhere else on the park.

Quality of service should aim to provide a reliable service at all times. Organisations aim to meet the customers' expectations in terms of reliability, but this needs to be checked frequently to assess whether these expectations are being met.

Staffing levels

No one likes to be kept waiting longer than necessary, so organisations need to consider the levels of staffing required at different times of the day, and possibly at different periods in the year. An attraction that is very seasonal may require the majority of the staff only during the main operating period, but there might be a need for some staffing at other times to maintain a minimum service.

The Tourism Office in Blackpool, for instance, requires maximum staffing during the main holiday season. But Blackpool has attractions that are open all through the year, and there is also demand from conference delegates and other events arranged during the quieter months, as well as people making enquiries about the next holiday season. So the varying staffing level needs to be considered in order to avoid excessive delays in providing information.

Extra staff may need to be employed at peak times for many facilities, so each organisation needs to be aware of when the peak times are (whether during a day or on certain occasions during the year) in order to meet customer's expectations of quick, efficient service.

Staffing qualities

If an organisation has to employ seasonal staff or extra staff for peak periods, it is just as important for these people to be trained in the customer service practices of that organisation, so that the customer does not experience a reduced quality of service because the employee is 'only temporary'.

Many major events employ casual staff for the period of the event only (perhaps for two or three days), but these people must deliver the same quality of customer service as permanent employees. Consider some major sporting events, such as the Grand National at Aintree and the Wimbledon tennis championships. Obviously the organisers will need a fair number of casual staff to provide services and products during these events. These people will often be employed only for the short duration of the event, but they will need to be selected according to their ability to provide a service consistent with the aims of the event. Their period of employment usually includes some time before the event to undergo customer service training and induction into the accepted practices to be followed.

Enjoyment of the experience

Whether you are visiting a theme park, going on holiday, travelling on business, or attending a sporting event, the experience you have should be as enjoyable as possible. If you come away unhappy, you are unlikely to repeat the experience. Therefore, organisations in the travel and tourism industry need to check that they are providing the quality of experience the customer expects so that they can hope to receive repeat business and increased sales.

Think it over ...

Think of a recent enjoyable activity related to travel and tourism you have undertaken. What made the experience enjoyable? Was it the service you received? Was it because you considered it to be value for money? Why might this activity have been more enjoyable than others you have been involved with? If you were asked to write an evaluation of the experience to the organisation providing the activity, what would be the main points you choose to praise in your letter?

Health and safety

Customers want to feel sure that their health and safety has been considered properly, so organisations need to monitor the maintenance of facilities and equipment. While they have a duty of care to all customers as a legal requirement, many organisations will undertake regular checks to ensure that they not only meet the minimum requirements of the legislation but also put into place additional procedures to avoid complaints about health and safety issues.

Obviously, all forms of transport need to meet the minimum standards of safety required by passengers, but sometimes extra actions are taken to ensure passenger safety. For example, some long-distance train services can become overcrowded, such as the one from Plymouth to Glasgow with peak passenger loading usually in the part of the journey from Birmingham to Scotland. The train manager will request passengers to make sure that their luggage is stored safely in the overhead compartments provided. If the service is exceptionally busy and there are many standing passengers with unstowed luggage, it might be necessary to close the on-board shop because it would be unsafe for passengers to carry hot drinks and food down the aisles and through lobbies.

✱ REMEMBER!

Employees need to know what actions they must take to ensure the health and safety of customers at all times.

Think it over ...

Have you seen signs warning of dangers or hazards at a venue? Why does the organisation display these? What other health and safety actions have you noticed at venues?

Cleanliness and hygiene

The appearance of premises or facilities, both inside and out, can affect how customers feel about the organisation. If these are clean, then customers get the impression the organisation cares about its environment – and if it cares about the environment it probably cares about its customers. If the area looks dirty or untidy then this is likely to create the opposite impression – that the organisation is uncaring of the customer experience. First impressions count when considering customers' expectations, and the appearance of staff and facilities does affect judgements made.

Hygiene is also important, particularly where food is being served or prepared. The presence of staff with dirty hands and nails or poor personal hygiene will affect customers' decisions, so many organisations set out practices and procedures for all staff to follow to try to maintain good customer relations.

To help the overall appearance of the environment, some train companies now employ people to clear away rubbish and litter from carriages to keep areas tidy and avoid problems that may affect health and safety. Catering companies often have signs in toilets and the kitchen to remind staff to wash hands regularly – they cannot afford to get a bad reputation through food poisoning or poor hygiene practices.

Accessibility and availability of products and services

Is the product or service available?

Nothing is more annoying than visiting a supermarket for a certain product only to find a notice saying 'Sorry, temporarily out of stock'. If you visit a travel agency, you expect to be able to access brochures from a range of companies for a wide variety of holidays in order to make an informed choice. When the brochures are not available for you to browse through, your reaction may be to try another agency, and if their shelves are more fully stocked it may persuade you to use that agency for your booking.

How broad is the access to the product or service?

Many organisations make their products more accessible by offering them through a range of media – on-line, direct sell, mail order or through intermediaries such as Tourist Information Centres.

Accessibility of products and services relates to how the customer can access them and the wider choice they have can influence their decisions. This can include opening times of an organisation – many travel agencies now open on Sundays to attract those customers who are not able to make bookings during normal business hours.

Is the product or service physically accessible?

Another aspect of accessibility is actual physical access to the products and services, especially for those who are not fully mobile. Can the customer reach the product on the shelves? Can the customer get into the premises – through the doors, up steps or stairs? These aspects are just as important when assessing the quality of customer service – a competitor may have better access and will therefore attract certain customers.

Where exactly is the product or service?

Can the customer find the facility? This is another aspect of access and availability that affects choice. Most tourist attractions now provide locational maps on their publicity, but there are often also signs on major routes directing customers to attractions. The easier it is to locate a facility, the more visitors it is likely to receive.

Is there a wide enough choice to suit different needs?

We have already seen that customers have a range of different needs, so the organisation must consider how these are to be met. Does it offer a variety of services or products to suit a variety of customers, or is its market so restricted that it will appeal only to one type of customer? This could limit the potential earnings of the organisation. Though an attraction may be targeted at a specific group, such as children, these are usually accompanied by adults. So the organisation must consider the needs of the adults as well and provide facilities and services to suit.

Theory into practice

Undertake a survey of travel agencies in your area. Consider accessibility of the brochures, physical access to the premises and space inside, location of the facility, and choice of brochures. Compare the features of the different agencies, then visit the web pages of the travel agencies to discover whether products are available through other media.

Customer care policies

A customer care policy sets out guidelines concerning the most effective ways of dealing with customers within the organisation. This policy is likely to be introduced to new employees during an induction programme, to ensure that all employees within the organisation understand the relevance of the policy and how it applies to them when dealing with customers in a range of situations.

It sets out the practices and procedures that employees should follow when dealing with customers in order to maintain a standard of performance for all. It can also lead to identification of training needs if an employee is not meeting those standards at all times. An example of a customer service policy is given in Figure 2.18.

- A good range of product knowledge

- Friendly and helpful staff

- Well-presented and appropriately dressed staff

- A diverse range of information to ensure that all customers are completely satisfied when they visit the TIC

- Prompt service when dealing with written, telephone and oral communications

- Adequate supplies of promotional materials displayed and available at all times

Figure 2.18 Key customer service quality criteria for a Tourist Information Centre

Monitoring the provision of customer service

In order to establish how well the organisation is meeting the needs of its customers and its customer service policy, it must undertake regular *quality checks* and obtain *feedback* from customers. It can remain competitive only if it is actually providing what the customer wants.

You need to be aware of the many ways in which this analysis can be undertaken, and the reasons for their usage. Some of the techniques are informal, others are more formal. Some are quality checks undertaken internally, others involve customers both internal and external. The findings should be fully considered by management in order to develop the quality of customer service.

Informal feedback

This can take the form of simple questions, preferably requiring little more than a standard 'Yes' or 'No' answer – even these simple answers can lead to development. For example, if you are dining in a restaurant and the head waiter comes to ask whether everything is satisfactory, or if you are enjoying your meal, this is not just being polite. It is a form of feedback. This is the time not only to comment on good or superb service or food, but also to identify anything that could be improved. The head waiter can note any relevant comments and discuss them with the management. If the comments seem valid they could lead to improved service.

Other informal feedback can come from the staff. They may identify a problem or an area that could be improved. Some organisations offer rewards for staff who suggest a positive development that is then taken up within the organisation. It could be something as simple as the order in which a buffet is laid out, or a physical change to the working area that improves the service given to customers.

Management may discuss issues not only with heads of department, but also with employees, as a way of checking that the service they provide meets the needs of customers. If this is done informally, employees do not feel threatened by the situation and may be more honest with their comments.

Suppliers may also be asked for feedback on the organisation's systems or procedures. They can also be forewarned of extra demand, such as when the organisation is aware of a probable increased demand for a product because of a special promotion. The suppliers will need to know so that they can ensure stocks are available. An exhibitor at a trade fair will want sufficient copies of brochures and publicity material, but may warn the suppliers that extra material may be needed if demand exceeds that anticipated.

Surveys

These might be face-to-face surveys with pre-prepared questions that can then be analysed. Alternatively, they might be pro formas left at venues for participants to complete. Most tour operators issue customers with pro forma survey forms to be completed, often with a prize or reward offered to encourage participation. These are designed to give immediate feedback to the operator on the services provided, the support from the operator, and the accommodation or location. These are also often used to obtain additional information about the customer in order to develop a profile of customers, to group them according to age, income, family size etc. which may be used in future marketing campaigns.

Part of a survey form from Cresta Holidays is shown in Figure 2.19. This was sent to customers with their tickets for the holiday they had booked. The postage for the form was prepaid so as not to discourage responses, and a voucher for money off a new booking was on offer.

Other organisations have simpler feedback survey forms for customers to complete, such as the one in Figure 2.20

A £20 THANK YOU FROM **CRESTA**

Firstly, I'd like to thank you for choosing Cresta. At Cresta we value service above all else and we would like your opinions on how we did so we can further improve our holidays for the future.

Please use this feedback form, when you return from holiday to tell us about you and how your trip went. Please complete before returning the form to us by FREEPOST.
Thank you again, on the receipt of a completed feedback form, we will send you a voucher worth up to £20 off your next booking with Cresta, please allow 28 days for delivery of your voucher from the day you post the questionnaire.

Thanks again,

Steve Kimber

Steve Kimber
Managing Director

One voucher per booking
Please write clearly using BLUE or BLACK ink in CAPITAL LETTERS

YOUR CRESTA HOLIDAY

1 **Your booking Reference:**

2 **Which Cresta brochure did you book from?**
☐ Cities ☐ Choices ☐ France
☐ Italy ☐ Golf ☐ Paris & Amsterdam
☐ Ireland ☐ Disney ☐ Worldwide
☐ Eurostar ☐ Spain & Portugal

3
a **How did your party travel?**
☐ Fly ☐ Eurotunnel
☐ Eurostar ☐ Ferry

b **Did you book car hire with us?**
☐ Yes ☐ No

4
a **Which country(s) did you visit?**
i) ii) iii)

b **Which City/resort(s) did you stay in?**
i) ii) iii)

c **Which accommodation(s) did you stay in?**
i) ii) iii)

5
a **How long prior to departure was your holiday booked**
☐ Within 1 month ☐ 1-3 months
☐ 4-6 months ☐ 7 months or more

b **What was your date of departure from the UK?**
☐☐ D ☐☐ M ☐☐☐☐ Y

c **How many nights did you stay for? (Please circle)**
1 2 3 4 5 6 7 8+

6
a **How many adults in your party? (Please circle)**
1 2 3 4 5 6 7 8+

b **How many children (3-16)? (Please circle)**
1 2 3 4 5 6+

c **How many infants (2 or under)? (Please circle)**
1 2 3 4 5 6+

Figure 2.19 A customer feedback form

ASTON BUSINESS SCHOOL

MANAGEMENT DEVELOPMENT CENTRE

We Value Your Opinion

We hope you had an enjoyable and successful event with us here at the Management Development Centre. We are dedicated to continuous improvement and would appreciate your help in filling in this quick questionnaire to evaluate the service we offer to our customers. Please rate the following questions and feel free to make any additional comments at the bottom. Thank you for taking the time to help us help you. (1=Poor 2=Fair 3=Good 4=Excellent)

	1	2	3	4		1	2	3	4
Was the Management Development Centre easy to find?	☐	☐	☐	☐	If applicable, how would you rate the audio equipment?	☐	☐	☐	☐
Was the venue clean, tidy and well maintained?	☐	☐	☐	☐	If applicable, how would you rate the visual equipment?	☐	☐	☐	☐
Were the staff helpful and friendly?	☐	☐	☐	☐	How do you rate the training facilities and standards of the meeting rooms?	☐	☐	☐	☐
How comfortable were the meeting rooms?	☐	☐	☐	☐	How do you rate the quality of the food and beverage?	☐	☐	☐	☐

Comments: ....

Client Name: (Optional) .... Name of Conference: ....
Date of Conference: .... Room Number: ....

Please leave this Questionnaire at Reception when you depart. Thank you.

Figure 2.20 A customer feedback form

from Aston Business School. This is for conference organisers and participants (as occasionally the views of organisers may vary from those of participants) to give immediate feedback on the facilities provided at the business school. Again, the form had postage prepaid.

While customers are vital sources of information for an organisation, many will also survey their own staff and management. This could be by means of a company image checklist or service level agreement. It could relate to a specific area, such as reception, or it might look at the organisation from a wider angle as in the example in Figure 2.21.

This type of survey may also set standards or 'benchmarks' to be followed. It is a valuable tool that can be used by internal or external customers to monitor and measure the quality of customer service. Each area would have criteria to meet, such as answering the telephone within three rings, greeting or acknowledging customers immediately on arrival at reception, etc.

Assessment guidance

When you come to prepare your own assessment of the customer service provision in your chosen organisation, you will need to consider the above areas and decide how you will measure that organisation's performance.

AREAS OF OPERATIONS CONSIDERED IN A SERVICE LEVEL AGREEMENT COULD BE:	
Telephone answering	Speed Quality Switchboard/extension standards Number of times callers are re-routed Quality of message taking Telephonist's organisational knowledge
Reception	Greeting Speed of response Maintenance of area (comfort, interest, tidiness) Knowledge of organisation personnel/roles Quality of surroundings (noise/distractions)
Paperwork	Quality of general correspondence Quality and accuracy of literature
Written/verbal communication	Response times Understandability Accuracy of details Face-to-face – friendly, helpful, professional Company/product knowledge
Customer contacts	Quality of relationships built Frequency of contact with customers
Company structure/identity	Visibility to customer Clarity of organisation Who's who Consistency between departments/individuals Consistent company image
Location/access	Clear maps/directions Suggested route clear and easy to follow Clear, accurate signage No exposure to health and safety hazards

Figure 2.21 Service level agreement for the whole organisation

Suggestion box or comments book

These, again, may be used by internal or external customers, and may identify areas not previously considered by management. Some organisations used to have a 'complaints book', but this was seen as a negative approach, as well as a missed opportunity to receive developmental feedback or compliments. The trend now is for a 'comments book' that can be used to write in both positive and negative feedback. This is seen as less threatening by some customers than a survey, and more a case of volunteering information than being pressured to answer set questions.

Instead of writing in a book, customers can sometimes fill in a form like the one from Virgin Trains shown in Figure 2.22.

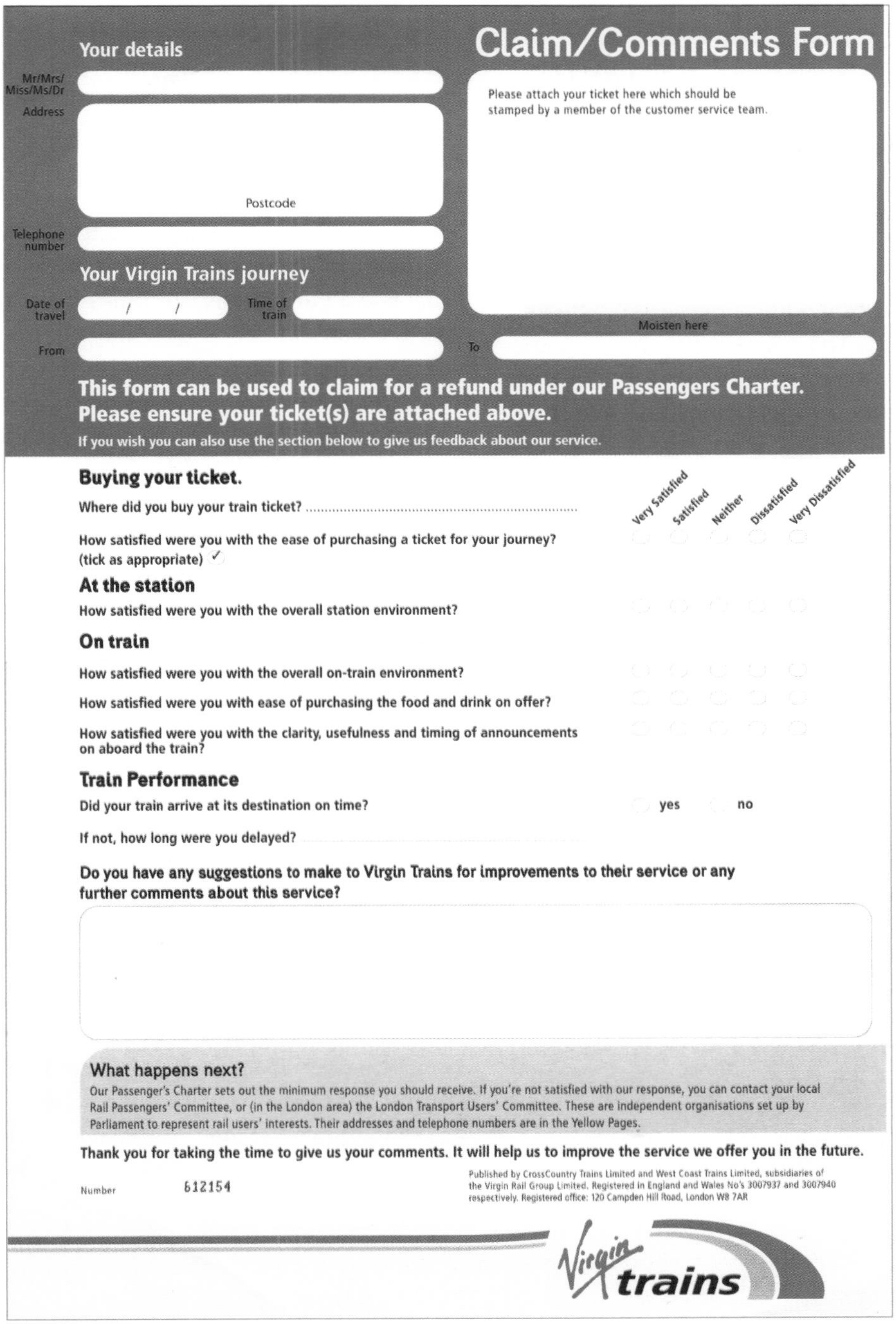

Your details

Claim/Comments Form

Mr/Mrs/Miss/Ms/Dr

Address

Postcode

Telephone number

Please attach your ticket here which should be stamped by a member of the customer service team.

Your Virgin Trains journey

Date of travel / /

Time of train

Moisten here

From

To

This form can be used to claim for a refund under our Passengers Charter. Please ensure your ticket(s) are attached above.

If you wish you can also use the section below to give us feedback about our service.

Buying your ticket.

Very Satisfied | Satisfied | Neither | Dissatisfied | Very Dissatisfied

Where did you buy your train ticket? ....

How satisfied were you with the ease of purchasing a ticket for your journey? (tick as appropriate) ✓

At the station

How satisfied were you with the overall station environment?

On train

How satisfied were you with the overall on-train environment?

How satisfied were you with ease of purchasing the food and drink on offer?

How satisfied were you with the clarity, usefulness and timing of announcements on aboard the train?

Train Performance

Did your train arrive at its destination on time? yes no

If not, how long were you delayed?

Do you have any suggestions to make to Virgin Trains for improvements to their service or any further comments about this service?

What happens next?

Our Passenger's Charter sets out the minimum response you should receive. If you're not satisfied with our response, you can contact your local Rail Passengers' Committee, or (in the London area) the London Transport Users' Committee. These are independent organisations set up by Parliament to represent rail users' interests. Their addresses and telephone numbers are in the Yellow Pages.

Thank you for taking the time to give us your comments. It will help us to improve the service we offer you in the future.

Number 612154

Published by CrossCountry Trains Limited and West Coast Trains Limited, subsidiaries of the Virgin Rail Group Limited. Registered in England and Wales No's 3007937 and 3007940 respectively. Registered office: 120 Campden Hill Road, London W8 7AR

Virgin trains

Figure 2.22 A customer claim/comments form

Focus groups

An unusual type of focus group is used by Blackpool Pleasure Beach. The organisation has what is called a Junior Board, and to be a member of this one can apply through the Pleasure Beach's website. There are age restrictions, but members visit the park at least three times a year and carry out a review of rides and services. The points they raise are then discussed at a full board meeting with management of the Pleasure Beach, who take the views seriously. The point is that these are the customers now and in the future, and the Pleasure Beach must meet their expectations if it is to thrive. By focusing on youngsters at a theme park aimed at young people, any ideas are seen as relevant and will be considered by the management when new developments are planned.

Mystery shoppers

These may be independent people hired by the organisation to undertake a 'shopping exercise'. In other words they act as potential customers and then report back to the organisation on their findings. Occasionally, the mystery shopper will be an employee from another part of the organisation, not known to the employees in the facility being surveyed. He or she is asked to report back, usually on a pro forma, but occasionally in more detailed format, identifying any areas where service is weak or service is good and where improvements or developments can be made.

Observation

Another form of feedback comes from observing the activities of the personnel in the organisation performing their usual duties and making notes of any specific areas that need to be considered. This may be undertaken by an internal colleague or a member of management, or it could be someone from another branch or department. All aspects of customer service should be covered, including body language, facial expressions, the quality and accuracy of information presented, and the attitude of the employee – as well as his or her performance of routine functions.

Conclusion

Most travel and tourism organisations undertake some form of customer care analysis, and may in fact use a variety of techniques in order to obtain an accurate reflection of what is happening in the organisation. The reports or findings need to be studied to identify areas for development, either in the procedures and practices or staff training requirements. It is essential to ensure that staff are maintaining the values and attitudes of the organisation as expressed in the mission statement, and are acting as good representatives of the organisation.

Preparation for assessment

In order to meet the requirements of Assessment Objectives 3 and 4 you have to undertake thorough research into the procedures and practices used by your chosen organisation to assess the effectiveness of its customer service before you can proceed to develop your analysis and evaluation. You should consider all the aspects of customer service as outlined in this unit in order to demonstrate that you understand the customer service principles and how they are applied by your chosen organisation.

You also need to consider what practices and procedures the organisation has in place to monitor the quality of its customer service provision and how these are used to develop the quality of service. You should undertake a review of these practices in order to suggest areas for development or improvement.

The following study and questions will set you on the right route to meeting the Assessment Objectives for this unit.

A study of Manchester Airport

Manchester Airport Group plc is the company that manages the airport. It is responsible for the buildings, taxiways, runways and land including car parks. It also makes sure the airport is safe to use by providing fire and security services. Other organisations, such as airlines and handling agents (referred to as service partners), are responsible for the many activities in and around the airport.

Customer service is the way in which Manchester Airport Group plc treats its customers, giving them what they want and need and making their experience enjoyable.

The customers of the airport are often assumed to be the passengers. But the only direct customers of the airport are the airlines, with their passengers being the end-users. There are other stakeholders in the customer chain – tour operators, the travel trade, service partners, employees and the general public. Service partners provide services such as catering, baggage handling, retail outlets, check-in facilities etc. They are also the internal customers of Manchester Airport. Service partner agreements are prepared as to service and quality required and signed by the airport management and the service partner.

Quality of service is checked regularly with meetings with service partners (who have their own customer service staff and policies), through surveys, analysing letters and telephone calls, face-to-face with employees on site, and comment cards from service partners. Checklists are used to monitor airport cleaning, which is contracted out. This is a computerised system and is the main tool used to assess the day-to-day cleaning operations. Specific standards are set for each of the 420 cleaning zones and there are three possible outcomes:

* not at the acceptable standard at the time of inspection

* meets the acceptable standard at the time of inspection

* exceeds the acceptable standard at the time of inspection.

Catering outlets and concessionaries have service agreements and contracts with Manchester Airport and these are monitored by the airport management. Contracts are agreed and signed and these include minimum delivery standards such as:

* retail units being kept in good repair

* Manchester Airport having 24-hour access for security and fire reasons

* all staff wearing an ID pass

* all concessionaries accepting credit cards.

Last year, Customer Relations received over 4500 comments and of these around 1000 were compliments or suggestions. The top two compliments received about the airport from passengers concerned the friendly and helpful staff and the wheelchair service. Complaints in the main related to catering, signage, baggage, terminal facilities, flight delays, car parking, the retail outlets, lack of waste bins and seating in the departure lounges.

An example of quality criteria as applied to Aviation Security officers is given below. The officers are assessed on the following criteria:

Makes no effort to discover who Security's customers are	1 2 3 4 5 6	*Is aware of who Security's customers are*
Does not exchange pleasantries	1 2 3 4 5 6	*Gives a friendly, cheerful service*
Displays a negative attitude to customers (e.g. surly, abrupt, unhelpful)	1 2 3 4 5 6	*Consistently displays polite and helpful consideration in dealing with customers*

Rating key:
1 unsuitable
2 falls short of requirements – considerable development needed
3 partially meets requirements – some development needed
4 meets requirements
5 does a little more than expected
6 exceeds requirements

Some of the criteria also given in the customer service policy include the following.

* Complaints by letter or telephone call have to be acknowledged within 3 working days.

* Complaints by letter or telephone call have to be dealt with effectively within 10 working days.

* Complaints by comment card are logged on to a database and replied to within 7 days.

* Telephone calls are directed to the appropriate department, company or service partner.

* Baggage is unloaded from aircraft within 15 minutes maximum (IATA standard).

* Maximum queuing time for Britannia and Monarch Airways is 15 minutes.

Theory into practice

1 Identify the customers of Manchester Airport Group plc, and state which are direct, and which are part of the customer service chain (stakeholders). Also classify them as either internal or external customers.

2 List the types of organisation classed as 'service providers'. What methods do Manchester Airport Group use to check the quality of service provided by these service providers?

3 What procedures are in place to monitor the performance of (a) cleaning contractors, (b) security personnel, and (c) dealing with complaints?

4 Explain why the airport sets minimum delivery standards with catering outlets and concessionaries.

5 Design an assessment tool that could be used to monitor the performance of a retail outlet, such as WH Smith, at the airport. Consider aspects such as opening times, staff presentation, cleanliness, availability and range of stock, speed of customer processing, queue management, layout of the outlet for access for all customer types, and any other criteria you feel are relevant.

Knowledge check

1 Explain the purpose of a mission statement.

2 Give *three* methods that organisations can use to measure the quality of customer service and explain the advantages and disadvantages of each.

3 Outline the benefits of staff training to the organisation in terms of efficiency and quality of customer service.

4 What is the difference between an external customer and an internal customer?

5 Identify at least *five* benefits to an organisation of providing excellent customer service.

6 Explain the customer needs of a group of Italian tourists visiting a museum.

7 Handling complaints requires practice and skill. What skills would you be expected to use when handling a complaint or dealing with a problem?

8 Explain the term 'value for money' when used in relation to customer service situations.

9 How can an organisation try to maintain consistency and reliability in the provision of its customer service?

10 Tone and vocabulary are important in customer service situations. Explain this in relation to dealing with customers face-to-face.

Resources

You can collect information and opinions about customer service from many sources. Here are some suggestions:

* regional tourist boards for Welcome Host training

* 'fly on the wall' TV documentaries such as 'Airport'

* television comedy programmes such as 'Fawlty Towers' and 'Brittas Empire'

* case studies in books such as this one

* websites of major travel and tourism organisations, such as Marriott Hotels, Thomson, Alton Towers, the National Trust, and so on (use a search engine such as Google to locate websites).

UNIT 3

Travel destinations

Introduction

Government statistics show that the British are travelling abroad more than ever before. Although the proportion of UK residents who did not take a holiday of four days or more has remained relatively unchanged over the past three decades, the proportion taking two or more holidays has increased from 15 to 25 per cent.

Between 1982 and 2002, the number of visits abroad made by residents of the UK almost tripled. However, spending on these visits in 2002 was more than seven times the spending in 1982. In real terms (taking inflation into account) UK residents' spending quadrupled over the 20 years. In 2003, visits overseas by UK residents rose by over 3 per cent to an all-time high of 61.5 million.

People travel for many reasons and it is usual to find both domestic and overseas visits being made for one of the following:

* leisure travel, such as a family holiday or short break
* business travel, such as attending a meeting, conference or an event
* to visit close family, relatives and friends.

The most common reason is for leisure purposes and for many people the summer holiday has become a well established highlight of the year. The actual selection of a holiday destination has become, for many of us, a major activity in itself.

How you will be assessed

This unit is assessed through your portfolio work. You will investigate *two* travel destinations, one of which is short-haul and one long-haul. You must show that you are familiar with the use of destination maps at different scales and are aware of how these can be used to display locational information. You must show an understanding of how the features of particular destinations appeal to different types of visitor. You will also have to show evidence that you have used various sources of information and how these provide clues about future tourism development.

What you need to learn

* the geographical location of major short-haul and long-haul destinations that attract UK tourists
* the key features of the major destinations
* the reasons why these features make destinations appeal to different tourist groups
* the reasons why some destinations may become more popular in the future whilst others will decline in popularity.

The choice of destination

Before we look at travel destinations themselves, it is important to recognise some of the influences that are at work when an individual traveller makes a decision to visit any particular location.

There are many forces at work that can influence our decision whether or not we will even consider visiting a particular destination. Several of these forces are depicted in Figure 3.1. However, our perceptions about places are often influenced mostly by the way in which we first hear about them. Furthermore, our perceptions can frequently be wrong, and we can easily form impressions about destinations that do not reflect a true image of the reality.

For most people the preferred way of spending their leisure time is to take a complete break from everyday life and to go on holiday, either within the United Kingdom or abroad.

Popular destinations

According to the World Tourism Organisation, by the year 2020 China will become the world's favourite destination – it is estimated that a total of 137 million people will visit the country. Germans are expected to be the world's most travelled people at that time with 163 million visits, or 10 per cent of the world market. The Chinese will be fourth, closely followed by the British who will make a total of 96 million trips. Figure 3.2 shows popular overseas destinations for UK travellers.

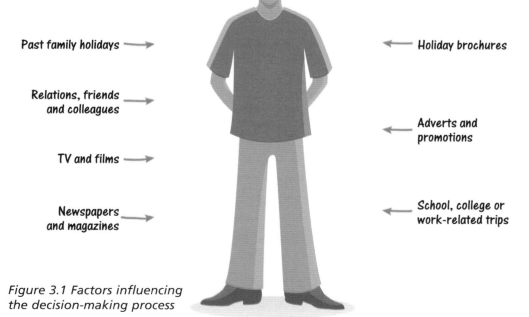

Past family holidays →

Relations, friends and colleagues →

TV and films →

Newspapers and magazines →

← Holiday brochures

← Adverts and promotions

← School, college or work-related trips

Figure 3.1 Factors influencing the decision-making process

SHORT HAUL		LONG HAUL			
Spain	Netherlands	Thailand	UAE	Barbados	China
France	Cyprus	Maldives	Mauritius	St Lucia	India
Greece	Belgium	USA	Singapore	Mexico	Jamaica
Italy	Germany	Sri Lanka	Malaysia	Antigua	South Africa
Portugal	Malta	Egypt	Kenya	Australia	New Zealand
Irish Republic	Austria	Hong Kong	Indonesia	Cuba	
Turkey					

Figure 3.2 Popular overseas destinations for UK travellers

Theory into practice

On a blank outline map of the world, name and locate each country listed in Figure 3.2. Then set up and complete the following table:

COUNTRY	CAPITAL	AIRPORT	CURRENCY	RESORT OR DESTINATION	RISK OR HAZARD
UAE	Abu Dhabi	Abu Dhabi	Dirham	Dubai	Heatstroke
		Dubai			
Spain	Madrid	Madrid	Euro	Salou	Seawater pollution
		Barcelona			
Australia	Canberra	Sydney	Dollar	Cairns	Bush fires

Influences on the choice of destination

All of us make decisions about where and when we are going to travel. Our final choice of destination to visit and details of our final travel arrangements are subject to a complex set of inter-relationships. Each individual traveller has certain constraints that, in effect, limit his or her ability to choose from the full range of alternatives that are currently available to the UK travelling public. Individual preferences will be subject to factors such as those illustrated in Figure 3.3.

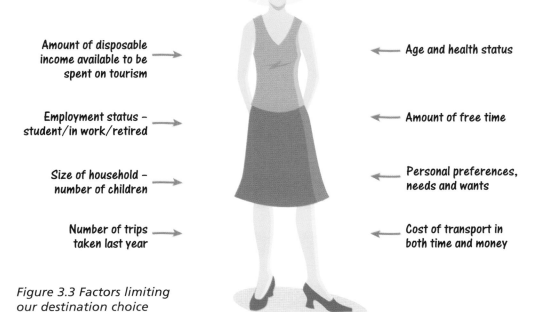

Amount of disposable income available to be spent on tourism

Employment status – student/in work/retired

Size of household – number of children

Number of trips taken last year

Age and health status

Amount of free time

Personal preferences, needs and wants

Cost of transport in both time and money

Figure 3.3 Factors limiting our destination choice

Use Figures 3.1 and 3.3 to help you suggest reasons why people with similar interests and preferences will visit very different destinations (as shown in Figure 3.4) in order to satisfy their requirements.

SEASIDE	NATIONAL PARK RECREATION	MOUNTAIN ADVENTURE	CITY BREAK
Southend-on-sea	Yorkshire Dales	Lake District	Chester
Benidorm	Ireland	The Alps	Amsterdam
Lanzarote	Canada	Norway	Rome
Barbados	Costa Rica	The Andes	New York
Fiji	New Zealand	The Himalayas	Sydney

Figure 3.4 Destinations for particular types of leisure holiday

People react in different ways to the opportunities available, even if their personal circumstances are virtually identical. Most people would like the 'perfect holiday', one that is tailor-made to satisfy every wish and desire. In reality we know that such a situation is most unlikely to arise, so we are content with a holiday that meets most of our personal requirements. In other words, most people are quite happy to behave as satisficers rather than optimisers. The operation of such influencing factors helps to explain the destination choices made by the UK travelling public.

Tourist destinations actively try to increase the number of visitors. Tourism is one of the world's biggest industries, with international tourism receipts now approaching the equivalent of 400 billion US dollars worldwide. Furthermore, these receipts have grown by 12 per cent a year over the last decade, and competition between countries for tourists' spending looks set to become even more intense. All destinations will therefore be trying to develop a consistent and high-quality tourism product to maximise their appeal and thus maintain the very valuable economic impacts that tourism can bring.

Leading tourism locations receive considerable benefits from their visitor numbers, so it is no surprise that established destinations like New York, Hong Kong and Dubai experience a significant contribution to their gross domestic product (GDP) from this sector. In an attempt to manage and sustain tourism growth, many countries have established specific development plans for the tourism sector.

In the UK, 'destination benchmarking' surveys are undertaken to update information from previous surveys on the profile behaviour and opinions of tourists in order to identify emerging trends. These surveys include the regional tourist boards' standard 'destination benchmarking' questions which are designed to measure levels of satisfaction with particular destinations. This allows comparisons to be made with competing destinations in terms of key variables such as:

* accommodation
* parking
* attractions
* places to eat and drink
* shops
* ease of finding one's way around
* public toilets
* cleanliness of streets
* upkeep of parks and open spaces
* choice of nightlife/entertainment
* overall impression
* security from crime
* safety from traffic
* overall enjoyment
* likelihood of recommending it to others.

All tourist destinations, whether in the UK or overseas, recognise that each potential visitor has available a choice of options. Each location is therefore in direct competition with many similar destinations. Variations in the quality of total visitor experience will result in variations in visitor numbers. The competing destinations will battle for our custom on three key fronts:

* quality – its beauty/uniqueness, levels of service and infrastructure
* price – of accommodation, transport and catering
* level of promotion – the ways in which the destination can be brought to the attention of potential visitors.

The geographical location of destinations

Any study of the world's travel and tourism industry will at some stage involve knowledge about where places are to be found. It is important that people who work in travel and tourism have a clear idea about the world's basic geography.

The position of any location on the Earth's surface can be described in terms of its *latitude*, measured in degrees, north or south of the Equator. This is very similar to the lines of *longitude*, which indicate the position east or west of Greenwich in London. The furthest point north is the North Pole (90°N) and the furthest point south is the South Pole (90°S). In each hemisphere, there are two additional important lines of latitude between the Pole and the Equator – these are the Tropic of Cancer (23.5°N) and the Tropic of Capricorn (23.5°S). The Arctic Circle is at 66.5°N and the Antarctic Circle is at 66.5°S.

The *lines of latitude* indicate divisions that allow us to make generalisations about the locational position of all points on the Earth's surface. It is quite common to see reference being made to the following:

* equatorial latitudes – between 5 degrees north and south of the Equator
* tropical latitudes – anywhere between 23.5 degrees north and south of the Equator
* sub-tropical latitudes – between 23.5 and approximately 30 degrees north and south of the Equator
* temperate latitudes – between approximately 30 and 50 degrees north and south of the Equator
* arctic latitudes – around 66.5 degrees north and south of the Equator
* polar latitudes – anywhere between the Poles and 66.5 degrees north and south.

Using and developing your research skills

All people working in the travel and tourism industry need to be able to find out about places because they will have to answer questions from prospective customers. This information has to be *up to date* and *accurate*. There is a wide range of sources of information. Being able to answer questions and supply accurate information is part of delivering good customer service.

When students or researchers want to get information on a topic, there is an orderly manner in which the investigation should be approached.

Assessment guidance

For the assessment of this unit you will be expected to show that you have:

- been clear what you are trying to find out
- been able to understand how to search for information
- been clear in deciding what might be useful
- presented the information obtained in an orderly way that is fit for its purpose
- drawn conclusions from the information that you have obtained
- acknowledged your sources of information, thus allowing for further references to be made.

You are also expected to choose appropriate sources of information.

A wide range of organisations provide information for anyone who wants to travel to virtually any destination in the world. Travel organisations can be categorized in terms of whether they are primarily marketing or non-marketing. Marketing organisations include tour operators, tourist boards and the overseas marketing departments of the destinations themselves. While any information about a destination can be of use to a particular individual, it is always worth remembering that the primary objective of marketing and promotion departments is to attract tourists who are able to spend money on their product or at their destination.

The amount of information that is currently available about most destinations for most travellers usually far exceeds what is required, so the problem is where to start.

Brochures

Most people planning a leisure trip will visit a local travel agency. Here they can find a wide range of brochures that are often arranged according to the type of holiday. There may be a section on cruises, sections arranged by country, types of package such as villas and self-catering breaks, special interest holidays such as skiing, coach tours and a host of others. There will also be brochures produced by transport providers such as ferry companies or airlines giving details

not only of their transport services but also of their particular range of inclusive tours. British travel agents distribute between six and ten brochures per person booking a holiday.

Brochures are a very good source of basic information about particular destinations. It is common to find the following included:

* a map giving the location of the destination relative to point of entry, together with resort attractions

* a table of climate figures indicating what the weather conditions will be like

* photographs showing aspects of the natural and built environment that people are likely to be interested in

* a description of the facilities to be found in selected types of destination accommodation

* brief details of local places of interest and attractions.

Guides and manuals

It must be remembered that the main purpose of glossy printed brochures is to create *awareness* amongst readers which will then lead to a positive decision to buy one of the featured holiday products. This will not be sufficient for anyone wanting to make a detailed study of the attractions to be found within a particular destination.

Travellers wanting to know more about particular destinations have a number of options. Travel agency staff should have immediate access to a selection of guides and manuals such as the OAG *Flight Guide*, OAG *Cruise and Ferry Guide*, OAG *Gazetteers*, OAG *Holiday Guides* and the OAG *Guide to International Travel*. They will be able to refer to these to answer specific questions about particular destinations. Travel employees cannot be expected to know the answer to every question but they should know where to look in order to obtain appropriate information. For example, the OAG *Gazetteers* contain independent reviews of resorts and accommodation in six volumes covering the following:

* Mediterranean hotels

* Mediterranean apartments

* European cities
* long-haul
* North America
* ski, lakes and mountains.

Both private individuals and agency staff can use the Columbus Press *World Travel Guide*. This is a huge publication and includes everything that travel staff will need to answer a general destination enquiry from a member of the public. The contents range from details of the climate in locations at a specific time to the social and cultural backgound of the destination. Information is provided about many destinations on a country-by-country basis, and an extract is shown in Figure 3.5. Further reference will be made to the Caribbean island of Dominica in a case study later in this chapter.

National Tourist Boards

Anyone who intends visiting a country can write to the relevant tourist board and ask for information. Most countries publish marketing brochures and leaflets that provide more detailed information than the tour operator's brochure, usually including details about climate, social conditions and currency regulations. Furthermore, because the UK is such an important generator of outbound tourists, many national tourist boards maintain a UK office to service this potential demand. The range of material available is sometimes quite impressive and we can look at an actual example to illustrate this point further.

The Government of Dubai operates a Department of Tourism & Commerce Marketing (DTCM). The DTCM actively promotes Dubai's tourism product and brings it to the attention of a global marketplace in an attempt to sustain and extend the number of visitors that the destination currently attracts. The DTCM has established a global network of overseas offices to aid its promotional strategy and in 2004 the following locations were operational:

DTCM in Dubai (www.dubaitourism.ae)
New York – North America
London – UK and Ireland
Paris – France
Frankfurt/Main – Germany
Stockholm – Scandinavia

Dominica (Commonwealth of)

ACCOMMODATION

HOTELS: The number of hotels has expanded in recent years; most of the hotels are small- to medium-sized, and well-equipped; the largest of them has 98 rooms. There are three hotels at the fringe of an area designated as a National Park. Information can be obtained from the Dominica Hotel Association, PO Box 384, Roseau. Tel: 448 6565. Fax: 448 0299. The Association also provides assistance in organising conferences and conventions in Dominica. **Grading:** Many of the hotels offer accommodation according to one of a number of 'Plans' widely used in the Caribbean; these include Modified American Plan (MAP) which consists of room, breakfast and dinner and European Plan (EP) which consists of room only.
APARTMENTS/COTTAGES: These offer self-catering, full service and maid service facilities and are scattered around the island.
GUEST-HOUSES: There is a variety of guest-houses and inns around the island which offer a comfortable and very friendly atmosphere. There is a 10% government tax and 10% service charge on rooms.
CAMPING/CARAVANNING: Not encouraged at the present time, though sites may be designated in future. Overnight safari tours are run by local operators.

RESORTS & EXCURSIONS

Roseau, on the southwest coast, is the main centre for visitors. From hotels around here it is possible to arrange jeep safari tours for seeing the hinterland of the country. Canoe trips up the rivers can also be arranged. The beaches are mainly of black volcanic sand, but there are a few white-sand beaches on the northeast of this island. Sports facilities include scuba diving, sailing and sport fishing.
Morne Trois Pitons National Park, covering 7000 hectares (17,000 acres) in the south-central part of Dominica, was established in July 1975. Places of interest in the park include the *Boiling Lake*, the second-largest in the world which was discovered in 1922, and the *Emerald Pool, Middleham Falls, Sari Sari Falls, Trafalgar Triple Waterfalls, Freshwater Lake, Boeri Lake* and the *Valley of Desolation.*
Cabrits Historical Park was designated a park in 1987. Attractions include the **Cabrits Peninsular** which contains the historical ruins of *Fort Shirley* and *Fort George,* 18th- and early 19th-century forts, and a museum at Fort Shirley. The usual touring spots in addition to the above include the **Carib Indian Territory**, the *Sulphur Springs,* the *Central Forest Reserve, Botanical Gardens, Titou Gorge, L'Escalier Tête Chien,* several areas of rainforest and a variety of fauna and flora.

Figure 3.5 Information on the island of Dominica, which is looked at again later in this chapter, taken from the World Travel Guide *published by Columbus Travel Guides*

Milan – Italy
Zurich – Switzerland and Austria
Moscow – Russian Federation, CIS and Baltic states
Johannesburg – South Africa
Mumbai – India
Hong Kong – China and Far East
Tokyo – Japan
Sydney – Australia and New Zealand

The DTCM produces a wide variety of promotional materials, including maps, destination guides and brochures that will attract leisure and business visitors. It produces information for a series of niche markets using titles such as:

The Classic Golf Destination
The Watersports Resort
Tours and Safaris
The Birdwatcher's Paradise
The Great Incentive
Heritage and Culture
Dubai: Cruise Hub of the Arabian Gulf
Conference and Exhibition Facilities

The worldwide promotional activities of the DTCM are widely credited with being one of the key elements in Dubai's current tourism boom. The government agency has won international awards and recognition as the leading exponent of destination marketing in the Middle East and it has become a model to be emulated by other destinations. We shall return to Dubai later in a case study.

Travel guides

Travel guides give a comprehensive coverage of destinations all over the world. Country and regional guides, such as those produced by Rough Guides and distributed worldwide by the Penguin group, include recommendations from shoestring to luxury and cover more than 200 destinations around the globe, including almost every country in the Americas and Europe, more than half of Africa and most of Asia and Australasia. Rough Guides also produce city guides which provide neighbourhood information and contain easy-to-use coloured maps for streets and city transport.

Lonely Planet is a similar source and it publishes over 650 guidebooks, in fourteen different languages, covering every corner of the planet. The organisation also offers a range of services to aid and inspire travellers at home or on the road. Many travel publishers publish pocket-sized city and country guides that are more suitable for short stays or business trips. Most travel guides have excellent photographs illustrating the culture and attractions of the destination.

Trade journals, newspapers and magazines

Trade journals such as *Travel Trade Gazette* and *Travel Weekly* contain a lot of information about destinations. Here the focus is on new developments and what is being planned or introduced into various tour operators' programmes, with comments about how sales to the travelling public might be affected. There are up-to-the-minute commentaries on featured destinations, and details of road shows and the various incentives available for travel agency front-line staff.

Newspapers and magazines frequently contain destination reports within their travel sections. These will feature best-value options and other advice for readers contemplating either a domestic or an overseas trip. Figure 3.6 shows an illustration about Barcelona, a destination that is the subject of a case study later. The significant point about this particular extract is that it clearly aims its advice at a range of visitor types. In terms of Barcelona being a visitor destination, the extract emphasises that travellers with a variety of needs and wants can be catered for by a range of local providers.

Television

Television programmes have featured reports about holiday destinations for over 40 years. Several programmes, such as the BBC's 'Holiday Programme' and ITV's 'Wish You Were Here', have introduced more than one generation of leisure travellers to the delights of locations scattered throughout the tourist world. Furthermore, the locational setting of particular programmes and films has increased viewer awareness as to the attractions contained in many destinations. Indeed, the visiting of locations featured on both the big and small screens has fuelled tourism development at various destinations.

In addition, over three million people make use of teletext as a source of information on their holiday arrangements.

BARCELONA

Where to stay, where to eat, what to do: Barcelona for every budget

ON THE CHEAP

Enter Hostal Oliva (Passeig de Gracia 32; 00 34-93 488 0162) through a traditional Modernista atrium. Rooms 10 and 11 are nice ensuite doubles (if you're okay with the traffic hum) — good value at £41, room-only. Hostal Fontanella (Via Laietana 71; 93 317 5943) is all flowery fabrics, gilt-edged mirrors and frilly armrests: a homely atmosphere, but you'll need to bone up on your Spanish. Ensuite doubles cost £48.

Can Culleretes (Carrer Quintana 5; 93 317 3022; closed Sunday evening and July) is Barcelona's oldest restaurant, serving meaty treats such as suckling pig in apricots and prunes (£8) and wild boar and game stew (£5). Or try Les Quinze Nits (93 317 3075), on the north side of the beautiful Placa Reial. It offers Catalan cuisine at Happy Meal prices (sausage with white beans costs just £3), but you have to queue for ages if you time it wrongly.

Get some salt in your hair with a sun-beaten stroll along the beach promenade. Bathe if you dare, but there are cleaner beaches up the coast. This one is better for eating and drinking beside.

MIDDLE OF THE ROAD

Nestled between two leafy, cafe-filled squares in the Barri Gotic is Hotel Jardi (Placa Sant Josep Oriol 1; 00 34-93 301 5900; doubles from £58). Rooms are basic — a little poky, but spotless — and the location is ideal. The brand-new and supertrendy Hotel Constanza (Bruc 33; 93 270 1910, www. hotelconstanza.com) is excellent value at £83 a double. Seven new rooms with sun terraces should be ready this autumn.

Agua (Passeig Maritim 30; 93 225 1272) is a bargain by the beach. Try seafood specialities such as sweet shrimps with tagliolini, garlic and chilli (£5). Or be entirely unmodern: reserve a downstairs window table at the Catalan classic El Gran Cafe (Avinyo 9; 93 318 7986) and order the duck with pear (£11).

The Palau de la Musica Catalana (Sant Francesc de Paula 2; 93 295 7200, www.palaumusica.org; closed Monday; £6) has an opulent stained-glass ceiling and an intricately decorated interior. Seeing it without music is pointless, so go to a concert if you have time. Tickets start at about £20.

NO EXPENSE SPARED

The Prestige Hotel (Paseo de Gracia 62; 00 34-93 272 4180; executive doubles from £190) lives up to its name. Near the Gaudi facades of La Pedrera and Casa Batllo, it does modern decor in a classic building. And the minibar's free. The central location of the supertasteful Hotel Neri (93 304 0655; www.hotelneri.com) doesn't mean it's noisy, and the doubles are a steal at £127.

El Bulli (Cala Montjoi; 97 215 0457, www.elbulli.com) is, relatively speaking, just around the corner, on the Costa Brava — and, as one of the world's top restaurants, it should not be missed. But tables book up for a whole season in one day in January, so chances are that it will be. Chin up — there are many other wonderful options, including the seafood emporium Botafumeiro (Carrer Gran de Gracia 81; 93 218 4230), where the extravagant shellfish platter for two costs £70.

A night at the opera. Gran Teatre del Liceu (93 485 9913, www. liceubarcelona.com) has been fully restored after the fire of 1994. The best tickets start at about £40.

Source: Harriet Perry from *The Sunday Times*, 5 September 2004

Figure 3.6 Information on Barcelona, which is looked at again later in this chapter

The Internet

Internet research of holiday destinations is now commonplace. Over 25 million people currently investigate aspects of their domestic and overseas travel in this way. Many people have access at work, home or via a third party, and most travel and tourism organisations maintain a website for information storage and to service the increasing trend for on-line bookings.

The amount of data available is extremely large and information about most destinations in the world can be found at the click of a mouse. However, some sites are more useful than others, so 'surfing the net' can easily become a very time-consuming and tiring process. It is for this reason that face-to-face contact with a travel advisor remains popular with members of the travelling public.

Five destinations around the world

Assessment guidance

Assessment Objectives 2, 3 and 4 for this unit require you to have made a study of *two* contrasting destinations. You have to examine the key features of each destination and explain how and why they appeal to different visitor types. You will use a range of sources to obtain information about each and then analyse your findings, leading to a reasoned explanation about future trends.

One way in which it is possible to examine the reasons behind the growth of certain locations as important travel and tourism destinations is to look at case studies. The rapid growth and expansion of Dubai as a tourist destination is a very good illustration.

Destination: Dubai

The United Arab Emirates (UAE) comprises seven members: Abu Dhabi (the capital city), Dubai, Sharjah, Ajman, Umm Al Quwain, Ras Al Khaimah and Fujairah. Dubai, with an area of 3885 square kilometres, is the second largest emirate. Dubai is situated on the banks of the Dubai Creek, a natural inlet from the Arabian Gulf, which divides the city into the Deira district to its north, and Bur Dubai to its south. The city ranks as the UAE's most important port and commercial centre. Along the Arabian Gulf coast there are offshore islands, coral reefs and sabkha (salt marshes). Stretches of gravel plain and sandy desert characterise the inland region. To the east, a range of mountains lies close to the Gulf of Oman and forms a backbone through the Mussandam Peninsula. The western interior of the country, most of it in Abu Dhabi, consists mainly of desert interspersed with oases.

The emirate embraces a wide variety of scenery in a very small area. In a single day, the tourist can experience everything from rugged mountains and awe-inspiring sand dunes to sandy beaches and lush green parks, from dusty villages to luxurious residential districts, and from ancient houses with wind towers to ultra-modern shopping malls. Having expanded along both banks of the Creek, Dubai's central business district is divided into two parts – Deira on the northern side and Bur Dubai to the south – connected by a tunnel and two bridges. Each has its share of fine mosques and busy souks, of public buildings, shopping malls, hotels, office towers, banks, hospitals, schools, apartments and villas.

Outside this core, the city extends to the neighbouring emirate of Sharjah to the north, while extending south and west in a long ribbon of development alongside the Gulf, through the districts of Satwa, Jumeirah and Umm Suqeim. At first glance, the city presents a predominantly modern face, an ever-changing skyline of new developments, from striking glass and concrete towers to gracious modern buildings incorporating traditional Arabian architectural motifs and features.

Statistics

Some of the statistics surrounding Dubai's recent developments are particularly impressive and few locations in the world can match the degree of economic diversification that the emirate has achieved in a short space of time (see Figure 3.7).

Figure 3.7 Key events in the development of Dubai as a tourist and business destination

DATE	DEVELOPMENT MILESTONE	
1971	The foundation of the United Arab Emirates 	
1979	World's largest artificial port opens at Jebel Ali	
1985	The Jebel Ali Free Zone opens Award-winning airline Emirates is established 	
1989	The Dubai Desert Classic, a European PGA tournament, tees off for the first time 	
1990	Five million passengers pass through Dubai International Airport 	
1993	Tourists exceed one million	
1996	First running of the Dubai World Cup, the world's richest horse race, at Nad Al Sheba First annual Dubai Shopping Festival attracts millions of visitors 	

Continued

DATE	DEVELOPMENT MILESTONE
1998	Tourists exceed two million
1999	World's only 7-star hotel, the Burj Al Arab, opens and the landmark Emirates Towers come into operation
2000	Dubai Internet City established, attracting the world's top IT firms including IBM, Microsoft and HP Sheikh Rashid Terminal developed at Dubai International Airport completing the first phase of a US$ 450 million expansion Second phase due for completion in 2007 raising annual capacity to 60 million visitors
2001	Dubai Media City opens, becoming the regional home of global media giants such as CNN and Reuters Construction begins of The Palm, the world's largest artificial islands Tourists exceed three million
2002	Emirates announces plans to double its fleet of aircraft by 2007 Tourists exceed 4.5 million Dubai International Airport handles 16 million passengers
2003	UAE first Middle Eastern country to host meetings of the World Bank and the IMF, in Dubai Dubai International Financial Centre opens Dubai Healthcare City opens Burj Dubai, the world's tallest tower, is announced Dubailand, the region's ultimate tourism, leisure and entertainment destination, is announced

دبي لانـــد
Dubailand

In 1989, Dubai recorded only 630 000 visitor arrivals but numbers increased to over 8 million in 2003, with at least 458 000 coming from the UK. Dubai has managed to increase its number of visitors by over 1200 per cent in little more than a decade and tourism is now, at 12 per cent of the gross domestic product (GDP), one of the emirate's more important and fastest growing sectors of the economy.

Dubai's significance as a global destination stems from the fact that it can be viewed from two main perspectives. It is not just a simple holiday destination, it is an important commercial, trading and business centre as well. Therefore visitors to Dubai provide examples of the three categories into which tourists are usually divided. A recent visitor survey in Dubai identified the following figures:

* leisure visitors – 44 per cent

* business visitors – 45 per cent

* visiting friends and relatives (VFR) – 8 per cent

* not classified – 3 per cent.

Previously viewed in tourism terms as little more than a 'duty-free stopover', Dubai today has become a highly acclaimed destination offering an outstanding range of facilities and services for both leisure and business travellers. We next look at some of the reasons behind Dubai's phenomenal growth.

Features

Figure 3.8 shows Dubai's geographical location (55°E, 25°N) on the southern shore of the Arabian Gulf. It is strategically located at the crossroads of three continents – Europe, Asia and Africa – a natural meeting place. Dubai is now a major aviation hub. The government's 'open skies' policy has resulted in Dubai International Airport being served by some 105 airlines, with connections to more than 140 cities worldwide. It is also the operational hub for the Emirates airline and so attracts visitors wanting a stopover. The UK is particularly well served with nearly 70 scheduled non-stop flights a week from Heathrow, Gatwick, Manchester, Birmingham and Glasgow. This high degree of accessibility, so important for the development of tourism, is clearly one factor in explaining the particularly high increase in UK visitors to Dubai between 1989 (only 32 000) and 2003 (over 400 000).

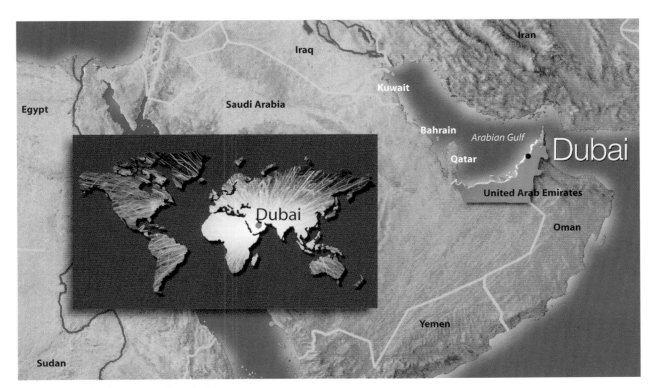

Figure 3.8 The location of Dubai

Dubai has a very accessible location. In terms of flying times, London is seven hours away, Frankfurt is six, Hong Kong eight and Nairobi four. These facts give Dubai a very wide catchment area. Business events in Dubai attract delegates and trade visitors from around the world. This catchment area covers the Gulf states, other Arab countries like Iran, the Asian subcontinent, East Africa, Central Asia and the CIS. This rapidly developing region boasts a population of around 1.5 billion people. A recent analysis of Dubai hotel guests identified the following breakdown:

* Europe – 27.3 per cent
* Asia – 22.4 per cent
* Gulf states – 20.2 per cent
* other Arab states – 10.4 per cent
* UAE – 6.8 per cent
* Africa – 6.3 per cent
* America – 4.6 per cent
* Australia and Pacific – 1.5 per cent

Dubai was also well placed to take advantage of the increasing global trend for leisure travel and to provide a different experience for an increasingly adventurous travelling public who constantly demand alternative destinations. The emirate contained a mix of natural and cultural attractions that formed the basis of a very marketable leisure tourism product. The existing natural attractions included:

* miles of clean uncrowded beaches along the shores of the Arabian Gulf

* a sub-tropical climate with average temperatures of 18°C in January, 33°C in July and annual precipitation of less than 150 mm, contributing to a year-long tourist season

* the availability of watersports all year round in the Gulf (and the Gulf of Oman is a diving centre of international significance)

* desert dunes for a variety of outdoor activities and leisure pursuits

* the Hatta Mountains for 'wadi-bashing' and other adventurous pursuits

* the Al Maha environmental conservation reserve, the base for the reintroduction of the Arabian Oryx.

Dubai is a migratory crossroads in both spring and autumn for many bird species. The Khor Dubai Wildlife Sanctuary is home to more than 1000 Greater Flamingos.

Dubai also had a strong cultural heritage to exploit for tourism purposes. Important elements of this cultural attractiveness to Western visitors included:

* the 'exotic' Middle Eastern atmosphere associated with the hustle and bustle of the souks and dhow wharves along Dubai Creek

* the distinctly Middle Eastern architecture of the wind towers, mosques and palaces

* the traditional welcoming and hospitable culture of the Arab world

* acceptance of a cosmopolitan lifestyle.

Although these natural and cultural assets have clearly contributed to Dubai's success as a destination, it is very important to emphasise that they have been greatly enhanced by ambitious investment in the tourism infrastructure on the part of both public and private sectors.

The Dubai government's Department of Tourism & Commerce Marketing (DTCM) is the main organisation for the promotion and development of tourism in the emirate. The department has taken over the licensing of hotels, hotel apartments, tour operators, tourist transport companies and travel agents. It has a supervisory role covering all tourist, archaeological and heritage sites, tourism conferences and exhibitions, the operation of tourism information services and the licensing and organisation of tour guides. The government provides ongoing development to the infrastructure, and the recent opening of the Port Rashid cruise line terminal is just one of a series of innovations aimed at widening the total tourism product base within Dubai. It is hoped that this terminal will do for cruising what the opening of Dubai Duty Free did for air traffic arrivals. The government has a direct stake in the tourism sector through the development and ownership of a number of the major hotels as well as spectacular theme parks such as 'Wild Wadi'. This investment is not just a matter of expenditure; it is clearly demonstrating that quality must be paramount.

Think it over ...

Identify the various ways in which destinations can demonstrate the quality of their various tourism facilities. For example, what quality standards are available in the UK?

The recent creation of the 7-star luxury Burj Al Arab Hotel is yet another illustration of this underpinning philosophy in the emirate's development. Government commitment to the tourism industry is further indicated by the fact that His Highness Sheikh Mohammed bin Rashid Al Maktoum, Crown Prince of Dubai and UAE Minister of Defence, is not only the DTCM Chairman but he has been the driving force behind many of the emirate's most spectacular development schemes. This level of government commitment to the tourism industry has helped to generate significant private sector investment. Hotel and apartment complexes have been extensively developed. There has been a rapid expansion in the number of local inbound tour operators offering a range of tourist experiences from 4-by-4 desert safaris to dhow cruises.

For example, the majesty and tranquillity of the desert can now be experienced in a choice of exciting half-day, full-day and overnight safaris. These action-packed trips cover varied terrain ranging from desert to mountain and frequently include remote camel and goat farms as well as isolated villages. Highlights of a Dubai desert safari will usually include the following:

* dune driving in four-wheel-drive vehicles (see Figure 3.9)

* wadi-bashing – exploring the wadis or dry beds of streams that flow after the winter rains from the Hajar mountains, with the option of a

Figure 3.9 Dune driving in Dubai

swim in one of the many rock pools (see Figure 3.10)

* sand-skiing, using special skis to negotiate the slopes of high dunes in the emirate's interior

* camel riding, a major tourist attraction.

Other attractions are desert feasts, which are popular with visitors as an evening activity. A traditional Arabian barbecue under the stars follows spectacular sunset views. These can be tailored to meet every taste from a romantic

Figure 3.10 Wadi-bashing in Dubai

peaceful experience to elaborate fun-packed evenings complete with music, belly-dancing and displays of falconry. Some operators offer the opportunity to experience the traditional desert way of life in a Bedouin village outside Dubai.

The result of these various developments has been the creation of a world-class tourism product for a world-class destination. We can now look in more detail at the nature of Dubai's built attractions in an attempt to identify the ingredients of a successful destination.

Built attractions

A recent survey of UK tour operators promoting Dubai identified sport as being a significant component of the destination's appeal. The findings of this survey indicated that:

❋ 65 per cent offered golfing holidays

❋ 10 per cent had packages based on water sports

❋ 28.8 per cent had packages associated with the Dubai Desert Classic (golf)

❋ 16.7 per cent had packages associated with the Dubai Rugby Sevens

❋ 12.5 per cent had packages in March for the Dubai World Cup (horse racing).

The DTCM now actively promotes Dubai as 'The Classic Golf Destination'. Dubai is home to the PGA Desert Classic and has several championship-standard grass courses that are open to visitors. Demand is so great that a central reservations office was created to manage bookings (www.dubaigolf.com). This is but one illustration of Dubai's well-deserved reputation for being the sporting capital of the Middle East. The calendar of events shown in Figure 3.11

EVENT AND TYPE	VENUE	DATE
Jet ski competition and races	Dubai Creek	Early August
Laser and sailing regatta	Dubai Creek	Early August
Traditional dhow sailing race (22 ft)	Dubai Creek	Early August
Emirates Grand Prix and Dubai Duty Free Grand Prix UIM Class One Offshore Power Boat Racing	Mina Seyahi	November
Dubai Rugby Sevens	Dubai Exiles Rugby Club	November/ early December
Eid camel races	Dubai Course	December
Dubai Marathon	To be announced	January
Dubai Tennis Open Men's & Women's	Dubai Tennis Stadium	February
Jebel Ali Hotel and Golf Resort Challenge Match	Jebel Ali Hotel & Golf Resort	February
Dubai Desert Classic Pro Am Tournament	Dubai Creek Golf & Yacht Club	March
Dubai Desert Classic	Emirates Golf Club	March
Dubai World Cup Races	Nad Al Sheba	March
Dubai–Muscat Sailing Race	Dubai Creek	March
UAE Marlboro Desert Challenge – Rally	Start at Hyatt Regency	November

Figure 3.11 Dubai's main sporting events

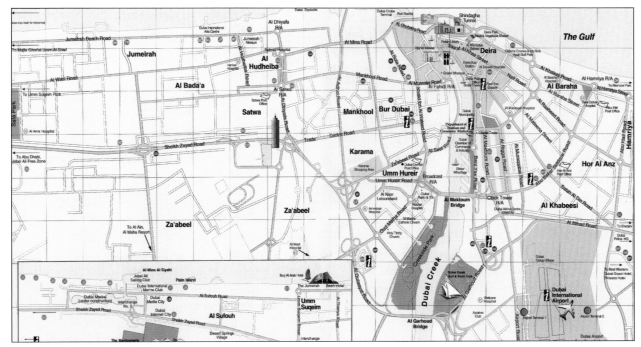

Figure 3.12 A detailed map of Dubai

attracts top personalities from all over the world and a varied programme of different sports helps Dubai to function as an all-year destination.

The variety of sports available is on a par with the best resorts in Europe and Asia, while there are others that are unique to the region. All the major hotels in Dubai boast very well-equipped sports centres. Visitors will find floodlit all-weather tennis, squash and badminton courts, swimming pools, snooker, table-tennis and fully equipped health and fitness centres at their disposal as part of their accommodation package.

Figure 3.12 shows features of central Dubai and it is possible to classify the built attractions in the following ways:

* shopping malls (e.g. Wafi City)
* traditional souks for gold and spices
* Dubai Museum and other historical buildings
* business tourism facilities (e.g. World Trade Centre)
* various luxury hotels in city-centre or beach locations.

Theory into practice

Identify and provide examples of the key leisure visitor attractions and facilities present in Dubai. Place these into suitable categories, such as:

* weather, climate and seasonal characteristics
* natural landscape and scenery
* natural vegetation and wildlife
* historical and cultural attractions
* modern built attractions
* opportunities for both indoor and outdoor activities
* types of accommodation
* events such as carnivals and festivals
* food, drink and entertainment.

This task will help you to meet the requirements of Assessment Objective 3.

A mixture of attractions and facilities

The concept of viewing a destination as an amalgam, with a combination of visitor attractions and facilities, is very appropriate in Dubai's case.

Figure 3.13 The lobby of Emirates Tower

The important aspect to be aware of is that the destination combines different types of attraction with a range of other facilities in a planned and organised manner. The mixing of the leisure and business tourism environments within Dubai illustrates this principle particularly well. Dubai is well established as the leading exhibition centre in the Middle East and it was recently voted the world's best conference venue. The city combines the facilities and services of one of the world's major international business centres with all the attractions of a top destination. This means that organisers and delegates alike can count on effective and successful events staged in a luxurious environment offering an outstanding range of recreational opportunities. The city now hosts more than 60 major exhibitions annually as well as numerous conferences, seminars, in-house corporate meetings and the like. This demand is serviced by a range of business facilities, including:

* Dubai Chamber of Commerce and Industry conference venue

* major hotel venues, such as Emirates Towers (see Figure 3.13)

* Dubai World Trade Centre, a 36 000 square metre exhibition hall

* Dubai Airport Exhibition Centre

* other special interest venues, such as Nad Al Sheba Club (see Figure 3.14).

The business sector is supported by major local companies that are well-equipped with a full destination management service covering hotel bookings, airport transfers, ground transport and a daily programme of tours and activities with multilingual guides. They also offer the required expertise for organising business-related travel, including original and exciting incentive programmes. The recent expansion of both leisure and business travel to Dubai has been matched by the growth in local inbound tour operations.

There is clear evidence to support the view that business and leisure tourism in Dubai have developed in parallel. Dubai's initial commercial development saw it rapidly become the leading port, trading centre and exhibition centre for the whole Gulf region. The city thus had the basic tourism infrastructure of hotels and travel-related services from the early 1990s, and these proved to be a very good starting point on which to build the leisure tourism product of the last decade. The DTCM markets Dubai as a destination for both leisure and business.

Figure 3.14 Nad Al Sheba racecourse

Assess the appeal of Dubai as a destination to each of the following UK visitor types: (a) a family with children, (b) a middle-aged ('empty nest') couple, and (c) a conference delegate. This exercise will help you prepare for the requirements of Assessment Objective 2.

The Al Maha desert resort

It is generally accepted amongst most nations that approximately 8–10 per cent of their land area should be put aside for the conservation of their indigenous habitats. The function of such a policy is to ensure that the nation's historic environment is permanently retained as part of its heritage and that the diversity of fauna and flora within the nation is kept intact as a representative sample of the original habitat. It is intended that such conserved areas can function without disturbance or undue intervention from human elements.

Al Maha is the first ecotourism resort in the UAE. Dubai has several environments worthy of conservation within such a framework. Apart from the dune environment at Al Maha there is also the mountain habitat around Hatta and the coast's intertidal strip. Each of these represents a separate, distinct and unique habitat type within Dubai. Each has its own fauna and flora, its own appeal to the visitor and its distinct historic, geological and archaeological merits. Al Maha has been developed with key ecotourism principles underpinning its commercial success.

As indicated on Figure 3.15, the environment must be free of intrusive disturbances which devalue the guests' experience of the surroundings. This includes the restriction of all artificial noise from the operation and ambient noise from the resort's surroundings. The restriction of any human structures which impinge on the natural landscape confines the development of the resort's own infrastructure to a minimum land area. The land making up the resort must provide a natural, original and unique environment for the guests, where they feel a part of the conservation process. This allows the guests to feel that their support is directly contributing to the conservation of the area they are experiencing.

One of the major contributors to the success of

Figure 3.15 Al Maha dunes

ecotourism resorts worldwide is the fact that the guests enjoy *exclusivity*. The rate charged is a function of the exclusivity enjoyed and paid for by the guest. The undisturbed settings, the personal attention and service standards not achievable in large public facilities are the basis of high-yield 'ecotourism' products. The guest must be assured of privacy, discretion and an unobtrusive environment. The experience must also be meaningful to the visitor, providing aspects which are educational, comfortable and divergent from normal lifestyle – thus assuring the guest that time spent in the resort is an enhancement to his or her quality of life.

The resort must meet the perceptions and expectations of the guests with regard to:

* accommodation
* facilities
* architecture and design
* surroundings
* ambience.

To meet these criteria, Al Maha has adapted traditional historic aspects, with operational requirements, to meet the guests' perception and expectation of the desert and Arabian heritage. A portion of land surrounding the core area of the resort has been demarcated for protection, and all activities capable of devaluing the environment are restricted. Isolation has been reinforced by means of the introduction of animal-proof fencing which will allow the establishment of indigenous species in viable breeding numbers within a free-roaming setting. The programme has been very successful and guests are now issued with their own fauna and flora checklist guide to record the various species that they have seen. The variety of headings used provides a suitable illustration of how far the desert resort has now developed in terms of conservation:

* grass (e.g. herb, dune, basket and cat's tail)

* shrub (e.g. broombush, dye plant and milkwort)

* herb (e.g. callous leaf, palm lettuce and Arabian cotton)

* plant (e.g. crimson wort, spiny disk and dwarf pea plant)

* tree (e.g. salam, ghaf and sidr)

* mammal (e.g. sand gazelle, Arabian hare and jird)

* reptile (e.g. monitor lizard, sand skink and sand snake)

* birds (common and may be resident or migrant – 300 species recorded).

Dubai's tourism future

The DTCM has set an aggressive target of attracting 15 million tourists by the year 2010. Projections for the immediate future are summarised in Figure 3.16.

YEAR	DUBAI HOTEL GUESTS (MILLIONS)	DUBAI HOTEL BEDS (THOUSANDS)
2003	5.24	39.8
2004	6.08	48.2
2005	7.06	55.9
2006	8.19	64.8
2007	9.49	75.2
2008	11.01	87.2
2009	12.78	101.2
2010	15.00	117.3

Figure 3.16 Targets for Dubai's tourism future

Such targets are not over-ambitious. Expatriates and foreign visitors can enjoy a relaxed and pleasant lifestyle in Dubai. There is virtually no crime, apartments and villas are modern and spacious, and the climate will appeal to those who enjoy warm weather. There are many clubs and societies in Dubai. Freedom of worship is allowed for all religions. Foreign newspapers, magazines, films and videos are all available. Alcohol may be consumed in hotels and in licensed club premises. Women can drive and move about unaccompanied.

In 2002, freehold ownership for UAE nationals as well as expatriates in certain select property developments was introduced in Dubai and 25-year mortgage loans became available. Initially, focus was centred on The Palm, Dubai Marina, and other developments of Emaar Properties. The potential for visiting friends and relatives will thus be substantially increased.

The Palm has already been described as the 'Eighth Wonder of the World' and is the sort of project that some say could only have taken place in Dubai. It consists of two massive, artificial islands: The Palm Jumeirah and The Palm Jebel Ali. Each island is being built in the shape of a palm tree, consisting of a crown of seventeen fronds, a trunk, and a surrounding 'crescent island', the back of which forms a protective breakwater. Each island will be approximately 6 kilometres long and 5.5 kilometres wide. Together they will add nearly 120 kilometres of much-sought-after coastline to Dubai. Approximately 3000 homes and at least 40 luxury hotels will be built on each island, capable of berthing a total of 400 yachts. It is expected that the first residents will move into The Palm Jumeirah before the end of 2004. The Palm is just one of several Nakheel residential projects; others include The World, Jumeirah Islands, Jumeirah Lake Towers and The Gardens.

Dubai will continue to improve the destination's infrastructure, and the following are just some of the developments that are already planned and in actual construction or development to support visitor growth targets:

* Hydropolis – the world's first underwater hotel

* Dubai airport expansion to handle 70 million passengers by 2016

* Dubai Festival City – a 4 km site along the Creek

* Dubai Land – the region's biggest tourism project aiming for 200 000 visitors a day – to include five themed leisure areas and the Mall of Arabia, the world's biggest mall

* Dubai Railway project for 2008

* Burj Dubai – the world's tallest tower.

We next look at some other types of destination to see how and why they appeal to different types of visitor.

Destination: Barcelona

Almost 4.5 million people live in the Barcelona metropolitan area. The city enjoys a prime location, bathed by the sea and having excellent transport links with the rest of Europe. The Mediterranean and Europe are the defining characteristics of Catalonia.

Barcelona is a modern, cosmopolitan city, but has inherited many centuries of history. Its geographic location and the open character of its inhabitants are the reasons why the city is being culturally enriched all the time. It has a valuable architectural and monumental heritage – five of its buildings have been designated World Heritage Sites. The entire city guarantees that visitors will enjoy taking a stroll around its streets which generate a sophisticated charm.

Barcelona enjoys a Mediterranean climate, with mild winters and warm summers. It is a coastal city and has over four kilometres of urban beaches and large areas of nearby forest. Although it is a large city, it is easy to get around using public transport and on foot. Furthermore, you can reach any point in the city by metro, bus and taxi. Barcelona is the capital of Catalonia. Its inhabitants are open and welcoming. The people of Barcelona speak Catalan, their own language, and Spanish. Many of them also understand a little English and French.

Barcelona has importance as a visitor destination. In 1990 the total number of visitors just exceeded 7.2 million, and that figure had risen to nearly 8.7 million in 2002 – a 20 per cent increase. Furthermore, the city regularly attracts large numbers of visitors from the UK and Ireland (see Figure 3.17).

YEAR	VISITORS FROM UK AND IRELAND
1990	4.1%
1995	7.2%
2001	15.6%
2002	14.4%
2003	11.8%

Figure 3.17 Visitors to Barcelona from the UK and Ireland

There are several reasons for this impressive recent growth and significant appeal to the UK market. A key factor is that 80 per cent of visitor arrivals come by plane and this has resulted in Barcelona becoming the world's 36th busiest airport, handling over 22 million passengers in 2003. Barcelona is now served with many low-cost flights from the UK, and airports providing services to the city include:

* Aberdeen
* Birmingham
* Bristol
* East Midlands
* Edinburgh
* Gatwick
* Glasgow
* Prestwick
* Leeds/Bradford
* Liverpool
* Luton
* Newcastle
* Stansted.

This means that Barcelona is a very accessible destination for UK visitors.

We have already seen that the city generates media attention and that it contains a range of affordable options. However, what other attractions does the city contain and why does it appear to be increasingly popular with visitors? The results of various surveys by the local tourist board indicate a high degree of visitor approval for the following aspects of Barcelona's total tourism product:

* architecture and culture
* leisure and entertainment
* shopping, restaurants and hotels
* character of the local people
* public transport
* value for money of restaurants

* value for money of shopping
* value for money of hotels
* access to Barcelona
* signs and information
* safety in the city

* general cleanliness
* low atmospheric pollution and low noise.

Figure 3.18 shows that there are a range of visitor attractions in the city and that six locations attract over a million visitors.

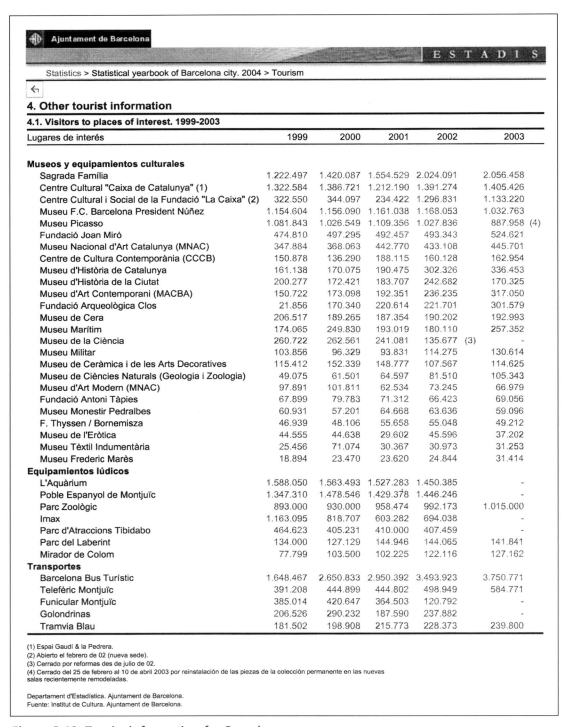

Ajuntament de Barcelona

ESTADIS

Statistics > Statistical yearbook of Barcelona city. 2004 > Tourism

4. Other tourist information

4.1. Visitors to places of interest. 1999-2003

Lugares de interés	1999	2000	2001	2002	2003
Museos y equipamientos culturales					
Sagrada Família	1.222.497	1.420.087	1.554.529	2.024.091	2.056.458
Centre Cultural "Caixa de Catalunya" (1)	1.322.584	1.386.721	1.212.190	1.391.274	1.405.426
Centre Cultural i Social de la Fundació "La Caixa" (2)	322.550	344.097	234.422	1.296.831	1.133.220
Museu F.C. Barcelona President Núñez	1.154.604	1.156.090	1.161.038	1.168.053	1.032.763
Museu Picasso	1.081.843	1.026.549	1.109.356	1.027.836	887.958 (4)
Fundació Joan Miró	474.810	497.295	492.457	493.343	524.621
Museu Nacional d'Art Catalunya (MNAC)	347.884	368.063	442.770	433.108	445.701
Centre de Cultura Contemporània (CCCB)	150.878	136.290	188.115	160.128	162.954
Museu d'Història de Catalunya	161.138	170.075	190.475	302.326	336.453
Museu d'Història de la Ciutat	200.277	172.421	183.707	242.682	170.325
Museu d'Art Contemporani (MACBA)	150.722	173.098	192.351	236.235	317.050
Fundació Arqueològica Clos	21.856	170.340	220.614	221.701	301.579
Museu de Cera	206.517	189.265	187.354	190.202	192.993
Museu Marítim	174.065	249.830	193.019	180.110	257.352
Museu de la Ciència	260.722	262.561	241.081	135.677 (3)	-
Museu Militar	103.856	96.329	93.831	114.275	130.614
Museu de Ceràmica i de les Arts Decoratives	115.412	152.339	148.777	107.567	114.625
Museu de Ciències Naturals (Geologia i Zoologia)	49.075	61.501	64.597	81.510	105.343
Museu d'Art Modern (MNAC)	97.891	101.811	62.534	73.245	66.979
Fundació Antoni Tàpies	67.899	79.783	71.312	66.423	69.056
Museu Monestir Pedralbes	60.931	57.201	64.668	63.636	59.096
F. Thyssen / Bornemisza	46.939	48.106	55.658	55.048	49.212
Museu de l'Eròtica	44.555	44.638	29.602	45.596	37.202
Museu Tèxtil Indumentària	25.456	71.074	30.367	30.973	31.253
Museu Frederic Marès	18.894	23.470	23.620	24.844	31.414
Equipamientos lúdicos					
L'Aquàrium	1.588.050	1.563.493	1.527.283	1.450.385	-
Poble Espanyol de Montjuïc	1.347.310	1.478.546	1.429.378	1.446.246	-
Parc Zoològic	893.000	930.000	958.474	992.173	1.015.000
Imax	1.163.095	818.707	603.282	694.038	-
Parc d'Atraccions Tibidabo	464.623	405.231	410.000	407.459	-
Parc del Laberint	134.000	127.129	144.946	144.065	141.841
Mirador de Colom	77.799	103.500	102.225	122.116	127.162
Transportes					
Barcelona Bus Turístic	1.648.467	2.650.833	2.950.392	3.493.923	3.750.771
Telefèric Montjuïc	391.208	444.899	444.802	498.949	584.771
Funicular Montjuïc	385.014	420.647	364.503	120.792	-
Golondrinas	206.526	290.232	187.590	237.882	-
Tramvia Blau	181.502	198.908	215.773	228.373	239.800

(1) Espai Gaudí & la Pedrera.
(2) Abierto el febrero de 02 (nueva sede).
(3) Cerrado por reformas des de julio de 02.
(4) Cerrado del 25 de febrero al 10 de abril 2003 por reinstalación de las piezas de la colección permanente en las nuevas salas recientemente remodeladas.

Departament d'Estadística. Ajuntament de Barcelona.
Fuente: Institut de Cultura. Ajuntament de Barcelona.

Figure 3.18 Tourist information for Barcelona

Barcelona is also popular because it is only an hour away from the purpose-built resort of Universal Mediterranea (see Figure 3.19). This giant theme park, which opened in 1994, attracts thousands of holidaymakers every year who journey through its five worlds (Mediterránia, Far West, Mexico, Polynesia and China) on its many rides and attractions.

Enjoying an enviable coastal location, between Salou and Vila-seca on Spain's Costa Dorada, this 117-hectare site boasts entertainment aimed at all age groups. There are nightly shows, including Fiestaventura in the Mediterranean world, as well as many other attractions, including the Sea Odyssey underwater adventure, the Stampida rollercoaster ride, and the Grand Canyon Rapids and Tutuki Splash water rides. Templo del Fuego, which opened in 2001, has the greatest number of fire and water effects ever used in any attraction, while the big attraction for the 2002 season was the new Costa Caribe Caribbean-themed water park. Visitors who wish to spend a few days in the park can stay in one of the many hotels on site, all of which share a beach area, Playa Larga, where guests can relax and soak up the Mediterranean sun. The park is owned by the Universal Studios Recreation Group, responsible for other theme parks around the world, including Universal Orlando and Universal Studios Hollywood.

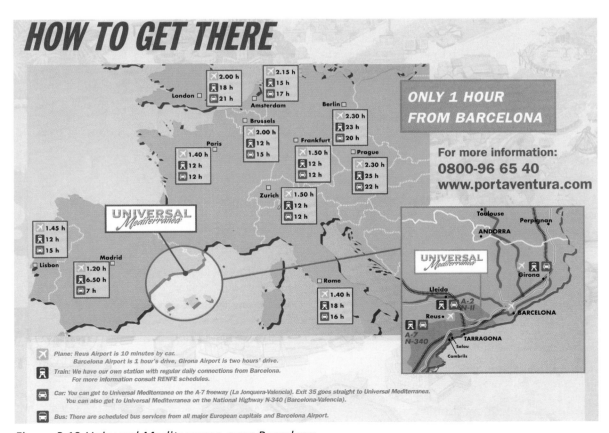

Figure 3.19 Universal Mediterranea near Barcelona

Destination: Southport

Southport has been recognised as a leading British seaside resort for many years. It is also famous for the internationally acclaimed Lord Street, a mile-long boulevard renowned for the quality of its shopping – along one side are shops with Victorian glass-topped canopies and on the opposite side are gardens, fountains and classical buildings.

There are miles of golden sands on the beach for holidaymakers to enjoy as well as excellent resort facilities such as a pier, baths, bowling greens, amusement park, marine lake, civic theatres, arts centre and art gallery.

The town was founded in 1792 when William Sutton opened a hotel and the name 'South-port' first appeared in proper use during the year 1798. Following a pattern common to all UK seaside resorts, the first major development was in 1848 when a rail service became available from Liverpool to the town (visitors travelled previously by canal and road). Then, from 1853, people could go by train to the resort from Manchester (via Wigan), and the seaside town attracted thousands of workers from the Lancashire mill towns.

The Victorian era left the town with a glorious legacy:

* its spaciousness
* the parks, gardens and wide tree-lined streets
* Lord Street, one of Britain's finest boulevards.

The town grew and developed as a traditional UK seaside resort. Now it shows many of the features that characterise such destinations. However, the following statistics show that tourism is still of great local significance:

* 5.1 million visitors per annum
* 550 000 staying visitors generating £65 million
* 4.6 million day visitors generating £119.4 million
* 86 hotels (about 2300 bedrooms)
* 1.6 million bed–nights
* employment for over 6700 permanent staff and about 5000 seasonal jobs.

The destination's tourism profile can be summarised as follows:

* main visitor origin regions – Merseyside, Cheshire, Manchester, Lancashire, West Yorkshire, Scotland, North Yorkshire and Staffordshire
* key markets – short breaks, conferences, festival and events, day-trip and group travel, golf, birdwatching, and walking/cycling.

Southport's reputation as England's golfing capital is well deserved. The resort is home to a number of premier links and parkland courses including Royal Birkdale, Formby, Hesketh, Hillside, Southport and Ainsdale, and Formby Hall Golf Club. Many have hosted top tournaments such as the Ryder Cup and the Curtis Cup. Royal Birkdale will host the Open Championships for the ninth time in 2008. With Royal Liverpool and Royal Lytham St Annes situated close by, the region is increasingly being recognised as a golfer's paradise.

Visitors are also attracted to a variety of events held in the Southport area each year. The following examples of visitor numbers illustrate different aspects of the destination's appeal:

* British Lawnmower Museum – 5000
* Southport British Musical Firework Championship – 45 000
* Southport Air Show – 230 000
* Southport Christmas Festival – 25 000
* Festival of Street Entertainment – 12 000
* Southport Flower Show – 120 000
* Southport Zoo – 58 000
* Southport Pleasureland – 2.6 million
* Southport Jazz Festival – 30 000
* Southport Pier – 250 000
* Summer Classics – 4500.

Theory into practice

Research a selection of these events and assess their relative appeal to different visitor groups.

Southport Pier, located on the seafront (see Figure 3.20), reopened in 2002 following a £7 million restoration programme. The pier, second longest in the UK, has proved to be popular with visitors, with well in excess of half a million people having taken a stroll along this unique attraction since it was redeveloped. The views at pier-end are truly panoramic. The beautifully designed Pier Pavilion is very popular with visitors. It houses a number of traditional style amusements – a throwback to Southport's golden era – plus an exhibition tracking the history of the pier itself. This is a specialised attraction for 'pier buffs', who are a significant special-interest group. The pier also regularly hosts a number of visitor events – a recent Pier Extravaganza event proved to be a huge success.

Recent investment in the development of Southport's Theatre and Floral Hall Complex has boosted the number and quality of conferences to the town and highlighted the need for further quality accommodation to serve the conference market. The complex is Merseyside's largest and most flexible multi-purpose venue, providing clients with full technical support, in-house catering and professional coordination. The complex is conveniently located on Southport's Promenade just a short walk from the town's wide range of accommodation, dining and leisure facilities.

The traditional tiered theatre auditorium has an impressive 1631 capacity which can be conveniently reduced for smaller numbers of 250. There are large roller shutter doors to the stage for ease of unloading and access. The 141 square metre stage with technical facilities can accommodate up to three vehicles, making it ideal for car and product launches. The spacious foyer area with its own amenities links the theatre to the magnificent Floral Hall ballroom. This can host an array of events such as conferences, seminars and dinners for 150 to 1200 guests, as well as exhibitions and trade shows with 850 square metres of floor space and a 100 square metre integral stage. The Floral Hall has the flexibility to be transformed to suit individual customer needs

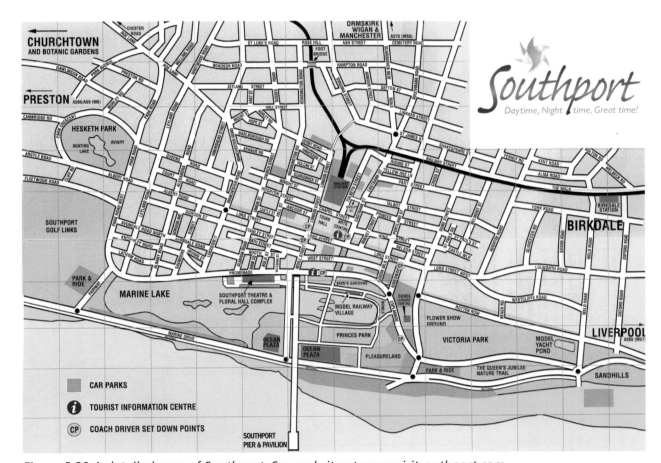

Figure 3.20 A detailed map of Southport. See website at www.visitsouthport.com

with in-house catering, technical and bar facilities. Five smaller suites complement the larger facilities and are ideal for more intimate events – seminars, weddings, private functions or receptions for up to 250 guests. There is on-site parking for up to 200 vehicles and level access to all suites for patrons with disabilities.

Environmentally, there have been significant strides over recent years, particularly the new £9 million sea wall and the general landscaping and enhancing of the facilities on the promenade and seafront, including some innovative sculptures. The Victorian architecture of the town has been preserved and enhanced. Outstanding and well-maintained gardens and open spaces have advanced the town's reputation as an attractive floral resort. The internationally renowned Southport Flower Show is thriving and moves from one successful event to another.

Southport is a major retail and shopping destination. Park-and-ride schemes have been introduced to improve visitor movements around the resort. Many new restaurants, bars and cafés have opened up and many have been refurbished. The resort has a lively atmosphere by day and by night. The nightlife is excellent, with a wide choice of clubs and musical tastes. Pleasureland, the theme park, is Southport's biggest attraction, with over 2.6 million visitors each year. After many years a £11 million scheme including a new rollercoaster, the 'Traumatizer', and a new family entertainment centre, 'Casablanca', including a bowling alley, amusement arcade, bar and restaurant has been developed, along with landscaping improvements in the theme park. Events continue to play a major role in attracting visitors to the area.

Southport has a varied tourism product and it is no surprise that its Tourist Information Service receives over 44 000 phone calls a year and 246 000 walk-in visitors. The resort's main website, www.visitsouthport.com, receives half a million hits each year.

Theory into practice

Use Figure 3.20 and your own research to explain why Southport attracts both leisure and business visitors.

Destination: Keswick and the Northern Lakes

Lake District National Park is the largest (230 000 hectares), most spectacular and most visited of Britain's national parks. It regularly has around 20 million visitors a year. The park was established by Parliament in 1951 with two principal aims:

* to conserve and enhance the natural beauty, wildlife and cultural heritage of the national park
* to promote opportunities for the understanding and enjoyment of the special qualities of the national park by the public.

The park as a whole contains many features that may attract different types of visitor. It has several unique selling points, such as:

* complex geology
* diverse landscape of the Lakeland fells
* the largest concentration of common land in Britain
* traditional livestock breeds like Herdwick sheep
* varied habitats, especially freshwater ones
* extensive semi-natural woodland
* the highest concentration of outdoor activity centres in the UK
* one of the most diverse range of tourist facilities, attractions and accommodation in the country
* internationally important archaeological sites
* distinctive settlement character
* its own dialects and distinctive sports such as hound trailing, fell running, and Cumberland and Westmorland wrestling.

Visitors flock to the area to take advantage of the peaceful scenery, the wildlife, the many good walks and the opportunities to take part in adventure tourism activities.

Theory into practice

Study Figures 3.21 and 3.22. List the various outdoor activities that different visitor types could undertake in both locations. This exercise can help you generate evidence for Assessment Objective 4.

Figure 3.21 A view of the tranquillity of the Lake District

Figure 3.22 A visitor activity location in the Lake District

Keswick retains the attractive appearance of a traditional small market town, the weekly stalls still set around the Moot market hall which dominates the town centre. The Tourist Information Centre is conveniently placed in this fine old listed building.

Despite its small size, Keswick's popularity as a visitor destination means that it contains a variety of indoor and outdoor attractions far wider than you might expect. Three very individual museums, a highly successful theatre, the cinema and art and craft exhibitions are balanced, for the very active, by the leisure pool, indoor climbing centre and the sports hall.

Figure 3.23 illustrates the appeal of the Keswick area to a variety of tourists. The map shows a range of both natural and built attractions. Some are quite specialised. Located in the Borrowdale valley near Grange, at the southern end of Derwentwater (www.lakelandscape.co.uk/derwentwater.htm), the Bowder Stone is one of Lakeland's most famous landmarks. The huge boulder weighs around 2000 tonnes, is 9 metres (30 feet) high and lies balanced precariously on its corner. It has become a local attraction for rock climbers and is visited on a regular basis throughout the year. A sturdy wooden ladder allows visitors to climb on top of the stone and it acts as a minor viewpoint. Educational groups will visit the site to conduct field investigations into footpath erosion and undertake assessment of the impacts of tourism within a national park.

Theory into practice

Study Figure 3.23 on the next page and identify the variety of both natural and artificial attractions to be found in the Keswick area. Research their appeal to different visitor groups. This exercise will help you generate evidence for Assessment Objectives 2 and 3.

The national park contains many facilities that attract student groups. Near the village of Threlkeld is the Blencathra Field Centre (see Figure 3.24), one of the properties run by the Field Studies Council (FSC). The FSC's mission statement is 'Environmental Understanding for All', and we can now look at some of the ways in which this has been put into practice.

The Blencathra Field Centre is owned by Lake District National Park but is managed by the Field Studies Council which is an educational charity. The centre was opened in 1994 and delivers part of the National Park Education Service. The centre provides residential courses for groups aged between 8 and 80 as well as

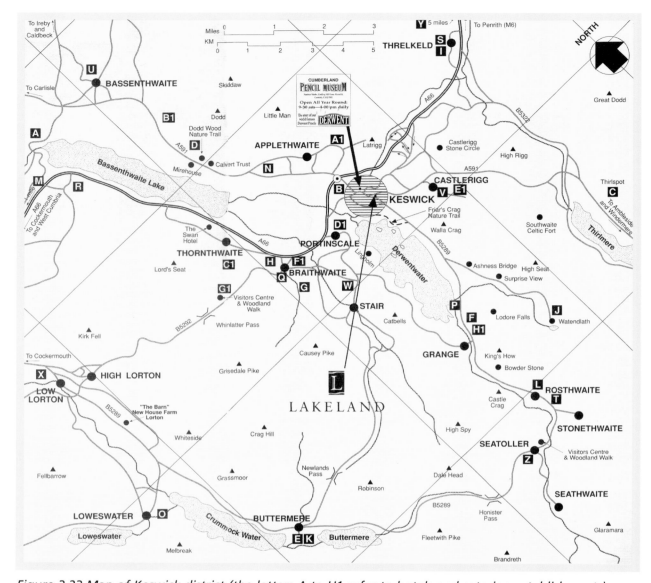

Figure 3.23 Map of Keswick district (the letters A to H1 refer to hotels and catering establishments)

providing a residential base for independent groups who wish to take advantage of this quiet location four miles from Keswick. The centre also has three self-catering cottages which are of three Cumbria Tourist Board Keys standard. It delivers courses for over 3000 people each year, with typical stays anything between two and seven nights. Depending on the season, there can be up to 100 visitors on site each night. It is not open to the casual bed-and-breakfast visitor market.

Traditionally, the main role of FSC centres was to provide courses for educational groups, especially for schools on a field trip. Blencathra, which is also an eco-centre, now finds itself frequently hosting courses for diverse outside groups. For these customers the main requirements are the accommodation, catering, specialist tutoring, and a high standard of customer care available at the centre. The centre has clearly adapted to customer needs and wants and it is now appealing to a much wider client

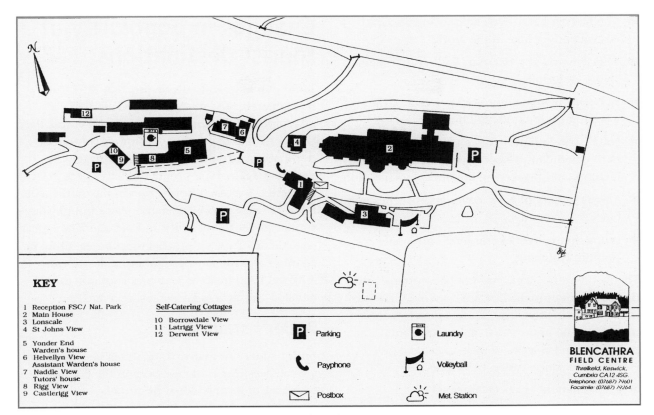

Figure 3.24 The Blencathra Centre in the national park

KEY

1 Reception FSC/ Nat. Park
2 Main House
3 Lonscale
4 St Johns View
5 Yonder End
   Warden's house
6 Helvellyn View
   Assistant Warden's house
7 Naddle View
   Tutors' house
8 Rigg View
9 Castlerigg View

Self-Catering Cottages

10 Borrowdale View
11 Latrigg View
12 Derwent View

P Parking

📞 Payphone

✉ Postbox

💿 Laundry

🚩 Volleyball

⛅ Met. Station

**BLENCATHRA
FIELD CENTRE**
Threlkeld, Keswick,
Cumbria CA12 4SG.
Telephone: (07687) 79601
Facsimile: (07687) 79264

base than it did in the past. Bookings are conducted on a one-to-one basis and individual requirements are given every attention. This has resulted in a customer base that is far more mixed than just school groups doing a coursework project visit. Even at this small scale, the significance of both leisure and business visitor requirements is very evident.

Theory into practice

Research the types of courses available at an FSC centre. Suggest reasons why Blencathra near Keswick would be a good location to deliver such products and services.

We shall end our destination case studies with an example from the tropics and briefly examine the visitor appeal of an unspoilt Caribbean island. Such a location has many attractions for the adventurous twenty-first century tourist.

Destination: Dominica

The Caribbean island of Dominica, shown earlier in Figure 3.5 on page 97, was discovered by Columbus in 1493. The island is situated towards the northern end of the Lesser Antilles, lying between the two French islands of Guadeloupe to the north and Martinique to the south. The island is 47 km long and 26 km wide. It is volcanic in origin and ruggedly beautiful, with towering green mountains covered with dense tropical forests, deep valleys and countless streams providing magnificent scenic views. Dominica's physical features are unique selling points that help to set it apart from other Caribbean island destinations.

Dominica now markets itself as 'The nature island of the Caribbean' and as 'The Caribbean's ultimate Eco-destination'. Visitors are attracted to the island to experience a range of natural wonders, including:

* Morne Trois Pitons National Park – UNESCO Natural World Heritage Site

* Valley of Desolation

* The Boiling Lake – volcanic springs, second largest boiling lake in the world
* Middleham Falls, Sari Sari Falls and Trafalgar Triple Waterfalls
* rich natural vegetation – 60 per cent of the island, the habitat for 172 bird species
* 3500 Carib Indians – descendants of the first native population – occupying their own territory and preserving the pre-colonial culture
* a wide variety of bays, coves and beaches with black volcanic sand
* scuba diving, reef exploration and whale and dolphin watching.

The fact that the island has not been extensively developed does make Dominica an excellent eco-tourism destination. The island's government recognises the importance of environmental protection and a series of measures have given emphasis to conservation principles:

* 1975 – national park established
* 1987 – Cabrits Historical Park established
* spear fishing prohibited
* removal of living sea organisms and artefacts from wrecks not allowed
* ecological resorts established (e.g. Papillote Wilderness Retreat).

The island is now becoming an established Caribbean destination because of the quality of its managed physical environment. The strategy has clearly worked and annual visitor arrivals have increased from 47 000 to more than 63 000 over recent years. It has become a niche destination and attracts a specialised market segment.

However, Dominica has certain seasonal disadvantages because of its tropical location. Each of the Earth's major climatic zones may contain natural hazards, depending on the time of year, which visitors will have to make allowance for. In this case it is the risk of late summer hurricanes that bring an annual threat to the tourism economies of the Caribbean and Florida. Dominica was hit by particularly violent storms in 1979, 1980 and 1999. The risk of such tropical storms explains why July, August and September are 'low season' in such destinations.

Changes in popularity of tourist destinations

What will happen to destinations in the future? It is generally accepted that the Canadian geographer R. W. Butler, writing in 1980, was the first person to liken the development of tourist destinations to a product passing through the various stages of the product life-cycle. He suggested that each destination in the world will follow a cycle of evolution and pass through stages similar to youth, maturity and old age. The logical conclusion of such a process must be the ultimate death of a particular destination, unless it can reinvent itself in some way and continue to develop – a process known as 'rejuvenation'.

Butler's stages

Butler's ideas fit many destinations very well and we can see clear evidence, both in the UK and overseas, of locations that fit into one of the six stages of development that he proposed.

1: Exploration stage
A small number of tourists make their own travel arrangements. Only a few visitors come to the country, maybe backpackers or some other type of independent traveller. There are no charter flights or tourist services and the cost to the traveller, both in time and/or money, can be high. No investment in tourist infrastructure has been made at this stage. However, the economic, social, cultural and environmental impacts caused by tourism will be virtually nil.

2: Involvement
Some local residents begin to provide facilities exclusively for the use of visitors. Visitor numbers increase and local businesses start providing services. The local population has accepted the arrival of visitors and the destination starts to grow, with locals actually becoming involved with promotional activities.

3: Development
Local suppliers and providers of tourism products and services become increasingly involved in the development process. The area becomes established as a tourist destination with a defined market. As

the visitors keep coming, more businesses enter the market which is now becoming profitable. Package holidays begin and the destination sees marked expansion with the arrival of foreign operators and investors. As the country becomes more popular and the infrastructure begins to take shape, more tour operators become interested and organise package tours to the country. A range of brochures become available at travel agents, advertisements appear in the media. Competition between businesses is growing, so prices start to fall and so do profit margins. With increased competition resulting in falling prices, different type of customers will now be able to visit the destination. This reflects a well-defined tourist destination shaped by heavy marketing in tourist-generating regions.

4: Consolidation

Tourism now starts to dominate the economic base of the area and starts to have an adverse effect on the traditional economy and lifestyle. Local agricultural land is given over to resort development but there is not a proportional increase in local wealth, per capita income or job creation. The rate of increase in numbers of visitors will have started to decline, although total numbers will still increase.

5: Stagnation

Peak numbers of visitors will have been reached. There is a growing awareness of negative environmental, social, cultural and economic tourism impacts. Sales go down as the country goes out of fashion and there is evidence that the original cultural and natural attractiveness of the destination has been lost. Profits are low, businesses may leave the market or diversify to other types of product. Furthermore, because there may be fewer businesses in the local tourism marketplace, prices can be increased, thus accelerating the decline.

6: Decline versus rejuvenation

Butler's model of destination development and evolution ends with a series of options that all resorts will have to face at some time. Figure 3.25 shows the following:

* Immediate decline (a) – Visitor numbers fall quite rapidly and the tourism base severely contracts, resulting in a local economic depression.

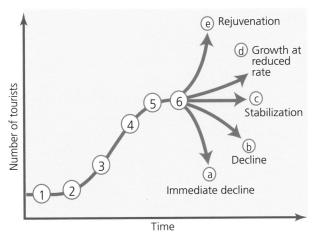

Figure 3.25 An illustration of Butler's six stages and the possible future trend

* Decline (b) – The destination will face a declining market and will be unable to compete with newer destinations or destinations which better meet the needs of the modern tourist.

* Stabilization (c) – The destination is able to maintain its market share but there is little, if any, continued growth and development.

* Growth at reduced rate (d) – The effects of competition mean that even with new development plans, the destination is never able to return to the levels of previous growth and development.

* Rejuvenation (e) – If major changes are made, such as improving the environment and tourism infrastructure, better marketing or the addition of more attractions for example, then the destination may experience a period of rejuvenation. This is a period of further growth and development brought about by innovation and renewed diversification. In effect, the destination reinvents itself and extends its appeal to different market segments.

Assessment activity

Identify locations in the world that would fit into each of these stages of destination evolution, giving reasons for your choices.

To help you with this task, consider the five destination studies that we have looked at and decide where they should be placed within the model. Some destinations, because of their long history, will have passed through several stages.

Other factors

In terms of travel from the UK, statistics show that visits between 2000 and 2002 to the following countries all went into decline: Israel, Iceland, Canada, the USA, Germany, France and India. Does this mean that each of these countries were at stage 6 of the Butler destination evolution model?

The answer is that the real world is a lot more complicated than this model might suggest. There are many factors that can influence the popularity of tourist destinations and, when examining the appeal of any one particular location, you have to be aware of wider issues and the conditions operating elsewhere.

Assessment guidance

Assessment Objective 4 requires you to make reasoned predictions about the future appeal of both your chosen destinations.

We shall now examine how certain factors can work together to influence the popularity of certain destinations.

Visits to the USA by UK tourists would have been badly affected during the years 2000 to 2002 by a number of circumstances. The following list of figures relating to New York City international visitors from 1998 clearly shows the effect of the terrorist attacks on 11 September 2001:

* 1998 – 6.0 million
* 1999 – 6.6 million
* 2000 – 6.8 million
* **2001** – 5.7 million
* 2002 – 5.1 million
* 2003 – 4.8 million
* 2004 – 5.1 million.

From the UK's point of view, 870 000 tourists visited New York City, still down on the million plus that went in year 2000. Fear of terrorist attacks may be only one factor that explains this drop. The weakness of the pound sterling against the US dollar was also a significant factor in that it made the USA a comparatively expensive destination to visit. However, 2004 saw a reversal with the pound strengthening against the dollar,

thus making the USA much more affordable for the UK outbound tourist. The major transatlantic carriers are always quick to maintain their flight volumes, and so cheap airfares to the USA (to New York in particular) are frequently available.

Therefore, in just a two-year period, UK residents travelling to New York will have been influenced by both *economic* and *political* influences. It was pointed out at the start of the chapter that individuals can form incorrect perceptions about particular destinations. Let us now try to identify current world destinations where particular factors and circumstances are influencing the number of visitors that are received.

Bulgaria is a very cost-effective destination for the UK visitor. It remains outside of the European Union and prices are low. The Black Sea coastal resorts around Varna attracted over 100 000 Britons in 2004, and with companies offering value packages for 2005 the trend looks set to continue. Some current packages are shown in Figure 3.26.

TOUR OPERATOR	PACKAGE HOLIDAY DETAILS
Balkan Holidays	Fourteen nights bed & breakfast at the Hotel Varshava in Golden Sands Prices start at £199 including flights
Airtours	Seven nights all-inclusive at the Grand Hotel in Sunny Beach Prices start at £339 including flights
Cosmos	Seven nights bed & breakfast at the Hotel Strandja in Sunny Beach Prices start at £319 including flights

Figure 3.26 Sample holiday packages to Bulgaria in 2004

The mass-market operators are now promoting the destination and the main resorts have clear appeal to both families and budget-conscious travellers. Charter flights into Bourgas and Varna airports mean that Bulgaria has the potential to rival Spain in terms of being a UK visitor destination.

Spain's Costa Brava was once at the forefront of mass tourism and during the 1970s was the leading destination for UK holidaymakers. However, in 2004, tour operators Cosmos and First Choice announced they were axing the destination from their 2005 holiday programmes. The resort has become a victim of its past success and is suffering from a combination of over-commercialisation, negative media coverage, rising costs and a dated image. In terms of the model of destination evolution, the Costa Brava is clearly at stage 6. Decline seems likely, but the Spanish Tourist Board hopes that the destination can be rejuvenated. The tourist board is now planning to market the Costa Brava as more than just a beach resort. It will now include the local region's countryside and culture in its marketing literature and will refer to the destination as Costa Brava Pirineu de Girona. It remains to be seen whether or not this rebranding will influence the UK travelling public.

The present UK leisure travel market is in a state of change. The summer of 2004 saw an 8 per cent drop in mass market sales. Many analysts put this down to rising UK interest rates rather than fears over the Iraq conflict or the threat of SARS infection. However, industry forecasts suggest that mass-market sales will show a further decline in 2005. This suggests that UK leisure travel consumer behaviour is altering, a development that will have a significant effect on destinations. Current UK leisure travel market research indicates the following:

* Forty-five per cent have taken at least four holidays in the past two years.

* Thirty-one per cent have bought a holiday through a travel agent.

* Thirty-two per cent have booked on-line.

* Thirty-eight per cent are likely to use a travel agent in the future.

* Thirty-six per cent are likely to use the Internet in the future.

This research suggests that the UK travelling public will become more independent and further shy away from the traditional mass-market product. Short breaks will continue to grow in popularity, which will favour established destinations such as Barcelona.

There are bound to be winners and losers amongst the various long- and short-haul destinations that are currently visited by UK tourists. Some destinations will continue to benefit from the positive impacts of tourism development, whereas others will suffer negative effects. Some examples of the key issues involved in tourist/host encounters within destinations are shown in Figure 3.27.

Positive aspects, such as
Increased employment opportunities
Preservation of traditional culture, folklore, festivals
Better recreational facilities
Better infrastructure
Negative aspects, such as
Decline in traditional employment
Population migration
Seasonal underemployment
Exposure to alternative lifestyle(s)
Increased crime
Decline in importance of traditional way of life.

Figure 3.27 Key issues in encounters within destinations

Environmental impacts of tourism within destinations can exert positive effects such as:

* conservation of heritage sites

* regeneration and redevelopment of derelict sites

* pollution controls

* traffic management schemes etc.

However, continued tourism development can equally result in negative effects such as:

* urban sprawl

* traffic congestion

* over-development at 'honeypot' sites

* footpath erosion and landscape degradation

* loss of open spaces

* water supply issues

* wildlife habitat disruption

* loss of bio-diversity

* water and air pollution.

Such issues will be viewed by potential visitors in terms of their own personal expectations, needs and wants. Many factors influence an individual's decision to visit a particular destination, as was indicated earlier in Figure 3.3. It remains to be seen how the travelling public will view the great variety of destinations that now actively compete for their custom.

Theory into practice

Make a copy of the following table and add as many correct illustrations as you can for each category, indicating the effect on UK visitor numbers. Some examples have been provided to start you off.

FACTOR	UK DESTINATIONS	SHORT-HAUL DESTINATIONS	LONG-HAUL DESTINATIONS
Cost of accommodation	Weekend offers		
Cost of transport		easyJet budget flights	Competition to key gateways (e.g. NYC)
Costs at destination	Remote areas		High value of sterling against many currencies
Tour operator promotional activity		Thomson's summer sale offers	
Destination promotional activity			Dubai DTCM
Over-commercialisation		Benidorm and other resorts	Niagara Falls
Crime and social problems	Nottingham city-centre drinkers	Rome thefts	Jamaica
Political instability/unrest		Gibraltar	
Terrorism		Basque Spain	Post-9/11 NYC
Positive media coverage			Dubai
Negative media coverage			
Positive tourism management	Lake District National Park Authority		
Negative tourism management			
Growth in independent travel		Timeshares and property in Spain	
Growth in short breaks			
Exclusivity		La Manga	Al Maha
Increased accessibility		easyJet new routes	Emirates direct flights from LHR, LGW, BHX, MAN & GLA
Water hazard	Cornwall floods		
Air hazard			Los Angeles smog
Noise pollution			
Natural disasters	Foot and mouth outbreak	Ski resort avalanches	Caribbean hurricanes

NYC = New York City; LHR = Heathrow; LGW = Gatwick; BHX = Birmingham; MAN = Manchester; GLA = Glasgow

The tsunami in south-east Asia

We end this study of travel destinations with a review of the effects of the terrible disaster that struck south-east Asia at the end of 2004.

On 26 December, at 0758 local time, an earthquake of magnitude 9 occurred off the west coast of northern Sumatra, Indonesia. This was the fourth largest earthquake in the world since 1900. The earthquake generated a tsunami (tidal wave) which swept across the Indian Ocean within hours of the event and brought devastation to a large number of coastal areas, including several important tourist destinations. The main areas affected by the tsunami are shown on Figure 3.28.

Over 280 000 people are thought to have lost their lives in this natural disaster. The overall local impacts caused by the wave were very variable, but Figure 3.29 identifies key aspects of the scale of the disaster.

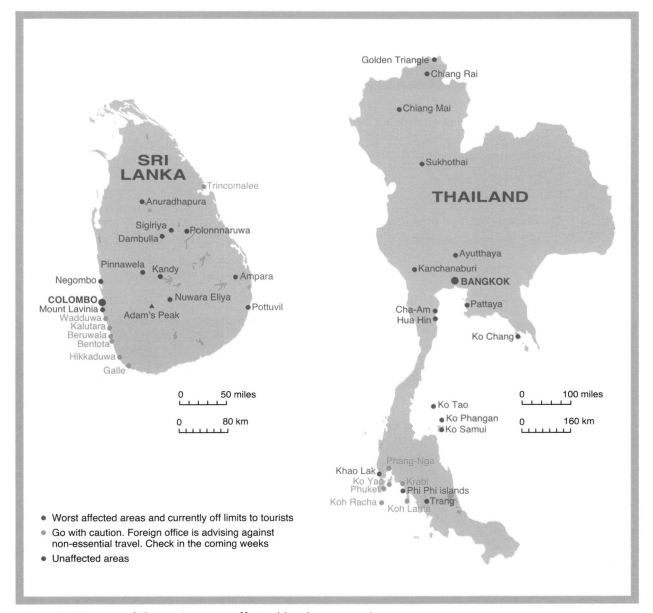

- Worst affected areas and currently off limits to tourists
- Go with caution. Foreign office is advising against non-essential travel. Check in the coming weeks
- Unaffected areas

Figure 3.28 Some of the main areas affected by the tsunami

COUNTRY	DEAD/MISSING	HOMELESS	DESTRUCTION
Indonesia	220 000	517 000	1550 villages
Sri Lanka	36 000	835 000	88 000 homes
India	15 700	627 100	157 400 homes
Thailand	9 000	8 500	Coastal resorts

Figure 3.29 Some provisional estimates of the human impact of the tsunami of 26 December 2004

Furthermore, a large number of European visitors to the above destinations were also victims of the disaster. Interim figures of casualties for the UK, Germany and Sweden are summarised in Figure 3.30.

COUNTRY	LOSSES
UK	51 confirmed dead 416 missing presumed dead 701 individuals whose whereabouts are not confirmed
Germany	784 dead or presumed dead 250 unaccounted for
Sweden	689 confirmed or presumed dead 1200 unaccounted for

Figure 3.30 Some provisional figures for casualties among travellers

Impacts on countries in the region

We shall now look at some of the impacts created by this extreme natural event, and we begin with a consideration of the disaster's immediate effects on tourism in Thailand.

Thailand

The Gulf of Thailand was unaffected by the disaster and all resorts located in this part of the country (Ko Samui, Hua Hin, Ko Pha Ngan, Pattaya and Ko Samet) remained open for business as usual. It was the areas of the west coast that took the full force of the giant wave, particularly Phuket, Krabi and Khao Lak (see Figure 3.31). The island of Phuket, the most popular resort on the coast, was the scene of some of the worst damage and loss of life. Twenty-four hotels were destroyed or severely damaged. A further 29 were still able to operate,

Figure 3.31 An example of the damage caused by the tsunami

but had sustained damage ranging from flooding and destruction of some rooms to loss of water and power.

Patong and Kamala were both particularly badly hit, with the large Merlin resort completely destroyed and the Holiday Inn and Amari Coral Beach badly damaged.

Khao Lak was devastated by the disaster, with most properties damaged beyond repair and hundreds of fatalities. On Ko Phi Phi, a favoured destination for backpackers, much of the accommodation was in budget beach huts, many of which were completely destroyed. At Krabi, resorts on high ground were unaffected, but there was destruction at beach level, where Rayavadee and the Krabi Resort Hotel were badly hit.

It has been estimated that Thailand's tourist island of Phuket lost US$10 million a day during the early new-year peak season in the wake of the tsunami. Beaches normally packed with tourists escaping the northern hemisphere's winter were practically deserted, and Phuket had just a 20 per cent hotel occupancy rate. The numbers were bound to remain low, especially in terms of European travellers from countries that suffered hundreds or even thousands of casualties from the waves.

Tourism accounts for some 6 per cent of Thailand's gross domestic product. Phuket alone generates 72 billion baht in tourism revenue each year. During the peak Christmas and new-year period, revenues can be expected to double and so the destination actually lost about 400 million baht per day. Most of the visitors to the destination in the immediate aftermath were rescue and relief workers, outside volunteers, and hundreds of diplomatic staff and forensic personnel tending to the needs of the thousands of foreign tourists who were on Phuket at the time of the disaster.

The heavy financial losses were expected to last through to March 2005, until many of the affected properties could be rebuild enough to reopen. However, the damage in the eyes of the international community may take many more months to repair. Many of the most dramatic video images of the waves crashing into resorts and towns were taken by tourists on Phuket's west coast. Local authorities quickly began a campaign to assure foreign governments and travel agencies that Phuket will bounce back quickly. However, nearly 20 000 people lost their jobs, and the government has promised to find jobs for displaced workers and offer relief measures to businesses.

We will now briefly explore the tsunami's effects on other destinations in the region.

Malaysia

Resort areas around Penang were most affected. No hotels were reported to have closed, although water damage and debris were widespread. On Langkawi, the Pelangi Beach resort was badly damaged and Berjaya resort also suffered damage to its beach area.

The Maldives

Some islands suffered severe damage but many areas were sheltered from the destructive force of the main wave. The tourist board estimated that out of 87 resorts only 19 had to be closed, due to varying degrees of damage. Within the destination as a whole, major hotels that were forced to close included Soneva Gili, The Four Seasons, Taj Exotica and Velavaru.

Sri Lanka

Just over half of Sri Lanka's 14 000 rooms were affected. Sri Lanka Tourism estimated that 48 large properties, mainly in southern resorts such as Bentota and Galle, suffered damage and almost half of these had to be closed. Among those damaged beyond repair was the Yala Safari Game Lodge.

India

The coast of Tamil Nadu was devastated and there were many casualties. In the town and temple site of Mahabalipuram, a popular attraction for Western tourists, fifteen people were reported dead and surrounding resorts were damaged.

Indonesia

Tourist centres such as Bali and Lombok were unaffected. The worst-hit areas were in Aceh, northwest Sumatra – about which the UK Foreign Office had already established a longstanding warning against non-essential travel due to civil unrest. The Foreign Office reinforced its warning in the light of the earthquake disaster.

The Seychelles

Three thousand miles from the earthquake's epicentre, the Seychelles were spared the worst effects of the tsunami. Three hotels located on Praslin were temporarily closed: the Paradise Sun, La Reserve I and Vacanze Cote d'Or Lodge. Other hotels with some flood damage included Cafés des Arts and Palm Beach.

East Africa

Kenya experienced unusually high swells, with slight damage in Mombasa, but all resorts were reported to be operating normally. Travel industry sources reported that tourist areas in Tanzania were also unaffected.

Possible effects on world tourism

The number of victims claimed by this unprecedented natural disaster, among both the local populations and the visitors in their midst, has been described as the highest in history. An immediate reaction is to ask to what extent it has affected world tourism, a source of economic activity and cultural enrichment for the countries concerned – as indeed for most other countries of the world. Taking world tourism as a whole, the answer has to be that the impact will be slight, for the following reasons.

Although the five most severely affected destinations – India, Indonesia, The Maldives, Thailand and Sri Lanka – are making tremendous strides in their tourism development and having considerable success as tourist destinations, they achieved a market share of only 3 per cent of total world tourist arrivals in 2004. In the other Asian countries hit by the tsunami, especially Malaysia, the affected areas are either not highly developed tourist destinations or are already recovering.

In 2004 this region of the world enjoyed the greatest expansion of both its economy and its tourism. South-east Asia's growth rate outstripped that of the region as a whole in a year marked by a vigorous recovery from the sharp downturn in growth caused by the SARS outbreak and the unstable climate of 2003. Asia made spectacular economic advances in 2004, as reflected in the results of many countries of the region and of the main generators of tourism in particular. It is estimated that, in 2004, gross domestic products (GDPs) rose by the following amounts:

* Australia – 3.6 per cent
* Japan – 4.4 per cent
* India – 6.4 per cent
* Republic of Korea – 8.8 per cent
* China – 9.0 per cent.

This has boosted every kind of tourism, especially that *within* the region which accounts for 79 per cent of the region's total arrivals. Furthermore, the human catastrophe and the material losses caused by the tsunami have been confined to a few coastal resorts in each country, and the damage in some cases is quite limited.

All in all, it can be assumed that the volume of tourism actually affected in the five countries in question will account for less than one per cent of total world arrivals. There are therefore solid grounds for hoping that a prompt recovery of those destinations will pave the way for co-operation and that tourism will help to mitigate the devastating effects on the local population.

The perception the tourist has of the disaster is that it was a freak and distressing event wholly unprecedented in the Indian Ocean. The disaster has brought tragedy to the local population and hit tourism hard. There is, however, a great divide between the perception people have of the event, owing to the considerable coverage given to it by the media – an example of the globalization phenomenon – and the expected consequences for the development of world tourism. Although there was great hardship initially, tourism is expected to recover in the short term and be only slightly affected during 2005.

Knowledge check

1 *To help you appreciate the varied nature of destinations and to understand the key factors in their development.*

Choose a destination and examine how it has changed through time (at least for the last 10 years or so) in terms of:

- new building developments
- numbers of visitors (day visits, overnight visits and overseas visitors)
- new events
- new attractions
- variety of locations within the destination and their uses
- the agents of tourism development and the roles of the private, public and voluntary sectors
- support facilities in place.

2 *To help you understand the ways in which particular locations appeal to particular types of tourist and visitor.*

Find an example of each of the following and obtain an image and description of each location:

- beach resort
- countryside area
- historical destination
- ski resort
- inclusive holiday centre
- conference/major event venue.

Using only the image, describe the reasons certain groups of tourist might be attracted to it.

3 *To help you to appreciate the major factors influencing destination appeal.*

For the six destinations previously researched and identified, provide full details of the following:

- location (landscape features)
- climate
- accessibility (internal and external)
- accommodation
- attractions (natural and built)
- culture (dress, arts and crafts, performance, language and religion).

Resources

The following long- and short-haul destinations currently actively promote themselves to the travel trade and encourage agency staff to take advantage of specialised destination training:

✳ Malta Tourist Office – www.maltawiz.com

✳ Singapore Tourism Board – www.singa-pro.co.uk

✳ Hong Kong Tourism Board – www.discoverhongkong.com

✳ South African Tourism – www.southafrica.net

✳ Caribbean Tourism Organisation – www.caribbean.co.uk

✳ Jamaica Tourist Board – www.visitjamaica.com

✳ Tourism Authority of Thailand – www.training.thaismile.co.uk

✳ Tourism Ireland – www.irelandexpert.co.uk

✳ Kiwi Specialist Programme – www.newzealand.com/travel/trade

✳ Spanish Tourist Office – www.tourspain.co.uk

✳ Jordan Tourism Board – www.jordanambassador.com

✳ Tourism Australia – www.specialist.australia.com

✳ Jersey Tourism – www.jersey.com/trade

✳ Dubai DTCM – www.dubaitourism.ae

✳ Seychelles SMART – www.aspureasitgets.com

✳ Bermuda Tourism – www.bermudatourism.com

✳ LA Travel Academy – www.seemyLA.com

✳ Bahamas Tourist Office – www.bahamacademy.co.uk

✳ Visit USA Association – www.visitusa.org.uk

✳ Canadian Tourism Commission – www.canada-counsellors.co.uk

You may also find the following websites to be of use:

✳ www.about.com

✳ www.tourist-offices.org.uk

* www.whatsonwhen.com
* www.musee-online.org
* www.unmissable.com
* www.worldclimate.com
* www.tripprep.com
* www.fco.gov.uk/travel
* www.viamichelin.com
* www.oanda.com/convert/cheatsheet
* www.travelknowledge.com
* www.americanexpress.com
* www.staruk.org.uk
* www.towd.com
* www.travelchannel.co.uk

Newspaper articles will often be stored on the paper's website and these are an excellent source of additional information. For example, if specific information were required about tourism developments in Dubai or the wider UAE, then items in the local press could be investigated at www.gulf-news.com from an on-line edition by selecting 'Search' from the footer bar. Similar arrangements will exist for other publications. Finally, the search process will reveal many other sources of appropriate information. It is well worth looking at some specialist geography sites as they frequently contain excellent travel and tourism material. In particular, www.geoprojects.co.uk and www.geographyonline.co.uk has further interesting resource material.

International travel

Introduction

The world's travel and tourism industry is growing, and prospects look promising according to the World Tourism Organisation (WTO). Furthermore, according to the WTO, the number of international tourist arrivals in the United Kingdom was heading for a new all-time record in 2004, as growth for the entire year was estimated to reach around 10 per cent.

For the entire January to August period in 2004, growth has been estimated at 12 per cent, corresponding to an extra 58 million arrivals. Of course it has to be taken into account that this leap was primarily a reaction to 2003's depressed figures due to the war in Iraq, the SARS outbreak and the weaker global economy. Nevertheless, compared to corresponding months of the previous record year, 2002, the increase still amounts to 42 million (9 per cent).

How you will be assessed

Unit 4 is mandatory for those seeking the double award and will be examined by means of an external assessment. You will be required to answer four structured questions, each one based around a piece of vocationally related stimulus material. The stimulus material will have been selected solely on the basis of its ability to reflect key aspects of the unit content as itemised below.

The questions will require short responses. However, the last section of each question will allow you to write more openly, with an invitation to respond more freely, to an identified topic or issue. Answers to these final section questions will be assessed using criteria related to your level of response. The overall allocation of marks will reflect the following Assessment Objective weightings: AO1 – 30 per cent; AO2 – 25 per cent; AO3 – 25 per cent; AO4 – 20 per cent. A sample question, together with its marks scheme, is provided at the end of this unit.

What you need to learn

* the types of international transport and the major routes used by international travellers coming to and going from the UK

* the transport products available to international travellers making journeys to and from the UK
* ancillary products and services provided for international travellers
* organisations that influence international travel from the UK
* consumer issues influencing the provision of international travel from the UK
* the factors influencing international travel.

Types of international transport and major routes

Air transport to and from the UK

International travel accounts for almost 90 per cent of all air travel in the United Kingdom in terms of terminal passengers. The increase in the number of people travelling by plane over the last two decades is both a continuation, and a quickening, of a long-term trend.

> ### Key term
> Terminal passengers do not include those in transit to other destinations.

Between 1952 and 2002, the number of terminal passengers at UK airports rose from 2.8 million to 188.8 million. The rate of increase was continuous and steady until the early 1970s, since when it has been much steeper, but also more erratic. For example, the numbers of passengers *fell* in the recession year of 1974, and again in 1991 – the year of the Gulf war – before continuing upward. There was also a marked flattening of the upward trend in 2001 – almost certainly the result of the outbreak of foot-and-mouth disease in the UK and the terrorist attacks in the USA on 11 September. However, numbers resumed their steep rise in 2002.

Figure 4.1 shows the passenger numbers at major UK airports in 2003. The figures clearly reveal that London Heathrow is one of the world's most important airports in terms of

AIRPORT AND CODE	NUMBER OF PASSENGERS	PERCENTAGE CHANGE
London Heathrow (LHR)	63 200 000	0.3
London Gatwick (LGW)	29 895 000	1.3
Manchester (MAN)	19 527 000	4.8
London Stansted (STN)	18 712 000	16.6
Birmingham (BHX)	9 083 000	13.1
Glasgow (GLA)	8 117 000	4.4
Edinburgh (EDI)	7 477 000	8.2
London Luton (LTN)	6 807 000	5.1
East Midlands (EMA)	4 269 000	31.9
Newcastle (NCL)	3 684 000	7.8

Figure 4.1 The UK's top ten airports

international passenger numbers, and that it dominates UK air travel. However, other UK airports are clearly in the world's top 100 in terms of passenger numbers, and the UK's smaller regional airports are experiencing a period of rapid growth.

To obtain a clearer picture of the factors that influence international air travel to and from the UK we can look at an actual example – Manchester Airport.

A study of Manchester Airport

Manchester Airport is the UK's third largest airport and currently handles 20 million passengers a year, offering direct flights to over 180 destinations worldwide by over 90 airlines (Figure 4.2). The airport is part of Manchester Airports Group plc (MAG), which is the second largest airport operator in the UK and comprises the airports of Manchester, Nottingham East Midlands, Bournemouth and Humberside. The group's role is to deliver overarching business and financial strategies for the business as a whole and to provide a policy framework within which targets for the individual businesses can be set and delivered.

Manchester Airport has an exciting and promising future, but an equally illustrious past which began in 1928. Here are some significant events in its development.

* 1953: Sabena (Belgian Airlines) introduce the first scheduled service to New York.

* 1955: The first inclusive tour flight operates to Ostend.

* 1962: The Duke of Edinburgh opens the new £2.7 million terminal, the first in Europe to incorporate the pier system, in which passengers remain under cover until ready to board the aircraft.

* 1969: The runway is extended to 2745 metres, allowing aircraft to take off with a full payload and fly non-stop to Canada.

* 1974: An inter-continental pier opens, capable of handling Boeing 747s. Unlike other piers, it features 'travellators', waiting lounges and air conditioning. For the first time, air bridges connect passengers direct to the aircraft.

* 1978: Fifteen scheduled airlines operate flights to 37 destinations in the UK, Europe and North America. Over a hundred companies operate at the airport, employing more than 5000 people.

Figure 4.2 Manchester Airport

* 1981: The runway is extended by 244 metres taking its total length to 3048 metres, so as to attract long-haul operators to destinations throughout the world.
* 1987: A throughput of one million passengers a month is achieved for the first time.
* 1993: Terminal 2 is opened by the Duke of Edinburgh, doubling Manchester Airport's terminal capacity to around 20 million passengers a year. The railway station is opened in May, providing direct links to many towns and cities in the North of England.
* 1995: Passenger throughput hits 15 million a year.
* 2001: Manchester Airport completed the purchase of East Midlands and Bournemouth Airport to become the second largest airport operator in the UK. Its second runway opened in February.
* 2004: The station is officially opened by Margaret Beckett MP, and the airport celebrates its 20 millionth passenger in the space of a year.

Figures 4.3 and 4.4 show Manchester's top 25 destinations served by scheduled flights and charter flights during 2003. The tables also indicate changes in passenger volume for both types of flight since 2002.

Manchester Airport handled 9.4 million international charter passengers during 2003. Eighty per cent of these passengers were carried by one of the five largest charter airlines. These figures clearly indicate that the airport attracts a substantial number of leisure travellers, mainly package holidaymakers. Further evidence for this comes from the fact that 300 tour operators use the airport as the starting point for their inclusive tours. Additionally, some 7 million passengers flew on international scheduled flights and a further 3 million passengers took domestic flights from Manchester. The high passenger volumes reflect the airport's wide catchment area, with one-third of the UK's population living within a two-hour travel time. Further growth and expansion will take place in the future as passenger numbers are expected to rise to 40 million by the year 2015.

Details of the main carriers of international

COUNTRY	PASSENGERS	PERCENTAGE CHANGE 2002/3
UK	3 042 394	11.7
USA	1 043 863	0.3
Germany	820 174	14.9
Spain	807 811	79.7
Ireland	747 414	−3.5
France	635 382	−7.5
Netherlands	490 387	−5.3
UAE	269 862	41.5
Italy	207 418	47.2
Denmark	198 660	−13.8
Belgium	192 223	−8.7
Pakistan	177 008	17.8
Switzerland	164 492	13.1
Singapore	139 953	−7.9
Malta	129 680	8.4
Cyprus	127 669	0.6
Portugal	117 967	11.2
Czech Republic	103 828	65.1
Malaysia	101 085	31.5
Finland	86 689	9.2
Turkey	78 446	18.4
Sweden	61 010	−18.8
Canada	58 082	3.0
Norway	41 337	7.1
Qatar	40 421	n/a

Figure 4.3 Manchester Airport's top 25 scheduled flights in 2003

travellers from Manchester in 2003 are shown on Figure 4.5.

As 2004 came to a close, Manchester airport announced details of new services for 2005 which were to provide additional routes and new destinations. The low-cost carrier Jet2.com will base

COUNTRY MARKET	PASSENGERS	PERCENTAGE CHANGE 2002/3
Spain	2 692 155	−4.8
Canary Islands	1 882 852	0.9
Greece	1 496 490	−3.2
Portugal	508 632	2.5
Cyprus	442 241	−3.7
Turkey	430 548	7.1
USA	310 670	7.4
Italy	296 799	12.2
Dominican Republic	157 095	16.5
Canada	130 016	0.5
Tunisia	118 127	−7.1
France	110 373	−3.2
Malta	97 499	−1.1
Mexico	96 724	−18.1
Egypt	92 200	45.9
Bulgaria	77 819	46.7
Austria	76 566	−6.6
Jamaica	62 171	13.9
Barbados	57 300	−13.8
Switzerland	46 299	9.8
India	40 970	31.6
Cuba	36 227	13.8
Gambia	33 994	16.9
Finland	28 515	33.9
Morocco	11 814	-8.1

Figure 4.4 Manchester Airport's top 25 charter flights in 2003

six Boeing jets at the airport and provide services to Budapest, Faro, Geneva, Malaga, Murcia, Nice, Pisa, Valencia and Venice. The arrival of Jet2.com will bring Manchester's total of low-cost operators to seven, joining the existing Ryanair, bmibaby, Hapag–Lloyd Express, FlyBe and Air Berlin.

MAIN SCHEDULE CARRIERS

- British Airways
- Monarch Scheduled
- bmibaby
- Lufthansa
- KLM
- Air France
- Aer Lingus
- Emirates
- Ryanair
- bmi
- Pakistan International Airlines
- SAS
- US Airways
- Continental Airlines
- Virgin Atlantic
- Singapore Airlines
- Delta Airlines
- Malaysia Airlines
- SN Brussels

Figure 4.5 Manchester Airport's scheduled flights

Sea transport to and from the UK

More than 45 million ferry journeys are now taken to and from the UK involving continental Europe and the Republic of Ireland, and on British domestic routes. The most significant destination is France.

Think it over ...

Ferry travel is often the easiest, simplest, cheapest and quickest way of reaching a particular destination. One reason for this is the fact that the only limit on the amount of luggage you can take is the capacity of your car, caravan or trailer. Furthermore, unlike on board trains and planes, the luggage will be within reach most of the time. You also have a choice of gateways, as in many cases final destinations can be reached by a variety of routes and sailings.

COUNTRY	NUMBER OF ROUTES	FASTEST JOURNEY TIME
France	12	50 mins
Holland	3	3 hrs 40 mins
Belgium	2	12 hrs 30 mins
Ireland	7	1 hr 40 mins
Norway	3	12 hrs
Sweden	1	18 hrs
Denmark	1	18 hrs
Germany	1	19 hrs
Spain	2	18 hrs
Faroe Islands/ Iceland	1	28 hrs

Figure 4.6 International ferry services from the UK

The ferry industry has been revolutionised with the introduction of the fast ferry concept. The majority of routes now offer a choice of vessels and facilities to suit all passenger requirements and time frames. Details of the major international ferry services are shown in Figure 4.6.

Within all cross-Channel ferry traffic, the Port of Dover is of the greatest significance. We shall now look at this gateway in some detail.

Case study of Dover

Ferry services

Dover is Europe's busiest 'ro–ro' freight and passenger ferry port (Figure 4.7). It operates two dedicated cruise liner terminals – a deep-sea cargo terminal specialising in fresh produce imports, and a 400-berth marina.

> **Key term**
>
> Ro–ro is short for 'roll on, roll off', which describes the nature of the traffic.

Thirty years ago the ferry terminal celebrated processing one million tourist cars along with 5.7 million passengers and 200 000 lorries. In 2002, the traffic throughput had risen to 2.6 million tourist cars, 16.4 million passengers and 1.8 million lorries.

Traffic growth slowed in 2003. The war in Iraq, competition from 'no frills' airlines, and the good summer weather combined to produce a boom in domestic holidays and thus a depression in the

Figure 4.7 The Port of Dover

YEAR	PASSENGERS	TOURIST CARS	COACHES
1985	13 783 840	1 611 738	117 669
1986	14 374 376	1 892 249	121 951
1987	14 041 376	1 918 062	121 457
1988	12 317 057	1 679 788	102 319
1989	15 044 651	2 122 387	120 718
1990	15 532 585	2 218 160	124 832
1991	15 989 318	2 413 287	126 012
1992	17 941 400	2 563 403	153 181
1993	18 458 557	3 003 398	148 606
1994	19 123 743	3 233 476	157 064
1995	17 872 712	2 893 835	158 167
1996	18 979 719	3 054 781	153 642
1997	21 463 570	3 558 355	165 002
1998	19 441 608	3 300 283	153 700
1999	18 276 988	3 003 364	156 725
2000	16 232 191	2 594 824	148 285
2001	16 002 464	2 554 931	136 702
2002	16 442 680	2 632 182	147 549
2003	14 681 003	2 581 573	125 224

Figure 4.8 Dover's annual traffic statistics for 1985 to 2003

day or three every hour around the clock throughout the year.

Figure 4.8 shows how passenger numbers have fluctuated since 1985.

Dover enjoyed a good start to the 2004 summer holidays, with 15 000 more travellers using its ferry services to France compared with in July 2003. A total of nearly 1.8 million passengers travelled on the port's 2500 ferry services to and from the French ports of Calais, Dunkerque and Boulogne in July 2004. While the number of car journeys remained constant at around 310 000, there was a 7 per cent rise in the number of coach journeys.

> **Think it over ...**
>
> The port's ferry business came to the rescue of Eurotunnel in early August 2004 when the Channel Tunnel was blighted by operating difficulties. UK airports, too, were hit by operating difficulties in the summer of 2004, and holidaymakers came to realise that the so-called 'low cost' airlines were not as cheap as advertised fares would have them believe.

The Port of Dover now carries five times more freight vehicles and passengers than the Port of Portsmouth, and more passengers to the near Continent than Heathrow, Gatwick, Luton and Stansted put together. Figure 4.9 provides details of Dover's 2004 ferry services.

Cruise holidays

The UK cruise industry is now a billion-pound business and represents 5 per cent of the total British foreign holiday market. More UK ports

cross-Channel tourist market. However, in that year the port still processed over 2.5 million tourist cars and 1.7 million lorries. The frequency of ferry services continued to increase, with over 27 000 departures in 2003 – an average of 74 per

ROUTE	COMPANY	SEASON	TIME
Dover–Calais	Hoverspeed	March–December	1 hr SeaCat
	P&O Ferries	All year	1 hr 30 mins
	SeaFrance	All year	1 hr 30 mins
Dover–Dunkirk	Norfolkline	All year	2 hrs
Dover–Boulogne	Speed Ferries	All year	50 mins

Figure 4.9 Dover ferry services operating in 2004

COMPANY	NUMBER OF CALLS	DOVER TRAFFIC	PORT OF CALL
Fred Olsen	31	25%	Oslo, Bergen
Saga	21	17%	Oslo, Lisbon
NCL	13	10.5%	Le Havre, Copenhagen
Celebrity	9	7%	Oslo, Le Havre
Costa	8	6.5%	Amsterdam, Cherbourg
Oceania	7	6%	Bergen, Zeebrugge
Crystal	5	4%	Copenhagen, Zeebrugge

Figure 4.10 Dover's cruise traffic in 2004

(41 in 2003) are being visited as ports of call or used as home ports than ever before. The popular destinations showing most growth are western Europe, the Norwegian fjords and the Baltic. The largest increase has been an 84 per cent rise in sales of western European cruises, the second most popular destination from the UK. This is clearly due to the greater range of UK home ports now being used by cruise lines, particularly along the southern and western coastlines.

Since 1994, Dover's standing as a cruise destination has grown dramatically. Today, with two spectacular cruise terminals and a yearly throughput of around 150 000 passengers, Dover is a premier world port and one of the busiest in northern Europe. Dover is visited by many of the world's leading cruise operators, including Norwegian Cruise Line, Fred Olsen, Cunard, Princess Cruises, Saga and many others. In 2004, Dover had over 120 cruise calls scheduled from April to November and the main features of this traffic are shown in Figure 4.10.

Rail transport to and from the UK

Eurostar is the fast train service linking London, Ashford in Kent, Paris, Brussels, Lille, Avignon, Calais, Disneyland Resort Paris and the French Alps (Figure 4.11). The Channel Tunnel rail link enables trains to run at speeds of up to 300 kilometres/hour (186 mph).

Since services began in 1994, Eurostar has transformed the travel market between London and Paris or Brussels. It has quickly become the rail/air market leader and doubled the total number of passengers travelling between London and those two cities. Eurostar carries more passengers between London and Paris than all of the airlines put together. Figure 4.12 shows the impact that the rail services have had on cross-Channel international travel.

Between London and Brussels, Eurostar had a 59 per cent share of the market, up from 47 per cent. Eurostar saw its year-on-year passenger volumes for the month jump by 26 per cent. Passengers have been attracted by the frequent services and by an 'all Belgian stations' ticket policy, which enables travellers to go to any station in Belgium at no extra cost.

On the London to Paris route, Eurostar had a 66 per cent market share, up from 60 per cent in

Figure 4.11 Eurostar

LONDON TO PARIS	JULY 2004	JULY 2003
Eurostar	65.88%	60.23%
Air France	12.58%	14.02%
British Airways	12.33%	15.62%
bmi	4.59%	4.91%
easyJet	4.42%	4.89%
Others	0.19%	0.33%
Totals	100%	100%
LONDON TO BRUSSELS	JULY 2004	JULY 2003
Eurostar	59.25%	46.57%
British Airways	23.14%	24.19%
bmi	15.18%	12.75%
KLM	2.18%	3.09%
Ryanair	0.00%	12.38%
Others	0.25%	1.03%
Totals	100%	100%

Figure 4.12 Cross-Channel market share statistics

July 2003. Passenger volumes increased by 22 per cent year-on-year, while all airline competitors on this service saw their market shares fall. These higher market shares are having a clear effect on other carriers, who continue to cut their services. British Airways closed its Gatwick to Paris service from the end of October 2004, while easyJet cut its Luton to Paris frequency from five flights a day to three. These moves follow service closures by Ryanair earlier in the same year.

Eurotunnel

Eurostar and Eurotunnel are two different companies. However, Eurostar is Eurotunnel's largest customer. Eurotunnel manages the infrastructure of the Channel Tunnel and operates accompanied truck shuttle and passenger shuttle (car and coach) services between Folkestone and Calais/Coquelles, France. It is market leader for cross-Channel travel. Eurotunnel also earns toll revenue from other train operators using the tunnel (Eurostar for rail passengers, and EWS and SNCF for rail freight). Eurotunnel is quoted on the London, Paris and Brussels Stock Exchanges.

Figure 4.13 shows traffic volumes through the Channel Tunnel in recent years.

Heathrow Express

The Heathrow Express is a train service from Heathrow Airport to Paddington station in central London, operated by the Heathrow Express Operating Authority, a wholly owned subsidary of the British Airports Authority (BAA). The service operates from approximately 5 a.m. until midnight with trains every fifteen minutes. There are two stops at Heathrow, one for terminals 1, 2 and 3 (journey from Paddington, about 15 minutes) and one for terminal 4 (about 22 minutes). The service costs around £13 for a single journey in standard class and around £22 for first class (2003 prices) and is non-stop from London to Heathrow. The service, which opened on 23 June 1998, offers trains that are modern by British railway standards, featuring on-board televisions and the ability to use mobile phones throughout the journey, even when in tunnels.

The service, whilst generally well-received – not least because steps were taken to reduce the environmental impact of the train line, such as disguising ventilation shafts as barns – has received some criticism principally because of its cost. Per kilometre, the journey is more expensive than travelling on Concorde used to be. However, over 4 million passengers use the service every year.

MODE OF TRANSPORT	2000	2001	2002	2003
Cars	2 784 493	2 529 757	2 335 625	2 278 999
Coaches	79 460	75 402	71 911	71 942
Eurostar (passengers)	7 130 417	6 947 135	6 602 817	6 314 795

Figure 4.13 Eurotunnel traffic figures for 2000 to 2003

Road transport to and from the UK

International travel by coach from the UK is dominated by the Eurolines group. This consists of more than thirty independent coach companies operating together to form Europe's largest regular coach network. This network connects over 500 destinations, covering the whole of continental Europe, and Morocco. Eurolines allows travelling from Sicily to Helsinki and from Casablanca to Moscow.

Eurolines members offer fares with no hidden extras – sea crossings, travel taxes and road tolls are all included in the price. Furthermore, most of the services bring passengers directly to a city centre, thus avoiding the need to pay for transfers by taxi or rail, for example.

Eurolines runs various day trips seasonally throughout the year. Their most popular day trip is to Cité Europe – France's answer to Bluewater, but with all the discounts that shopping in continental Europe brings. Collections and drop-offs for this service are offered in London, Lewisham, Dover and Canterbury. Major destinations are offered by themes such as:

* *Food & Drink* (to Brussels, Paris, Dublin, Munich, Bordeaux and Bruges)
* *Families* (to Disneyland Resort and Paris, Cité Europe, Poitiers, Amsterdam and Dublin)
* *Culture* (to Lille, Amsterdam, Budapest, Barcelona, Milan and Madrid)
* *Clubbing* (to Amsterdam, Berlin, Tallinn, Prague, Frankfurt and Ghent)
* *Romance* (to Paris, Tours, Bruges, Cologne, Vienna and Florence).

Special offers are frequently made available. Below is listed a selection of recent offers for 30-day advance return fares, starting from London:

Paris – from £29
Amsterdam – from £29
Brussels – from £29
Dublin – from £29
Belfast – from £29
Cork – from £33
Cologne – from £44
Lyon – from £49

Milan – from £49
Barcelona – from £49
Prague – from £49
Nice – from £49
Frankfurt – from £49
Munich – from £59
Vienna – from £59
Madrid – from £69
Budapest – from £69.

Demand is high, and there are plenty of options with four services to both Paris and Amsterdam each day. These scheduled services boost Eurotunnel's passenger statistics and contribute to the 2.6 million overseas trips made by coach from the UK each year.

Who travels

This section ends with a look at the relative balance between British residents and overseas residents travelling to and from mainland UK between 1981 and 2002. The relative importance of air, sea and the Channel Tunnel can be clearly seen in Figure 4.14.

Transport products to and from the UK

Going by air

International air transportation to and from the UK is available from both scheduled and chartered carriers.

> **Key term**
>
> A charter service is used mainly within the package holiday market. A tour operator may pay the airline for the whole flight or for a bulk booking of seats, and then either sell them on at whatever price they choose or put them together with accommodation to form a package.

Operators and services

While there are many charter airlines, several are owned by tour operators such as Thomsonflights (operated by Britannia Airways). Others are independent. Monarch is the UK's largest

	1981	1991	1996	2000	2001	2002
Visits abroad by UK residents (millions)						
Air	11.4	20.4	27.9	41.4	43.0	44.0
Sea	7.7	10.4	10.7	9.6	9.7	10.0
Channel Tunnel	–	–	3.5	5.8	5.6	5.3
All visits abroad	19.0	30.8	42.1	56.8	58.3	59.4
Visits to UK by overseas residents (millions)						
Air	6.9	11.6	16.3	17.8	16.1	17.1
Sea	4.6	5.5	6.2	4.3	4.0	4.4
Channel Tunnel	–	–	2.7	3.1	2.8	2.7
All visits to UK	11.5	17.1	25.2	25.2	22.8	24.2

Figure 4.14 International travel to and from the UK between 1981 and 2002

independent charter airline. Each year it carries some five million passengers and works with a large range of tour operators – from the household-name companies to specialist travel businesses. Monarch visits nearly 100 destinations from its major bases at London Gatwick, London Luton, Manchester, Birmingham, and other regional airports.

Think it over ...

London Gatwick is near Crawley, in West Sussex. *London Luton* is near Luton, in Bedfordshire. Why do you think each has 'London' in its name?

There is no guarantee with a charter flight that it will operate. If few seats have been sold then two flights may be consolidated – one service will be cancelled and any passengers booked on it may be moved on to another flight. This will avoid two flights going out half empty. The prices of charter flights can change at any time. The tour operator monitors the sale of seats and will vary prices according to demand.

In contrast, a scheduled service operates to a regular timetable and the flight will go regardless of how many passengers are booked on it. Scheduled flights are becoming increasingly

popular with leisure travellers because of their flexibility, wide choice of fares and range of destinations served. They remain popular with certain sections of the business community because of the facilities that are made available. Furthermore, the expansion of 'low cost' carriers offering scheduled services, such as easyJet and Ryanair, has proved attractive to both leisure and business travellers.

Monarch is an interesting airline because it offers both scheduled and charter services. Monarch Scheduled provides the international traveller with low-cost, convenient flights that can be booked direct on-line or by telephone, or alternatively through a travel agent. Passengers are able to enjoy food and drinks and in-flight shopping and entertainment. Monarch Scheduled gives leisure and business travellers flexibility to choose from popular destinations in Spain, Gibraltar, Portugal, the Balearics and the Canaries, with services from London Luton, London Gatwick and Manchester airports:

* London Luton – Alicante, Faro, Gibraltar, Gran Canaria, Lanzarote, Malaga, Menorca, Tenerife

* Manchester – Alicante, Barcelona, Faro, Gibraltar, Malaga, Palma de Mallorca, Tenerife

* London Gatwick – Alicante, Faro, Malaga.

The airline operates a timetable of midweek and weekend departures, with low one-way prices. This means greater flexibility because there are no minimum or maximum stay requirements. Typical customers are property owners, independent holidaymakers, 'ex-pats' visiting the UK, business travellers and people visiting friends and relatives. Vantage Club, their frequent flyer programme, offers a range of additional benefits and services. After a qualifying period, members are awarded Vantage Club points each time they fly and these points can be redeemed for free flights.

Scheduled air services are provided by several international carriers. The Dubai-based Emirates is one of the fastest growing airlines in the world and has received more than 250 international awards for excellence since its launch in 1985. With the recent addition of new routes to Moscow, Auckland, Perth, Mauritius and Cochin it can now fly international passengers to more than 70 destinations in 50 countries in Europe, the Middle East, the Far East, Africa, Asia, Australia and the USA.

The Emirates fleet of aircraft is constantly being upgraded to keep it one of the youngest in the skies. After recent additions it now has a fleet of over 50 aircraft, which includes twenty-nine Airbus A330-200, nine Boeing 777, and twelve larger 300-series Boeing 777 aircraft. As a highlight of its future growth, Emirates announced the biggest order in civil aviation history, worth $19 billion, at the Paris Air Show in 2003.

In December 2003, the first of 28 ultra-long-range Airbus 340-series aircraft joined the Emirates fleet. These spacious four-engined planes can travel over 14 000 kilometres (8700 miles) without refuelling – allowing Emirates to take passengers all the way non-stop from Dubai to Australia, Japan or North or South America. An additional twenty-six Boeing 777s will also extend capacity on existing routes. Emirates will be one of the first airlines that will fly the newest and largest passenger aircraft in the world, the Airbus double-decker A380, which holds over 550 passengers and will have come into service by October 2006. Emirates has 45 of these advanced aircraft on order.

Classes

Most aircraft used on international scheduled services are split up into different cabin sections with different prices being charged for the product and services that are delivered. Figure 4.15 shows the main features of the different cabin sections to be found on scheduled flights.

CLASS OF TRAVEL ON FLIGHT	FEATURES OF THE CABIN/SERVICE
Economy	Largest section of aircraft Adjustable seats Complimentary meal service Complimentary drinks service Duty-free shopping In-flight entertainment
Business	Wider, adjustable seat with more legroom Meal service with more choice Complimentary drinks service with wider choice Larger choice of in-flight entertainment Designated check-in desks at certain airports Access to lounges at certain airports Increased free baggage allowance
First	Normally a small section at front of aircraft with fewer seats Wider seats, with plenty of legroom, which can convert into a flat bed Special meals with extensive choice Selection of fine wines and other complimentary drinks Largest choice of in-flight entertainment Designated check-in areas and later check-in times Access to prestige lounges at major terminals Additional free baggage allowance

Figure 4.15 Features of classes on scheduled international flights

Not all routes operated by scheduled carriers will offer all three classes. Most European routes offer only business and economy. However, the European scheduled marketplace has been transformed in recent years by the arrival of an increasing number of budget airlines. There were only two main budget carriers at the start of the twenty-first century but there are now over 50. This heightened competition means that Europe now has some of the lowest airfares ever known, which in turn is generating huge growth in the numbers of passengers taking short breaks.

Generally, low-cost carriers do not provide the same level of service that is available to passengers travelling on a full-fare scheduled airline such as British Airways, Air France and Emirates. Furthermore, they tend to use regional airports where landing slots will be cheaper, and this can limit passenger accessibility to certain destinations.

Competition is now intense on many international routes, and London to Dubai is a good example. Figure 4.16 shows an advertisement for Gulf Air's new service. This is the type of stimulus material that might be included in the external assessment for this unit, to help illustrate some of the characteristics of scheduled air services for international travellers. The advert gives emphasis to the following:

* The service is scheduled, operating on a daily basis.
* The flight offers three types of cabin for the journey.
* The service is aimed at both leisure and business travellers.
* Gulf Air point out two of their unique selling points: passengers on the flight will have access to a 'Sky Chef' and a 'Sky Nanny'.
* Promotional fares are available in all classes.

Theory into practice

To help you understand air services to and from the UK, complete the following exercises.

1 Choose an important international carrier serving the UK market and identify its route network.

2 Investigate frequency of service on UK routes.

3 Provide details about what is available for first-class, business-class and economy-class passengers on these routes.

4 Compare the chosen carrier with British Airways or another UK carrier that operates a service on these routes. Suggest reasons for the various differences that you identify.

Theory into practice

Read the following account of a journey from Manchester to Kuala Lumpur on Malaysian Airlines. Identify the main features of the service provided and come to a conclusion about which class the passenger was travelling in.

'Once I reached the airport I had to get the elevator to the correct level and then head for the Malaysian Airlines check-in. Once checked in and gone through the passport control, I went towards the departure gate, and this is where I spent my time shopping and eating at the restaurants. On board the aeroplane, which is large, I was shown to my seat by the staff. Once the safety instructions had been given and we had taken off, the staff distributed the in-flight menu, and then, when they had served drinks, they collected the menus in and gave us a lemon refreshment flannel. Shortly after this the in-flight entertainment was available for the duration of the flight, either the 40 radio stations provided, the interactive quiz and computer games or my favourites, the in-flight movies of the most recent releases. The flight staff were very helpful and would regularly bring drinks and snacks between the meals if asked, or would bring extra blankets if you were too cold. The meal was served half way through the flight and was very enjoyable. Choices ranged from satay dishes to rice, depending on what time of flight you were on.'

Athens —— Alexandria — Al Ain —— Dubai —— Riyadh — Abu Dhabi — Islamabad — Bangalore — Kolkata — Colombo —— Bangkok
Frankfurt Cairo Amman Jeddah Salalah Bahrain Karachi Chennai Mumbai Dhaka Hong Kong
Istanbul Casablanca Beirut Kuwait Sanaa Muscat Lahore Cochin Thiruvanan- Kathmandu Jakarta
Larnaca Khartoum Damascus Mashad Shiraz Peshawar Delhi thapuram Kuala Lumpur
London Dammam Ras Al Khaimah Tehran Manila
Paris Doha Singapore
Sydney

DUBAI TO LONDON DAILY

"Ahlan wa sahlan"
(Welcome to our home)

Introducing our new daily flight to London from
21 June with special introductory fares. Every flight
comes complete with gourmet dining, care of our
Sky Chef, and quiet, content children, thanks to our
Sky Nanny. So whether your customers are travelling
for business or pleasure, we'll make their London
experience begin the best way it can. For more
information, please contact Gulf Air on (04) 2729500,
(04) 2713222 or visit us at www.gulfairco.com

CLASS	FARES FROM
Economy	AED 1,999
Business	AED 6,999
First	AED 8,999

- For our special fare, tickets must be purchased before 30th June,
  to complete travel by 30th September 2004
- Taxes extra
- Terms and conditions apply.

Figure 4.16 An advertisement placed by Gulf Air

Going by sea

Services available on board ferries vary according to the length of the crossing, but will usually include catering, accommodation in berths or bunks for longer routes, entertainment, amusements and shopping facilities.

Some ferry crossings can almost be classed as mini-cruises, such as those from the UK to Scandinavia, where the facilities provided for passengers are quite extensive. For example. the DFDS Seaways service from Harwich to Esbjerg departs from the UK at 18:00 and after an overnight crossing arrives in Denmark at 12:00 midday local time.

This route is served by the *Dana Sirena*, which was a brand new ship in April 2003. This vessel can cater for a wide range of passengers, from those on a relaxing short break to those travelling with their car and caravan on holiday to Scandinavia. The ship offers three main categories of cabin: Standard, Sirena Class and Commodore De Luxe. It can carry up to 600 passengers and over 350 cars, with a cruising speed of 22.5 knots. The onboard shop offers perfumes, sweets, confectionery, clothing and tobacco all at advantageous prices compared to UK retail prices. Souvenirs, newspapers, magazines and books are also available. There are two restaurants and a café. Finally, there are two evening entertainment areas and a children's playroom.

Cruise ships usually provide passengers with an all-inclusive holiday of three days or more. Passengers are provided with:

* fully equipped accommodation
* stewards to provide cabin service
* a choice of dining options
* fully detailed brochure about the cruise: ports of call, length of time there etc.
* leisure activities and recreational facilities
* various forms of entertainment.

Cabins will frequently range from a basic two-berth, usually on one of the lower decks, to luxurious state rooms on the highest deck which have their own verandahs and/or sitting rooms attached to the sleeping accommodation. Prices are set according to the level or standard of facilities, length of cruise and type of accommodation.

The UK leisure traveller has a very wide choice of cruises to pick from. Websites of the main operators are listed in Figure 4.17 (on page 146).

Websites of the main operators are listed in Figure 4.17 (on page 146).

Theory into practice

1 Choose an example of an important international ferry route from the UK, and an example of an international cruise used by UK passengers.

2 For each, identify the main service operators.

3 Provide details of the vessels used.

4 Describe the products and services available on-board.

Going by rail

Eurostar

On Eurostar, Standard class offers a reserved seat in a spacious, air-conditioned carriage with the opportunity to buy refreshments from the on-board bar/buffet. First class offers more space and a reclining seat, and passengers will be served champagne, followed by a three-course meal with wine or soft drinks.

On the London to Paris route, Premium class offers the best of Eurostar, with all the benefits noted above plus dedicated check-in and ticket office facilities and access to its lounges. On board, passengers can enjoy the maximum of space and privacy in the dedicated Premium carriage, with a four-course meal. On arrival, a chauffeur will be waiting to take passengers to any central city address.

Eurostar's pricing offer the following options:

* Business fares combine first-class on-board service with dedicated ticket office and check-in areas, and access to the exclusive lounges in London, Paris or Brussels.

* Business 'value' first-class passengers enjoy these benefits at a reduced price on certain trains (special exchange and refund conditions apply).

* Full-fare business first-class offers a streamlined check-in of just 10 minutes, and is

CRUISE OPERATOR	WEBSITE
Carnival Cruise Lines	www.carnivalcruise.co.uk
Celebrity Cruises	www.celebritycruises.com
Costa Cruises	www.costacruises.co.uk
Crystal Cruises	www.crystalcruises.com
Cunard Line	www.cunard.co.uk
Fred Olsen Cruise Lines	www.fredolsencruises.co.uk
Hebridean Island Cruises	www.hebridean.co.uk
Holland America Line	www.hollandamerica.com
Island Cruises	www.islandcruises.com
MSC	www.msccruises.com
Norwegian Coastal Voyage	www.norwegiancoastalvoyage.com
Norwegian Cruise Line	www.uk.ncl.com
Ocean Village	www.oceanvillageholidays.co.uk
Orient Lines	www.orientlines.com
Orient-Express Cruises	www.orient-express.com
P&O Cruises	www.pocruises.com
Page & Moy	www.cruisecollection.com
Peter Deilmann Cruises	www.peter-deilmann-river-cruises.co.uk
Princess Cruises	www.princess.com
Radisson Seven Seas Cruises	www.rssc.co.uk
Royal Caribbean International	www.royalcaribbean.com
Seabourn Cruise Line	www.seabourn.com
Seadream Yacht Club	www.seadreamyachtclub.com
Silversea Cruises	www.silversea.com
St Helena Line	www.rms-st-helena.com
Star Cruises	www.starcruises.com
Swan Hellenic	www.swanhellenic.com
Thomson Cruises	www.thomson-cruises.co.uk
Windstar Cruises	www.windstarcruises.com

Figure 4.17 Cruise line services available to UK travellers

fully exchangeable and refundable.

* Disneyland Castle class offers the luxury of a wider seat and more legroom as well as a snack and cold drink.

Eurostar attempts to appeal to a wide variety of international travellers such as large groups, wheelchair users, those travelling with a guide dog or passengers with special meal requirements (e.g. Muslim, Kosher or vegetarian). The company has put in place special arrangements to cater for their needs:

* Staff are on hand at Eurostar terminals to help passengers with restricted mobility and other special needs. Those who think that they might need help getting to or from the train are asked to arrive early, preferably at least 45 minutes prior to departure, at the check-in area and notify a member of staff.

* Eurostar provides a range of baggage services for its customers such as lost property, left luggage facilities, oversized baggage and more.

* The wheelchair-user fare enables passengers to travel in their own wheelchair in a special part of the train. One travelling companion can accompany the user at a reduced rate, but they must travel together on Eurostar for the companion fare to be valid.

* For groups of ten up to 766 on one train, tailored group packages are available to fit the needs of any internationally bound group.

* Eurostar does not operate an unaccompanied minors service, and children under 12 years cannot travel unaccompanied by an adult. The procedure for unaccompanied minors aged between 12 and 17 varies depending on circumstances.

* Passengers travelling in Premium or First class can have special meal arrangements. They can be provided with vegetarian meals if they give 12 hours' notice. However, Kosher, Muslim or vegan meals require at least 36 hours' notice.

* There are toilets in all terminals and in each carriage of the train. Baby changing facilities are accessible throughout the journey from all carriages, located in carriages 1 and 18.

* Eurostar can now accept guide dogs on board. However, no other animals can travel on Eurostar.

The Heathrow Express

Heathrow Express is the fastest and most convenient way to travel between Heathrow Airport and London Paddington. Passengers can check in their luggage and collect their boarding cards at Paddington, at any time on the day of travel, right up to two hours before the flight (one hour with hand luggage only). With their boarding card and seat number issued, passengers can then sit back and relax on the Heathrow Express and proceed straight to their departure gate at Heathrow. Check-in facilities are open from 5 a.m. to 9 p.m. daily. There are nine airlines currently checking in at Paddington:

* Air Canada
* Austrian Airlines
* Singapore Airlines
* bmi
* Varig Brazilian
* LOT
* Lufthansa
* Thai Airways
* SAS.

The Orient Express

The Venice Simplon-Orient-Express operates between London/Paris and continental Europe. The most regular journey, however, is between London, Paris and Venice, which can be experienced in either direction. There are additional departures between Venice, Florence and Rome, as well as from Venice to Vienna, Prague and Lucerne and from Paris to Istanbul and Istanbul to Venice.

The traditional route between London and Venice takes two days, with one night on board. This service uses the original carriages dating from the 1920s, the heyday of luxury train travel. Original designs and marquetry have been restored by craftsmen with minute attention to detail. In 1982, some £11 million was spent carrying out these refurbishments. As well as the carriages being restored to their former glory, the refurbishment also ensured the safety of passengers and the smooth running of the service.

Passengers travelling from or to London will experience the British Pullman carriages of the Venice Simplon-Orient-Express between London and Folkestone. The comfort of passengers is paramount, so the Channel crossing may be by coach and the Eurotunnel shuttle or by surface vessel, either Sea Cat catamaran or ship. An Orient Express hostess will escort passengers throughout the cross-Channel journey.

Table d'hôte meals are included in the fare. Continental breakfast and afternoon tea are served in the passenger's own compartment, while lunch and dinner are enjoyed in the sumptuous surroundings of the dining cars. The gourmet meals and discreet service are all part of the Orient Express experience. An à-la-carte menu is available for lunch and dinner, and there is a 24-hour compartment service for light snacks and refreshments. These are at an additional cost and paid for at the time of ordering.

Passengers departing from London on the British Pullman train are served lunch, together with a complimentary glass of champagne and half a bottle of wine. Passengers ending their journey in London will be served afternoon tea on board the British Pullman. On the Orient Express, overnight passengers are given their own compartments, complete with wooden marquetry and brass fittings in original 1920s detail.

Service on board this luxury form of transport is outstanding. Each passenger has a cabin steward who is responsible for one carriage on the Continental train. He or she will be available at all times and may be called by the bell inside each compartment. The steward will take care of passports during the journey, change the compartment from day to night configuration, and serve passengers breakfast, afternoon tea and other refreshments as required. The Maitre D' will come to each compartment to take lunch and dinner reservations. The Train Manager is on hand throughout the journey to help with any queries.

Theory into practice

1 Choose an example of a major rail journey, popular with UK international travellers.

2 Provide details of the itinerary and describe all the products and services available for passengers.

3 Compare the chosen journey with a luxury package featuring a train such as the Orient Express.

Going by coach

The Eurolines group referred to earlier in this chapter (see page 140) developed for all its members common *quality standards* and harmonised the sales and travel conditions. This means that all passengers using the network are guaranteed the same level of quality and assistance. The Eurolines operating members use modern coaches with reclining seats, large picture windows, washroom facilities and adequate legroom. All services are non-smoking.

Eurolines has launched a new Eurolines Plus service from London to Paris. This features improved levels of comfort for passengers, including:

* increased legroom in reclining seats (85 cm or 33.5 in for each passenger)

* individual headphones at each seat for music and video entertainment.

The service has been able to maximise passengers' comfort on Eurolines Plus by using the additional space in longer coaches to provide more legroom. It is now a greater amount of space than on most airlines operating to Paris. Eurolines Plus has also reconfigured seating in other existing coaches on this route to guarantee all services will offer passengers the same experience.

Theory into practice

1 Compare a fly/drive holiday package with an international coach tour package.

2 Consider the advantages and disadvantages of each for different types of customer. Aspects to consider might include: car hire options; flexibility and convenience; cost; health and safety; families versus singles and retired.

Ancillary products and services for international travellers

Tourist Information Centres and related services

Mersey Tourism runs three Liverpool Tourist Information Centres (TICs) on behalf of Liverpool City Council at Liverpool Airport, the Albert Dock and a purpose-built facility that it shares with Mersey Travel in Queen Square in the city centre.

It also operates an Accommodation Call Centre. These four facilities are very much in the front line for product and service delivery.

Figure 4.18 illustrates the range of services available. All the TICs deal with an extensive range of counter, postal and telephone enquiries, operate an accommodation booking service, sell tickets for theatres, guided tours and events, as well as National Express, Isle of Man and Irish ferry tickets. They also have on sale local, Beatle and football souvenirs, publications and postcards, many of them made and printed on Merseyside. There is also a Bureau de Change facility.

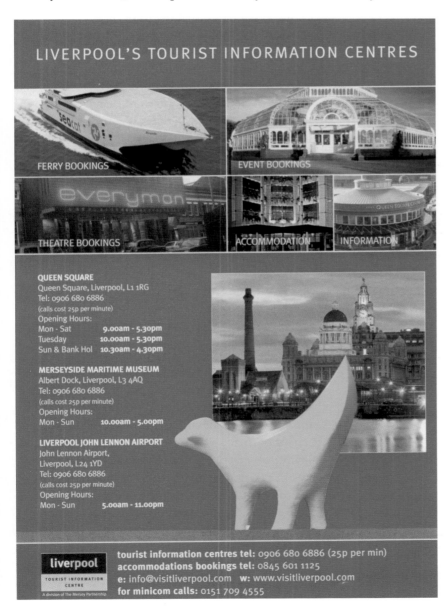

Figure 4.18 Liverpool's Tourist Information Centre leaflet

Information services supporting international travel include the promotional materials, the face-to-face service provided at the TICs, and the telephone service provided by the call centre. Use is made of the MISTIC reservation system. To support leisure visits, Mersey Tourism produces a *Travel Trade Guide* to help tour operators organise packages to the destination. Services provided to the trade include:

* brochure supplies
* itinerary planning
* Blue Badge guide bookings
* attraction discounted admissions
* group bookings and special offers
* private tours.

Mersey Tourism is also involved with the recruitment, training and administration of 'MerseyGuides' and 'BeatleGuides'. The MerseyGuides operate an extensive programme of public walks, car, coach and minibus guided tours. They provide guide/courier services for the travel trade, talks and illustrated lectures as well as 'quality of life' tours on behalf of the Mersey Partnership. This latter function deals with a relocation service, emphasising the benefits of Merseyside for new employers and employees. They also conduct urban regeneration tours for students and various other groups.

It is to be expected that many destinations will try to maximise their business tourism receipts. Mersey Tourism has responded to the opportunities presented by a growing business tourism market through the services provided by the Mersey Conference Bureau. Merseyside is now able to supply the conference organiser with a specialist customer service package that gives attention to:

* help with the choice of venues appropriate to the scale of the event
* supporting visual material (e.g. promotional leaflets/brochures to help sell the destination/venue)
* costed bids (to help secure a booking)
* a range of accommodation options, if required

* transport/transfers to make visitor/delegate movement easier
* audio-visual and stage/set quotations arranged to meet an organiser's specification
* arranging social and partners programmes to ensure visitors/delegates enjoy the venue and will want to return
* providing support services (e.g. business and communication facilities).

This approach to the conference business market has resulted in an increasing number of bookings, such that the value of Merseyside business tourism generated through the Bureau is £1.4 million. An example of the important events arranged by the Bureau in July 2001 was the British Council Conference held at the Liverpool Crowne Plaza Hotel which attracted delegates from every corner of the world.

Conferences, exhibitions and events can all be staged in a variety of venues. It is now quite common to find several types of host venue trying to attract these types of business tourism. Examples of such providers include:

* purpose-built conference centres
* hotel facilities
* sports venues
* civic buildings
* stately homes
* university and academic institution facilities
* other types of accommodation provider.

The accommodation used by international travellers has already been looked at, to a certain extent, during our investigation of destinations in unit 3. The focus of attention now is the range of ancillary services that they can provide for the benefit of their leisure and business guests. A visitor to Liverpool may be advised to stay at the city's Crowne Plaza Hotel and details of the facilities available at this property are shown on Figure 4.19. A good way to get an appreciation of what is available in various types of accommodation is to make a study of your local area.

CROWNE PLAZA
LIVERPOOL

Crowne Plaza Liverpool

Outstanding service, facilities and décor make the four star de-luxe Crowne Plaza Liverpool the city's premier hotel. Blend this with a stunning location, adjacent to the Royal Liver Building and the majestic River Mersey and you have a truly unbeatable combination.

Facilities
- 159 Luxurious, air-conditioned guest bedrooms, many with fabulous views of the Liver Building and the River Mersey
- The Plaza Brasserie serving award winning cuisine with a global flavour
- The Lounge, a stylish bar and lounge area and a great place to relax
- 24 Hour room service
- Modem points in all bedrooms
- The Harbour Club, a superb health and leisure facility
- A smoothly efficient team of staff to cater for your every need

Business
- Stylish air-conditioned conference facilities for up to 700
- Ground floor access to primary conference suite
- Executive boardroom facilities
- ISDN lines to all conference suites
- Secure on-site car parking
- Fully staffed and equipped Business Centre
- Close to Liverpool's business district

Leisure
- Superb waterfront location
- Close to the shops, museums and galleries of Albert Dock
- Health Club with pool, gym, sauna, dance studio, beauty therapy suite and tanning facilities
- Award winning cuisine

Room Name	Reception	Theatre	Classroom	Boardroom	Banquet	Dimensions	Height	Door H/W	Natural Daylight	Location
Princes Suite (1+2+3)	800	700	340	-	500	34 x 15	3.3m	2	✓	G
Princes Suite 1	300	300	140	50	260	19 x 15	3.3m	2	✓	G
Princes Suite 2	240	100	48	36	70	15 x 6.5	3.3m	2	✓	G
Princes Suite 3	240	100	48	36	70	15 x 6.5	3.3m	2	✓	G
Brunswick, Canada & Salisbury Suite	-	32	24	18	-	6.5 x 7.5	2.5m	2	✓	1
Harrington Boardroom	-	-	-	14	-	3.5 x 6.5	2.5m	2	✓	1
Syndicate Rooms	-	12	-	8	-	3.5 x 4.5	2.5m	2	✓	1

Crowne Plaza Liverpool, St Nicholas Place, Pier Head, Liverpool, L3 1QW
Tel: +44(0)151 243 8000 Fax: +44(0)151 243 8111
Email: enquiries@cpliverpool.com Web: www.cpliverpool.com

Figure 4.19 An advertisment for Crowne Plaza

Major transport terminals

We have already looked at some aspects of Manchester Airport's operations and we now turn our attention to the types of ancillary services provided for the benefit of international passengers at Manchester.

Check-in facilities

An earlier section drew your attention to the experience of an international passenger travelling from Manchester to Kuala Lumpur on Malaysia Airlines (see page 143). Figure 4.20 shows a situation that will be familiar to many of you who have travelled overseas from the UK. It shows passengers in the Departure hall at Manchester airport.

Malaysia Airlines provide passengers with a choice of at least five check-in desks to report to prior to starting their journey. The airport makes trolleys available to help them move their luggage within the terminal building, and the airline has a queuing system in operation to prevent overcrowding and congestion. The check-in process takes place in the 'land-side' part of the terminal building.

In Terminal 1 at Manchester, there are a variety of services provided for international travellers,

Figure 4.20 Departure hall at Manchester Airport

including these shops: Allsports (open 05:00–20:00), Boots (05:00–20:00), Claire's Accessories (05:00–20:00), Cotton Traders (05:00–20:00), Impulse (05:00–20:00), La Senza (05:00–20:00), Monsoon/Accessorize (05:00–20:00), Salisburys (05:00–20:00), Sunglass Hut (05:00–20:00), Dry Cleaning Centre (07:00–19:00), Thorntons (05:00–20:00), Travelcare (08:00–20:00), WH Smith (03:00–20:00).

Other services in the 'land-side' part are:

* *Bureaux de change:* Thomas Cook (05:30–20:00) and ICE (Monday–Thursday, 05:00–23:00; Friday–Sunday, 05:00–24:00). The Co-op Bank offers a full banking service.

* *Cash dispensers:* Barclays, Link and NatWest in the main Arrivals concourse accept most cards.

* *Children's play area:* The unstaffed play area is open 24 hours a day. Parents must remain with their children at all times.

* *Information desk:* The main information desk is located in Arrivals. Courtesy phones link passengers directly to the information desk – look for the blue phones. There is no information link from Departures.

* *Left luggage:* Luggage may be left on the Arrivals level in the corridor to Airtours check-in. This facility also deals with lost and found property. Open 06:00–22:00.

* *Luggage trolleys:* These are plentiful and free on the lower-level Arrivals floor and on the terminal forecourt.

* *Payphones:* These are situated in catering and shopping areas.

* *Places of worship:* A prayer room is available for all faiths. At the end of the Terminal 1 concourse, follow the corridor on the left.

* *Postal services:* There is a post box before Security Control. The nearest Post Office is in Arrivals.

* *Restaurants and bars:* All food and drink outlets are now located on the mezzanine level with good choice and excellent views of the airport.

* *Smoking:* This is currently allowed at meeting points and in some seated areas of lounges.

* *Toilets:* Before passport control there are four toilet facilities. Baby changing rooms are located in the women's toilet in the shopping area and also in the food concourse. Most toilets have facilities for disabled people. After passport control there are two toilets, one with disabled and both with baby care facilities.

'Air-side' services in Terminal 1 available for the benefit of departing international passengers include:

* *Bureaux de change:* One bureau, Travelex, opens from first flight to last flight.

* *Entertainment:* Video games are available in the Departures lounge after Security Control.

* *Food and drink:* After passport control are a small number of food and beverage outlets.

* *Payphones:* These are throughout the lounge.

* *Postal services:* There are none air-side. Travellers must mail letters before clearing security and passport control.

* *Smoking:* This is currently allowed in some seated areas of lounges.

* *Toilets:* There are two toilet areas, one near the cafe and one near the bar.

These services have been developed using the latest technology and they all contribute towards a pleasant passenger experience. Signage is extensive in both 'land-side' and 'air-side' areas of the terminal and the electronic display boards act as a constant reminder to passengers about the status of their intended flight.

Duty-free and tax-free shopping in Terminal 1 includes: Allombra (open 05:00–20:00), Alpha Airport Shopping (24 hours), Boots (05:00–20:00), Dixons (05:00–20:00), Fashion Gallery (05:00–20:00), Goldsmiths (05:00–20:00), House of Champions (05:00–20:00), Tie Rack (05:00–20:00), Waterstones (05:00–20:00), WH Smith (04:00–23:00).

Taxis

Taxi ranks are situated at the following places:

* Terminal 1 – outside International Arrivals
* Terminal 2 – adjacent to Arrivals
* Terminal 3 – outside Arrivals.

All taxis on the ranks at Manchester Airport are licensed by Manchester City Council. In addition, drivers approved by the airport hold a supplementary licence issued by Manchester Airport plc. Within the City of Manchester licensed area, the fare applicable is that shown on the meter. All drivers holding a Manchester Airport licence have agreed a maximum tariff which is shown in leaflets available from the drivers and on the tariff boards displayed at each taxi rank. The journey to central Manchester takes about 20 minutes and costs approximately £12.

Car hire

Car hire firms are located at the airport, most of them open daily between 7 a.m. and 9 p.m. Companies supplying Manchester Airport are: Manchester Car Hire, Avis, Budget, Europcar, Hertz UK, National Car Rental, and Sixt Kenning.

Passengers with special needs

Services for passengers with special needs are given high priority. Manchester Airport endeavours to ensure its facilities are available to all passengers, including those who are visually or hearing impaired or otherwise disabled.

* Aviation and Airport Services is appointed by the airlines to provide services for disabled passengers.
* A wide cross-section of staff has received training in sign language.

* An inductive coupler system is built into all public telephones.
* There are signs to assist passengers who are hard of hearing.
* A minicom system is available at the Information Desk, in Terminal 1 International Arrivals.
* Those with hearing aids with a 'T' position can receive enhanced announcements over the public address system when standing close to the induction loops indicated by the ear symbol.
* Special vehicles are provided to convey non-walking passengers and their companion and/or attendant.
* Designated parking facilities, adjacent to lifts, are available in the multi-storey car parks at all three terminals.
* Ramps and lifts are provided throughout the airport. All lifts have tactile buttons and voice synthesisers.
* Telephones with good accessibility for wheelchair users are available throughout all three terminals. A public text payphone is situated in Terminal 1 International Arrivals.
* Specially designed toilets can be found in most areas of both terminal buildings and are clearly signposted.

Car parking

There are a variety of car parking options available for the benefit of international passengers. Short-stay parking is recommended for stays up to five hours and is available at all three terminals, with covered walkways connecting to the airport's terminals. Disabled bays are available in all short-stay car parks, near lifts. Prices for parking start at £1.80 for up to 30 minutes.

The long-stay car parks located at all three terminals offer secure parking facilities, conveniently connected to the airport's terminals via transfer services that run every 5–15 minutes (depending on which car park you choose).

Airport parking can be booked on the day, but it is advisable to pre-book in order to secure a space. Booking in advance is usually also more economical, with most car parks offering discounts for phone and online bookings.

If you do not wish to have to transfer from the car park to the terminal you might choose the Meet and Greet valet parking service. This involves a chauffeur meeting you at a prearranged time at your departure terminal and parking the car for you in a secure compound. Upon your return, the car will be delivered to you at the terminal.

Travel agents

Most UK international travellers making their travel arrangements through a travel agency will be offered a wide range of ancillary services. Travel agents welcome the opportunity to provide these 'add-ons' because they generate additional income and thus increase overall shop/outlet profitability. Depending on the type of travel arrangements being made, customers can have any of the following provided for them at an additional cost:

* return taxi transfers to point of arrival
* car hire
* crèche
* welcome packs for apartments (including special occasion packs with flowers, champagne or cake and kids' beach packs)
* hotel accommodation for the night before the journey
* theme park tickets (Disney, Terra Mitica, Port Aventura etc.)
* walking tours
* pre-booked seats, upgraded meals, increased baggage allowances
* travel insurance
* hotel vouchers for fly/drive customers
* VIP airport lounges before departure in the UK
* chauffeur-driven car to airport
* airport parking or 'meet & greet'
* city break excursions, dinners, theatre trips
* coach tickets
* rail tickets
* foreign exchange.

Agents do not emphasise the price of these services, they give emphasis to the amount that the customer is saving by pre-booking. For example, the drive-in gate price for Manchester's long-stay car park is currently £6.10 a day or £48.80 for eight days. However, Holiday Extras offers eight days' parking with a night at the Britannia Airport Hotel for just £79. It would be quite easy for agents to sell this particular add-on to passengers flying from Manchester because of its reasonable cost and the convenience that it offers.

Using similar arguments, agents can tempt their customers with flight upgrades from as little as £259 per sector on long-haul scheduled services. Similarly, accommodation can be upgraded, as can car rentals. Travel agents are now offering even more services to their customers to boost income. It is becoming increasingly common to see the following more specialised services being offered to clients, where and when appropriate:

* balloon flights and helicopter rides
* Ibiza club passes
* swimming with dolphins/manatees
* spa days and massage packages
* diving packages
* wedding planner services
* Broadway show tickets
* New York 'Sex and the City' tours
* USA cell phone hire.

This trend to increased ancillary service provision is being further fuelled by the increase in the number of suppliers entering the global travel marketplace. For example, HolidayTaxis.com is Europe's leading provider of pre-booked transfers. They have identified that pre-booking a transfer is the fastest growing segment of the package holiday add-on market. They offer services in over 1200 resorts worldwide, including ski-shuttles, and have now expanded into the Caribbean. Agents can earn an average 18 per cent commission and can book the transfer on-line, receiving confirmation in seconds. The delivery of this service is both easy to arrange and profitable for the agents and will clearly remain much in demand by clients.

Tour operators

We end this section of the cha[...]n look at how the major operators offe[...]f ancillary services in addition to their s[...]urs. They are happy to take bookings from customers for particular services, and many of these have been indicated in the previous section. However, we will now focus on one specific type of tour that attracts many UK customers, the inclusive wedding package market.

Figure 4.21 shows an extract from the Tradewinds Worldwide Holidays' 'Weddings and romantic holidays' brochure. This is also an example of the type of stimulus material that will be used in the external assessment for this unit.

Tradewinds offers all clients White Horse's wedding insurance. They also offer a wedding gift service whereby family and friends can purchase extras and upgrades for the bride and groom. Access to executive lounges and flight upgrades are also available. Tradewinds also advise about the possibility of other extras, depending on the destination selected, such as:

* extra champagne
* extra flowers
* spa treatments
* room upgrade
* photography
* video of ceremony
* elephant ride in Sri Lanka
* Elvis impersonator in Las Vegas
* romantic cruise in the Seychelles
* dinner and trishaw ride in Penang
* deluxe honeymoon packages
* excursions.

You will have noticed that these services are simply offshoots of the services offered by most travel agents and that Tradewinds have merely contextualised them within a wedding package. Similarly, the packages featured in Figure 4.21 contain various add-ons that will be included if the clients wish to select them and others are simply offered as an incentive.

Organisations that influence international travel from the UK

Foreign and Commonwealth Office (FCO)

British nationals make over 53 million overseas trips each year. 'Know Before You Go' is a Foreign Office campaign that aims to help travellers have a safe and enjoyable holiday by encouraging them to be better prepared before going overseas. The key messages are to take out comprehensive travel insurance and to read the FCO's travel advice before starting a trip.

FCO travel advice is designed to help British travellers avoid trouble by providing information on threats to personal safety arising from political unrest, terrorist activities, lawlessness, violence, natural disasters, epidemics, anti-British demonstrations and aircraft/shipping safety. Furthermore, special advice is provided for UK international travellers in terms of:

* backpackers
* women travellers
* gay travellers
* young travellers
* mobile phone tips
* retiring abroad
* sustainable tourism
* visiting friends and relatives overseas
* financial protection organisations
* sports travellers
* alpine sports travellers
* short breaks.

In a recent 12-month period, the FCO's consular services provided assistance and advice to over 53 000 British travellers, issued over 460 000 passports abroad, and received around 700 000 page views per month on the Travel Advice website.

British Consuls will do everything they properly can to help British people in difficulty abroad. Figure 4.22 lists advice about what help a

Figure 4.21 An advertisement for a trip to Shangri-La

British international traveller can expect to receive from an overseas British Consul.

UK law states that the FCO will have to charge for some services.

- Issue emergency passports and in some places full passports

- Contact relatives and friends to ask them to help with money or tickets

- Give information on how to transfer money

- In an emergency, cash a sterling cheque worth up to £100 in local currency, if supported by a valid banker's card

- Help to get in touch with local lawyers, interpreters and doctors

- Arrange for next of kin to be told of an accident or a death and advise on procedures

- Visit you if you have been arrested or put in prison, and arrange for messages to be sent to relatives and friends

- Put you in touch with organisations who help trace missing persons

- Speak to the local authorities on your behalf

- Only as a last resort, in exceptional circumstances, and as long as you meet certain strict rules, give you a loan to get you back to the UK, but only if there is no-one else who can help you

Figure 4.22 The British Consuls' checklist

Civil Aviation Authority (CAA)

The Civil Aviation Authority, which is a public corporation, was established by Parliament in 1972 as an independent specialist aviation regulator and provider of air traffic services. Following the separation of National Air Traffic Services from the CAA in 2001, the CAA is now the UK's independent aviation regulator, with all civil aviation regulatory functions (economic regulation, airspace policy, safety regulation and consumer protection) integrated within a single specialist body. The UK government requires that the CAA's costs be met entirely from its charges on those whom it regulates. Unlike many other countries, there is no direct government funding of the CAA's work.

The CAA:

* ensures that UK civil aviation standards are set and achieved

* regulates airlines, airports and National Air Traffic Services economic activities and encourages a diverse and competitive industry

* manages the UK's principal travel protection scheme, the Air Travel Organisers' Licensing (ATOL) scheme, licenses UK airlines and manages consumer issues

* brings civil and military interests together to ensure that the airspace needs of all users are met as equitably as possible.

In addition, the CAA advises the government on aviation issues, represents consumer interests, conducts economic and scientific research, produces statistical data and provides specialist services.

The role of the CAA's Safety Regulation Group (SRG) is to ensure that UK civil aviation standards are set and achieved in a co-operative and cost-effective manner. SRG must satisfy itself that aircraft are properly designed, manufactured, operated and maintained; that airlines are competent; that flight crews, air traffic controllers and aircraft maintenance engineers are fit and competent; that licensed aerodromes are safe to use; and that air traffic services and general aviation activities meet required safety standards.

The responsibilities of the Consumer Protection Group (CPG) are to:

* regulate the finances and fitness of travel organisers selling flights and package holidays in the UK

* manage the UK's largest system of consumer protection for travellers, ATOL

* license UK airlines and enforce European Council requirements in relation to their finances, nationality, liability to passengers for death or injury and insurance

* enforce certain other legal requirements and codes of practice for protection of airlines' customers.

The ATOL scheme

The ATOL scheme is very significant for UK travellers. ATOL protects passengers from losing their money or from being stranded abroad. It does this by carrying out financial checks on the firms it licenses and requiring a guarantee, called a bond, to be lodged with the CAA. If a firm goes out of business, the CAA will make a refund to the passenger, or if the passenger is abroad, it will arrange for him or her to finish the holiday and then fly home. The number of ATOL licences in force is now the highest it has ever been. At June 2004 there were 2009 valid licences, compared with 1855 the previous year.

International Air Transport Association (IATA)

The International Air Transport Association was founded in Havana, Cuba, in April 1945. It is the prime vehicle for inter-airline co-operation in promoting safe, reliable, secure and economical air services, for the benefit of the world's consumers. The international scheduled air transport industry is now more than 100 times larger than it was in 1945. Few industries can match the dynamism of that growth, which would have been much less spectacular without the standards, practice and procedures developed within IATA. Today IATA has over 270 members from more than 140 nations in every part of the globe.

International air transport is one of the most dynamic industries in the world. IATA works with its membership to make the industry safer, more profitable and efficient. IATA deals with a wide variety of issues affecting international air travel, including:

* aircraft operations
* airport development and infrastructure
* cargo
* finance
* industry initiatives

* passenger issues
* regulatory and public policies
* safety
* security.

Furthermore, IATA publishes in-depth information about the airline industry, available in printed or digital format. It organises international conferences, exhibitions and industry meetings designed to provide industry leaders with a forum for discussion, insight and co-operation. It also runs extensive training programmes to help industry professionals strengthen administrative and leadership skills essential to their operations.

Passenger Shipping Association (PSA)

The Passenger Shipping Association was formerly known as Ocean Travel Development (OTD). OTD was formed in 1958 as an Association of Passenger Ship Owners. The year 1957 had seen, for the first time, the number of passengers travelling across the North Atlantic by air exceeding the numbers travelling by sea in the great liners. OTD's main objective was to focus public attention, and that of the travel trade, on sea travel as a holiday leisure pursuit, and as the modern alternative to transportation from place A to place B. The shipping lines conceded that they could no longer compete with the developing airlines with regard to travelling time and cost. They also recognised that their future lay in full-time cruising.

In 1986, consumer protection methods were established for all cruise companies selling in the UK, as well as being imposed on the package tours operated by PSA member ferry companies. Bonding, to provide financial protection to the passenger, and independent conciliation and arbitration procedures are now administrated by the association. The PSA is also an important corporate contact for the media, seeking information on both cruising and ferry markets.

The PSA has several key objectives:

* to promote public travel by sea
* to encourage expansion in the volume of passenger travel, by sea and river

* to work towards the removal or prevention of the imposition of restrictions or taxes on passenger travel by sea

* to advise members to ensure that passengers travel in a safe, healthy and secure environment.

Association of British Travel Agents (ABTA)

The Association of British Travel Agents is the UK's main trade association for tour operators and travel agents. ABTA's 1043 tour operator and 6356 travel agency offices are responsible for the sale of some 85 per cent of UK-sold holidays with a turnover of £26 billion.

ABTA provides assistance to customers having a complaint against companies that carry the ABTA logo. The quality of the holidays and services provided by ABTA companies is crucial to the reputation of the industry.

ABTA-regulated travel agents and tour operators must comply with strict financial rules. These rules are to protect the customer's money and allow ABTA to make sure that claims are paid in the event of a company failure. Customers can book their holidays knowing that if an ABTA regulated tour operator or travel agent goes out of business while they are away, then the customers should be able to continue as originally planned, and ABTA will ensure that they are able to get back home. Even if the customer has not yet started the holiday, he or she will get a refund or be given help to make alternative arrangements for the holiday to proceed. Many ABTA tour operators also provide bonds to the Civil Aviation Authority under the ATOL scheme, as discussed earlier in this section.

ABTA currently has bonds valued at £201 million for travel agents and £170 million for tour operators. To protect consumers' monies and holidays in 2001, ABTA paid out £2.2 million in respect of travel agents' failures, and £90 000 in respect of tour operators' failures. In 2003, ABTA dealt with nearly 17 thousand complaints. Of these, over 1200 went to ABTA's independent arbitration scheme, an alternative to a small claim's court.

Code of Conduct

As a regulatory body, ABTA maintains a strict *Code of Conduct*. ABTA companies agree to be bound by the code which governs the relationship between customer and company, and also the company's relationship with ABTA. The code aims to ensure that all customers receive the best possible service from ABTA travel agents and tour operators. This covers:

* the period before actual booking takes place

* the booking process itself

* after-sales service

* the handling of any complaints.

Here are some illustrations of the ways in which the code influences holiday booking procedures:

* When you book with an ABTA member they must give you accurate information to help you choose the travel arrangements that are right for you (code 1.1).

* ABTA members must follow all the necessary legal requirements such as the ATOL regulations and must make you aware of the terms and conditions that apply (code 1.4).

* ABTA members must give you guidance about any health requirements and the passport and visa requirements for your travel arrangements (code 1.6).

* If you have any special requests concerning a disability or other medical condition, ABTA members must ensure that these are dealt with properly and confidentially (code 1.4iii).

* ABTA members must also give you information about travel insurance (code 1.7).

* Before completing a booking, ABTA members must tell you if the Foreign and Commonwealth Office has issued advice about your destination (code 1.6iii).

World Tourism Organisation (WTO)

The World Tourism Organisation is a specialised agency of the United Nations and is the leading international body in the field of tourism. It serves as a global forum for tourism policy issues and practical source of tourism know-how. In 2004, the

WTO's membership consisted of 144 countries, seven territories and more than 300 affiliated members representing the private sector, educational institutions, tourism associations and local tourism authorities.

The WTO plays a central and decisive role in promoting the development of responsible, sustainable and universally accessible tourism. The WTO has the aim of contributing to economic development, international understanding, peace, prosperity and universal respect for, and observance of, human rights and fundamental freedoms. In pursuing this aim, the organisation pays particular attention to the interests of developing countries in the field of tourism.

Each region of the world – Africa, the Americas, East Asia and the Pacific, Europe, the Middle East and South Asia – receives special attention from its regional representative based at the WTO headquarters in Madrid. The regional representation for Europe strives to ensure that WTO members in the region fully benefit from the transfer of technology generated by the organisation's programmes, activities and research. The regional representation for Europe also pays particular attention to the specific needs of the National Tourism Administrations, local authorities and tourism enterprises in the region, conducting seminars and conferences on topics of interest to the tourism industry, including courses on tourism human resource development.

WTO is unique among international inter-governmental organisations in that it is open to membership by the operating sector and promotes various methods of co-operation amongst its members. Airlines, hotel chains, tour operators, trade associations, consultants, promotion boards and educational institutions make up approximately 350 members of the Business Council (WTOBC).

Website

The WTO's 'Facts & Figures' section aims to provide comprehensive information on international tourism worldwide. On its website (www.world-tourism.org/facts) it offers a selection of the latest available statistics, as well as analysis focused on *inbound tourism* (tourist arrivals, tourism receipts, travel by purpose and means of transport) and outbound tourism (outbound tourism by region of origin and tourism expenditure). The website also makes available an analysis of the world and regional tourism major trends, an overview of the evolution of world tourism since 1950, as well as WTO's long-term prospects.

Consumer issues influencing the provision of UK international travel

Travel from the UK is influenced by the operation of several pieces of legislation. Organisations involved with the provision of travel services for British international travellers come under the influence of these various pieces of legislation, so it is important to understand and appreciate their significance. It is important to understand that customers have rights and that legislation now has an impact upon the types of information that should be provided about travel and tourism products and services.

Acts of Parliament such as the *Consumer Protection Act 1987* makes it a criminal offence for anyone in the course of a business to give to consumers, by any means whatever, an indication that is misleading as to the price at which any goods, services, accommodation or facilities are available. Similarly, the *Supply of Goods and Services Act 1977* states that customers are entitled to work that is carried out with reasonable skill, in a reasonable time and at a reasonable price. If not, the supplier is in breach of contract and is obliged to sort the problem out.

The Data Protection Act 1998 was passed to regulate the use of information for processing systems which relates to 'individuals and the provision of services in respect of such information'. The Act requires users of personal data to comply with the following:

* Data must be obtained and processed fairly and lawfully.

* Data must be held only for specific lawful purposes.

* Data must not be used in any other way than those related to such purposes.

* Data should be adequate, relevant and not excessive for those purposes.

* Personal data should be accurate and kept up to date.

* Data should be held no longer than is required.

* Individuals should be entitled to access their data and, if necessary, have it corrected or erased.

* Data must be protected with appropriate security against unauthorised access or alteration.

The *EU Directive on Package Travel 1995* has resulted in all UK tour operators offering package holidays being subject to the *Package Travel Regulations*. Although the legal definition of a package is complex, it is clearly understood that transport (flights), accommodation (hotel) and an ancillary service (transfers), when supplied and paid for in combination, constitute the package. The two principal sections of the regulations provide financial protection for prepayments and require tour operators to provide what is promised.

A direct responsibility is placed on tour operators for the safety of their customers. Tour operators are legally responsible for the components of their packages if negligence is proved. They cannot avoid responsibility by attributing the blame to their sub-contractors. Also, UK customers can sue operators in UK courts and no longer have to pursue action against contractors in overseas courts, which can be more costly and complicated. Furthermore, the regulations prohibit inaccurate brochure descriptions and allow penalties for non-compliance. Surcharges under two per cent of the package price cannot be levied and have to be absorbed by the operator. The holidaymaker is entitled to compensation for any non-compliance with the regulations.

Consumers are guaranteed entitlement to a refund if the operator goes out of business. The provision of financial protection for holidaymakers is now well established throughout Europe and is incorporated in EU laws and regulations. Everyone buying a package holiday in the UK or in another EU country legally should now be financially protected. This means that if their tour operator fails, customers will receive their money back. If they are abroad at the time of the failure they will be brought back without charge and may well finish their holiday as planned.

As well as giving rights to consumers, the regulations create certain criminal offences. Examples are providing misleading or inadequate information in brochures, and not providing customers with key information about the package. The criminal provisions of the regulations are enforced by trading standards officers.

All travel and tourism organisations with more than five staff come within the ramifications of the *Health and Safety at Work Act 1974*. Such organisations must have a health and safety policy and certain key issues should be addressed:

* Accidents must be recorded in an accident book.

* There must be adequate lighting and covers for computer screens.

* Seats must be adjustable.

* Fire extinguishers must be provided.

* There should be a first aid box.

* Room temperatures should be comfortable.

* Adequate toilet and washing facilities should be provided.

Theory into practice

The following offers appeared in a local travel agency:

*One week self catering in Majorca £149
from Manchester*
Manchester to New York £199

Now read the revised versions that were placed in the same agency following a complaint.

* *One week in Majorca £149*
  *Self-catering in accommodation allocated
  on arrival*
  Based on four people sharing
  Available May/October

* *Manchester to New York £199*
  Departures 1 April to 15 July 2005
  Book before 21 March
  Minimum stay 7 nights
  Valid Monday to Thursday

Explain what was wrong with the first two adverts.

Factors influencing international travel

You have now had the opportunity to examine some of the features of international travel to and from the UK. In this concluding section to the study of unit 4 it is appropriate to review some of the points in unit 3.

Travellers are *consumers* of travel and tourism *products* and *services*. We have already seen that individuals are strongly influenced by various combinations of the following:

* past family holidays
* relations, friends and colleagues
* TV and films
* newspapers and magazines
* holiday brochures
* adverts and promotions
* school, college or work-related trips
* amount of disposable income available to be spent on tourism
* employment status – student/in work/retired
* size of household – number of children
* number of trips taken last year
* age and health status
* amount of free time
* personal preferences, needs and wants
* cost of transport in both time and money.

Consumer tastes and preferences change, whether they are coming to or going from the UK, and this explains much of the variation that is shown on Figures 4.1, 4.3, 4.6 and 4.10. When international travel experiences periods of rising demand new products and services will be offered. There will be new suppliers trying to obtain market share and specialised products will be aimed at particular segments or niche groups. Figure 4.23 shows a recent Travelbag advertisement placed in the UK weekend press. There are a wide range of products being offered to British international travellers, such as:

* business and economy flights to various worldwide destinations
* five-night city breaks to Cape Town
* seven-night fly/drive package to California

Figure 4.23 An advertisement placed by Travelbag

* Qantas Australia flights with stopover options
* Cathay Pacific New Zealand flights with a Hong Kong stopover
* Dubai mini-breaks
* three types of Bermuda package
* round-the-world offers.

Each of the advertised products will appeal to different types of customer. Some products have a niche focus, such as the New Zealand Wine Trail, while others will appeal to those wanting a conventional beach holiday at a reasonable price.

Figure 4.23 also provides clear evidence of other changes that are taking place in the UK international travel marketplace. The pricing in the advertisement reflects the growing affluence of the UK traveller, as well as the economies that have resulted from the comparatively high value of the pound sterling (£) against other currencies. Furthermore, the actual destinations offered may reflect new services on particular routes that have encouraged price competition and thus more affordable fares. This is very much the case with

destinations such as New York and Dubai where there is always keen pricing between the scheduled carriers.

The advertisement also provides evidence of the changes that are progressively taking place with respect to the various channels of distribution. Travelbag is part of the ebookers group and there are several ways in which customers can access the advertised products, such as:

* a personal visit to one of the named branches
* telephoning one of the stated numbers
* visiting the website.

Reservation technological improvements mean that bookings can be requested, checked for availability and confirmed very swiftly. This will be the case for each of the above three methods. Speed is very important because several advertised products have limited availability, such as the £468 Thailand Beach package. This is clearly a seasonal offer and sales maximisation will depend on doing a certain volume of business very quickly.

Theory into practice

This is a typical external assessment exercise based on a piece of vocationally relevant stimulus material. Refer to Figure 3.12 in unit 3, a tourist information map produced by the Dubai Department of Tourism.

1 Suggest four services that are likely to be provided for the benefit of incoming visitors at Dubai International Airport's Tourist Information Centre.   [4 marks]

2 Using *only* information shown on Figure 3.12, explain two reasons why a Hilton hotel located at the Satwa end of Sheikh Zayed Road is likely to be popular with business visitors.   [4 marks]

3 Many UK residents travel to Dubai using scheduled flights provided by carriers such as Emirates and British Airways. Explain the services that such airlines usually provide for (a) unescorted children, and (b) disabled passengers.   [6 marks]

4 Assess the reasons for the increase in popularity of long-haul holiday packages from the UK.   [6 marks]

Marking scheme

Q	Expected answer	Marks	AO
1	You will receive one mark each, to a maximum of four, for valid services, such as the following in What You Need To Learn: special event information; hotel bookings; guidebooks and guiding services; excursions; transport tickets etc.	4	AO1
2	You will receive one mark for each of two valid reasons identifiable from Figure 3.12, and then a second mark for an appropriate explanatory statement or comment for each. Correct responses will include: adjacent to World Trade Centre, so convenient for business meetings/events; away from the hustle and	4	AO2 (2) AO3 (2)

bustle of city centre, so less congested environment; international chain, so recognisable brand name and quality standard; accessible location near to airport etc.

3	Although the question is divided into parts (a) and (b), you will receive marks for identifying a maximum of two valid services in each category, with a maximum three marks for appropriate service identification. You can then be awarded up to a further three marks for clear explanatory comment about these services. Valid *children* reasoning will include: looked after during pre-boarding formalities, to keep safe and secure; seated near cabin crew for monitoring in-flight; child meal and activity pack to keep them occupied etc.; escorted through arrivals (meet guardian). Valid *disabled* reasoning will include: accessibility (remain in wheelchair until boarding); wheelchair stowed last (unloaded early at arrival); called first for pre-boarding (aisle seating etc.); cabin crew briefed about special needs etc.	3 + 3	AO2 (3) AO3 (3)
4	This question requires you to assess the reasons for the popularity of long-haul packages amongst UK consumers. Details of at least two valid reasons must be present to progress beyond level 1 in the level of response criteria that will be used to allocate marks. Further progression will reflect the amount of evaluation offered and the use of evidence to reach conclusions.	6	AO1 (2) AO4 (4)

Knowledge check

The answers are given at the end.

1 Which of the following islands are *not* Caribbean holiday destinations: (a) Barbados, (b) Cuba, (c) St Lucia, (d) Bermuda, (e) Dominica?

2 What term best describes the climate of Milan: (a) tropical, (b) sub-tropical, (c) temperate, (d) arctic, or (e) equatorial?

3 Which of the following ancillary services are *not* usually available in large hotels: (a) currency exchange, (b) excursions, (c) rail tickets, (d) travel insurance, (e) restaurant reservations?

4 Which of the following are part of an important destination's infrastructure: (a) airport, (b) main roads, (c) dry sunny climate, (d) skilled workforce, (e) an annual major sporting event?

5 Which of the following are important personal skills required by many travel and tourism employees: (a) honesty, (b) verbal communication skills, (c) numeracy, (d) good timekeeping, (e) computer literacy?

6 Which of the following are *not* national air carriers: (a) British Airways, (b) Emirates, (c) KLM, (d) Qantas, (e) Ryanair?

7 Which of the following are positive impacts of tourism: (a) less unemployment, (b) more pollution, (c) fewer people under-employed, (d) restoration of historic sites, (e) high-season overcrowding?

8 Which of the following seas contain important international ferry routes: (a) North Sea, (b) Irish Sea, (c) Dead Sea, (d) Caspian Sea, (e) Black Sea?

9 Which of the following are *not* cultural attractions for international visitors: (a) traditional food, (b) traditional dances, (c) traditional beach resorts, (d) traditional houses, (e) traditional festivals?

10 Which organisation has a responsibility for air ticketing: (a) ABTA, (b) ATOL, (c) CAA, (d) WTO, or (e) IATA?

11 Which of the following are associated with all-inclusive holidays: (a) Leading Hotels of the World, (b) Club Med, (c) Amtrak, (d) Holiday Inn, (e) Sandals?

12 Which of the following are natural hazards for visitors to tropical areas: (a) monsoon rains, (b) cyclones, (c) famines, (d) oil spills, (e) civil unrest?

13 Which of the following destinations have their local time in *advance* of GMT: (a) Berlin, (b) Dublin, (c) Lisbon, (d) Accra, (e) Cape Town?

14 Cruise ships will frequently call at which of the following locations: (a) Madeira, (b) Malta, (c) Nairobi, (d) St Moritz, (e) Madrid?

15 Which of the following attractions would you expect to be listed in a local tourist board guidebook: (a) theme park, (b) heritage site, (c) art gallery, (d) shopping centre, (e) concert hall?

16 Explain the current trend for many providers of travel services to belong to large integrated companies.

17 Explain why tourism development in certain locations can produce a variety of negative social impacts.

18 Outline some of the ways in which a national tourist board can promote tourism internationally.

19 Show how the needs of the international business traveller are met by a variety of travel service providers.

20 What are the main functions of a tour operator's overseas representative?

Answers

1: (d). **2:** (c). **3:** (c) and (d). **4:** (a) and (b). **5:** (b), (c) and (e). **6:** (e). **7:** (a), (c) and (d). **8:** (a), (b) and (e). **9:** (c). **10:** (e). **11:** (b) and (e). **12:** (a) and (b). **13:** (a) and (e). **14:** (a) and (b). **15:** all.

16: This question is about the advantages of integration. Large companies can benefit from economies of scale. This means, for example, when two operators combine they can achieve cost savings during their negotiation with suppliers because of their increased purchasing power. The larger company enjoys a competitive advantage because it can sell its product at lower prices due to its economies of scale. Furthermore, the integrated company can impose quality control standards throughout its chain of distribution and this, in turn, can lead to increased levels of customer satisfaction and further profitability.

17: This question is about the negative effects that tourism can have on an area's social (and cultural) conditions. The 'demonstration effect' is one aspect of the host/tourist encounter that can create social problems when locals adopt visitor values leading to a loss of their cultural identity. A variety of related conditions can follow resulting in increased crime, unbalanced population growth as migration swells tourist destination resident population numbers (often to the detriment of surrounding rural areas), loss of traditional ways of life and the frequent exploitation and trivialisation of traditional culture – e.g. dress/costume, dance/performance, arts and crafts, religion/festivals etc.

18: International promotion is one aspect of destination marketing and there will usually be a variety of promotional and publicity activities undertaken. The national board will participate in various international exhibitions, make marketing visits to key tourism generating areas, undertake a series of presentations and roadshows, provide and fund familiarisation and assisted visits for the travel trade, undertake advertising campaigns in key markets, produce and distribute brochures, manage all media relations to maintain a destination image, and establish enquiry information services (offices and internet) to maximise visitor numbers.

19: Essentially there are three sets of requirements during an international business trip – travel organisation, accommodation, and meeting venue. Each of these will involve specific services that the average leisure traveller will not require as a matter of course:

- *Travel* will usually involve a business or club class scheduled flight with access to a range of facilities and services, both in-flight and on the ground. Speed, efficiency and the opportunity to work will be prime considerations, whereas cost will be a secondary issue.
- *Accommodation* will be in a business class hotel where the range of leisure facilities and services, so important for other types of guest, will be only of secondary importance. Access to business facilities and a convenient, accessible location will be the major concerns.
- *Venue facilities* for holding a meeting/conference/event will be of the greatest significance as this is the reason for undertaking the overseas travel in the first place. Most international destinations will have a range of venues, with appropriate facilities, capable of hosting such business functions.

20: Overseas representatives are responsible for ensuring that clients have an enjoyable holiday experience. They are in frequent guest contact and are thus responsible for delivering a high standard of customer service. The duties of such staff will usually include:

- airport duties and coach transfers
- hosting regular welcome meetings
- maximising the sales of excursions and days out on offer at the resort(s)
- dealing with complaints and solving problems
- clinic and police station visits when required
- guiding company excursions
- taking part in entertainment days and evenings
- ensuring all paperwork, health and safety checks and accounts are accurate and meet deadlines
- ensuring all information books and boards are kept to a high quality and are always up to date.

Resources

In addition to the comprehensive list provided for Unit 3, the following websites will be of use:

* www.statistics.gov.uk
* www.baa.co.uk
* www.bhx.co.uk
* www.manchesterairport.com
* www.liverpooljohnlennonairport.com
* www.london-luton.co.uk
* www.grandukholidays.com
* www.contiki.com
* www.wallacearnold.co.uk
* www.shearingsholidays.com
* www.cosmostourama.co.uk
* www.leger.co.uk
* www.insightvacations.com
* www.titanhitours.com
* www.orient-express.com

UNIT 5

Tourist attractions

Introduction

Tourist attractions have the power to draw visitors to a destination, so they have a vital role in the UK travel and tourism industry. This unit, which has links to unit 1, offers you an opportunity to examine what contributes to the success of tourist attractions. You will find that they are often pivotal for enticing visitors by providing amusement, entertainment and education. Indeed, without a range of good quality attractions, many tourist destinations would struggle to survive.

How you will be assessed

For your assessment, you will need to investigate *two* contrasting UK visitor attractions and identify and describe the factors that contribute to their success. One attraction should be from the private sector and one from the public or voluntary sector.

What you need to learn

* ownership, funding and management operations at visitor attractions
* enhancement of the visitor experience through technological developments
* the importance of visitor and traffic management
* evaluation of the popularity of visitor attractions.

Types of tourist attractions in the UK

Attractions, by definition, have the ability to draw people to them and they are often the main motivation for travel. If you think about travelling to a destination, what is it that makes it worth visiting? The beach? The rollercoaster rides? The shopping? Are these all examples of tourist attractions? In local town leaflets and tourist board brochures you will often find tourist attractions listed under the 'places to visit and things to do' section. A tourist attraction can therefore be described as any facility or event which draws visitors to that particular place.

The following definition is one that the national tourist boards of England, Northern Ireland, Scotland and Wales use:

> [A place] *where it is feasible to charge admission for the sole purpose of sightseeing. The attraction must be a permanently established excursion destination, a primary purpose of which is to allow public access for entertainment, interest or education; rather than being a primary retail outlet or a venue for sporting, theatrical, or film performances. It must be open to the public, without prior booking, for published periods each year, and should be capable of attracting day visitors or tourists, as well as local residents.*

Using this definition, a questionnaire is forwarded to each attraction annually in order to gather data regarding the number of visitors they receive, admission charges, type of ownership and seasonal opening times. This data is published annually in July and can be found on the Staruk website, www.staruk.org.uk (the official website of the UK Research Liaison Group, which is made up of representatives from the tourist boards and the Department of Culture, Media and Sport).

✷ REMEMBER!

It is important to recognise that some built attractions were not originally intended for tourism purposes. Examples are churches, stately homes, industrial sites, railways, reservoirs and factories. Also, attractions are not necessarily purpose-built or human-made places. They might be areas that occur naturally, such as rivers, coasts, forests and hills.

Theory into practice

As a group, think of examples of tourist attractions in your local area, such as museums or an art gallery. You may even have a local zoo or a famous landmark such as a castle. Also as a group, gather together leaflets and brochures for as many local attractions as you can and design a poster to display.

Key terms

Natural attractions incorporate landscape features of the countryside found in mountains, forests, coastlines, lakes and waterways, national parks, areas of outstanding natural beauty and heritage coasts. **Purpose-built attractions** include sites such as theme parks, indoor arenas, cultural and heritage centres, purpose-built venues and major shopping centres.

Natural attractions

It was not so long ago that the countryside was considered to be unsafe to visit. Throughout history, mountains and mountainous areas have been seen as frightening, barbaric wastelands and barriers to other lands. Well into the eighteenth century, writers were describing the mountains as places where dragons and evil spirits lived!

How differently we see things today. Areas once thought of as threatening are now some of the most popular places to visit. Many people use their holidays or spare time to visit our countryside and enjoy a wide variety of recreational pursuits there.

The countryside allows for all kinds of 'passive' pursuits, such as picnicking, reading, watching sports, sunbathing, or just sitting in the car to view a scenic landscape. More 'active' pursuits include walking, mountain climbing, riding horses, cycling, canoeing and sailing.

Landscape features, therefore, are often the very reason why some people like to visit the countryside. You may be fortunate enough to have a park, garden, river or wood near to where you live. Many people enjoy travelling into a larger and sometimes a wilder expanse of the countryside. There is no doubt that water always attracts many visitors. Rivers, streams, lakes and

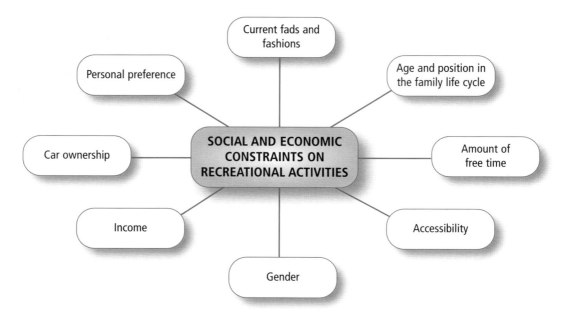

Figure 5.1 Social and economic constraints on recreational activities

reservoirs can provide the backdrop for an interesting and refreshing visit.

Recreational pursuits in the countryside can, however, be dependent upon social and economic constraints, as outlined in Figure 5.1. These constraints will influence a person's ability to travel and visit places.

Using a car to travel to the countryside is still the most popular method of transport. It is convenient and offers a great deal of flexibility. However, a certain amount of disposable income and free time is needed for these visits to be possible. The ability to travel freely into the countryside and visit many beautiful places is further enhanced by the opening up of accessible rights of way.

Land protection and conservation

There are many forms of land protection and conservation. These are often introduced to preserve the landscape as well as making it accessible for all of us to visit. We shall now look at some of these important measures.

Coastlines

Mainland Britain is an island with many miles of beautiful coastline (see Figure 5.4 on page 172). Some of the coastline is considered special enough to warrant protection by being designated as a Heritage Coast. There are currently 43 in England and Wales. Scotland has a different system of Preferred Conservation Zones.

Heritage Coasts were initiated in 1972 with the aim of protecting coastlines of special scenic and environmental value from undesirable development. The National Trust owns many of these designated coasts. Heritage Coasts are a non-statutory designation but are instead defined by agreement with the relevant maritime local authorities and the Countryside Agency which oversees their management and administration. These coastlines not only provide stunning scenery and footpaths for walks – they are also habitats for all kinds of birds and animals. Some coastal areas have also become significant for specific human-made facilities which in themselves have become attractions (e.g. lighthouses).

Areas of Outstanding Natural Beauty

An Area of Outstanding Natural Beauty (AONB) is designated for its landscape and scenic beauty – by the Countryside Agency in England, by the Countryside Council in Wales, or by the Scottish Natural Heritage in Scotland (where an AONB equivalent is known as a National Scenic Area).

Classification of interesting walks

The Ramblers' Association puts together interesting facts and advice on walking in the country. These are the main categories of promoted routes and long-distance paths.

National trails

These are nationally recognised trails in England and Wales designated and managed by the Countryside Agency or the Countryside Council for Wales. They include some of the best-known routes in Britain, passing through some of its most beautiful countryside and areas of great historic interest. They are all waymarked using the standard acorn symbol (Figure 5.2).

Long-distance routes

These are the Scottish equivalent of national trails, designated by Scottish Natural Heritage and managed by the local authorities through which the routes pass. They pass through countryside of exceptional beauty and interest and are waymarked by the thistle symbol (Figure 5.3).

Recreational routes

In addition to the nationally recognised trails, there are many more waymarked routes, usually created with the involvement of local authorities and with the help of local ramblers.

Figure 5.2 The acorn symbol for a national trail

Figure 5.3 The thistle symbol for a long-distance route

1 On a map, locate the positions of the following famous walks: the South Downs Way, the North Downs Way, Offa's Dyke path, the South West Peninsula coastal path, the Cleveland Way, the Pembrokeshire coastal path, the Pennine Way and the West Highland Way.
2 Cycling is a popular pastime in the countryside. There are many cycle routes that attract locals and visitors to a variety of areas. Find out about Sustrans and the National Cycle Network. Do any of the cycle routes coincide with footpaths?
3 British Waterways is a public corporation which manages and cares for more than 3200 kilometres (2000 miles) of canals and rivers in England, Scotland and Wales on behalf of the British people. Use the British Waterways website (www.britishwaterways.co.uk) to find out more details on their work. What are their current projects?

An AONB can cover many types of land use, including towns and villages. Most of the areas are privately owned. An AONB usually has special funding to help promote good management and sustainable development.

One AONB, the Malvern Hills, consists of a north–south ridge that is often described as a miniature mountain range. It is situated approximately 50 kilometres (30 miles) south-west of Birmingham. The rocks that make up the hills are some of the oldest on Earth, having been formed some 600 million years ago. The hills were designated an AONB in 1959 so that the landscape could be conserved and protected for the nation's interest.

The highest point of the Malvern Hills is the Worcestershire Beacon which is at 425 metres. The summit gives breathtaking views of the pastoral farmland patchwork of the Severn Vale. On a clear day you can see the Cotswolds. Tourists have flocked to Malvern since the early 1800s. Today it is popular with day-trippers who mostly travel

Figure 5.4 A view of Britain's coastline

from the Midlands. The town of Great Malvern holds events and festivals celebrating the town's cultural heritage.

Sites of Scientific Special Interest

An AONB is not necessarily an area with high nature-conservation value. This is in contrast to Sites of Special Scientific Interest (SSSI). There are over 4000 SSSIs in England alone, covering around 7 per cent of the land area. These sites are generally felt to be internationally important for their wildlife and geology. English Nature administers SSSIs, with the aim of preserving and protecting the natural heritage of the land by controlling development, pollution and climatic problems. SSSIs include wetlands, heathlands, beaches, remote moorlands and rivers.

National Parks

In 1872 the Americans designated Yellowstone as their first National Park. Owned and run by the state, the status of a National Park was designed to protect and conserve the land from unwarranted development.

In the UK, such parks were established in 1949 within the provision of the National Parks and Access to the Countryside Act. Today there are twelve parks, the most recent additions being the Norfolk Broads, set up by a special Act of Parliament in 1988, and the New Forest and the South Downs proposed in June 2004 (see Figure 5.5). In Scotland, Loch Lomond and the Trossachs

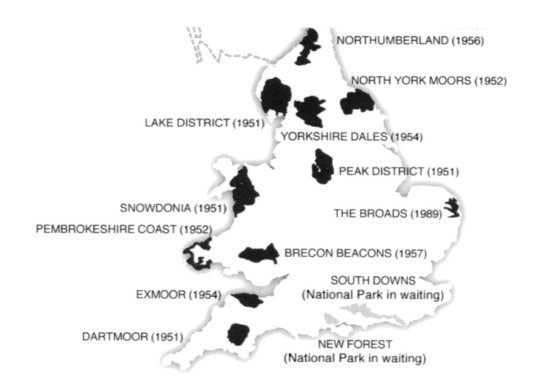

Figure 5.5 National Parks in England and Wales

LOCATION	DESIGNATION YEAR	DESIGNATION ORDER	AREA (HA)	POPULATION	VISITOR DAYS (MILLIONS PER YEAR)
Breacon Beacons	1957	10th	135 144	32 000	7
Dartmoor	1951	4th	95 570	29 100	4
Exmoor	1954	8th	69 280	10 645	1.4
Lake District	1951	2nd	229 198	42 239	22
Northumberland	1956	9th	104 947	2 200	1.5
North York Moors	1952	6th	143 603	25 500	8
Peak District	1951	1st	143 833	38 100	19
Pembrokeshire coast	1952	5th	62 000	22 842	4.7
Snowdonia	1951	3rd	214 159	26 251	10.5
Yorkshire Dales	1954	7th	176 869	17 980	9
The Broads	1989	11th	30 292	5 500	5.4

Figure 5.6 National Park general statistics

were included in 2002 and more recently the Cairngorms in 2003. The website of the Council for National Parks has more information (www.cnp.org.uk).

National Parks have two main purposes that were updated in the 1995 Environment Act:

✳ to conserve and enhance the natural beauty, wildlife and cultural heritage of the parks

✳ to promote opportunities for public understanding and enjoyment of the special qualities of the parks.

Figure 5.6 shows general National Park statistics, including visitor-days per year. Unlike the parks in America, National Parks in the UK are not state-owned. Much of the land belongs to private individuals and companies such as the Forestry Commission, the Ministry of Defence, water/utility companies, the National Trust, and English Nature.

Constructed and purpose-built attractions

Constructed and purpose-built attractions are often the easiest ones to think of because you might have visited some of these – especially ones within easy reach of where you live.

Purpose-built attractions are those places to visit that have been planned to entertain and make a profit (e.g. Alton Towers), or to educate (e.g. the Natural History Museum).

There are, of course, many constructed sites that were built not for entertainment or education but for other purposes. Cathedrals and abbeys were built for religious purposes, but today they can be tourist attractions too – think of York Minster, Lincoln Cathedral and Fountains Abbey. Other examples include castles that were built to protect against invaders, palaces that were homes for kings and queens, and mansions or stately homes for the rich landowners of the past. Today they are amongst some of the most popular tourist attractions for domestic and overseas visitors alike.

Constructed and purpose-built tourist attractions can be sub-divided into these seven categories:

* entertainment sites
* sports and recreation
* theme parks
* culture and heritage
* shopping centres
* wildlife centres
* parks and gardens.

There is sometimes a blurring of the categories. You might visit an historic monument that is set within beautiful gardens and may also have important cultural links. For example, Hampton Court was home to the kings and queens of Britain since the time of Henry VIII. Today, it is one of the most famous visitor attractions in the country. Although perhaps better known as a Tudor palace, with its magnificent buildings, it also has world-famous gardens and a priceless art collection.

We will now look at each of these seven categories in more detail.

Entertainment sites

What do we mean by an entertainment site? Surely all attractions could be said to provide some form of entertainment? For the purposes of this definition, entertainment sites cover indoor arenas, nightclubs, discos, concert halls, theatres, cinemas, bowling alleys and arenas.

Many towns and cities use their entertainment sites as a major selling message to attract visitors. Newcastle, Sheffield and Liverpool all boast good nightlife, bars and clubs, whilst London is popular for its West End theatres.

Sports and recreation

Leisure centres have traditionally catered for locals and visitors alike. Facilities are varied to cover a range of interests and community needs.

An increasing number of local authority centres have had their management transferred to charitable trusts in order to enable greater investment and development.

As facilities are updated, there has been an increase in the number of fun pools with flumes and chutes. Many gyms have been upgraded, often at the expense of traditional squash courts. This is in response to a change in sporting trends. There has also been a move away from sauna and solariums towards more modern spa and beauty treatments along with a growing interest in health, fitness and well-being. There has been a decrease in the provision of sunbeds by local authority facilities and leisure centres due to health and litigation concerns. Facilities today have also had to change in response to new water treatment technology and health and safety regulations and recommendations.

Many leisure centres hire out their large sports halls to companies or groups for non-sporting occasions – perhaps a dog or cat show, or an antiques or computer fair. They may also rent out rooms for conferences, meetings and wedding parties. This helps to bring in extra revenue and use facilities during the quieter or off-peak periods.

Spectators at leisure centres or sporting events are also important for raising extra revenue (e.g. a swimming gala competition using the swimming pool or European cup football match at a large football stadium). These events can attract domestic and overseas visitors. A large football stadium may hold some 50 000 spectators. This will bring income not only from ticket sales, but also from the sale of food and merchandised products.

Major sporting venues include the National Cycling Centre in Manchester, the Aintree racecourse near Liverpool, the Wembley Stadium in London, the Millennium Stadium in Cardiff, Hampden Park in Glasgow, and the Don Valley Stadium in Sheffield. Many events are held at sporting arenas, such as the Commonwealth Games at the City of Manchester Stadium.

Theme parks

Love them or hate them, theme parks are popular tourist attractions in the UK. They attract visitors from a national catchment as well as having regional appeal.

Theme parks try to incorporate unusual rides and shows to differentiate them from the other parks. For example, Valhalla at Blackpool Pleasure Beach is currently the world's biggest dark ride and was officially opened in 2000. The Pleasure Beach also likes to be called 'The Entertainment Adventure Capital of the World'.

Theme parks are typically situated within a two-hour journey from large centres of population. They tend to market themselves to families and groups. Legoland in Windsor (Figure 5.7) analysed its visitor statistics and found the following:

* The average party size is four people.

* Half of all parties include 3- to 5-year-olds, just ahead of parties including 6- to 8-year-olds.

* A quarter of all adult guests are in their thirties.

* About three-quarters of guests are on a day trip.

* A quarter of guests are resident in the local area, London or Middlesex. One-third are residents elsewhere in the south-east of England. One-third are from the rest of Britain and 6 per cent of guests are from overseas

* Two-thirds of guests are first-time visitors.

Figure 5.7 Legoland

Legoland is able to retain visitor numbers by continuous developments and upgrading of the park. Recent years have seen an increase in visitor numbers from 1.49 million in 2000 to 1.63 million in 2002. Although these numbers sound high, it must be remembered that theme parks generally have only seasonal opening times (between Easter and October), and will therefore not receive visitor income for the late autumn and winter months.

The corporate hospitality market is also vital for many parks. They make use of the business and education sectors to supplement their income. Some parks adopt a theme (e.g. Camelot), whilst others use their ever more frightening rides and live shows to entice the general public.

Many theme parks now have hotels attached to them. This enables guests to have easy and direct access to the park, sometimes allowing early entry and breakfast or party treats with mascots. Blackpool's Big Blue Hotel is new and, due to its success, the owners are already planning an extension which is due to open in June 2005.

Theory into practice

On a map of the UK, locate five theme parks that have not been mentioned in this section. Find out about their most famous rides.

Culture and heritage

The word 'heritage' is an increasingly popular description of tourist attractions. Some people think that it is used as a good description for marketing history. It certainly gives an attraction more interest and possibly a stronger appeal to a different target market. You can probably think of at least one 'heritage' centre or attraction close to where you live. Here are some examples:

* Rochdale Arts and Heritage Centre
* Margrove Heritage Centre, Cleveland
* Almond Valley Heritage Centre, Livingston
* Honeywood Heritage Centre, Carshalton.

Of course there are many tourist attractions which use heritage as their *theme* but not necessarily in their title – for example, Jorvik, Ironbridge Gorge, Robin Hood and Beamish. Heritage is often linked to the culture of a destination, so often towns and cities market themselves as centres of cultural heritage. Consider York, Chester and Carlisle – all have fascinating cultural and historical connections. In fact, by promoting the culture and heritage of an area the regional tourist boards are helping to contribute to a strong regional identity.

The UK has a rich and diverse culture. Clearly, this is the main reason why so many overseas tourists choose to visit this country. Our culture and heritage are often the main motivation to visit. The royal family is often given as the main reason to visit the UK by overseas tourists. Buildings associated with the royal family become important attractions – such as Buckingham Palace, Kensington Palace, the Diana memorial fountain, and Balmoral. Events linked to the royal family and pageantry also become important – such as the Queen's birthday parade or the changing of the guard.

Think it over ...

The European Union conducted a survey of young people during the late 1990s and asked them to name the first five things that sprung to mind about the United Kingdom. The top responses were: the BBC, the royal family, the Beatles, Shakespeare, and London. If this survey were repeated today, what do you think would be the top five responses?

It is important to remember that our culture is constantly evolving and that the elements of our modern country contain plenty of reasons why someone would wish to visit. Many towns and cities have realised that they can use their culture and heritage to attract visitors on city or short breaks.

More cultural and heritage breaks in the UK

Here are some examples of promotional texts used for town/city breaks available in the UK. It is interesting to note the reasons given for making each place sound unique and worth a visit.

Glasgow *does not follow fashion, it creates its own. The people of Glasgow are unique – renowned for their banter, they add a charm to the city that cannot be replicated. Glasgow offers the visitor culture, entertainment and an abundance of stylish bars and restaurants. Reasons to visit include: the cathedral, Scottish Maritime Museum, Charles Rennie Macintosh Museum, City Chambers, The Lighthouse, theatres, art galleries and football.*

Bradford *has claims to be the UK's first industrialised inland tourist destination. Attractions include the Victorian industrial heritage and Haworth, the home of the Bronte sisters. It also has one of the most popular provincial museums in the country – the National Museum of Photography, Film and Television. It has IMAX, one of Britain's largest cinema screens, and new digital interactive galleries. It is home to over 200 Asian restaurants and successfully sells curry-themed short breaks.*

Chester *was founded by the Romans 2000 years ago. The picturesque old city boasts a Roman amphitheatre, medieval half-timber buildings, unique two-tiered rows, a central cross, ancient churches and a cathedral that is 900 years old. It also has a famous racecourse and riverside.*

Nottingham *promotes heritage open day events in celebration of England's architecture and culture. Nottingham Castle holds a re-enactment of life during the Wars of the Roses. The former Museum of Costume and Textiles is open to the public along with the*

Museum of Nottingham Life at the Brewhouse Yard Museum that offers free behind-the-scenes tours of the different aspects of putting a collection together.

CASE STUDY

Liverpool – European City of Culture 2008

By 2008, many of the visitors arriving in Liverpool will step off one of the ocean-going liners that will dock at the new cruise terminal at the Pier Head. From there, it will be a short walk to visit Liverpool's world-famous waterfront which is a World Heritage Site along with the Albert Dock – home to a fantastic collection of museums and visitor attractions. They will then be able to jump on board a tram and travel into the redeveloped city centre, with an extra two million square feet of retail and leisure space, including top department stores and designer boutiques. In the evening, they may watch a pop concert at the Kings Dock arena, before enjoying a drink at one of the city's growing number of bars and clubs.

Winning the title is not just about attracting tourists. A large section of the population of Liverpool will be involved in the 1000 events that will form part of the year, bringing people together and strengthening links between communities. In 2008, Liverpool will be an international visitor destination, with people flocking to Merseyside and £2 billion being pumped into the local economy.

Source: Liverpool, Capital of Culture 2008 – A Thrilling Voyage, Sir Bob Scott, Chairman Liverpool Culture Co.

1 **Identify all the different tourist attractions mentioned and list them under each attractions category.**
2 **Discuss the benefits of being designated a European Cultural Capital. Are there any negative points to achieving such a status?**

Shopping centres

Shopping is big business and many people love it. Large shopping outlets now draw hundreds of people daily. After Saturday, Sunday is the second most popular day to shop. In 2004, Sunday trading commemorated its tenth anniversary.

Many shops, such as Harrods and Hamleys, have become tourist attractions in their own right. Large shopping outlets such as Bluewater in Kent, Trafford Centre in Manchester and Cribbs Causeway near Bristol provide all the purpose-built facilities and services you could possibly want from a shopping experience. These outlets may also feature bowling alleys, cinemas and countless restaurants. Factory outlets also draw visitors who search for bargains in stores offering 'designer goods' at reduced prices.

CASE STUDY

Peak Village

The following text is an example of an advertisement for one of the popular factory shopping outlets, Peak Village. Notice how it uses the other tourist attractions in the vicinity as an added incentive to visit.

Discount factory outlet shopping at its best, with major brand names at 30–70 per cent off high street prices. Where else will you find Grenson, Adidas, Farah, French Connection, Cat, Ben Sherman, Lee Cooper, Regatta and Karrimor discounted all of the time?

Nestling in the Derbyshire Dales between the tourist towns of Matlock and Bakewell lies Peak Village, home to 26 shopping outlets and a variety of shops and attractions usually found only in large towns. It's leisure shopping at its best with a 200-seater restaurant and coffee shop.

Peak Village is on the edge of the world-famous Peak District National Park which receives over 6 million visitors every year. The centre is easy to find whichever way you are travelling.

Peak Village is only one mile from Chatsworth House and is a must for coach and group organised visits. Fifteen free coach spaces and 400 free car parking spaces make Peak Village the perfect place to spend the day. There are disabled parking spaces, drop curbs and ramps for easy access. Wheelchair hire is available at no cost.

Peak Village is part of a marvellous day out for the family. On top of great value-for-money shops, restaurant and coffee shop, and the Wind in the Willows attraction, Peak Village has free entertainment most weekends.

On a map, locate the factory shopping outlet nearest to where you live. Make a list of everything that is on offer, such as shops, extra facilities and services. Compare your list with that for Peak Village.

Wildlife centres

The present-day interest in environmental issues cannot be overestimated. Consequently, many tourist attractions have incorporated conservation and preservation policies into their philosophies.

Although the traditional zoo is still popular (e.g. Chester and London), many new wildlife attractions attempt to make us think about our environment and appeal to our conscience. A good example of this is the South Lakes Wild Animal Park in Dalton in Furness, Cumbria. The park is privately owned and run, but supports directly and works closely with many conservation organisations throughout the world. An average of 15 per cent from every admission fee is donated directly to wildlife conservation and protection in the wild. The park is now the largest fund-raiser for the Sumatran Tiger Conservation in the world (Figure 5.8).

The mission statement for South Lakes Wild Animal Park has the following aims:

* to provide a facility for the maintenance and propagation of wildlife – in particular the breeding and protection of species that are under threat or no longer exist in their natural environment

* to inform and educate park visitors, students and the general public about the role of the park, wildlife, the environment and other matters, using the resources of the park and elsewhere

* to contribute towards the conservation of the natural environment and the species therein

* to generate an income to fulfil the above and for the provision of facilities in the park for the enjoyment and cultural enrichment of the population at large and the people of Furness in particular.

Theory into practice

Find another example of a mission statement from a zoo or wildlife park. Compare their work with that of South Lakes Wild Animal Park.

Figure 5.8 The endangered Sumatran tiger

CASE STUDY

The Deep based in Hull

The Deep (Figure 5.9) was designed to educate visitors about the world's oceans and to provide entertainment. The work of the Deep is ongoing and a new phase is expected to be completed by the summer of 2005.

Figure 5.9 The Deep in Hull

The attraction asks important questions for the visitor to consider regarding the environmental issues surrounding the many uncharted spaces in the depths of the sea.

Its funding reflects the fact that it is pivotal to the regeneration of the town of Hull itself. Creating local jobs and new infrastructure, it has helped the area gain national and international recognition while at the same time bringing income into the town. Funding was broken down as follows:

- Millennium Commission – £21.48 million
- European Regional Development Fund – £7.7 million
- Single Regeneration Budget – £3.8 million
- Yorkshire Forward – £3.37 million
- Kingston upon Hull City Council – £5.4 million
- University of Hull – £0.8 million
- Garfield Weston Foundation – £0.25 million
- private finance – £2.66 million.

1 **What was the total funding of The Deep?**
2 **How useful are tourist attractions in educating the public?**
3 **How do tourist attractions attempt to give serious study to important ethical, environmental or spiritual issues?**

> **Key term**
>
> **Regeneration** is the renewal of an area through development and investment.

Parks and gardens

The beauty of parks and gardens attracts overseas and domestic visitors. Gardens are particularly favoured by special-interest and coach groups and, generally speaking, do not appeal to teenagers. However, school and college trips often take place where aspects of parks and gardens can be linked to the curriculum. Some garden attractions such as Kew Gardens in London and the Royal Botanic Gardens in Edinburgh are just two examples of places schools and colleges are encouraged to visit through the provision of educational packs and details supplied to

teachers. Talks and tours of the gardens are provided.

You have probably heard of the Eden Project, based in Cornwall, which opened fully to the public at Easter 2001 (Figure 5.10). Although purpose-built, it has large biospheres that look like huge bubbles sunk into the hillside. These are, in fact, large conservatories.

The area was developed in an old clay pit and became a tourist attraction even as it was being built. In 2002 it received nearly two million visitors and has even starred in a James Bond film.

The owners believe that their role is to educate and conserve many interesting and exciting flora and fauna to bring pleasure to the public at large. However, it is a unique botanic garden where the focus is on plants that are useful to humanity, including many rarely found in other gardens.

Figure 5.10 The Eden Project in Cornwall

Tourist attractions linked to the running of events

Strictly speaking, events do not fall under the definition of a tourist attraction you read at the start of this chapter. However, events are often used by attractions to draw visitors to that place. Examples are flower shows at Hampton Court Palace and music festivals at Leighton Hall near Lancaster. Visitors from overseas will often use events as the main focus for their visit.

Consider the success of the Commonwealth Games in Manchester in 2002 that attracted one million spectators to the Manchester venues and was watched by a worldwide TV audience of one billion people. The Manchester Games has acted as a catalyst for attracting inward investment, and over the next 10–15 years it is hoped that Manchester will attract a total inward investment of more than £400 million. Games such as these also leave behind the valuable legacy of new or improved facilities. London is currently bidding for the 2012 Olympic Games. With every successful bid comes government-backed funding and a great deal of prestige.

The City of Manchester Stadium is one such example. It once held the main athletics and rugby competitions and now hosts football matches as it is the home ground for Manchester City Football Club. Other physical improvements were made, including the development of Piccadilly Plaza and gardens and the Ancoats Urban Village.

A taster of events in the UK

The following list gives a selection of popular events occurring around the country:

* Cowes Week – a prestigious annual, week-long sailing regatta attracting a thousand yachts, 8000 sailors and 100 000 spectators

* Great British Beer Festival – more than 400 real ales from British brewers and 200 beers from around the world, including the competition to find the Champion Beer of Britain

* Edinburgh Festival – theatre, dance and opera

* Notting Hill Carnival – colourful floats and costumes in the streets, and soul, calypso, reggae and garage music entertaining more than two million people

* London Marathon – an annual event with 30,000 competitors from all over the world ranging from some of the top runners in the world to the fun and amateur runners raising money for charities

* Glastonbury – large music festival run each year on farmland in July.

Theory into practice

1 Draw up a list of events in your region. Use a calendar and try to find one event for each month of the year.

2 Find out who organises at least two of your local events.

Ownership, funding and management operations

From your studies in unit 1 you will know that there are many sources of funding and ownership within the travel and tourism industry. How an attraction is funded depends on whether it operates in the private, public or voluntary sector. This in turn will affect how an attraction is managed and operated. Naturally, every attraction will have its own aims and objectives, but these, too, are influenced by how it is funded and operated. Figure 5.11 shows some examples.

Ownership and funding

Private sector organisations

The travel and tourism industry now tends to be dominated by the private sector, which operates attractions ranging from the small and medium-sized to the very large.

Key term

The **private sector** includes organisations that are owned and operated by private individuals or groups of individuals. It is privately funded, possibly by shares traded on the stock market. The main target is to make a profit for the shareholders.

Private sector organisations exist in a number of forms. These include the sole trader, owned and run by a single individual (also known as sole proprietor). In contrast, a private limited company is set up as a body that is separate from its owners. The company shares are usually held by a small number of individuals (they may be family members). The owners of a private limited company may decide to sell their shares on the stock market, whereby they would become a public limited company.

Public limited companies (PLCs) are owned by the general public who have shares in the company. The company will need to make a profit in order to pay shareholders a share of the profits. This is known as a dividend. For example, the Tussauds Group own Alton Towers and Warwick Castle.

The principal private sector funding sources are:

* entrance fees

* sales and retail outlets

* advertising revenue

* personal finance – savings (in smaller privately funded attractions)

SECTOR	MAIN TYPES OF ATTRACTIONS	REASON FOR OWNERSHIP
Private or commercial	Theme parks	To make a profit
Public, government, local authorities	Galleries, museums, leisure centres	Education, public access, increased opportunities for the local community
Voluntary, trusts, charities	Heritage centres, steam railways, wildlife conservation centres	Conservation, education, protection

Figure 5.11 Ownership of attractions

* bank loans (including mortgages on property and overdraft facilities)
* share investors
* sponsorship
* grants from Defra (Department for Farming and Rural Affairs), DCMS (Department of Culture, Media and Sport), the Countryside Agency, English Nature, the Forestry Commission and English Heritage.

* DCMS (Department of Culture, Media and Sport)
* National Lottery
* tax (from residential and commercial properties)
* European Union
* sponsorship
* Arts Council
* Sport England.

Theory into practice

Visit the website of the DCMS at www.culture.gov.uk. Follow the visitor attractions link and research up-to-date information on the newest visitor attractions.

CASE STUDY

Trafford Centre

The Trafford Centre in Manchester lists its objective as to maintain a first-class service to customers through:

* the accurate interpretation of customer needs
* the prompt delivery of meaningful advice relating to those needs
* provision of sincere committed high standards
* continuing care of the customer's interest
* the regular monitoring of factors affecting the provision of customer service delivery
* communication of the quality objectives to all employees involved with the provision of services on behalf of the centre.

Find out how *two* other visitor attractions in the private sector aim to fulfil their objectives. Either visit an attraction or check its website.

Public sector organisations

Public sector organisations gain funds from local or central government. Local tourist attractions such as museums, art galleries and leisure centres are examples of these. Public sector organisations are generally run to provide a service for both the local community and visitors from out of town.

The principal public sector funding sources are:

* entrance fees
* sales and retail outlets
* advertising revenue

CASE STUDY

English Heritage

English Heritage is a non-governmental public body, established by the National Heritage Act 1983 and sponsored by the Department of Culture, Media and Sport. It is the government's official adviser on all matters concerning the conservation of the historic environment and is the major source of public funding for rescue archaeology, conservation areas, and repairs to historic buildings and ancient monuments.

It is responsible for over 400 historic properties in the nation's care. Among these are many places which feature as landmarks in England's history. Visits to English Heritage properties not only generate income which is invested into their conservation work but also make a substantial contribution to the national economy via domestic and overseas tourism.

The sites provide exemplars of the best conservation practice, enabling standards to be set in visitor management, educational provision and site interpretation, whilst acting as local centres to increase awareness of English Heritage as a whole and to build local commitment to the conservation of the heritage.

Source: Adapted from English Heritage, *Tourism Facts*, 2002

Find out how many properties belong to English Heritage in your county.

Voluntary sector organisations

Voluntary sector organisations generally exist for the benefit of their members and often have charitable status. They do not necessarily set out to make a profit, but they do need to make a surplus which can help with the running of the organisation and ultimately benefit its aims and objectives. Most voluntary organisations tend to have a conservation and/or education objective, but they can vary in size and purpose. For example, the National Trust owns many properties of significant historical importance. Other examples of voluntary sector organisations are the Royal Society for the Protection of Birds (RSPB), and regional art galleries and workshops.

The voluntary sector relies heavily on an army of volunteers who are sympathetic to their cause. These volunteers are essential in the development and support of many voluntary sector organisations such as heritage centres and steam railways. They can help reduce labour costs for these attractions by assisting with the selling of memberships, patrolling as wardens around landscapes or properties, and assisting with construction and decoration of exhibits.

The principal voluntary sector funding sources are:

* membership subscriptions
* entrance fees
* advertising revenue
* sales and retail outlets (including mail order products and services usually included in catalogues and website advertising)
* National Lottery
* gifts, donations and bequests
* grants from the local authority, Countryside Agency and Arts Council.

CASE STUDY

National Trust (NT)

The National Trust (www.nationaltrust.co.uk) was founded in 1895 by Sir Robert Hunter, Canon Hardwicke Rawnsley and Miss Octavia Hill. Concerned about the impact of uncontrolled development and industrialisation, they set up the trust to act as a guardian for the nation in the acquisition and protection of threatened coastlines, countryside and buildings. The NT now cares for over 248 000 hectares of countryside in England, Wales and Northern Ireland, 600 miles of coastline, and over 200 buildings and gardens.

The objectives of the National Trust are achieved by practical conservation, educational activities, and encouraging millions of people to visit and enjoy NT areas.

The NT is an independent charity which relies completely on the support and generosity of its supporters. It employs 4000 full-time and 4000 seasonal staff. However, it also relies on some 38 000 volunteers who contribute two million hours of their time.

The NT has many long-term programmes in place in order to educate about the importance of the environment and preserve the heritage for future generations to enjoy. The trust invests over £160 million a year in the nation's environmental infrastructure and works with over 40 000 companies, including 2000 specialist conservation businesses.

Source: Adapted from National Trust, *What We Do*

1 **Find out the NT membership fee for a family of four.**
2 **Find out the equivalent membership fee for the Royal Society for the Protection of Birds (RSPB).**
3 **From Internet research, compare the aims and objectives of these two voluntary sector organisations.**

Funding opportunities

As you have seen, tourist attractions are funded through many different sources. Naturally, raising funds is essential to any organisation in order that it can function and carry out its objectives to the full. There are a variety of funding opportunities, some of which can apply to more than one sector. It is important to realise that even though tourist attractions fall into these different sectors they can still work together and co-operate on many projects, such as joint marketing and funding initiatives.

Tourist attractions now rely heavily on *secondary spending* by the public. This is the source of funds received from visitors at attractions from their retail outlets, shops, cafés, restaurants, etc. It also includes funds from corporate hospitality, educational visits and events. These 'extra' products and services provide a diverse mix of funding opportunities which can often sustain the tourist attraction and in some instances may be the main motivation for people to visit. Consider, for example, a medieval banquet at a stately home, an award winning café in a museum or a Christmas craft fair at an historic house.

Marketing and promotion of tourist attractions

Marketing is all about helping an organisation to achieve its aims and objectives. It concerns the whole organisation and not just one aspect of it.

There are many definitions, but the British Institute of Marketing defines marketing as 'the management process responsible for identifying, anticipating and satisfying customer requirements profitably':

✻ *identifying* – who the customers are and their needs

✻ *anticipating* – trying to predict and forecast the needs and wants of the customers

✻ *satisfying* – providing precisely what the customers want

✻ *profitably* – making a profit.

An attraction with a non-profit objective may still make a profit and then use the extra funds to develop and sustain the attraction.

The function of marketing is therefore essential in attracting and retaining customers for all tourism businesses and not just tourist attractions.

Marketing concepts

What is the target market (potential customers)?

Market research takes many forms and helps tourist attractions to know their customers and understand what their customers want and need. This helps a tourist attraction to plan and coordinate future strategies.

What product or services are we to deliver?

A *marketing strategy* is put together by the tourist attraction. This is a plan or programme designed specifically for the tourist attraction that gives guidelines to staff on the proposed marketing work to be carried out.

Marketing strategies are usually updated annually. However, marketing is not a static, one-off process. It is vital that tourist attractions stay up to date. Customers can change, they will be influenced by media, fashions, new fads and tastes. It is essential for a tourist attraction to review its marketing strategy regularly to ensure that it is not missing new clients, that it is still targeting the right type and number of visitors and adapting its product/service in accordance with the demands of customers.

How shall we price the product/service?

Consider cash discounts, promotional pricing, seasonal discounts, 'bogof' promotions etc.

> ### Key term
>
> **'bogof'** stands for 'buy one, get one free', which is an increasingly common marketing initiative.

How shall we deliver the product/service?

Market research here is vital so that customer satisfaction is always achieved. Information gathering on the current product or service shows any improvements that could be made.

Persuading the customer

This can be through a mix of advertising, brochures/leaflets, direct mail campaigns, sponsorship deals, sales missions at exhibitions and workshops, promotional campaigns on radio and/or television, newspaper coverage and public relations (PR).

CASE STUDY

National Museums Liverpool

National Museums Liverpool is England's only national collection based outside London. The group consists of eight venues that are home to varied collections covering everything from social history to space travel, entomology to ethnology, dinosaurs to docks, arts to archaeology. The collections are designed to encourage everyone, regardless of their background or ability, to discover and enjoy the arts and sciences.

The Marketing Department and Public Affairs Department devise and coordinate all media activities and campaigns for National Museums Liverpool. They develop and implement promotional campaigns for the different venues with their individual exhibitions and events programmes. The public is informed by means of leaflets, posters, street hoardings, adverts on sides of buses, the local and national press, radio and television.

A detailed guide along with leaflets on events is sent to the local Tourist Information Centres, libraries and hotels. They are also mailed out to people on their mailing list free of charge.

There is ongoing market research into visitor attitudes towards different aspects of the museums' facilities.

Public relations provides news for press stories including photo shoots and interviews with curators and films of artefacts. The press can influence public opinion, so it is crucial that all communications with the media be well managed and planned.

There are tourism initiatives linking together with other tourism bodies to promote their joint tourism products and services (e.g. Wirral Consortium, British Tourist Authority and hotels).

The group takes part in exhibitions/trade fairs, such as attendance at Wirral History Fair, Southport Flower Show, British Travel Trade Fair, Wirral County Show, Great Days Out in the North West and World Travel Market.

1 **Use a search engine to find the website of National Museums Liverpool.**
2 **In how many languages is the site available?**
3 **What are the eight venues covered by National Museums Liverpool?**

Staffing of tourist attractions

The roles and numbers of staff at a tourist attraction obviously depend on the type and size of the organisation. Who owns an attraction, along with how it is funded, also influences the staff numbers and structure of the organisation. Employing and training good staff is vital to any tourism business. The attitudes and behaviour of staff can help visitors enjoy their visit. A good experience at a tourist attraction will result in word-of-mouth recommendations and repeat visits.

For tourist attractions, staffing costs are likely to be their highest expenditure. Attraction managers must therefore ensure that they employ the right staff and that they receive appropriate training.

Jobs in attractions are generally seasonal. They may also have irregular hours and be extremely demanding – such as dealing with customer complaints and problem-solving.

Generally, organisational structures help to provide a clear framework for the channels of responsibility and lines of communication. Different departments will be able to see levels of responsibility, which helps with the process of decision-making and at the same time allows individuals to see where they fit in. Figure 5.12 shows an example of a staff organisational chart at Rheged, the Upland Kingdom Discovery Centre in Penrith, Cumbria.

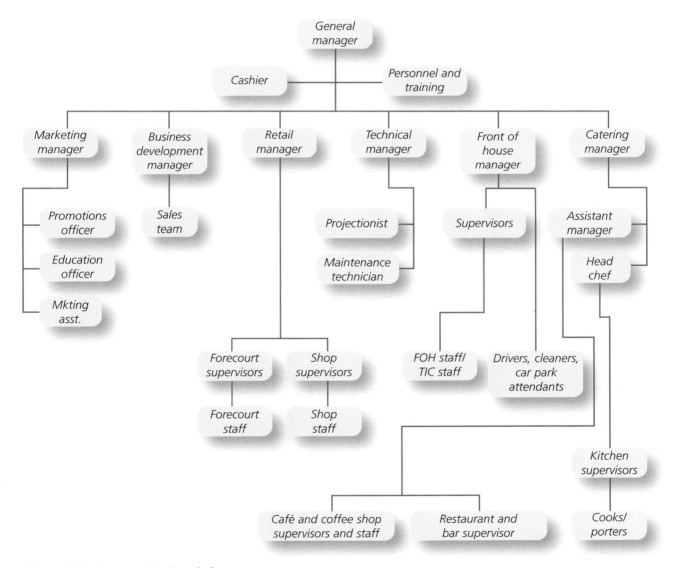

Figure 5.12 An organisational chart

CASE STUDY

Figure 5.13 The London Eye

London Eye

The following job descriptions reveal the type of skill requirements to work in a major tourist attraction, the London Eye, which is situated on the south bank of the River Thames, opposite Big Ben (Figure 5.13). The jobs come under Guest Services (Customer Assistants).

Ride and Queue Assistant: *Working outside, no matter what the weather, this role is vital to ensure guests are welcomed into a safe environment. Providing guests with relevant information, you will need to be extremely safety conscious and confident in dealing with large groups of people.*

Retail Assistant: *Responsibilities include assisting guests with their enquiries and offering them help when choosing a unique gift from retail areas. Experience in cash handling, sales, visual merchandising and stock control are a real advantage.*

Admissions Assistant: *Responsibilities include assisting guests with various enquiries, processing their bookings via a computerised till system and proactively selling guidebooks to enhance the guests' experience. If you have knowledge of computerised booking systems this would be advantageous.*

The positions are full-time and require working five days out of seven on a roster basis. This will include evenings, weekends and bank holidays, so will suit those who want to avoid the routine 9.00 to 5.00 job!

What you'll bring to the job

- *At least one year's proven experience within a customer service environment*
- *Common sense in difficult situations*
- *Delivery of first-class customer service at all times*
- *A proven record of working well in a team*
- *A positive attitude towards your job, customers and colleagues*
- *Fluency in spoken English (other European languages and/or Japanese would be useful).*

What we offer

- *Competitive salary*
- *Membership of the company profit sharing plan*
- *Complimentary tickets to attractions like Madame Tussauds, Warwick Castle and Alton Towers*
- *Discounted British Airways flight packages.*

1 **Find out who owns the London Eye.**
2 **Does the company own any other tourist attractions?**
3 **What is meant by a 'competitive salary'?**

Employment figures collected in a survey in 2002 found that 2744 visitor attractions in the UK accounted for a labour force of around 111 000 people. Of these 56 000 were paid employees (full- or part-time) and around 55 000 were volunteers.

Health, safety and security

For tourist attractions to operate successfully, consideration must be given to the health, safety and security of staff and visitors. Occasionally, the media picks up on accidents that have occurred at certain attractions and the news stories can have a damning impression on future visitor numbers – along with the possibility of closure through contravening health and safety regulations.

Following the Hillsborough disaster in 1989 where 96 people died during an FA Cup semi-final between Liverpool FC and Sheffield Wednesday FC, a report was published by Lord Justice Taylor highlighting both the failings and inadequacies of stadiums catering for large numbers of visitors. As a result, new guidelines and regulations were recommended, such as tighter controls on seating provision, crowd control measures, policing, and first-aid facilities and personnel.

Accidents and injuries can occur anywhere and at any time. The newspaper article in Figure 5.14 highlights how vigilant fairground ride supervisors need to be.

An organisation that has effective health, safety and security policies can not only save lives and prevent injuries but can also maintain a very positive public image – a good grounding for successful repeat visits.

Risk assessments

In order to assess any potential risks and prevent them from happening, a tourist attraction should conduct a risk assessment. This is a useful way of checking and ensuring that appropriate measures are in place ready to deal with any incidents that might occur. Staff should be trained on a regular basis in order to establish first-class responses to emergency situations.

Holiday boy killed at fairground

A HORRIFIED pensioner saw his four-year-old grandson thrown to his death from a fairground ride in Spain.

Little Jack Innes was too small and slid under the safety bar as he was whirled around above the ground on a ride known as The Octopus at the fair at Torrevieja, south of Alicante. Paramedics tried to save him but he died within minutes. The boy was staying with his grandparents, Mr and Mrs Anthony Innes, who live at Torrevieja, a favourite retirement spot with Britons. He had been taken to the fairground on the front as a Sunday evening treat.

Jack's grandfather was on the ride with him. But as it spun round the G-force pushed the little boy forward. He was about 12ft above the ground when he slid beneath the safety bar and was hurled more than 20ft on to concrete. Felix Perez, 51, who owns the three-year-old ride and has worked all his life in fairgrounds, said last night: 'I'm absolutely destroyed. I can't explain how I feel for the parents of this boy.

'This attraction is meant only for adults, not for children of four years old. But I didn't notice this man take his little grandson on with him.'

Jack's parents, who live in Four Marks, near Alton, Hampshire, were told of the accident by his grandparents early yesterday.

Figure 5.14 News of an horrific accident (Source: *Daily Mail*, 7 September 1999)

Site management and equipment

Preparation of a site for tourists to visit is often a mammoth task and one that is not usually seen by the public. Maintenance programmes should not be so intrusive that they spoil the experience for the visitor. Imagine walking around an art gallery as someone is emptying rubbish bins and trying to polish the floor. Your perception and enjoyment at that particular place would be marred by the noise and activity of workers.

However, at many tourist attractions such as theme parks, cleaners and maintenance staff are often clearly visible. Where an attraction is receiving thousands of visitors each day during the peak season it will need to have good systems in place. Fast-food outlets, ice-cream vendors etc. have the potential to create a great deal of litter, so the provision of adequate bins and cleaners is essential. In some fast-food outlets the turnover of visitors is so high that, without constant cleaning and tidying, the site would soon become unworkable or unhealthy.

In order to prevent problems with both the site itself and its equipment there needs to be in place a system of planned and corrective maintenance.

Planned maintenance

This is a system of scheduled activity – regular servicing of rollercoaster rides, testing and checking equipment, cleaning and lubricating machines etc. Some tourist attractions close during the winter period and set aside a time to replace and update equipment.

Inspections and checklists are used by many tourist attractions. For example a local leisure centre will have weekly, monthly and yearly checks on different areas of the centre.

Corrective maintenance

Corrective maintenance is necessary when problems occur suddenly – a ride breaks down or a storm causes structural damage, etc.

Security

Security for staff and visitors is important. Many of the larger tourist attractions incorporate:

* closed-circuit televisions (CCTV)

* fire-alarm warning systems

* access control systems

* public-address (PA) systems

* barriers with a guard at the entrance to prevent unwanted visitors

* lost-and-found designated areas

* first-aiders and first-aid rooms

* emergency callout procedures

* food preparation and hygiene systems.

The site team should be well trained and drilled to handle any emergency. All attractions will have an *emergency plan*, consisting of procedures that have been agreed and written down for all staff to follow. In some instances, these procedures will be prepared with the assistance of the police, fire brigade and the health and safety executive.

Health and safety legislation affecting tourist attractions

The following are some of the important Acts and Regulations that are relevant to tourist attractions. What might be called the most important piece of legislation is the Health and Safety at Work Act 1974. The Act covers the health and safety of employers, employees and visitors to an organisation. The Act sets out to:

* secure the health, safety and welfare of people at work

* protect people other than those at work

* control the keeping and use of dangerous substances

* control the emission into the atmosphere of noxious or offensive substances.

Other relevant Acts and Regulations include:

* Data Protection Act 1998

* Disability Discrimination Act 1995

* Control of Substances Hazardous to Health Regulations 1994 (COSHH).

CASE STUDY

Madame Tussauds

The following is the Good Practice statement issued by Madame Tussauds, London:

'The quality and safety of our attraction is of the utmost importance and therefore a considerable amount of time and effort is spent on making all visits a safe and fun experience. The Tussauds Group who own Madame Tussauds in London is Europe's leading operator and developer of visitor attractions.'

Below is a summary of the main health and safety requirements covered by Madame Tussauds.

- *Legal requirements*. Under the Health and Safety at Work Act 1974 many regulations relate to work activities, the principal requirement being to undertake risk assessments to identify 'hazards' and assess the risk under the Management of Health and Safety at Work Regulations 1999.

- *The health and safety policy*. This is signed by the Chief Executive Officer for the Tussauds Group and the Divisional Director.

- *Risk assessments*. These are undertaken by all departmental managers with reference to the work activities that they manage. Risk assessments are reviewed annually.

- *Insurance*. Madame Tussauds is covered by public liability insurance.

- *Safe practice*. For the Spirit of London Ride (a mechanical passenger ride in the basement and ground floor levels of Madame Tussauds) and fairgrounds and amusement parks, guidance on safe practice is adhered to. The guidance develops good practice concerned with the overall safety management of attractions with emphasis on risk assessment, management of safety and the inspection stages known as design review, assessment of conformity to design,

initial test and 'in-service' annual inspection for all rides. The rides are also subject to outside independent inspection engineers to ensure the safety and integrity of the ride for each season.

- *Attraction operation*. During the hours of public access there are competent and qualified staff on duty in all areas. A nominated Site Controller is present with a Duty Manager available at all times.

- *Food safety and hygiene*. The food units operate in accordance with the Food Safety Act 1990 and are regularly inspected by the local Environmental Health Department.

- *First-aid facilities*. A dedicated team of qualified first-aiders is on hand at all times.

- *Emergency planning*. An emergency plan has been prepared to cover incidents such as fire, bomb, ride/attraction disaster.

- *Fire safety*. There is a fire danger management system (fire alarm) with sprinkler and portable fire extinguisher equipment in all areas. All are inspected and maintained to the highest standards. There is also a Fire Safety Manual. A full programme of fire safety evacuation drills and staff training are undertaken regularly.

- *Security*. A security team patrols the site. The team is also trained to deal with any emergency incidents that occur on site.

1 **Visit a local tourist attraction.**
2 **Design a health and safety notice for that attraction. You should make your notice eye-catching. It can be A4, A5, folded or unfolded – the design is your choice. However, it must be informative for the general public.**
3 **Find out who is responsible for health and safety at that attraction. Try to obtain a copy of the health and safety policy.**

Developments in technology

Today, new and established tourist attractions are keen to encompass modern technologies so that they can meet the needs of all customer types. Tourist attractions use technology to enhance:

* exhibits
* booking and communication systems
* guiding and interpretation
* access.

The many developments becoming commonplace include exhibits, rides, simulation and virtual reality, photographic and sound effects, robots and animated figures, laser- and computer-generated equipment, and cyber cafés.

Exhibits

With many people now having direct access to computers, game consoles and interactive television channels, it is imperative that tourist attractions move with the times. Even established museums such as the Science Museum in London incorporate interactive galleries.

Rides
Rides are becoming more and more adventurous, with visitors being pushed to extremes of endurance.

Simulation and virtual reality
The real-life world in computer games and virtual reality is now expertly brought to visitors in many tourist attractions. Rock Circus (sister to Madame Tussauds) in the Trocadero in London has fascinating robotic figures, lasers and videos. The London Planetarium has a virtual-reality trip through the gallery of astronomy and space travel.

Photographic and sound effects
A visit to Dynamic Earth in Edinburgh takes the visitor inside the planet and tours round the globe. The wind, rain and thunder all come crashing together in the rainforest display. The power of the waves is demonstrated by the authentic sound and movement of large sail sheets.

Robots and animated figures
Many attractions use robots and animated figures. Madame Tussauds feature many moving waxwork models as well as the traditional static ones. Legoland incorporates Lego Racers, which is a computer-simulated attraction involving interactive software and state-of-the-art touch-screen technology. It is based on the Lego Media PC game.

Laser and computer-generated equipment
Laser zones are now becoming increasing popular with visitors of all ages. They are set in semi-darkness. The idea is that you try to laser shoot other players. The game is played with lighting effects, fog and heart-pounding music. Players compete against each other and the interactive arena tags players when their reactions are too slow.

Cyber cafés
Many attractions incorporate their own cybernet cafés allowing visitors to make easy and quick Internet access.

Booking and communication systems

Today, tourist attractions must understand the need to provide a variety of methods of purchasing tickets and finding information.

* Credit card bookings enable bookings via the telephone and Internet. Sometimes attractions charge an extra fee to the customer for booking this way.
* Fast-track tickets are booked and paid for in advance, giving a specific time to return to gain instant entry to a site or ride.

CASE STUDY

Segaworld and Dynamic Earth

Segaworld at the Trocadero Centre, Piccadilly, is Europe's first interactive theme park, opened in 1996. Sega is one of Japan's major games groups. Segaworld sells itself as the largest one-stop entertainment house in Europe. It is housed in an enormous building covering six floors. It boasts white-knuckle rides, state-of-the-art video games, hi-tech exhibitions, screen entertainment and themed restaurants. Unlike the more traditional theme parks, Segaworld combines virtual reality and computer graphics to create an interactive world where you can experience all the thrills of adrenalin-fuelled trips in front of one screen. Naturally as it is an indoor theme park it is not affected by the adverse British weather.

Dynamic Earth is based in Edinburgh and is part of a major regeneration plan using former industrial land at the end of the Royal Mile. The project attracted funds from the Millennium Commission and houses a permanent exhibition and education centre which is designed to give the public better understanding of the processes that have shaped the Earth. The tour of the site takes approximately 90 minutes. There are ten zones that take the viewer through different facets of the Earth, beginning 15 000 million years ago with the Big Bang theory. Volcanoes, earthquakes and dinosaurs all feature along with a spectacular reworking of a tropical rainforest where rain and thunderstorms occur every 30 minutes. Dynamic Earth also features extra products and services available that include a soft play area, food, shop, toilets, provision for non-English speakers, disabled access, subscription to an Internet newsletter, conference facilities, children's parties, season tickets and group tickets.

1 **Use a search engine to find the websites of both Segaworld and Dynamic Earth.**
2 **Compare and contrast the new technologies at both tourist attractions. Decide which one you would prefer to visit.**

* Electronic point-of-sale (EPOS) systems are particularly useful with retail and catering outlets, saving time and enabling efficient auditing and tracking of payments.

* Integrated computer systems are vital for quick and easy communication between staff. They are particularly good for video conferencing and links between heads of departments who may not be in the same town or even the same country.

* A website is essential for any tourist attraction, to advertise and communicate with the public. Some web pages will give a virtual tour and offer a variety of sources for bookings. Contact details are also given, allowing potential customers to email requests and find the answers to specific enquiries.

An example is the booking system at Legoland. Tickets can be booked in advance by telephone, with the customer paying by credit or debit card. The booking system is linked to a credit card clearance system. This saves customers queuing when they arrive. Computer software has been designed specifically for the park. There is also a call centre with operators answering queries and taking bookings. When all lines are busy, the call is automatically diverted to an overflow system.

Legoland has also implemented a quick address system, whereby the telephone caller is asked for his or her postcode and the operator then checks the correct address against details on a database. Any ticket purchased is encoded for a specific day. When a customer puts this ticket through the main park turnstile, the number will be matched against either the purchase that day or against the advance booking entry. This admission system is linked to the accounts system which tracks payment for tickets.

These procedures in place at Legoland are now typical of those at other large attractions.

Guiding and interpretation

How an attraction uses guiding and interpretation techniques can benefit the visitor experience by providing greater understanding and enjoyment.

The traditional way is to make available a printed leaflet or a booklet with maps or directions to follow around a site. These may be in large print and/or Braille, and might be available also in audio.

Signposting can be a useful way of simply directing visitors around a site. It can be made more enjoyable by using techniques such as 'Follow the dinosaur footprints ...' or by providing coloured lights on the floors to create different sections and direct members of the public around a specified route. Signposts can be useful for imparting vital information such as environmental implications at a wildlife park.

Touch screens are a newer way of accessing information at an attraction. Touch screens can be particularly useful for members of the public who are unable to use keyboards.

Guided tours may be available with audio-visual aids or simply with a human guide. Some guides will be dressed up in keeping with their surroundings (e.g. in Victorian/Edwardian dress at Beamish). At Worcester's Commandary, visitors might come across a guide dressed as a pikeman, giving advice to visitors on how to fight with Oliver Cromwell's Roundheads.

Self-guided tours may be enhanced with press-button telephones at various points (e.g. at Britannia Yacht moored in Edinburgh). Another common technique is to have tape recordings that are started when a visitor steps on a mat that has an electrical micro-switch concealed underneath, or when the visitor steps through an invisible light beam. Self-guided tours are popular with visitors because they allow the enjoyment of an attraction to be taken at their own pace. It is possible also to go back to particular areas of interest and repeat favourite sounds and sites.

Viewing galleries give the visitor a variety of better views to enjoy the attraction, in a safe and controlled environment. There are platforms in the White Scar caves in Yorkshire where you can thread your way around the beautiful paths to see spectacular sites of stalagmites and stalactites.

Demonstrations provide an excellent educational opportunity for many visitors. They can watch – and sometimes participate in – particular arts and crafts such as pottery, painting and restoring, or even learn the finer points of tiling and thatching.

Access

Given the variety of tourist attractions available today, it is important that all types of people be catered for. A swimming pool may use a pool hoist to help visitors into the pool. In buildings, lifts and escalators are now commonplace. Computer touch screens and automatic doors make for easier entrance to and exit from a building. Large retail outlets also provide Shopmobility chairs for visitors who are unable to walk long distances.

An example is the Bluewater shopping complex in Kent, which provides access and facilities for all kinds of visitors. They have a Shopmobility scheme whereby, for an annual membership of £10, users can have unrestricted access to manual wheelchairs whenever they visit the shopping centre. If they wish to use an electric wheelchair this is provided for an extra £2. They also provide disabled car parking in all of their main car parks. There is help on hand also for blind or partially sighted people – a way-finding system is in operation which is free of charge.

At Bluewater, as at many other visitor attractions, there is a range of baby-care rooms, changing facilities, bottle warming, and a private mothers' feeding area. The use of high chairs and space for pushchairs is made available along with a daily crèche.

Visitor and traffic management

Visitor and traffic management are vital for the success of a tourist attraction. It's obvious that the position of a natural attraction cannot be altered. The Lake District National Park, for example, regularly receives 15 million visitors each year, and the majority arrive by car. This can cause problems with road congestion, pollution and overcrowding. The policymakers and transport planners try to ease traffic problems by providing suggested routes. They also suggest alternative modes of transport and encourage different times of the year to visit.

Theory into practice

Research the visitor and traffic management policies used in the city of Bath. How do they prevent overcrowding?

Links with transport providers

The Lake District National Park Authority has devised a set of leaflets to encourage car users to think about using different forms of transport. Entitled 'Give the driver a break ...', the leaflets outline various modes of transport – buses, trains and boats – and show prices. This is all linked to suggested itineraries for places to visit (see Figure 5.15).

Give the **driver** a break...

Discover the fruits of Grizedale Forest

Lake District
carefree
your route to a relaxing day out

Providing sustainable transport in your National Park

'Go Ape' on a high rope course, take idyllic forest walks or escape on your mountain bike in this inspirational setting.

For a great CareFree summer day out...

Cross Lakes Shuttle

From Bowness use the Cross Lakes Shuttle service, a combination of ferry and Mountain Goat minibus. and take the ferry (10.50) from Pier 3 (see timetable for later services). Across the lake at Ferry House the connecting Cross Lakes Shuttle bus (11.10) will take you, via Hawkshead, to Grizedale Forest (11.40). Nestling between Coniston and Windermere, this internationally famous forest sits in a superb location, a land that escapes some of the tourist hurly burly. It is ideal for families, walkers, cyclists or those who just want to picnic in a beautiful, inspirational setting. Idyllic forest walks, stunning views, cycle routes (and cycle hire) suitable to all levels of fitness and the chance to 'Go Ape' on a unique high rope course are just a few of the forest's temptations.
If you intend to walk up to the highest point (Carron Crag 317m) for the splendid views, remember to wear suitable footwear and clothing and to take food and drink as the weather can change quickly on the higher hills.

After a throughly enjoyable and exhilarating day the Cross Lakes Shuttle bus will be at the visitor centre (15.45 - see timetable for later services) ready to return you via the ferry to Bowness.

Wood carvings in Grizedale

Figure 5.15 A leaflet promoting the no-car day out

At the same time, the leaflets give an explanation of the necessity of providing sustainable transport within the park. Here is what the Grizedale leaflet says:

'The Lake District National Park Authority is committed to the promotion, development and use of sustainable travel choices to reduce the adverse impacts of motor traffic on people, the environment and landscape character.

'Giving the driver a break helps to give the environment a break – so relax and escape from the pressures of driving and finding parking spaces and help to preserve the beauty and tranquility of England's finest landscape.

'Together with our partners, Cumbria County Council, Friends of the Lake District and Stagecoach, we have produced this series of 'Give the Driver a Break' CareFree itineraries – ideas for great summer days out in the National Park without using your car. You'll find lots to do without travelling by car, and you can easily explore many of the Lake District's best loved places by bus, boat, bike or boot.

'Travel by steam train, open-topped bus, traditional timber launch, or even take a bike for the day from one of the many hire outlets. ...

'A little effort from a lot of people can have a big effect – help to protect this special corner of England.'

Some other tourist attractions have worked hard to encourage visitors to consider new and alternative methods of travel. Hadrian's Wall, a World Heritage site, produces leaflets and web information giving a directory on the best ways to travel to the wall. They detail the bus services that run from May to September and give further information on the reduced winter service. These services are made even more popular by the addition of guides who join some of the bus journeys to add to the visitor experience. Guided walks are also recommended with a list of rambling experts willing to join walkers. Information is also given on suggested self-guided walks to the wall, giving Ordnance Survey map information. Links with public transport are also highlighted, with suggestions from both the east and west, giving connections from the Metro Centre in Newcastle and the coastal railway stops at Maryport and Ravenglass in Cumbria. Both website and promotional leaflets also provide public transport information contact details. By providing such a wealth of detail, they actively encourage visitors to leave their cars and promote the use of public transport.

Many natural attractions have visitor/study/field centres attached to them. These purpose-built facilities are placed in areas which best suit the natural attraction. They fulfil an appropriate role, such as an education workshop, shop or café.

Purpose-built attractions are designed deliberately to draw from large numbers of the population. The catchment area of theme parks is generally within a two-hour drive time. A small local museum, in contrast, may mostly be of interest to its local community and a few interested enthusiasts.

The impact of tourism

Large numbers of visitors, no matter how they arrive, can have an enormous impact upon an area. How an area copes with the influx depends on where it is situated and how an attraction is managed. The management and operation of an attraction must take into consideration the way people attempt to visit the site along with putting in place measures to deal effectively with large groups of people.

When studying tourism you will read of the *positive* and *negative* tourism impacts. You may also sometimes see them discussed as the *costs* and *benefits* of tourism. They are often divided into environmental, social and economic effects, but these categories are interrelated. Figure 5.16 shows positive and negative impacts of a tourist attraction.

Today, many tourism policymakers believe it is essential to maintain our valuable natural and human-made resources. This has led to a growth in *sustainable tourism* (alternative terms are green tourism, eco-tourism, responsible tourism, etc.). The aim is to provide new tourism development that does not create negative impacts and will not impinge in a negative way on the community or the environment.

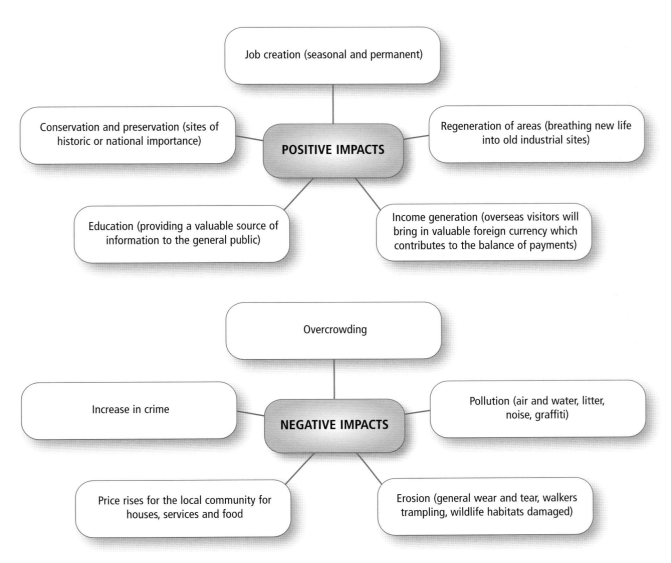

Figure 5.16 A tourist attraction has positive and negative impacts on its environment

One tourist attraction with such principles is the Earth Centre in Doncaster, opened in 1999 on the site of the former Cadeby Colliery. The attraction promotes sustainable development and, through a series of exhibitions and activities, asks visitors to look at how they live and how it will impact upon the environment now and in the future.

Land use and facilities nearby

Many issues surround the amount and type of land needed for tourist attractions, particularly for those that are new and looking for appropriate areas to establish themselves. They may wish to locate close to large centres of population, or position themselves near to local hotels and transport facilities. This gives good opportunities to develop a visitor base and possibilities for joint initiatives. Good links to infrastructure and services may be vital in reducing the costs of development and running. The availability of parking facilities is often at a premium – if visitors find it difficult to park they may move on and visit elsewhere.

New attractions will usually require planning permission from the local authority. The government sometimes actively encourages new developments on land that was formerly an industrial site or areas considered to be in a regeneration zone.

Giant's Causeway

The Giant's Causeway in Northern Ireland was formed about 60 million years ago. It has about 40 000 six-sided columns of basalt stones formed from volcanic actions (Figure 5.17). Local folklore says the columns were fashioned by the legendary giant Finn McCool as he tried to stride across the sea to the Hebridian island of Staffa where a lady giant lived.

The causeway is Northern Ireland's most popular tourist attraction. The area covers 71 hectares and has been designated a World Heritage site, a national nature reserve, an area of outstanding natural beauty and an environmentally sensitive area.

The National Trust is the owner and manager of the site and promotes it cautiously, concentrating on four specific aspects of the site:

- landscape and nature conservation
- education
- interpretation
- visitor safety and management.

The NT aims to provide sustainable access to the Giant's Causeway. Its objectives are:

- to conserve the natural processes, flora and fauna of the area

Figure 5.17 The Giant's Causeway in Northern Ireland

- to maintain the public footpaths and where appropriate establish new ones
- to educate and inform the public about the site
- to remove existing unsightly structures and prevent new ones.

Source: Adapted from *The Making of the Causeway*, National Trust

With a partner, draw up a suitable Code of Conduct for visitors to the Giant's Causeway.

Making use of industrial land

Many attractions now make good use of land that was previously used for industry.

- The Tate Gallery in Liverpool is one of the largest galleries of modern and contemporary art. It is situated in a converted warehouse that is part of the historic Albert Dock (completed in 1846).
- Wigan Pier Heritage Centre is situated in two restored eighteenth-century warehouses.
- The Leeds and Liverpool Canal passed through the pier area and the warehouses belonged to the British Waterways Board.
- The Eden Project in Cornwall is built on the site of an old clay pit.
- The Don Valley Stadium is built on land formerly used by the steel industry.

1 **With a partner, find out the significance of brown- and green-field sites in relation to planning developments. You could start by checking with your local authority.**
2 **In a small group, research regional examples of attractions being built on old industrial sites. Use a map to highlight what you find.**

Queue control techniques

A combination of well thought out entrances, exits, car parks and routing helps to alleviate queues. Some attractions adopt speed restrictions and speed ramps to create a safer environment for both visitors and staff.

Enabling visitors to flow around a system can reduce stresses on local roads and access areas. Busy attractions will ideally consider peak-time traffic issues and will tailor their opening times so that they do not coincide with these peak periods. Busy theme parks may also adopt queue entertainment for visitors while they wait. Generally, good IT systems and more sales booths can assist with quicker selling of tickets and movement of visitors.

One of the most popular forms of queue control is timed-ticketing or fast-track tickets. Many of the theme parks operate such schemes and find the organisation provides smoother running of the parks.

Some smaller visitor attractions may also find themselves in difficulty if their visitor numbers exceed the capacity of the attraction. Hill Top and the Beatrix Potter Gallery in Hawkshead have found ways of dealing with the huge number of visitors it receives. The 'Hill Top' house is quite small and the exhibits fragile. Therefore, during school holidays and at other peak periods visitors must buy tickets which stipulate a specific time for entry, so controlling the number of visitors entering the house at any one time. It also allows the owners to keep a check on who is entering and at what time. Members of the public cannot just simply turn up and wander in.

Accessibility

Access is concerned not only with the routes for entry and exit, but also with how accessible the attraction is for *all* types of people. Accessibility covers physical access and the price of entry (see Figure 5.18).

An attraction can be physically difficult for people to visit for a number of reasons. Personal transport opportunities might be limited, and a person's mobility restricted. Opening times might be inconvenient.

Tourist attractions today try to overcome these issues by adopting good public transport links, and by adhering to the Disability Discrimination Act to provide good physical access for everyone.

Tourist attractions organise their opening times and charges according to visitor type or age. A common structure is: adult, child (5–15), under-5s, senior citizen, student.

> ### Key term
>
> The term often used to indicate a reduced price for certain categories of customer is **concessions**.

Some attractions offer discounted family tickets and group prices. Very often teachers in charge of a school party, carers or guides gain free entry. Many attractions operate joint ticket facilities, which encourage people to visit a sister organisation or another attraction nearby.

Often tourist attractions will change their pricing structure for different seasons. Many regional tourist boards actively encourage the tourist attractions within their areas to extend their opening seasons outside the period Easter to October. Some attractions may therefore operate a limited winter opening scheme, usually with reduced hours. For example, Dartmouth Castle opens from April to October daily from 10 a.m. to 6 p.m., but from November to March is open from Wednesday to Sunday from 10 a.m. to 4 p.m.

Clearly, it is not viable for some attractions to remain open during the winter months when so few visitors are received and daylight is restricted. Some of the larger attractions are able to remain open all year, such as London Eye. Many attractions find it useful to close for a period of maintenance and repairs.

Accessibility for visitors with specific needs means some attractions offering facilities such as an induction loop, braille or large-print options, guides or assistants around a site, wheelchair access, parking close by, and accessible toilets. Some museums provide level access to entrances, along with lifts. Reading Museum provides tactile signage throughout its building, whereby each separate gallery has its own icon to help visitors

EXCELLENCE IN ENGLAND TOURISM FOR ALL AWARDS

Seven tourism establishments have been voted as the most accessible in England for people with disabilities and will go forward for the tourism 'Oscars' – the Excellence in England Tourism Awards 2004, in association with Enjoy England. The winner was announced at the national awards ceremony at Kensington Palace in London on 22 April 2004 at which our Chairman, Sir William Lawrence was present. The seven finalists' details as given by Visit Britain are:

Norfolk Cottages
www.norfolkcottages.net
Newly converted farm buildings in rural East Anglia. The four cottages nestle around a secluded paved courtyard with colourful scented flowers in raised beds. An extra-warm swimming pool and Spa are both accessible by hoist. Subtle adaptations to the cottages allow every member of the party to enjoy their stay, and an extensive range of disabled living aids is available free.

Poole's Cavern and Buxton Country Park
www.poolescavern.co.uk
This two million year old cavern has opened up to a wide audience, with an audio system throughout for hearing and visually impaired visitors, and there are high resolution controllable underground CCTV cameras to give people the opportunity to stay in touch with family members exploring the

caves. They have a new fully accessible website, and an extension to their wheelchair path has just been announced.

National Portrait Gallery
www.npg.org.uk
There is a dedicated Access Officer to deliver their commitment to embracing the needs of all disabled visitors to the gallery and archive. Emphasis is placed on providing disabled access to regular events such Sign Language tours. There are portable induction loops and sound-guide with portable neck loops for the hard of hearing.

Manchester Art Gallery
www.manchestergalleries.org
A recent £35m grant has made all parts of the building physically accessible. The Gallery has been particularly innovative for visually impaired visitors with the development of a new tour with touchable artworks, a handling trail, audio-described events, a free sighted guide service and information in alternative formats.

Bladgon Farm Country Holidays in the South West
www.blagdon-farm.co.uk
Eight 4 and 5 star cottages, some with four poster beds, overlooking a lake. Extensive grounds include a fishing lake, play area, pet's corner and walks. Facilities include a bar/bistro, an indoor pool, with a hydrotherapy jet and

track hoist. Also facilities to assist visually and hearing impaired, and guests with learning difficulties and respiratory problems are well catered for, with an extensive range of equipment available.

Farming World
www.farming-world.com
A family-run farm in the South East, with a proven record of caring for those with special needs, including 'hands-on' sessions with some of the quieter animals; highly scented and textured plants known to have a calming effect on autistic children; and trained staff for signing and guided tours; integrated play for all children with mixed abilities.

National Coal Mining Museum
www.ncm.org.uk
The museum has made a substantial investment in facilities for the disabled, having acknowledged this as a potentially huge market. Huge barriers have been overcome in order to ensure that all areas are accessible, including travelling 140 metres underground in an old mining cage and exploring the hidden world of the coal face.

> **Stop Press**
> **The winner was the**
> **National Portrait Gallery**

Figure 5.18 The tourism 'Oscars'

find their way around the museum.

Many attractions now appreciate the benefits of providing information and assistance to non-English speakers. The City of Portsmouth provides

guides and leaflets in several languages such as French, German, Italian, Japanese and Spanish.

It is important to realise that tourist attractions are a dynamic component of the travel and tourism industry. They are continually changing and evolving. You should now be able to understand exactly what an attraction is and realise that one all-encompassing definition is quite difficult to give.

Theory into practice

1. Choose a tourist attraction and find out what products or services are provided for people with specific needs. The information may be in leaflets or brochures.
2. If possible, visit the attraction and draw a plan to show all the different forms of accessibility.

Assessment guidance

To complete Assessment Objective 3, you should research the importance of visitor and traffic management at each attraction. You may wish to draw plans of the attractions to show how visitors arrive and flow around each site.

Popularity of tourist attractions

According to the Department of Culture, Media and Sport:

'The UK's 6500 visitor attractions are at the very heart of our £76 billion tourism industry, with the top twenty major paid admission attractions accounting for 45 million visits alone in 2003.'

The popularity of visitor attractions can be judged on the number and types of visitor they receive. As you have seen, some attractions are not run on a commercial basis so that monetary gain or profit cannot then be considered a means to judge success.

Visitor numbers at popular attractions

Facts about UK tourism are displayed on a useful website at www.staruk.org. Visitor figures are calculated for major paid and free admission attractions (Figures 5.19 and 5.20). Data is drawn from the survey of Visits to Visitor Attractions, which includes data from attractions that provide visitor figures and give permission to publish their figures.

ATTRACTION	LOCATION	VISITS IN 2002	VISITS IN 2001
London Eye	London	4 090 000	3 850 000 (est)
Tower of London	London	1 940 856	2 019 183
Eden Project	St Austell	1 832 482 (est)	1 700 000
Legoland	Windsor	1 453 000	1 632 000
Flamingo Land theme park and zoo	Kirby Misperton	1 393 300 (est)	1 322 000 (est)
Windermere Lake Cruises	Ambleside	1 266 027	1 241 918
Drayton Manor family theme park	Tamworth	1 200 000 (est)	960 000 (est)
Edinburgh Castle	Edinburgh	1 153 317	1 126 680
Chester Zoo	Chester	1 134 949	1 060 433
Canterbury Cathedral	Canterbury	1 110 529 (est)	1 151 099 (est)

Figure 5.19 Major attractions with paid admission

ATTRACTION	LOCATION	VISITS IN 2002	VISITS IN 2001
Blackpool Pleasure Beach	Blackpool	6 200 000	6 500 000
Tate Modern	London	4 618 632	3 551 885
British Museum	London	4 607 311	4 800 938
National Gallery	London	4 130 973 (est)	4 918 985 (est)
Natural History Museum	London	2 957 501	1 696 176
Victoria & Albert Museum	London	2 661 338	1 446 344
Science Museum	London	2 628 374	1 352 649
Pleasureland theme park	Southport	2 000 000 (est)	2 000 000 (est)
Eastbourne Pier	Eastbourne	1 900 000 (est)	2 000 000 (est)
York Minster	York	1 570 500 (est)	1 600 000 (est)

Figure 5.20 Major attractions with free admission

Theory into practice

1 Using the staruk website, look up the latest visitor figures.

2 Compare and contrast these with previous years.

3 Who has made the biggest improvement? Why do you think this is the case?

CASE STUDY

European Tourism Conference 2004

The importance of thousands of visitor attractions came under the spotlight as the Secretary of State for Culture, Media and Sport, Tessa Jowell, gave the keynote address at the First National Conference of Visitor Attractions on 12 October 2004.

Owners and senior managers of visitor attractions, opinion-formers and tourism and heritage professionals were urged to sign up for the conference at London's Queen Elizabeth II Conference Centre. The conference was organised by the industry on a not-for-profit basis by the Association of Leading Visitor Attractions (ALVA), the British Association of Leisure Parks, Piers and Attractions, and the

Visitor Attractions Forum. It was supported by the Department for Culture, Media and Sport, VisitBritain and the Tourism Alliance. The event was developed around a number of key themes, including:

- the latest industry developments and opportunities for the sector
- evaluating strategies to stay one step ahead of competitors
- innovative marketing strategies to maximise tourism spending
- up-to-the-minute market research
- the expert views and analysis of key industry speakers.

The event coincided with the launch of VisitBritain and the National Tourist Boards' Visits to Visitor Attractions Survey of 2003, which lists visitor figures for nearly 3000 individual attractions and outlines the top-line trends by attraction category.

Source: Freely adapted from an article in Travel Daily News, 12 July 2004

1 Research the Association of Leading Visitor Attractions (www.alva.org.uk). What are its objectives? Who are its members and what benefits do they gain?
2 Obtain a copy of the latest Visitor Attractions Survey. Assess which attractions are the most successful year on year.

Factors influencing the popularity of attractions

Factors other than marketing, research and promotional techniques that can influence the popularity of a tourist attraction include:

* its features
* target groups
* customer service and staff training
* awards
* souvenirs.

Features

Generally the features of a tourist attraction are a combination of all its exhibitions, interactive displays and events (regular or ad hoc). Many attractions will also provide extra facilities and services that help to encourage all types of visitors and fulfil the needs of customers as much as possible (see Figure 5.21).

Providing seating around a site helps people who are unable to stand for long periods. Providing waste bins and litter collectors enhances the overall ambiance of an attraction – not many of us would be impressed to walk around a site where litter is blowing around or where toilets are blocked and appear to have been neglected.

Target groups

The types of visitor expected at an attraction will depend not only on the type of attraction itself, but also on where it is located, how easy it is to

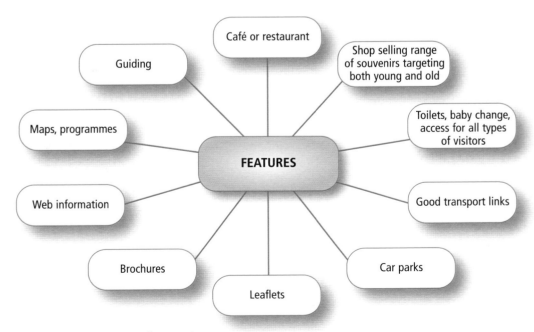

Figure 5.21 Features of a tourist attraction

reach, how close accommodation/other facilities are to the attraction, and how much it costs to visit.

One way of trying to distinguish between different groups of people for marketing purposes is the technique of *market segmentation*. There are four main ways in which markets are segmented:

* *geographical* – categorising people on the basis of where they live

* *demographic* – categorising people on the basis of age, sex and race

* *psychographic* – categorising people on the basis of their attitudes and opinions

* *behaviouristic* – categorising people in terms of their relationship with products (e.g. first-time buyers).

Key term

Market segmentation divides the potential market into groups having similar characteristics.

Generally, tourist attractions can identify the types of customer most likely to visit them. They can be drawn from the following:

* individuals
* couples
* families with young children
* families with older children
* senior citizens
* groups – school/college
* groups – special interest
* visitors with specific needs
* hospitality and corporate visitors
* overseas visitors.

Repeat visitors are important to a tourist attraction. If a tourist attraction can keep customers happy they may return. However, many attractions will need to offer new and exciting features so that visitors will have a reason to return. For example, museums and art galleries have changing exhibition programmes. Some attractions have guests or stage artefacts or paintings that are on tour. Themed or promotional events can also create new business as well as repeat visits. Examples are festivals, anniversaries, workshops, Christmas fairs and antiques roadshows.

Theory into practice

Copy out the following grid and complete it with the likely needs of each group in the family life-cycle.

Family life-cycle	Likely needs at an attraction
Small child (under 5 years)	Soft/safe environment to play in Other children to play with Parental assistance and guidance
Child (5–12 years)	New and interesting places to see and experience Other children to see and play with Parental guidance
Teenager	
Couple	
Family group	
Empty nester	
Senior citizen	Ease of accessibility into and around the attraction Company of others Plenty of seating and viewing galleries

---

Customer service and staff training

Meeting the needs of customers at a tourist attraction is achieved through the work of well-trained staff. Staff who display a good attitude and behave professionally create a good impression for visitors.

Good customer service leads to *customer satisfaction* leads to *appreciation of the staff* leads to *staff satisfaction*.

Many attractions display customer charters to indicate to the general public the terms and conditions of service that customers can expect from an attraction.

Awards

Raising the profile of a tourist attraction can influence the number of visitors. Some attractions have invested time and resources in applying for industry awards, such as England for Excellence and the Investor in People scheme. As you will have read, some areas are already designated a certain status, such as National Parks, AONBs, SSSIs, and Heritage Coasts.

There is also a special award for beaches. The Blue Flag scheme is operated by the Foundation for Environmental Education in Europe. Flags are awarded to individual beaches that meet criteria covering the quality of the water, the quality of the environment and how the beach area is managed.

Visitor Attraction Quality Assurance Service

VisitBritain (www.visitbritain.org) have introduced a Visitor Attraction Quality Assurance scheme (VAQAS). Designed to include a wide range of attractions, large or small, it is an assessment scheme whereby attraction operators can learn how to enhance their quality of operation and spread best practice within the attractions sector. An annual assessment is made by a quality assurance assessor who looks at the following areas:

✱ *pre-arrival* – including telephone enquiries, leaflet and website design

---

CASE STUDY

World Heritage sites – a status to be proud of

The World Heritage site list was established at a United Nations Educational, Scientific and Cultural Organisation (Unesco) conference in 1972, under the convention concerning the protection of world culture and natural heritage. Under the convention, the World Heritage committee promises to publish and keep up to date the *World Heritage List*.

The committee provides technical co-operation under the World Heritage Fund to enable sites to be safeguarded. Emergency assistance is also available where properties become damaged by disasters such as earthquakes and floods.

Naturally, World Heritage sites attract many tourists. Today there are 788 properties now inscribed on the *World Heritage List*, twenty-six of which are in the UK. Below are listed some of the UK sites along with their year of listing.

1986	Giant's Causeway and Causeway Coast
	Durham Castle and Cathedral
	Ironbridge Gorge
	Stonehenge
1987	Blenheim Palace
	City of Bath
	Hadrian's Wall
1988	Tower of London
	Canterbury Cathedral
1995	Gough Island Wildlife Reserve
1997	Maritime Greenwich
1999	Heart of Neolithic Orkney
2000	Blaenavon Industrial Landscape
2001	Saltaire, West Yorkshire
2003	Kew Botanical Gardens
2004	Liverpool – Maritime Mercantile City

Research the *World Heritage List* to gather information on one of the sites in the UK. Present that information to the rest of your class.

* *arrival* – including initial signage, car park and welcome and efficiency of staff

* *the attraction* – including range of content, quality of presentation and quality of interpretation

* *toilets* – including layout, maintenance and cleanliness

* *catering* – including layout and design, range, presentation and quality of the food, and appearance, attitude and efficiency of staff

* *retailing* – including design, presentation of merchandise and appearance, attitude and efficiency of staff.

Every assessment is followed by a debriefing and a formal report. Finally the attraction is awarded the accreditation 'Quality Assured Visitor Attraction'.

Souvenirs

Tourism is about having an experience – one that may be unique and not easily replicated. For many visitors, therefore, the souvenir becomes the tangible part of the holiday experience, and in some cases can be the very reason for taking the trip in the first place. Many tourist attractions sell a range of souvenirs to entice and reinforce the visitor experience. This also becomes a vital source of secondary spending by visitors and helps an attraction to make valuable extra income.

Think it over ...

When did you last visit a tourist attraction? What souvenirs did you buy? How much did you spend? Did you travel deliberately to buy a souvenir?

Assessment guidance

To complete Assessment Objective 4, you must evaluate the success of each tourist attraction. You should find visitor numbers and assess visitor types. You must also investigate the popularity of each attraction. A visit to local attractions would help you to find more detailed information.

Knowledge check

1 Give a definition of a tourist attraction.

2 What is the different between natural and built attractions?

3 What do the initials AONB and SSSI stand for?

4 What are the two main purposes of National Parks in the UK?

5 List five National Parks in England and Wales.

6 List the seven tourist attraction categories.

7 Explain the term 'target market'.

8 Name and explain the three sectors of ownership for tourist attractions.

9 Explain the importance of risk assessments at a tourist attraction.

10 What is the Visitor Attraction Quality Assurance Service?

11 Name three health and safety Acts or legislation relevant to tourist attractions.

12 Give three examples of queue control techniques at tourist attractions.

13 List the factors that influence the popularity of tourist attractions.

14 Explain the difference between planned and corrective maintenance.

15 List the factors that may influence the decision to visit a tourist attraction.

Resources

* Historic Houses Association (www.hha.org.uk) was formed in 1973 by owners of some of Britian's best known heritage properties. It represents over 1500 owners and guardians of historic houses, parks and gardens in private ownership in the UK.

* Association of Scottish Visitor Attractions (www.asva.co.uk).

* Association of Leading Visitor Attractions (www.alva.org.uk) seeks to represent to government, the tourism industry, the media and the public, the views and achievements of the country's major visitor attractions whilst

promoting co-operation and high standards among its members.

* National Piers Society (www.piers.co.uk) was founded in 1979 under Sir John Betjeman and aims to save piers for future generations.

* British Association of Leisure Parks, Piers and Attractions (www.balppa.org) is a non-profit-making trade association that represents the interests of owners, managers, suppliers and developers in the UK's commercial leisure parks, piers, zoos and attractions sector.

* Millennium Commission (www.millennium.gov.uk) invests around £1.2 billion in the construction and development of more than 200 projects in the UK. These range from large attractions to the smaller community-based developments.

* Department of Culture, Media and Sport (www.dcms.gov.uk).

* VisitBritain (www.visitbritain.org).

UNIT 6

Organising travel

Introduction

This unit looks at how travel is organised and booked and will be of particular relevance to you if you wish to work in the retail travel sector of the industry. As this is a very dynamic sector, changes in methods and systems will occur, so you will need to be aware of these changes and how they affect organisations in the sector.

The work you have undertaken for unit 2 relates very closely to this unit. The concepts covered in unit 1 also have some relevance, as you will need to understand the structure of the travel and tourism industry to identify where retail travel fits in. Knowledge of travel destinations from unit 3 will also help you identify why specific destinations appeal to particular client groups, and the locations of various destinations in the world.

Finally, the work you undertake for unit 4 on international travel will introduce you to concepts of travel service providers and their roles within the industry.

How you will be assessed

You will need to produce portfolio evidence which will be marked internally and will probably form two sections. The first section will show the results of your investigations into types of travel organisers (looking at two providers in detail), how they operate and their role in the chain of distribution. You will need to demonstrate an understanding of the application and importance of technology for these travel organisers, and explain how this technology affects their popularity within the sector. Then you will need to research the different marketing techniques used by travel organisation providers and analyse the impact and effectiveness of these techniques. Although this is not a full study of marketing, it will form a basis for study of this important subject at level A2.

You also have to demonstrate your practical application of the knowledge acquired about retail travel with the production of two complex travel itineraries.

Providers of retail travel

Think it over ...

Are you aware of the wide variety of travel agencies operating in the UK marketplace? Most high streets in large towns have at least one, if not more, travel agencies – you might have visited some of them already.

Before we go on to look at types of retail travel provider, we must consider the *chain of distribution* of travel products. You will have already looked at this in unit 1, but it will be useful to have another look at it here (Figure 6.1).

Figure 6.1 Chain of distribution

Note particularly that a travel agent is a *retailer* who acts as a go-between for the *wholesalers* and the *customers*. Travel agents are thus the 'face' of the travel industry and tend to be the contact the majority of people currently use to purchase travel products. This unit will be looking mainly at the retail market – whether through travel agencies or through direct selling – but also at other methods of buying travel products and services.

Think it over ...

Think of as many ways customers buy travel products as you can. Compare your list with others in the group.

Professional associations

In your study for unit 4 you will have learned about the *professional organisations and legal bodies* which affect travel agencies and other travel providers. You are strongly recommended to revisit that work to identify how organisations such as ABTA set the codes of conduct for travel agencies.

Association of British Travel Agents

Most travel agents that we will be considering in this section (apart from business travel specialists) will want to be members of the Association of British Travel Agents (ABTA). This organisation acts as a regulatory body for travel agencies and tour operators. All members must comply with strict financial rules laid down to protect the customers' money, and offer repayment in the event of company failure. This cover includes the air transport component of package holidays, as well as coach- and rail-based holidays.

ABTA also stipulates that any customer buying a holiday from a member has the benefit of professional advice, and there must be at least one fully qualified member of staff employed by the travel agency. Agents will be expected to answer questions on visa and medical requirements and give any relevant Foreign Office advice about the chosen destination.

Theory into practice

Visit the ABTA website (www.abta.com) where you will find a useful section on the benefits of buying package travel through a member travel agent or tour operator. This has been produced for both members and customers. It provides information about the security of monies paid for air travel, accommodation or any other travel product, and compensation paid. Look carefully at the benefits – this may help you when you are completing your assignment for this unit.

Air Travel Organisers' Licensing

This body (ATOL) is managed by the Civil Aviation Authority (CAA). It is the UK government's licensing mechanism for air holidays and flights sold by tour operators and travel organisers. ATOL is the UK's biggest holiday protection scheme. It protects holidaymakers from cancelled flights or being stranded abroad. The body regularly checks the financial status of the firms it licenses, who have purchased a guarantee (called a 'bond') which is lodged with ATOL.

Retailers

We will start by looking at various types of retailers (who are usually travel agencies).

Independent travel agencies

This type of travel agency is usually set up by someone working for himself/herself, or as a partnership or limited company. The business is managed and run by the owners, though there may be other staff working within the agency. It has no direct links with any specific tour operator, so the travel agent is able to offer a wide choice of brochures and services and will earn *commission* on sales that are made.

The information provided by the independent travel agent should not be dependent on or affected by commission rates offered by tour operators, and the quality of service should be very individual, unique and unbiased. The independent travel agency could also pay a fee to join Worldchoice and enjoy override commission which would improve income levels. These are additional commission payments made by tour operators when independent travel agencies meet sales targets.

Aims and objectives

Usually an independent travel agency is a single business – there are no branches of the business in other towns. However, there are examples of chains of independent travel agencies, but these will be considered further under 'miniple' ownership. Their aims and objectives are still the same.

The business comes from developing customer loyalty from those who prefer individual attention and service, with no bias towards specific suppliers. The advice given may relate to specific suppliers, but this has come from the agent's experiences with those suppliers and recognition of the quality of service provided. The recommendations often come from experience developed over a period of time or from incentive visits made with various suppliers and operators.

The major aims and objectives are to provide the customer with an independent, individual service to meet the customer's specific needs and to build a local reputation for quality of service and support to the traveller.

Advantages and disadvantages of using an independent travel agent

If the customer wishes to look at a wide range of operators for a specific location or type of service, then the independent travel agency will usually have access to any major provider. Although the agency might specialise in a specific product (e.g. cruises), other types of travel products and services can be offered. As independents need to attract and maintain customers, they will often offer extra services to attract and retain the business. One example is to offer a taxi service to and from the airport for all fly/cruise passengers, such as that offered by Fylde Travel Services who use a local provider (Figure 6.3).

You will notice that this business is a member of both ABTA (Association of British Travel Agents) and ASTA (American Society of Travel Agents) as the company does a lot of business with customers who wish to travel to the USA. It also holds an IATA (International Air Transport Association) Domestic licence. These trade associations set codes of conduct for members and are recognised internationally. They also provide assurance to customers that the

Fylde Travel Services Ltd.

7 Church Street, Poulton-le-Fylde, Lancashire, FY6 7AP, England.
Telephone: (01253) 883335/885322 Fax: (01253) 899499
Email: fyldetravel@aol.com Website: cruisespecialoffers.com

with Compliments

ABTA
30805
TID NO.
9600 3165

43244
IATA DOMESTIC
9100 4701

Figure 6.3 An independent travel arranger

organisation is a reputable one and the agent is qualified to ABTA standards.

The independent travel agency may be prepared to take more time to find the most advantageous price for the customer, or the best value for money. It might produce a tailor-made package for the customer.

One disadvantage of using an independent travel agency is that fewer late deals and special offers may be available. However, the agency should be able to access useful information from computer reservation systems such as Easysell. Another potential disadvantage is that there might not be sufficient staff available to deal with enquiries immediately, so customers may need to be prepared to wait longer for attention.

The high costs of advertising also mean that independent travel agencies are not able to take advantage of wide coverage and name recognition through national newspapers, and so they rely more on local publications and word of mouth. This means that the agency's name may not be as familiar to customers who are considering making reservations.

Often, to supplement the services offered, independent agencies will act as retail agents for local tour operators, such as coach companies, or offer theatre or entertainment tickets and use these as a promotional tool.

How independent travel agencies make reservations

Many independent travel agencies act also as ticketing agencies for major airlines and are able to book flights direct with the supplier. Some offer a service whereby a customer is able to purchase tickets for any of the major airlines as well as budget airlines such as Ryanair and easyJet. This service avoids customers spending their own time searching Internet sources for cheap air fares or special offers.

Most travel agencies use a viewdata system, such as Traveleye, to access all providers of travel products. However, the high cost of these has to be borne by the smaller agencies, so many are considering reviewing their systems and using direct Internet connections instead. Due to the competition from the large multiple agencies, many independent agencies must look for cheaper methods to access products for customers.

Any bookings made by the agency acquire commission from suppliers, and this varies enormously between the suppliers. Some offer 2 per cent of the price whilst others may offer 10 per cent. Others such as British Airways pay a flat rate per booking, regardless of the cost of the ticket – so a round-the-world first-class flight ticket would yield a commission identical to that paid for an internal flight ticket. Thus, when there is a choice of supplier, the independent travel agent will try to use a provider who offers the better commission rate.

Commission is earned also on other products sold to customers, such as ferry tickets, car hire and accommodation. Specimen commission rates are:

* package holidays – 10 per cent
* airline tickets – 7.5–9 per cent
* ferry bookings – 9 per cent
* travellers' cheques – 1 per cent
* travel insurance – 35–40 per cent.

From this you will note that the biggest potential earner is the sale of travel insurance – which is why agencies encourage customers to purchase insurance through them. However, regular travellers nowadays tend to purchase annual travel insurance policies which are not available from travel agencies – due to a deal between ABTA and the Financial Services Authority which now requires 'linking' of an insurance sale to a specific travel product. This can result in a loss of a large percentage of earnings for small independent travel agencies.

Theory into practice

An independent travel agency, GoWithUs, takes a booking for a 12-night package holiday for a family, which totals £1896. This earns commission at 10 per cent. To insure the two adults costs £42 per person, which earns commission at 35 per cent. Cover for the children aged between 2 and 7 is free when travelling with an insured adult. They pre-book five days' car hire at the resort, costing £37 per day, which earns commission at a rate of 15 per cent. Calculate the total commission this booking would earn for GoWithUs.

Setting targets and measuring performance

Some principals offer *incentive commission*, which can rise with the volume of sales. So if, for example, a travel agency sells its target of £50 000 worth of holidays with one company, it could earn £5000 commission. If the agency exceeds that target it may be offered 12.5 per cent commission on sales of £50 000. So the volume of sales

achieved may form the basis for the targets and will be looked at in terms of performance measurement.

As these tend to be smaller businesses, they will set their own target sales in order to provide sufficient income to remain viable. They will not be competing with other group branches to meet those targets, unless they are part of a miniple. Rather, they will measure their performance against past years and probably recommend suppliers who are able to offer higher commission rates in order to earn extra revenue. They will also maintain contact with regular customers to retain the custom in order to encourage further bookings and business.

Theory into practice

Visit a local independent travel agency to study the range of products and services on offer. If possible, invite the owner of a local independent agency to your school or college to discuss methods of setting targets, as well as the advantages and disadvantages of being an independent.

Miniple travel agencies

Some independent travel agencies expand to open more branches, and these are then classed as 'miniples'. The business owns and manages several branches but limits the region in which it operates. For example, Global Independent Travel Group had ten shops in the south-west of England in 2004 and is considering opening up to ten new branches.

Aims and objectives

Miniples operate in the same way as the independent travel agency. They have no ties to specific tour operators or providers, and earn commission in the same way. But with more branches, they are more likely to achieve higher sales and so earn higher commission income.

Their aim is to compete with the larger travel agency chains but offer a more personal service. In order to achieve this, they may be able to spend more on advertising within their region to increase their market share and raise awareness of the products and services they offer. Their objectives will always be to increase sales and therefore earn more income for development.

To continue with the example of Global Independent Travel Group, they are considering the introduction of foreign exchange bureaux within their agencies in order to increase profit margins. As they are larger than the small independent retailer, they will be able to afford the insurance cover necessary when holding quantities of currency and travellers' cheques.

The introduction of the euro within Europe has reduced the range of currencies it is necessary to hold, so they can concentrate on supplying mainly euros and US dollars, the two major currencies requested by travellers. They obtain supplies of other currencies as and when required.

Advantages and disadvantages of using a miniple travel agency

These are very similar to those for an independent travel agency, as described earlier. However, customers have the option of using a variety of branches if they are not able to return to the original branch. Communication should be transferable between the branches and the quality of service provided by each should be similar. The management should ensure that all employees are offering the same level of service within the various branches, so that the reputation of the company is maintained.

Setting targets and measuring performance

As there are several outlets within a miniple organisation, management may well set individual targets for each branch. Targets might be in relation to volume of sales or local population. A branch in a rural area would have a lower target than one in a major town or city, but each branch would have to aim to meet the targets set in order to justify their operation.

Performance can be measured and compared between the different branches in order to identify areas of concern. This could be training of personnel, or it could lead to more promotion within a specific locality to encourage more business.

CASE STUDY

Expansion

Here is a brief report published in *Travel Trade Gazette* on 19 August 2004:

> Independent agency chains are embarking on significant shop-opening programmes and recruitment drives, just as the multiples are scaling back. Australian-owned chain Flight Centre, south-west miniples Lets Go Travel and Global Independent Travel Group, and north-east group Hays Travel are just three companies about to expand their high street presence.
>
> Flight Centre has 71 stores across the UK and plans to open another ten by June. It is also recruiting 250 sales staff to meet demand for seven-day opening. Three or four of the new shops would be for student flights. They are launching Overseas Working Holidays ... on 1 September 2004, offering advice on work permits and casual labour, concentrating on Australia to begin with.

Discuss possible reasons for the expansion of miniple independent travel agencies.

Multiple travel agencies

Branches of multiple travel agencies are seen on nearly every high street in the United Kingdom and tend to be the names that are more easily recognised by the general public. The parent organisation has many branches within the country and the chain is often owned by tour operators, so providing an automatic route for sales of that tour operator's products.

As these travel agencies have direct links with the tour operators concerned, the products they will promote first are those of the parent company. Though they display brochures from other operators, their focus is on their own products.

Complete the table below:

Tour operator	High street travel agency
TUI/Thomson	
Mytravel	
First Choice	
Thomas Cook	

Aims and objectives

The aim of the multiple travel agency is to promote the products of the parent company or operator in order to increase the sales of these holidays. They specialise in the package holiday market, so holidays offered usually consist of transport, transfers and accommodation. Many also offer entertainment or all-inclusive packages that include meals and drinks. As the 'big four' (those listed in the task above) also operate their own fleets of aircraft and cruise ships, this concentration on their own products helps to maintain occupancy rates and control over the product marketed to the consumer.

Their objectives therefore are to ensure that all their hotels, ships and aircraft are filled to maximum capacity so that their earnings stay within the same organisation. They also compete very heavily with each other in order to maintain their market share. They tend to produce brochures 6–9 months ahead of the relevant season in order to encourage early bookings, and try to stay ahead of the competition with new features and offers.

The multiples have huge buying power, so they are often able to negotiate special advertising rates and will usually undertake large-scale advertising campaigns nationally. This is one reason why customers are so familiar with the names of the 'big four' travel agencies.

Advantages and disadvantages of using a multiple travel agency

One of the main advantages of using multiple travel agencies is the prices charged for products, which can be more favourable than those demanded by the independents. There is also the added advantage of the availability of the outlets – they are to be found in all major towns.

One disadvantage of using a multiple travel agency is that the products being promoted most heavily tend to be the company's own, though they do display some brochures from other providers. Employees are encouraged to sell own-brand products and have been trained to work with customers to persuade them to purchase. They are also encouraged to sell the complete package, and may not be as interested in selling components of a package, such as airfare only. Their destination knowledge will tend to relate to the destinations offered within their own brochures, so consultants often have to refer to these brochures for the information, rather than having first-hand knowledge or wider geographical knowledge of destinations.

Advice may not be as unbiased as that from an independent travel agent and may not be as complete in detail. Though the range of products on offer is broad, customers need to be aware that there are disadvantages if looking for a more individual package.

Making reservations

There are standardised systems used by each of the multiples, who also have their own viewdata systems to access information and to make reservations. The computer terminals at branches are all linked to a central reservation system – particularly for those packages booked through their own operating company. They are also able to access systems of other operators and providers within the agency.

A consultant will complete a booking enquiry form which should give all the relevant details prior to undertaking a search for possible matching holidays. Figure 6.4 is an example of an enquiry form.

When this form is completed with the necessary basic information, the consultant will proceed with the search. After locating a package that is acceptable to the customer, booking details will be completed, usually on-screen, with a printed confirmation being produced for the customer to sign and authorise. This becomes the

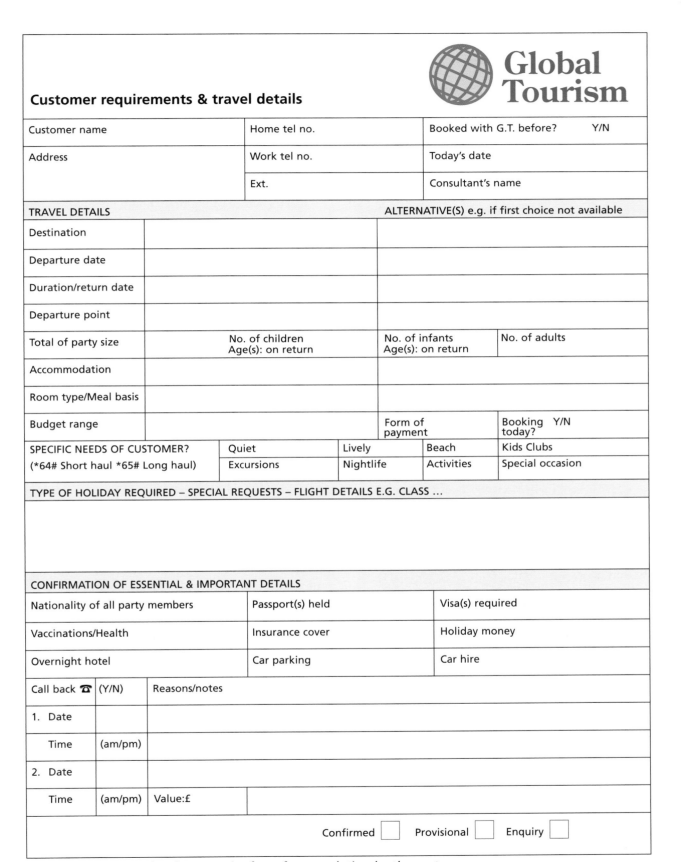

Customer requirements & travel details

Global Tourism

Customer name	Home tel no.	Booked with G.T. before?　　　Y/N
Address	Work tel no.	Today's date
	Ext.	Consultant's name

TRAVEL DETAILS		ALTERNATIVE(S) e.g. if first choice not available		
Destination				
Departure date				
Duration/return date				
Departure point				
Total of party size	No. of children Age(s): on return	No. of infants Age(s): on return	No. of adults	
Accommodation				
Room type/Meal basis				
Budget range		Form of payment	Booking　Y/N today?	

SPECIFIC NEEDS OF CUSTOMER?	Quiet	Lively	Beach	Kids Clubs
(*64# Short haul *65# Long haul)	Excursions	Nightlife	Activities	Special occasion

TYPE OF HOLIDAY REQUIRED – SPECIAL REQUESTS – FLIGHT DETAILS E.G. CLASS ...

CONFIRMATION OF ESSENTIAL & IMPORTANT DETAILS		
Nationality of all party members	Passport(s) held	Visa(s) required
Vaccinations/Health	Insurance cover	Holiday money
Overnight hotel	Car parking	Car hire

Call back ☎	(Y/N)	Reasons/notes
1.　Date		
Time	(am/pm)	
2.　Date		
Time	(am/pm)	Value:£

Confirmed ☐　　Provisional ☐　　Enquiry ☐

Figure 6.4 An example of an enquiry form for completion by the customer

contract between the tour operator and the customer, with the travel agency as the go-between. It records not only the details of the flight, accommodation and any other requirements, but also the cost of the package and the deposit taken.

This data is then stored on the branch system as well as the central system. It will trigger the issuing of tickets to the branch when the final payment has been made. The computer system records monies received as deposits and monies outstanding, as well as the date these are due for payment.

If the reservation is being made with another provider, then similar procedures will be followed, and the transaction recorded on the central computer system.

It is also possible to make reservations through other methods with the large multiple retail travel agencies. Look at the Lunn Poly flyer in Figure 6.5 to see different methods of making reservations.

Setting targets and measuring performance

Each branch of the multiple will be set a sales target by the head office management and will be expected to achieve this. The target will be for all sales made, but the branch will be expected to achieve a certain percentage of own-brand products as a minimum requirement.

Performance of the branch will be measured against its target, which may be set monthly or quarterly. Assessment will be made also of the performance of that branch compared with others within the group or region. Managers are expected to monitor this performance regularly at each branch and, where necessary, encourage staff to complete more sales.

The salary of the manager and staff may also be influenced by achievement of targets, with bonuses being paid if targets are exceeded in any quarter or measurement period. If necessary, successful managers might be moved to branches that are not achieving the set targets in order to improve performance.

Specialist travel agencies

Business travel management agencies

Business travel is a very specialised market and operates differently from the retail travel market. It is more a travel management function, whereby the specialist is contracted by the businesses concerned to provide travel products for their employees.

This service used to include a travel agent's employee based at the offices of the corporate customer. With advanced technology this is no longer the case. Instead of an agent, there will be a computer terminal at the office of the corporate customer that can access tickets and documents for travel.

Agencies catering only for business travellers or for corporate clients may be located at business parks to be nearer their customers, where land rents and costs are lower. This location is not essential, however, as most offer a 24-hour service through call centres to supply corporate clients with travel products as and when required. An

Figure 6.5 Four easy ways to book with one travel agency

example of this specialist service is Business Travel Plus, based in Blackpool.

These agencies build up relationships with providers and may have contracts with providers by which they receive preferential rates (such as for accommodation). They aim to supply the services businesses expect to receive, and earn sufficient revenue from commissions and sales to be able to negotiate better rates with providers. If they are based within a large organisation, they will undertake all the travel arrangements for that organisation. If they fail to provide an efficient service, then they will lose that client – so they must work in the best interests of the client at all times.

Aims and objectives

The aim is to provide a service to corporate customers which is a combination of sales for a contracted fee. The business travel management company will negotiate rates with the corporate customer to provide a specific service for a period of time.

The objectives are to provide a value-added service to the corporate client, to increase the customer base, and to sell more services to each client. The business is not operated on a commission basis at all, so this is very different from the other types of retail travel agencies you will study. They tend to act as travel *advisers* for the corporate client rather than as a travel agency.

Making reservations

The business travel manager will negotiate directly with airlines, accommodation providers etc. for preferential rates to see which provider will offer the best rate for the period of the contract. If, for example, a corporate client has just won a contract with another business in Singapore, the business travel manager will contact various airlines to see which will provide the best service at the best price for a specific period on behalf of the client. The same would be done with accommodation and other service providers. The business travel manager would then sign contracts with these suppliers to provide the services that have been negotiated.

Making bookings can represent less than 50 per cent of the fee charged to the corporate client for the services of the business travel manager.

Reservations will be made through a combination of Sabre and a proprietary Internet-based reservations system, where there is access to the wide range of products and services required by the business traveller.

Setting targets and measuring performance

Targets are based on revenue from fees charged to corporate clients for a wide variety of travel services.

The needs of business clients are often very different from those of the leisure tourist. Business clients usually have to use scheduled services because of the short notice for travelling. Their accommodation needs may be more business-orientated – the availability of support services such as fax, modem points, 24-hour room service etc. They may also require car hire or limousine services to be arranged. Many business travellers use railways for internal travel and the specialist will open business accounts with rail operators to make bookings.

Performance is assessed regularly over set periods to identify areas that need to be developed. As many business travel management organisations are individual businesses providing services to corporate clients, it would be the owner(s) of the business who measure performance and set targets for the overall business.

Destination-specific specialist travel agencies

Specialist travel agents are similar to the independents in that they are not linked to any one principal, but will use a wide variety of providers. However, in this case the specialism is in a specific destination. Examples are Austravel or Journey Latin America. They specialise in packages or components of the package to that specific destination, so are likely to have superior knowledge of that destination and its features.

Aims and objectives

The aim will be offer value-for-money products to attract customers in order to increase the volume of sales to that specific destination.

The objectives will be to obtain the larger share of the market for customers to the specific destination because efforts can be focused on obtaining the best rates for accommodation and transport. The staff employed will be expected to have excellent destination knowledge to provide customers with the most appropriate packages to suit their requirements.

Advantages and disadvantages of using a specialist travel agency

As the employees at a specialist travel agency have such good destination knowledge, they are able to provide the customer with a wider choice of products and services at that destination. Their focus will be on providing individual packages to suit the needs of the customer for that destination and they are not tied to any specific provider.

The disadvantages of using a specialist travel agency are few if the customer has a specific destination in mind. But if that customer is looking for a wider choice of destination options, he or she would be better advised to visit an independent travel agency or one of the larger multiples.

Interest-specific specialist travel agencies

These are similar to the destination-specific agencies, except that they specialise in a particular type of product, such as the cruise market, or in a specific age group, such as STA Travel for the student and under-26 market, and Saga for the over-fifties.

The aims and objectives of these are similar to those of the destination-specific travel agency except that the focus will be on the specific products or target groups.

Hypermarkets

Hypermarkets for holidays tend to be based in out-of-town industrial sites or major population areas and come as a result of customers using these sites as leisure facilities, with a variety of major superstores to visit. Holiday Hypermarkets was developed and then bought by First Choice Holidays as one of their ventures into the retail sector, but the idea was developed by other major travel agency multiples.

The focus is very much on making enjoyable the experience of buying a holiday. The stores often feature displays and exhibitions, and might also include cafés or catering facilities.

Hypermarkets are large stores offering a broad travel experience with activities. Some of the stores are very large with many employees. Holiday Hypermarkets opened what was claimed to be the world's largest travel agency outlet in Croydon in June 1999, which created 70 jobs.

The capital outlay for the actual hypermarket may be high initially, but the land is usually cheaper to buy or rent on out-of-town sites than on high streets. There is usually ample free car parking to attract families and make the outlet more accessible.

CASE STUDY
Fforestfach

According to an article on http://news.bbc.co.uk, Lunn Poly opened a new store in Swansea in January 2003 with 'an all-out attack on the senses of its sun-seeking customers'. To get people into the holiday mood, the store in Fforestfach welcomes visitors with music, the smell of coconuts and displays filled with shells, driftwood and photographs. The idea is that the coconut aroma reminds people of holiday suntan lotion.

The shop, which includes a Parisian-style café area, is the first of a wave of ten similar Lunn Poly stores across the UK. It marks a new venture for the firm, and arises because the way people book their holidays is evolving. The travel industry is looking at newer and more interesting ways of marketing holidays. The First Choice Holiday Hypermarket which has branches in Cardiff and Newport have ski simulators, driving games and Cadillac cars to add to the relaxed atmosphere and improve interactivity – which is regarded as important to attract customers.

How does a hypermarket differ from a high street branch? If possible arrange a visit to one to experience its features.

Aims and objectives

The aim of the hypermarket approach is to attract the maximum number of customers through the activities on offer, in order to encourage sales of holidays and to broaden the experience of buying holidays and make this more enjoyable.

The objective is to maximise sales and encourage increased as well as repeat business.

Advantages and disadvantages of using hypermarkets

As hypermarkets are usually linked to major travel product providers, such as First Choice and TUI/Thomson (Lunn Poly), the selling focus will be similar to that of multiple retail travel agencies, but on a much bigger scale. There will be more consultants available to assist with enquiries and bookings, and the atmosphere will be more relaxed with activities and cafés while customers consider various options. The pressures on purchasing will be just as great, but the sensation will appear more leisurely and relaxed.

Making reservations

Hypermarkets will make reservations in just the same way as multiple or miniple retail agencies. Refer back to the relevant sections to remind yourself of how this occurs.

Setting targets and measuring performance

Targets for hypermarkets will be much higher than for smaller branch agencies. The costs of setting up the hypermarket mean that the commission earned from sales will need to be higher in order to earn the extra revenue.

Performance will be measured in terms of both the overall performance of the agency and the individual performances of employees. Each employee has a target to achieve, and if that is not met then further training will be undertaken or the employee may be moved to a different type of retail agency within the same organisation.

The pressure to reach performance levels is greater within the hypermarket environment. Often hypermarkets are compared with each other in order to increase performance at individual sites.

Home-based travel agents

A home-based travel agent is anyone engaged in marketing and selling of travel products from a home office. It can be someone who works from his or her own home or as an outside sales representative for an accredited travel agency (usually referred to as the 'host agency') – such as Travel Counsellors, the fastest growing company in 2003. The home agent must find the customers. He or she acts as an independent contractor, so there is more freedom in determining how and with whom to do business.

The business may be specialist – such as cruise only, adventure holidays, educational tours, or villa/apartment bookings only. Alternatively it might offer wider travel products.

The home-based travel agent can work full-time, part-time or only occasionally – it is up to the individual how much time is put into the business and whether the person sets out to earn a substantial income or just 'pin-money'. Virtually anyone can become a home-based travel agent, provided he or she has a minimum of two years' ABTA experience.

Aims and objectives

The first aim is to earn income, through commission from sales, according to the effort put into the business. There are websites giving information on how to set up the business (for example, www.hometravelagency.com). There might be other aims too – it depends on how the business is set up. If the home-based travel agent is working as an outside sales representative then part of the commission earned will be paid to the host agency. If he or she is fully independent, all income belongs to the home-based travel agency.

The objectives are to reach the maximum number of customers which the agent can manage in order to earn commission from sales, either for the host agency or for the individual. In a specialist field, rather than general retail travel, contacts will have to be made with suppliers of the products concerned in order to negotiate commission rates and discounts. However, most agents will not deal with suppliers directly to negotiate commission but will join a consortium (e.g. Travel Trust Association, Global Travel Group), who will negotiate better commission rates for all members.

The customer who contacts a website will not always be aware whether the agency is home-based or not, as all communications will be via the Internet.

Any agent selling travel including flights must have an Air Tour Operators licence (ATOL). Agencies selling more than 500 flight packages a year apply for a mini ATOL licence now required by law, and additionally some form of bonding with either ABTA or TTA would be required. Joining IATA would be expensive for the home-based agent.

Advantages and disadvantages of being a home-based agent

The advantage for the owners of the home-based travel agency is that they can work in their own time, and at their own pace, creating the size of business they can manage effectively. They own their own business and the revenue earned from the business but will have to develop the techniques to manage the business effectively. If the agency is acting as a referral agency for a host agency, then the onus will be on the home-based travel agency to find the customers initially.

One disadvantage may be in finding the customers, achieving credibility and becoming recognised within the industry. Another, if working for a host agency, is deciding how the commissions will be split between the two forms of agency to reflect the amount of effort made in initiating a booking.

Making reservations

It will depend largely on how the business is organised as to who makes the reservations. If the home-based agent is acting for a host agency, then the latter will make the final bookings and reservations. If the home-based agent is an independent contractor, then reservations will be made in similar ways to other retail travel providers, but usually using the Internet as the medium through which bookings are made. The business will need to construct its own documentation and will act very much as an independent travel agency – but working from home, rather than the high street.

Setting targets and measuring performance

As for independent travel agencies, targets will be set according to the amount of time the agent wishes to spend at the business, and how much income he or she hopes to achieve through operating the agency. Performance will be measured against these targets season by season, or year by year.

Direct booking with tour operators

The majority of tour operators offer direct booking facilities, rather than through a travel agency. Tour operators have call centres where these bookings are handled, or on-line websites where bookings can be made. This method of operation means that the tour operator does not have to pay commission to the travel agency, and thus earns more on the actual reservation.

Some tour operators only take direct bookings through their operators or call centres. Examples of these include Saga Holidays, Direct Holidays and Travelsphere. Portland Direct is the direct-selling branch of TUI/Thomson, and Blue Sky is the direct-selling branch of Thomas Cook (Figure 6.6).

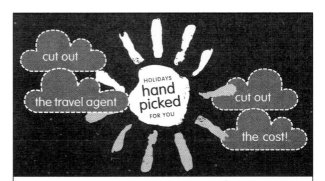

Figure 6.6 Advertisement placed by a direct-sell agency in the national press

Where the tour operator offers holidays through direct selling as well as by way of regular brochures in travel agencies, there may be similar accommodation listed, and the flights are usually with the parent company, but the price is often cheaper owing to the reduced cost of offering this option.

Theory into practice

1 As a group, obtain a copy of Portland Direct's brochure and a copy of TUI/Thomson's Summer Sun. Try to identify holidays that use the same property. Compare the flight information and details, then compare the prices.

2 Discuss the differences in the extra facilities provided or options given to the customer between these brochures.

Aims and objectives of direct selling

From the tour operator's point of view, this is another method of filling accommodation and aircraft capacity to achieve good occupancy rates.

It is of interest to those customers who do not wish to book through the usual travel agency channels, and the main attraction is generally the lower price of the product. It is also of interest to customers who are searching for a more specific holiday – whether it be a tour to a particular destination with a smaller operator such as Travelsphere, or a trip with people of similar age such as a Saga holiday. The tour operator still makes revenue from the booking, but does not have to pay commission to travel agencies for the bookings.

The principal objective is to maximise profit by making use of all sales opportunities. Major operators also want to achieve a larger share of the overall market.

The smaller specialised direct-selling companies may have slightly different objectives – to attract a specific sector of the market and offer holidays that appeal to that sector in order to increase their market share within that specialised market. They will still aim to achieve the maximum profit, but may not have the buying power of the major operators when it comes to negotiating rates with transport providers. They will purchase a certain number of seats on a specific flight (which may be scheduled or charter) and their objective will be to fill those seats to meet their commitment to the airline.

Accommodation purchasers will have similar objectives. They will reserve a certain number of rooms of various types (single, double, twin) and their principal objective is to fill all those rooms with paying customers.

Advantages and disadvantages of direct selling

For the tour operators, the advantage of direct selling is that they can assess the sales of specific products very quickly and respond by either reserving more rooms or aircraft seats, and undertaking specific marketing to target customers in order to increase sales. The tour operators do not have to pay commission to travel agencies, so they have more control over the price of the packages or products.

For the customers, the advantage is that the type of holiday may be more original and the operator may offer more 'extras' within the price. For example, with Saga Holidays, there is often an area of the hotel reserved solely for Saga customers with a special free bar and meeting facility. There are usually excursions included within the price, and there will be permanent representatives just to deal with Saga customers.

Customers using specialist direct-selling operators may see that the price appears slightly higher than the mass market tour operator price, and the flights offered may not be as convenient or frequent. For coach tours there may be only one specified departure date in any one week, and tours run for set periods of time, which may not always suit the customer's holiday arrangements.

The disadvantage to the tour operators is that they have to undertake all the marketing costs themselves. They do not have travel agencies offering their products and raising customer awareness. The costs of advertising and distributing brochures can be high, and there is no guarantee that an enquiry for a brochure will lead to a booking. Much of the follow-up by the tour operators is through mailshots, which may be ignored by potential customers. They have to be more original in their marketing in order to attract and maintain customers.

Making reservations

Bookings are made through call centres run by the tour operators or through Internet sites set up and managed by the operators. They will have made the initial reservations with transport and accommodation providers in anticipation of sales for a specific period. The customer will contact an operator and make a reservation directly. Any special requirements must be stated at the time of booking, and a booking reference number will be issued to the customer on receipt of a deposit.

Some direct-selling operators charge an additional fee of, say, 1 per cent for credit card bookings, which adds to the cost of the holiday. The operator must ensure that the customer is fully aware of the terms and conditions of the sale prior to confirming a booking, and these are usually printed in the brochures.

Confirmation notices and final invoices will come direct from the tour operator, as will tickets once the final balance has been paid. The customers must communicate directly with the tour operator, and they cannot use travel agencies to follow up any problems or cancellations.

Setting targets and measuring performance

This aspect will be very similar to the retail travel agency. Targets will be set at the call centre for each of the consultants, as they are the main intermediary between the customer and the operator. The customer service qualities of operators must be excellent if they are to encourage bookings, so their training will include development of selling skills.

The performance of consultants will be compared not only between the consultants but also from one period to another, to ensure that they are meeting targets. It will be up to the consultant to persuade a hesitant customer of the features of the holiday being discussed in order to close the sale.

Internet searches

Many individuals prefer to put together their own packages after searching the Internet for the various components of the holiday – transport, accommodation and other services. In this way, the customer is booking what is specifically required and will pay only for the specified products. Extras such as transfers might have to be purchased during the travelling.

Advantages and disadvantages of Internet searching

This method of arranging travel and accommodation can be very time-consuming. The consumer usually has to search a wide variety of websites in order to obtain the best deals. He or she may choose to use one of the specialist 'late-deals' sites, such as www.lastminute.com or www.expedia.co.uk, or may undertake wider searches across a variety of airlines, ferries and accommodation providers to identify the service which meets the needs best (Figure 6.7).

According to *Travel Weekly* in August 2004, the use of Internet sites is increasing. In 2002, 90 per cent of travel agency business was direct to the operator by the agency. Now 60 per cent of on-line bookings are direct and 40 per cent are from

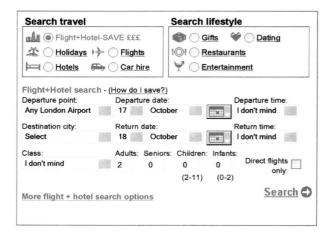

Figure 6.7 Two on-line booking forms

thetrainline have carefully selected partners to offer the following services and may be of interest to your booking.

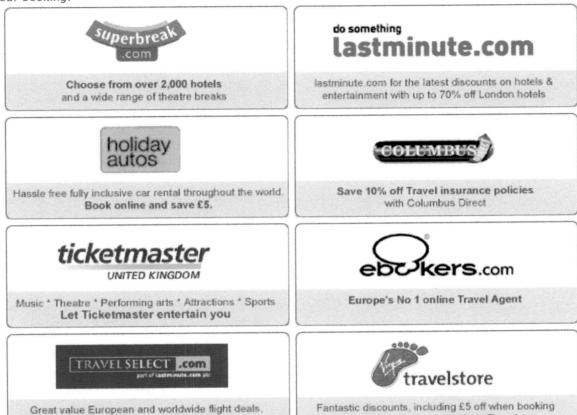

Figure 6.8 An example of group advertising of support services

agents. Lastminute.com splashed out £20 million in 2003 on developing its dynamic packaging capability in preparation for a surge in Internet usage in 2004.

Many websites also offer links to other services. An example of products and services contacts offered at www.thetrainline.com is given in Figure 6.8.

One of the major benefits can be a reduction in the cost of the overall package when compared with a tour operator's package. Also the consumer can choose the transport provider offering the most competitive prices and the most convenient departure point. Then the search will be continued for accommodation providers, and many of these websites offer virtual tours of the hotels/villas etc.

which give more information than a brochure may do. Bookings will then be made direct with the accommodation provider for the periods required. It is also possible to book attraction tickets through the Internet, so all components of a package can be paid up-front prior to departure.

One drawback may be that the accommodation availability does not match the flight availability, which then necessitates a further accommodation search. Another disadvantage is that the customer does not have the financial support of ABTA should any part of this package fail to be delivered (e.g. the airline goes bankrupt, the hotel denies the booking, and so on).

If the search is being undertaken at short notice, the best prices may not always be available. Many of the no-frills airlines offer the cheapest tickets early in the booking period, with prices rising steeply nearer to the departure date.

Making reservations

Reservations made will be direct contracts between the consumer and the providers. The consumer will be expected to retain copies of all booking confirmations and read the terms and conditions of all providers to ensure that he or she is aware of any clauses that might affect the booking. The customer also needs to visit airline websites on the day of departure to check that there has been no change in the scheduled departure time – a task normally undertaken by a travel agency for customers.

There is also the issue of financial protection and exposure to company failure if the booking is not purchased with a credit card. The customer could be left high and dry in a foreign destination with no return flight reserved if the airline has failed. He or she would have to purchase another ticket with an alternative airline – there would be little chance of recovering any loss of money.

Market share of agencies

It is quite difficult to obtain statistics on market share in the retail travel market, but there are occasionally features in the national press or in *Travel Trade Gazette* which comment on this.

Figure 6.9 shows the retail market share percentages at February 2004 (it does not include the direct channels of distribution). These give you some idea of the hold the large multiples have over the market.

First Choice Retail	6.70%
Mytravel Going Places	11.50%
Thomas Cook shops	13.00%
TUI Lunn Poly	18.00%
Co-op	11.90%
Independent agencies	11.90%
Total	73.00%

Figure 6.9 Market share at February 2004

Assessment guidance

The first part of your portfolio for Assessment Objective 1 will contain the results of your investigations into *two* types of travel organiser, and you will need to select them from the variety of travel providers covered so far in this chapter. You must show that you understand where each stands in the chain of distribution and their operating procedures. It might be of benefit to arrange a meeting with the managers of the different types of travel provider in order to get more specific information about their operating procedures than is given in this section of the chapter. Different providers may well have their own individual systems, and these are what you will need to explain in detail.

While discussing these issues with the manager, it would also be advisable to look ahead at the material you will need to cover for Assessment Objective 2. That relates to the impact of technology on the working environment in the travel providers you have chosen. You must ensure that the information you have is as current as possible – things are changing very quickly in terms of technology use in retail travel.

Products and services offered by providers

Retail travel agencies offer their customers much more than package holidays. We will now look at each of the products and services separately, though you need to remember that not all travel agencies will offer everything explained here. When you are undertaking your research, you need to establish which specific products and services are offered by each of the agency types you are investigating.

Think it over ...

As a group, discuss all the products and services a travel agency might offer apart from package holidays. Why are these products offered? How are they relevant to customers' needs?

Types of products and services

Package holidays

We have already mentioned package holidays frequently when considering the different types of retail travel provider. But what exactly is a package holiday?

This type of package has been offered by major tour operators for many years – since the early 1960s. Prices quoted in brochures were those from the main hub airport (e.g. Luton for Thomson) with additional supplements for flights from other regional airports. It was possible for the customer to be able to calculate the cost of the holiday according to the time of year it was taken, as again there were variations in price according to season. These price variations took account of the seasonality of the holiday market, as peak booking times for families were during school holidays (usually July and August) when demand was high.

There have been some changes to this definition made more recently by JMC and TUI/Thomson to 'unpack the package'. This offered the holidaymaker a little more variety, in that they did not have to include transfers to and from the accommodation or meals on the flight etc. as part of the package. The companies reduced the cost of the basic holiday, with these being offered as extra costs to be added to the published package price.

Accommodation costs *usually* include 'bed and breakfast', although some of the packages offered – particularly to the Caribbean areas or America – are room only. 'Bed and breakfast' means that the cost of breakfast is included in the package. Alternatively, 'half board' means that breakfast plus one other meal (usually the evening meal) is included. Other prices may quote for 'full board', meaning that all meals are included. More recently, there has been an increase in holiday packages that are 'all-inclusive', meaning that all meals, drinks and entertainment are included.

Obviously, accommodation prices in brochures vary considerably according to the meal plan offered, and more variety has been given by tour operators to meet different customer needs. If you are acting as a travel agent you must ensure that the customers understand exactly what is included in the cost of their 'package holiday'.

Package holidays are the main focus of the major multiple travel agencies and form a large part of the business for miniples and independent travel agencies. They are the products expected from a travel agency.

Car hire

Not all travellers wish to take part in excursions organised by tour operators. Some want to be more independent to explore the area or country themselves. Car hire is often offered as an extra to the main package, and customers can usually select the size of car that best suits their needs – a couple may not want as large a vehicle as a family of four or more. The travel agency will have contacts with various car hire firms, though might promote one company over another. Often there has been some negotiation between the tour operator and car hire providers to offer preferential rates.

Many tour operators now sell 'fly/drive' packages. These include the flight, the first (and possibly the last) night's accommodation, and the hire of a car for the period of the holiday. The customer collects the car from the destination airport and drives to the choice of accommodation. The customer is then free to tour the area, visiting locations and attractions and staying in accommodation of his or her own choice for the rest of the holiday. The last accommodation is usually near the airport so that the customer can return the car conveniently when arriving back at the airport.

Car hire is convenient also for people who own property at the destination and wish only to have flights and car hire made available to them. They would not have any accommodation provided as part of a package, but the travel agent is able to include car hire within the price of the flight in the 'package' proposed to the customer.

Foreign exchange

Not all travel agencies have a bureau de change within their premises, but the majority are able to order foreign currency for customers. Recall that a travel agency can earn 10 per cent commission on sales of foreign currency, so this is potentially a significant part of the agency's income. Customers can alternatively obtain foreign currency from a variety of sources (banks and post offices, for example), so the travel agency will be keen to offer this service as a way of retaining customers and earning extra revenue.

An agency that has its own foreign exchange section will need to have good security arrangements – the money held on the premises will be considerably more than at an agency not offering this facility.

There is usually a member of staff trained to deal with currency exchange. He or she must be very numerate and methodical. The person will probably deal with a variety of currencies (euros and US dollars, in particular, but also currencies of other nations) and have access to information on exchange rates. Some agencies use computerised systems that are automatically updated with currency exchange rates, and the system will also perform the necessary calculations for the cashier.

Customers may also wish to purchase travellers' cheques in either sterling or the currency of the destination, and these should be available in bureaux de change. If the customer is buying in sterling, he or she will receive cheques to the exact value of the payment made, but if buying in another currency then commission will be charged on the transaction. However, when the person comes to exchange these at the destination,

he or she will normally receive the face value of the travellers' cheque.

You will notice on foreign exchange boards that there are two rates – one for buying the currency and one for selling the currency (Figure 6.10). Part of the difference between the two rates accounts for the income earned for making transactions, but some agencies will also charge a commission rate for the exchange service. The market is becoming increasingly competitive, so many agencies now advertise '0 per cent commission' for foreign exchange transactions. However, there may still be variations between their buying and selling rates compared to other foreign exchange providers.

Figure 6.10 An electronic display of exchange rates

Theory into practice

A bureau de change is selling euros at 1.382 per pound sterling and buying them at 1.526 per pound sterling.

1 Calculate how many euros a customer would receive for £300.

2 If the person brings back 80 euros in cash, and wants to exhange them for pounds sterling, how much would he or she receive?

3 If the traveller decided to purchase euro travellers' cheques instead of cash, what would be the value of the cheques?

Insurance

The sale of travel insurance can earn good commission rates for travel agencies (see page 212), so this is a service offered by all the travel providers. Even direct selling providers, such as thetrainline.com, offer insurance with their tickets – customers must opt out of the insurance if they do not wish to purchase it.

Insurance policies cover a wide variety of problems that can arise – personal accident and medical cover, repatriation, delays and cancellation of flights, loss of personal belongings. All travellers are encouraged to purchase insurance cover. In fact, some operators will not accept a booking unless there is adequate travel insurance in place.

People who travel frequently can purchase annual travel cover, so this is a potential loss of income to the travel agent, who cannot provide such cover (see page 212).

Car parking and hotel accommodation at airports

Travellers usually make their own arrangements to get to an airport when this is not part of a holiday package. Many tour operators use charter flights that leave early in the morning or arrive back late in the evening. If the customer is some distance from the airport, the travel agent may suggest hotel accommodation to avoid a very early departure time from home. Some of the accommodation providers near airports also offer car parking at reduced rates or free for the period of the holiday, and will provide minibus or transport services from the accommodation to the airport.

Otherwise, car parking can be reserved at airports by the travel agency and the traveller has the choice of on- or off-site parking with transport to the terminal building.

By offering this type of extra, the travel agency is earning commission from the sale of the product and offering a more comprehensive service to the customer. The customer could come away from the agency with all the various components of the holiday fully arranged.

Ticketing

All travellers will require a ticket or proof of booking, and one of the services provided by the travel agency is the tickets or vouchers required for transport. If the product is a package holiday, tickets and vouchers will be received by the agency about two weeks before departure. These must be kept secure until such time as the customer collects them after being informed of their arrival.

How these are stored is important. For the large agencies this will often be by departure date and surname of the lead name on the ticket. They are not kept in the front office of agencies, but in a secure area behind. The agent is responsible for the tickets until such time as the customer collects them. When tickets arrive, the agent must go through the details on the tickets to ensure they are correct according to the records they hold, and must also check them carefully with the client when they are being collected. Details such as names of passengers, airport departure and arrival points, flight times, accommodation and meal arrangements all need to be fully checked with the client.

Some agencies are also licensed to issue airline tickets for specific flights booked through them. There has been a development in the e-ticket market, whereby electronic versions of the tickets are produced for the client. These tickets must clearly state the name of the client, the flight number, date and time, departure airport and arrival airport.

No-frills airlines use confirmation or booking references to identify the customer, but the details given on this voucher must match any that would be provided on the tickets themselves (Figure 6.11).

Ferry/Eurostar bookings

The majority of travel agencies will act as booking agent for ferry services and rail services, including Eurostar. They will store the timetables for the major ferry routes or be able to obtain these details through searches on the Internet or other viewdata system.

Bookings can be made in the same way as for flights. Ferry or other transport tickets will be sorted, stored and issued in the same way as flight tickets and vouchers.

YOUR CONFIRMATION NUMBER IS: JN2GEL

You will need this confirmation number and VALID ACCEPTED FORM
OF PHOTO ID(as detailed below)at check-in to receive your boarding card.

ITINERARY/RECEIPT - All times are local.

PASSENGERS
 1. FLORANCE ROWE   ADT

GOING OUT
From London Stansted(STN) to Jerez(XRY)
Sat, 07Aug04 Flight FR8398 Depart STN at 17:25 and arrive XRY at 21:20

COMING BACK
From Jerez(XRY) to London Stansted(STN)
Wed, 11Aug04 Flight FR8397 Depart XRY at 11:20 and arrive STN at 13:10

PAYMENT DETAILS
********89.98 GBP Adults
*********3.50 GBP Fees
*********8.93 GBP Service Charges
*********4.36 GBP Ins/whcr Levy
*********5.00 GBP UK Air Duty
*********2.63 GBP Government Tax
*********0.89 GBP Airport Taxes
*********0.00 GBP Car rental
*********0.00 GBP Insurance

Figure 6.11 An email confirmation message

Visa and passport advice

The travel agent must be able to advise customers on the regulations that should be followed when leaving the UK. All passengers are required to carry a passport, and the agency will be able to assist with completing documentation to apply for a passport or give advice on how this can be obtained.

Visas are required for travel to many countries – the travel agent must be aware of which countries require visas and how these can be obtained, and advise prospective passengers accordingly. Often, the brochures from the tour operators give details of which countries require a visa.

Visas and passports can take some time to be processed by the government departments of the countries concerned, and the agent needs to give suitable advice to customers in order to ensure that these are received prior to the journey taking place.

Theory into practice

Look in a travel brochure of an operator offering holidays to destinations outside Europe. Find the section on visas and make a list of countries requiring one. You may then like to extend this activity by establishing how much a visa would cost and how long it is valid for.

Health advice

Health issues are very important for travellers, so offering advice on this is part of the function of the travel agent. This is particularly necessary when travelling to countries in Latin America or tropical climates, or countries where the hygiene is not as rigorous as our own.

Some countries set down exactly what inoculations or preventative treatment is required. Then travellers have to provide documentary proof that they have followed the regulations and have had any necessary injections. Some countries only recommend that preventative measures be taken, but the travel agent must advise customers of any issues regarding health when discussing various locations with clients.

The most up-to-date information on this is provided by the Department of Health and Social Security website, and clients can also visit their local health centres for the necessary treatment or advice.

Theory into practice

Two gap-year students are hoping to spend time in South America, visiting Peru, Argentina and Chile. What advice is given by the Foreign & Commonwealth Office on travel to these countries? What immunisations would these students need? Is there anything else they need, such as visas, work permits, etc?

Flight-only bookings

This facility should be offered by all travel agents, but the independent travel agent, miniple or business travel management company are the most likely to provide the better service for this type of product. They can access the various airlines through their viewdata systems and provide the relevant tickets or e-tickets for the booking. Though the commission rates for the service are not always as high as that paid for insurance or foreign exchange, they are valuable sources of revenue. If these travel agents provide the service for flight-only bookings, then that customer may well use them again for other services.

Other flight-only bookings are likely to be made by individuals using the Internet directly to research airline prices, or specialist airline bookings firms, such as Airline Network which aims to provide the cheapest flight to worldwide destinations. The customer may receive normal or electronic tickets, but any other arrangements regarding travel are a matter for the customer.

Theatre or entertainment bookings

Many of the travel agencies also offer the facility of booking theatre or theme park and entertainment tickets with the package. Others will sell tickets for entertainment venues or attractions as part of their overall service, advertising these within the agency. The benefits of offering this service are good commission earnings from the sales, and customers attracted into the agency who wish to purchase these tickets may be suitably persuaded to return when planning their holiday.

Rail and coach tickets

Some travel agencies also act as agencies for the rail network and coach companies, whether national ones such as National Express, or specialist coach operators who organise tours, such as Wallace Arnold and Shearings. The market for rail tickets is probably not as high as that for coach services, both being easily available on the Internet. These are, however, additional products that earn commission, and are more generally sold through independent or miniple travel agencies.

Tailor-made holidays

These have been discussed at various stages during this chapter. They are holidays that are produced to meet specific client requirements. They will usually cover flights, accommodation, attractions and special transport services, and may be for holidays of longer duration than the one- or two-week package variety. All the client needs are noted in order to organise a specific package to suit that client.

Many people are now using the Internet to form their own tailor-made holidays. Therefore the bulk of purchases for this type will be either through independent travel agencies or the individual searching websites for the components to make up the complete package.

Cruise bookings

Cruises are a growing area of the holiday market and are available through most agencies. Cruise lines themselves advertise holidays under direct selling.

Cruise bookings are really no different from package holidays. Some include flights but others may sail from the UK. The management of bookings will be similar to other bookings made by the travel agency. Some agencies offer additional services. For example, a client booking a UK cruise may need transfers to and from the dockside as part of the package, so the cost of taxi services might be a free extra or enticement to the customer.

Tangibility, seasonality and perishability of products

Tangibility

> **Key term**
>
> A tangible product is one that you can hold. For example, if you go into a sports shop to buy a tennis racket, you have a tennis racket in your hand when you have purchased it.

It is important to remember that products and services retailed by a travel agent are very rarely tangible. With a holiday, you purchase only a booking confirmation until you receive the tickets, but you don't ever have a product or service in your hand. You are buying a dream and hope that the product or service will meet your expectations from the information in the brochures or promotional material. This means that large amounts of money may be spent on something you cannot test, which may lead to disappointments if the real thing does not match your expectation.

Perishability

A hotel has only a fixed number of rooms, and if any are not occupied at any one time the potential income from those days is lost forever. The owners must try to ensure that they have adequate occupancy all the time, or achieve a minimum occupancy rate that they have budgeted for in their anticipated earnings.

The same applies to airline seats, ferry space or cruise bookings. If they are not sold for a particular journey, then this is a loss of income. This is one reason why there is often very heavy discounting on prices of products that are being offered as late bookings – the provider is attempting to fill those empty spaces in order to earn at least some income from them.

Seasonality

The industry markets its products and services according to the season. You cannot sell skiing holidays in Switzerland in the summer as there is no snow, nor in the winter could you sell sun holidays in resorts where the weather is very poor. So there are variations of products and services available according to the seasons.

Brochures are produced to reflect the seasons. For example, TUI/Thomson have Summer Sun and Winter Sun brochures, for those who want sunshine at different times of the year. Summer sun might be more European-based, whereas winter sun may feature destinations such as the Caribbean or Maldives – and are available for booking usually about nine months before the season starts.

If early sales are good, there are fewer special offers or late deals available nearer the start of that season. If sales are not as good, then there will be more late deals available in order to sell the holidays rather than lose potential income. This will become more clear when we look at marketing and advertising techniques used by travel agencies to encourage sales and bookings.

Marketing and advertising

This section of the syllabus will give you an opportunity to look at marketing techniques used by travel agencies in order to attract business. You will be familiar with many of the techniques, having seen them used in the high street travel agencies and also in the media. The aim of marketing is to attract customers to that organisation and the product or services it can offer.

This section also summarises the legal requirements in this area.

Techniques used by providers

Window cards

Travel agencies frequently use their window space, particularly for special offers and late deals. Sometimes it is difficult to see inside the agency because of the number of cards displayed on the windows (Figure 6.12). These cards may be grouped into types of holiday (e.g. family, cruise, flight-only), but the information given on them is displayed in bold print and colours, usually with the name of the destination largest. Other brief details such as date of availability, departure airport and length of stay are given. The aim is to appeal to customers looking for bargains in the holiday market, to encourage custom.

Posters

Posters are displayed either in the shop window or on the walls inside the travel agency. They may display images of idyllic beaches, action-packed skiing or snowboarding. Again these are used to catch the eye of customers and attract business by appealing to emotions. The agency shown in Figure 6.12 also has an A-board (not in the picture) outside the premises – this may or may not be allowed by local council regulations.

Some posters may be informative rather than display destinations – such as *'Unbeatable Special Offers – ask inside for details'*. These aim to attract customers looking for bargains, but also encourage potential customers to actually speak to a consultant – which might lead to a booking.

Leaflets

Leaflets may be distributed at travel fairs to inform customers of offers, or be posted to customers whose names are on a mailing list for a

Figure 6.12 A typical high street travel agency with many window displays

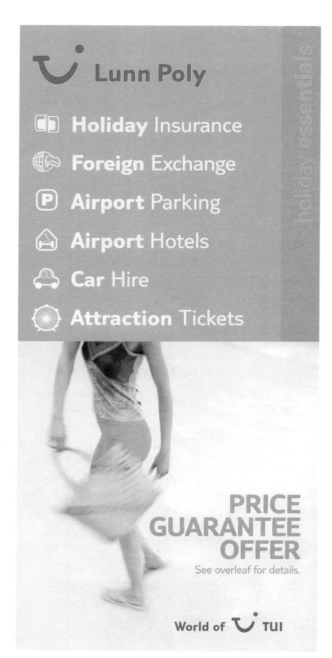

Figure 6.13 Ancillary services on offer

The use of colour is important here, to attract the eye. Often leaflets are produced in the brand colours of the agency to differentiate between different travel providers.

Media

Various forms of media are used as promotional tools. *Videos* may be playing on screens in the agency – these tend to show holidaymakers enjoying their experience doing a variety of activities. Some tour operators also make videos available for purchase showing features of a destination, or in the case of cruises the ships themselves. These are informative but also promotional as they highlight the better features of the product to encourage bookings. Videos are frequently used at travel trade fairs and exhibitions to appeal to visitors.

Interactive displays are used to highlight features of a resort or type of holiday. The purpose of this is to involve the customer in the display and so encourage business. Holiday hypermarkets often use some form of interactive display within the store – this may attract people to try the activity and so encourage them to consider that type of holiday or package. The aim is to involve the customer in the activity by showing movement, which is not possible with a poster. Many attractions use interactive displays as this could encourage visitors to resorts near the attractions.

Press releases can be invaluable marketing tools. The retailer produces the information in an eye-catching format in the hope that other forms of media – such as press and television – may feature news items covering the information. This ensures that the name of the provider is brought to the notice of the general public without the company having to pay for advertising. It raises awareness of new products and may well encourage enquiries and bookings.

Use of colour

Effective use of colour is essential as a promotional tool. When preparing promotional material it is necessary to think of the impact of the various colours. Some are considered to be warm and others are cool. These are used according to the season being promoted and the effect on the

travel agency or tour operator. They are used also at 'point of sale' in travel agencies. They can highlight specific features of an offer, or additional services that can be provided. There is the chance to give more detail than would be available on a poster or window card. Figure 6.13 shows the front of such a folded A4 leaflet, but there is a lot more information inside.

viewer. Bright colours obviously create immediate impact on the eye and attract customers.

Use of colour is also important in brochures produced by tour operators. Customers are more likely to study brochures that are in full colour than those produced in black and white. However, black and white may be used for circulars distributed with promotional material as these are obviously cheaper to produce and support the coloured promotional materials.

Special events

Providers of travel services may arrange promotional events to encourage further bookings, and the travel agencies will invite certain customers based on information held on their databases. These events could be to promote cruises or skiing or adventure holidays. Customers are invited to the events, entertained and usually provided with refreshments, and have an opportunity to ask questions. The atmosphere must be welcoming, and the selling skills (such as those covered in unit 2) will be vital tools in achieving sales targets at these events.

Another type of special event is a holiday exhibition, or travel fair. These are often used as promotional tools during the winter months, to encourage people to book ahead and think of their main vacation. Different agencies and providers will have stands at the exhibition and use most of the various forms of marketing and promotion we have already discussed.

Theory into practice

Arrange a visit to a travel fair, these are often held at weekends when it is felt more people are free to visit. Study the marketing techniques used by the various agencies and make notes of features of each – such as the use of leaflets, video or interactive displays, the availability of brochures and information, and the selling skills of those promoting the product or service.

Telephone numbers for direct booking

Agencies must attract a variety of customers and not everyone can visit their local agency to make enquiries. Direct-booking telephone numbers are usually given on brochures and in advertisements or flyers. The more accessible the product is to the customer, the greater the possibility of attracting business. These direct numbers should be displayed on all advertising materials – flyers, brochures, leaflets, websites – to give maximum coverage of the market.

Websites

As many customers now look for products through Internet searches, website details should be made available at the same time as direct booking numbers. Customers are able to search websites in their own time. For those businesses which rely on Internet selling, the details of the website are crucial to their existence. Some websites also have interactive pages where you can preview a resort, hotel and local attractions.

Internet search engines

Many travel agencies use industry-produced search engines such as Amadeus, Galileo, Sabre and Opodo in order to access information from providers such as accommodation and airlines (Figure 6.14). These are global distribution systems that enable research into providers as well as destinations. They are accessible to retail travel providers, and retailers will pay to use the system.

Others use viewdata systems produced for their own products and services while still having access to wider product information. Agencies subscribe to the services but then have open access to all the information in order to assist customers.

Internet search engines are a vital tool in the agency market, as the latest information and prices are available immediately and bookings can be made on-line.

Theory into practice

Discuss with a representative from a travel agency the Internet search systems used in an organisation. Identify the types of information available to them and how bookings can be made through the system.

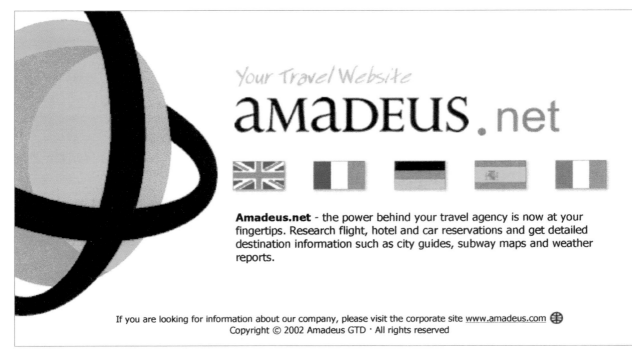

Figure 6.14 Opener to a global distribution system

Teletext advertising

Teletext or television travel shop features are used to raise awareness of the organisation and of special offers.

There is a complete section on holidays on teletext systems on ITV1 and Channel 4, and advertisements are classified under various headings – types of holiday, named providers such as Thomas Cook, destinations and so on. Customers are then able to view the information in their own time, and follow up any specific item by logging on to a website or through direct-booking numbers displayed on the screen.

At times the teletext pages displayed may be out of date, and some sections contain very large numbers of pages (perhaps 80 or more), so it may take some time before the viewer reaches the pages of a specific agent.

TV travel shops include features on specific destinations, give visual images of the accommodation or location, and may also give advice to travellers. The presenters are promoting specific products but also encouraging enquiries. They frequently give direct-booking numbers or website pages for customers to follow through the promotion.

Theory into practice

Go to the teletext pages on your television, and locate the holiday section.

1 Note the range of providers and products on offer.

2 Identify which agents are specialists, which are multiples, and which may be direct-selling organisations.

3 Look at the groupings of destinations offered, and how the control buttons can be used to move to different sections of the teletext pages (e.g. European destinations on different coloured control buttons).

4 You may want to follow through one of the holidays offered with the company concerned to check its availability and compare the price on the teletext with the price you are being quoted.

The impact of lead prices

Customers in the UK have become so used to prices being advertised that are below those in the brochure – and therefore appear to be 'a bargain' – that most travel agencies use the cheapest possible price as a feature of promotional material. This is called the *lead price* or *lead-in price*, because it entices customers to contact the organisation in the hope of getting a bargain holiday.

Most of the offers on teletext pages are lead-in prices to attract customers, but it has been known for those offers to no longer exist when callers contact the organisation. However, once the caller has made contact with the business, then selling skills will come into effect in order to encourage purchase of an alternative product.

On teletext pages, some providers highlight a certain price and flash this during the period of the display. This is another enticement to the customer, with the intention of attracting his or her business.

Window cards in high street travel agencies also tend to quote lead-in prices in order to attract customers.

Legal requirements in relation to marketing and promotion

There are various regulations which travel agencies must adhere to when considering marketing and promotion. You need to have some awareness of these and how they affect the industry.

Trade Descriptions Act 1968

This Act makes it an offence for a trader to apply false or misleading statements or knowingly make such statements about services provided and offered. It is enforced by local authorities' Trading Standards Officers and would apply specifically to information in brochures or leaflets. If holidays are marketed at a specific price, then there must be some available at that price; if a hotel is promoted as being one kilometre from the nearest town, then it should be no more than one kilometre away. All consultants in a travel agency need to be aware that information given to customers must comply with the Act.

Supply of Goods and Services Act 1977

This Act will apply more to products than to services, as the good itself must be fit for the purpose and of serviceable quality. However, agencies do need to consider the requirements of the Act in terms of any products they are selling that are tangible.

Consumer Protection Act 1987

This Act stipulates that the price quoted on promotional materials – such as window cards, advertisements etc. – should be the full price that the customer will pay. Extras (e.g. fuel charges, airline meals, transfers) must be stipulated. Lead-in prices that are unrealistic are outlawed. Failure to meet the requirements of this Act could result in legal action being taken by the Trading Standards Institute.

Consumer Credit Act 1974

This Act will affect those customers who are paying for their holiday in instalments, as the terms of the agreement must state the actual price of the product and display the interest rates and effects on that price over the period of repayment. Most travellers will pay using other forms of credit, such as a credit card, rather than with a credit agreement, but consultants need to be aware of this Act in case a customer wishes to pay via a credit agreement. Any agent offering credit terms must be licensed by the Office of Fair Trading, and any agreements must be set down in a specified way and contain specific information that includes the terms of the loan or credit and interest to be paid.

EU Package Holiday Directives of 1993 and 1995

These will have been considered during your study for units 1 and 4. They aim to give the consumer protection and the right to compensation if the products sold as a package do not meet the minimum standards laid down or as conveyed to the customer. It is recommended that you review the work done in this area and relate this to the role of retail travel products and services.

ASA and Ofcom

The Advertising Standards Agency (ASA) is an organisation that controls the advertising industry. It sets out a code of practice that advertisers in the non-broadcast media are expected to follow. This code is a body of rules that members of the industry agree to abide by. Advertisements must be legal, decent, honest and truthful and must be prepared with a sense of responsibility to consumers and society at large.

The Office of Communications (Ofcom), on the other hand, enforces codes of practice for advertising in the broadcast media, but advertisers still need to consider the restraints of the ASA.

Technology and its effect on the travel industry

There have been many references during the course of this chapter to the changes in the industry due to developments in technology. These effects are on-going and you will need to keep abreast of developments during your course of study, as many new processes and procedures are likely to be introduced over the next few years.

Developments in information technology

There has been increased use of the Internet by both agents and consumers, and changes in the way viewdata systems operate. Both customers and agents can access much more information from websites and viewdata systems, with many websites offering on-line booking services linked to providers. This has resulted in an increased number of e-tickets or vouchers being issued to cover services, which consumers present at the point of use (e.g. airline tickets, accommodation vouchers).

Website services are available 24 hours a day, which is convenient for those people who work unsocial hours and cannot access a high street agency during normal business hours, or even a holiday hypermarket with their extended opening hours.

Methods of organising travel

From the range of travel agency providers we have covered earlier in this chapter, the choice open to the consumer when organising travel is vast. A consumer can tailor-make his or her own package, can buy components from different travel agencies, or buy a complete package through a retail travel agency.

The business travel market has changed from having travel agency implants in companies to having 24-hour call centres with their travel management company.

Selection of particular forms of transport

You will have looked at the various forms of transport in your study for units 1 and 4, so you will realise there are many ways of booking transport.

Choice of transport

The choice of transport might depend on several factors, such as cost, convenience and accessibility – not only for departure but also for bookings. Some customers may wish to arrive at their chosen destination quickly, so would choose air transport. But they still have a choice between scheduled full-service airlines (e.g. British Airways, Qantas, British Midland, Monarch), scheduled no-frills airlines (e.g as Ryanair, easyJet, bmibaby) or charter airlines (e.g. Mytravel, Air 2000, Thomas Cook Airways).

Others may wish to adopt a more leisurely route, and take a coach, hire a car or use rail services. For travel across the English Channel, there are a variety of routes to consider – ferry, Eurostar and Channel Tunnel car transport services. There are also customers who use the transport as the central focus of their holiday, which is why cruises are becoming so popular.

Most of these forms of transport can be booked using Internet connections through the providers' direct-sell websites or net-based travel companies such as lastminute.com and expedia.com. Retail travel agencies can use their viewdata systems to search and make bookings.

Advantages and disadvantages of different forms of travel

There are advantages and disadvantages of using each transport form, and these need to be considered in relation to the expectations and requirements of the customer. A family with young children, for example, may prefer a flight rather than a rail journey as it could be quicker to reach the destination. However, the volume of luggage they need may mean that baggage allowances are very restricted. If they are hiring a car they will probably require a larger car with more storage space than a person travelling alone.

Cost may be a deciding factor in the selection of transport. For example, the cost of a taxi to the airport for a family of four may work out considerably cheaper than rail travel for the same purpose. It could also be more convenient, because it is door-to-door and no other form of transport would be needed to get to the station.

A hired car may be more convenient for a family or an elderly couple on holiday. It can be used as and when required, the journey can be undertaken in stages, and visits to attractions can be made to suit a personal programme. Also, there are no great restrictions on the amount of luggage that can be taken. Consideration does have to be given, however, to driving requirements at the destination – an international driving licence and insurance will be required, and some hire companies have mileage limitations during the period of hire.

If you are working in a travel agency you will need to be aware of advantages and disadvantages of various forms of travel in order to advise customers appropriately to meet their needs and requirements.

CASE STUDY

Trends in retail travel provision

According to research carried out by Mintel, a market research company, by July 2004 there had been a decrease of 6 per cent in package holiday bookings by British travellers since 1999.

The most significant factor in this decline was the use of the Internet for bookings. People were choosing different types of holiday from the usual package – looking for adventure and more individualised holidays, in all age ranges. Many of the bookings are now made on-line one month ahead of the departure date, in contrast to the earlier practice of booking around four months ahead.

In 2004 there was also a campaign being started to encourage travel agents to introduce a fee for advice given to the public. Many customers visit a travel agent to collect information, advice and brochures, then go away and make an independent booking. Travel agencies are therefore having valuable selling time taken up giving this advice and information, with no income generated. If they charged a fee of, say, £20 for a consultation this would earn some income (this fee being refunded if the customer went on to book a holiday with the travel agency).

The public, however, may react unfavourably to this type of charge. Some agents (e.g. Lunn Poly) make a £10 administration charge for bookings of less than £100, to help recover some income.

From what you have learned so far, consider the reasons for these developments and any effects on the retail travel market.

Use of global distribution systems

Earlier in this chapter we mentioned global distribution systems, such as Amadeus. These systems are available to registered agency members and allow access to a wide variety of providers and services. However, agencies are charged for the use of these systems, and not all airlines or providers are available on every GDS system.

The information is always current regarding availability. Most systems also have an added advantage of providing destination guides which can give relevant information to consultants about features of a specific destination.

Self check-in at airports

Developments in information technology have increased the efficiency and reduced the processing time at check-in points. In October 2004, Nottingham's East Midlands Airport was the first in Europe to introduce self-service check-in. This is an express service with passengers being processed by machines that identify them by their passport, booking reference or credit card. The passenger then selects a seat on the aircraft while the check-in staff print luggage tags, weigh bags and ask security questions. The check-in assistant can thus deal with up to four passengers at one time using one staff member to two kiosks. Other systems available allow check-in at rail stations (such as Gatwick Express) to avoid delays in departure halls.

Sources of information used for travel organisation

We have already considered some of the sources of information which travel organisers have available to assist customers. Other sources need to be considered for their value to both the retail agency and the consumer.

Guides, gazetteers and atlases

Travel agents should have access to the *World Travel Guide* which gives details of worldwide destinations, travel routes, maps and features. This is also available on-line at www.worldtravelguide.com and is constantly updated.

Many travellers will not visit a new destination without having consulted or used a *guidebook*. These are produced by specialised publishers, such as Rough Guides, Lonely Planet, Berlitz, AA City Pack, Dorling Kindersley Top 10, to name but a few. The guides may cover a whole country or region, or focus on a specific destination. The information varies in style and presentation, but the aim is to give the traveller details of history and culture of the destination, accommodation and transport, maps, visitor attractions, food and entertainment available in the location. The information is unbiased and current. Climate and topography may also be included in the information presented, and some of the guides are designed to be easily portable.

Gazetteers are similar to guides, but may contain more listings of facilities at a destination. There is usually less information about opening times, costs etc., but gazetteers can be useful sources.

Atlases and maps are invaluable when locating a destination. Many brochures produced by tour operators provide an outline map of the area and indicate the location of accommodation, but provide little detailed geographical data. An atlas will assist in locating the relationship of a specific destination to the country concerned. People may refer to 'an island in the Caribbean', for example, but have little awareness of its physical location within the Caribbean or its proximity to other islands. An atlas will help to identify the geographic location.

> **Think it over ...**
>
> Maps can be misleading, as this true story recounted by a travel agent in the USA demonstrates:
>
> *One person complained furiously about a package vacation in Orlando, Florida. When asked what was wrong with the package, he said he had been expecting a room with an ocean view. The travel agent explained that that was not possible, since Orlando is in the middle of the state. He replied: 'Don't lie to me. I looked on the map, and Florida is a very thin state!'*

Another customer could have benefited from looking at a map before telephoning the same travel agent:

> The caller enquired about a package trip to the island state of Hawaii. After mulling over all the cost information, the person asked: 'Would it be cheaper to fly to California and then take the train to Hawaii?'

Directories

Familiar directories include *Yellow Pages*, *Thomson's Directory* and the telephone directory. These list businesses either by type or alphabetically, and the same type of directory is available at locations for accommodation. Often it is possible to obtain street directories, such as *A-Z London*, which indexes all the street names with grid references. Directories are invaluable for large cities, but are also useful tools when searching for a specific location or destination. Even for Internet searches, information is displayed in directory format alphabetically to enable fast searches.

Timetables

Tour operators' brochures include timetables, often at the back, giving flight departure and arrival times. Timetables are provided also by other transport services such as ferries, railways and airlines. Timetable information can be obtained on-line and is available also at railway stations and departure points for ferries.

> ### ✱ REMEMBER!
> You will need to develop good skills in reading and interpreting timetables when you come to prepare your itineraries for the final part of your assessment.

When reading timetables for overseas travel, it is essential to consider the journey's duration. Timetables quote arrivals and departures using local times at the two locations, and these can vary. Consider time zones used across the world and features such as Greenwich Mean Time (GMT), which is in London, and the International Date Line (IDL) in the Pacific Ocean (Figure 6.15).

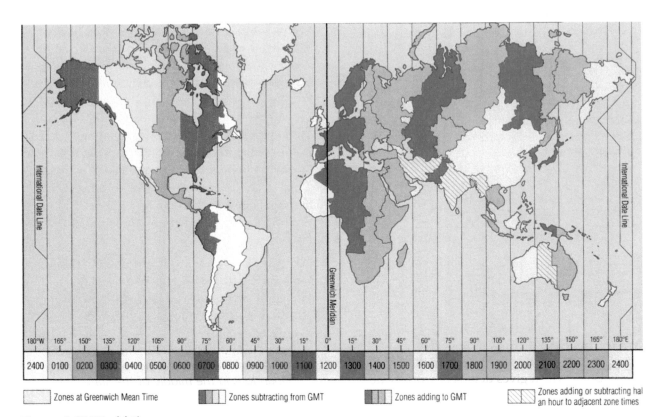

Figure 6.15 World time zones

Examples

* From the world time zones chart you can see that at 12 noon in the UK it is 0700 in New York on the east coast of the USA and 0400 in Los Angeles on the west coast. If a plane leaves London Heathrow at 1300 local time and the flight to New York takes seven hours, what would be the local time of arrival? [*Answer*: 1300 plus seven-hour flight = 2000 hours – minus the 5-hour time difference. So the plane is due to land at 1500, New York time.] Now calculate the time of arrival if the plane left at the same time, but flew to Los Angeles.

* Going east from London to Singapore, a flight leaving at 2150 takes 13 hours. At what time would it arrive in Singapore? [*Answer*: 2150 plus 13-hour flight = 1050 the next day – plus the 7-hour time difference. So the plane is due to land at 1750, Singapore time.]

* If the passenger then left Singapore at 2000 on a flight of 7 hours 15 minutes to Sydney, Australia, what would be the arrival time? [*Answer*: 2000 plus 7.15 flight time = 0315 – plus the 2-hour time difference. So the plane is due to land at 0515, Sydney time.]

> **Think it over ...**
>
> When using information sources, you need to realise that some of them will provide more appropriate information about itineraries than others. If you do not know what information is available in each of these types of sources, you will not be able to make the best use of them. Obtain a variety of the sources described in this section, and study them for the types of information they give.

Planning and costing travel itineraries

Getting the necessary basic information

Before an itinerary can be planned, it is necessary to establish exactly what the customer wants, including any special requirements. This can all be noted down using a customer enquiry form such

as that shown earlier in Figure 6.4 on page 215. It should include the following basic information:

* *Dates and times of travel.*

* *Number of people travelling* (and, where relevant, their ages – particularly if there are children as some operators have limits as to what age a youngster can be before an adult fare becomes due or has a free child's place).

* *Arrival and departure points.*

* *Preferred types of travel* – rail, air, coach etc.

* *How much they want to pay*. Usually a maximum figure would be given here and the consultant would aim to match the total costs of the journey to this budget.

* *Time available to complete the journey*. A traveller going to Australia and having to be there by a specific date might want a more leisurely journey to allow a stopover in Dubai, Singapore or Hong Kong.

* *Any special circumstances that might may affect the booking*. Are twin beds required rather than a double room? Do any of the travelling group have disabilities? If children are travelling unaccompanied, many airlines need to be made aware of this so that they can arrange escorts to accompany the child through terminals etc. Animals can be transported and taken on holiday, but special arrangements need to be made for their care and protection on the journey. If there are very young babies, these must be named on the passenger list, but would not be provided with a seat. However, the airline needs to be aware of these so that special baby carriers can be provided, particularly if the flight is a long one or overnight.

Having obtained this basic information, then a search can be undertaken to find holidays matching the criteria. The consultant must aim to meet all these requirements, or match them as closely as possible.

However, if these cannot be met, or are no longer available, then the consultant must search to find the next best alternative. It may be the departure airport being reconsidered, or the accommodation. It could be consideration being given to alternative aspects of transport – such as Channel Tunnel car transport rather than a ferry, or an alternative ferry departure point, or a no-frills airline instead of a full-service scheduled service, or a charter plane instead of a scheduled flight. There may not be flights available to the destination airport of first choice, so the consultant needs to know which airports are in the same locality to provide a suitable alternative.

The budget

The overall price is very relevant, and the consultant might not be able to meet the budget set by the holidaymaker. Alternative accommodation may need to be considered which does come within the budget. Many other things can affect the cost.

✱ Supplements will need to be added for extra services. Examples are a room with a sea view, first-class rail travel, taxi transfers at the destination rather than coach transfers, low occupancy rates for apartments, or a single-room supplement.

✱ Taxes will need to be added to the basic cost, such as UK airport duty, airport taxes, and any government duties or taxes. These can mount up considerably as they are charged per passenger, not per booking.

✱ It can happen that the basic cost of the holiday is within the budget given to the consultant, but when extra costs are added, this budget is exceeded. If car hire is seen as a separate item to the main budget costs, then this will not affect final decisions. But if the cost of car hire has been presumed to be within the total budget, then the consultant would need to look at cheaper alternatives for transport and accommodation.

✱ Travel insurance needs to be added if the customer does not have a current annual policy.

Discounts

Another costing feature to be considered when searching for possible matches to the basic requirements are discounts. There may be a discount available on account of age, for children

or for senior citizens, or those which relate to the size of the group. Often with large group bookings there is an allowance of one person free per number of other people in the group. Certain companies also allow discounts or special offers for family groups, such as free child places. Figure 6.16 shows examples of group discounts.

FREE Child Places and Kids Reductions

(All reductions apply only to selected holidays)

| | 1st Child | | Additional Children | |
Departures on or between	FREE PLACES	After sold out	European Family Value Price	All Other Accommodation
1st May – 21st May	FREE	£79	£99	50%
22nd May – 29th Jun	FREE	£139	£179	35%
30th Jun – 17th Aug	FREE	£189	£239	20%
18th Aug – 7th Sep	FREE	£149	£189	25%
8th Sep to End of Season	FREE	£99	£149	40%

*Must share a room or an apartment with 2 full-fare paying adults

NEW for 2004 – Single Parent Savers Kids from £99

(When 1 adult shares with 1 child under 12yrs) at selected properties – on selected charter flights

Departures on or between	Price
1st May – 21st May	£99
22nd May – 29th Jun	£179
30th Jun – 17th Aug	£239
18th Aug – 7th Sep	£189
8th Sep to End of Season	£149

*Must share a room or an apartment with 2 full-fare paying adults

NEW for 2004 – Teenage Discounts 12–15yrs

(At selected properties – on selected charter flights)

Departures on or between	When 2 adults share a room with a teenager
1st May – 21st May	50%
22nd May – 29th Jun	35%
30th Jun – 17th Aug	20%
18th Aug – 7th Sep	25%
8th Sep to End of Season	40%

FREE Places for Groups

| | | GROUP SIZE | | | | |
Departures on or between		8 to 12	13 to 18	19 to 25	26 to 34	35 plus
01-May	21-May	1	1.5	2	3	5
22-May	29-Jun	0	0.5	1	2	3
30-Jun	20-Jul	0.5	1	1.5	2.5	3.5
21-Jul	17-Aug	0	0.5	1	2	3
18-Aug	07-Sep	0.5	1	1.5	2.5	3.5
08-Sep	31-Oct	1	1.5	2	3	5

N.B. This grid shows the maximum number of free places given in selected accommodation. Our Groups Department will confirm the exact number of free places applicable at the time of booking.

Figure 6.16 Examples of reductions for groups and others

Examples of other special offers are three weeks for the price of two, or two for the price of one (Figure 6.17). These offers are often advertised near to the departure dates, as tour operators are anxious to achieve occupancy rates and earn whatever income they can from bookings. It is therefore more difficult to plan them in an itinerary.

Planning the itinerary

There is a standard industry layout for itineraries, though some computer systems produce slightly different formats. The main information that must be included is:

* booking reference and date of issue
* date, time (local times given) and point of departure which may include terminal number
* check-in details at all departure points if on flight or Eurostar
* flight code and name of airline if travelling by air
* number of passengers
* resort and name/details of accommodation
* identification of special requirements fulfilled (e.g. single room, sea view).

Some itineraries also include details of costs for the booking and these should be broken down into basic costs, discounts and supplements, airport and/or government taxes.

Figure 6.18 shows a final invoice which gives the basic details.

However, if the itinerary is for a tour, more information will be needed. This includes nights at specific destinations. An example is shown in Figure 6.19. This example does not show specific costs, but these would be included on the final invoice for the vacation tour.

Figure 6.19 depicts quite a complicated itinerary. The sources used to research the tour would be the Singapore Airlines timetable, accommodation providers at all the destinations en route (though these are not given on this itinerary), the Union Limited Train timetable and the Blue Train timetable. As this is to be a guided tour, specific details of departure and arrival for the train journeys would be given by the tour manager. They could have been included on this itinerary, but that would have given possibly too much information for the passenger's needs.

FREE excursions on selected cruises

GO POSH!

WHY WAIT?
GET THE BEST OFFERS NOW!

2-for-1 prices

OCEAN-GOING CRUISES IN GOLD-STAR LUXURY

Alaska ★ Bermuda ★ Canary Isles ★ Caribbean ★ Greek Isles ★ Madagascar ★ Mauritius ★ Mediterranean ★ Seychelles ★ Tahiti ★

Early bookings only!
Pick the best suites
Select your favourite destinations
Choose when you travel

PRICES DOWN for LIMITED PERIOD ONLY!

7-night cruises from £1, 010pp*

* strictly for early bookings and subject to availability

24-hour call lines
080 5050 1234 for brochure
080 5050 4321 for reservations

www.poshcruises.com   **POSH CRUISES**

Figure 6.17 A cruise offer advertised in a newspaper

P&O ✈ Cruises

BOOKING CONFIRMATION
PASSENGER COPY

Date Printed	Booking Ref	Group Name		
19 JUL 04	6L6NDR			
Tour	Cruise No		Agency Contact/ABTA	
	F416	HELEN		000G4376
Departure	Grade/Cabin		Ship Name/Registry	
04 OCT 04	JB/A405	ADONIA / BRITISH		
From Port		To Port	Number of Cruise Nights	
SOUTHAMPTON		SOUTHAMPTON	7	

Richmond House, Terminus Terrace
Southampton
SO14 3PN
Reservations: 0845 3555333
Facsimile: 02380 523720
Internet www.pocruises.com

VAT Reg No: GB 761 4300 58
ATOL 6294

Payment Schedule

Deposit w/o Ins	Deposit w/ Ins
120.00	
Due Date:	By Return
Balance Amount	Balance Due
Total Costs	

Mail payments to:
Cruise Payments
P&O Cruises
PO Box 1306
Southampton, SO14 3ZG

ATTN HELEN
CRUISE2CRUISE.COM
CORINTHIAN COURT
80 MILTON PARK
ABINGDON
OXFORDSHIR OX14 4RY

Currency

POUNDS STERLING

Description	Amount
NET FARE	1196.00
TOTAL	1196.00

CRUISE2CRUISE
PRICE £1064

Important Notice

WITH EFFECT FROM 27 FEBRUARY 2004, THE CONTRACT FOR YOUR P&O CRUISES PRINCESS
HOLIDAY TRANSFERRED FROM P & O PRINCESS CRUISES INTERNATIONAL LIMITED TO
CARNIVAL PLC, OUR PARENT COMPANY. THIS IS PURELY A CHANGE OF LEGAL ENTITY
FOR OUR BUSINESS AND WILL NOT HAVE ANY IMPACT ON OUR DAY TO DAY OPERATIONS.

Dining

NON-SMOKING
CONFIRMED — FIRST

Comments

BEDS IN TWIN CONFIG

Passenger(s)

Passenger(s)	Age	City	Air	Ins	Occ Ship	Occ Land	Comment
1. ROWE, FLORENCE MRS	61	LON	N	OWN	DBL		
2. DUGDALE, HANNAH MRS	83	LON	N	OWN	DBL		

Itinerary

```
AIR TRANSPORTATION NOT PROVIDED
MON 04/10 SOUTHAMPTON              05.00PM
          EMBARK FROM 02:00PM
TUE 05/10 COBH            02.00PM 11.59PM
WED 06/10 AT SEA
THU 07/10 LA CORUNA       08.00AM 05.00PM
FRI 08/10 BILBAO          08.00AM 06.00PM
SAT 09/10 LA ROCHELLE     08.00AM 06.00PM
SUN 10/10 ST PETER PORT   01.00PM 06.00PM
          TENDER REQUIRED
MON 11/10 SOUTHAMPTON     07:00AM
AIR TRANSPORTATION NOT PROVIDED
```

IMPORTANT NOTICE: The terms and conditions which govern this booking are printed in the back of the P&O Cruises brochure from which you booked.
A copy of these terms and conditions is available from your Travel Agent or from P&O Cruises. Please read all conditions carefully as they affect the passengers
legal right, particulary with respect to the provision of medical care (conditions 11 and 12), cancellation conditions (conditions 17), matters of security and safety
(condition 28), and the Carrier's liability and your right to claim (condition 43 to 46).
P&O Cruises is a business name of Carnival PLC, registered office: Carnival House, 5 Gainsford Street, London SE1 2NE, registered number: 4039524

Figure 6.18 A printed booking confirmation for a cruise

NAME(S) OF PASSENGER(S): MR JOHN AND MRS ANN JONES
ADDRESS: 1534 CAUSEWAY, SINGAPORE
18-DAY 17-NIGHT TOUR TO SOUTH AFRICA

No. of day	Date	Itinerary	Depart	Arrival	Remark
0	6 Feb	Check in at Singapore Airport		2320	Min 2 hours before flight
1	7 Feb	Singapore to Cape Town on Singapore Airlines SQ406 Arrive & overnight at Cape Town	0120	0915	Total of 5 nights in Cape Town
2–5	8–11 Feb	Cape Town			
6	12 Feb	Depart Cape Town Transfer to Union Ltd Train Night on Garden Route	1030		Total of 4 nights on Union Ltd Train
7–9	13–15 Feb	Union Ltd Train Night on Garden Route			
10	16 Feb	Leave Union Ltd Train Board Blue Train, overnight	1200	1600	Total of 1 night on Blue Train
11	17 Feb	Leave Blue Train Arrive Pretoria, overnight	1200		Total of 2 nights in Pretoria
12	18 Feb	Hotel in Pretoria, overnight			
13	19 Feb	Depart Pretoria Arrive Pinalesberg Game Park, overnight in lodge	0900	1500	Total of 2 nights in Pinalesberg Game Park
14	20 Feb	Pinalesberg Game Park, overnight in lodge			
15	21 Feb	Depart Pinalesberg Game Park Arrive Johannesburg, overnight	0930	1600	Total of 3 nights in Johannesburg
16–17	22–23 Feb	Johannesburg, overnight			
18	24 Feb	Check in at Johannesburg Airport Depart Johannesburg to Singapore on Singapore Airlines SQ405	1215 1415		Total no of nights: 17
19	25 Feb	Arrive Singapore		0615	

Figure 6.19 A detailed itinerary

Case study: London to Scotland on business

Let us now go through the process of planning an itinerary. Imagine you are acting as a consultant in a travel agency and receive an enquiry from a business person who lives in London.

He first has to travel to Glasgow for a meeting at 3.30 p.m. He will then go to visit two other companies, one in Edinburgh with a meeting at 10.30 a.m. the next day, and one in Stirling at 2.30 p.m. There is an evening function at his Edinburgh hotel which he will attend, and he has to be back in London by 3.00 p.m. the following day. You now have some basic information about the customer. What else do you need to know? Figure 6.20 shows what your enquiry form might contain.

Armed with this additional information, you can undertake a search for the best possible routes and times to suit the customer.

> **✳ REMEMBER!**
>
> All airports have check-in times – they are normally a *minimum of one hour* before the flight departure time for UK internal flights. Rail journeys do not require check-in times, but the customer will require booked seats.

Having obtained the necessary information, you have to contact the client with two itineraries with costs, one for air and one for rail. If the client chooses the air option, this could be presented as in Figure 6.21.

You also have to give the client a note of the cost. The major elements for this itinerary are:

✳ Heathrow Express return

✳ British Airways flight return, including tax

✳ Hertz car hire for 3 days

✳ single room at Barnston Thistle Hotel for two nights, bed and breakfast rate.

Finally, obtain confirmation from the client that the itinerary is acceptable. You will often have to be prepared to modify the details if required.

QUESTIONS	RESPONSES	SOURCES
How does the customer wish to travel?	Fastest method, rail or air	Rail and air timetables
If by air, which airport would the customer prefer?	Heathrow	Air timetables from Heathrow and flight prices
If by rail, does the customer want first or standard class?	First class	Rail enquiry lines for timetables and ticket costs
How will the customer get to the departure point?	If air, by Heathrow Express If train, by tube from home	Heathrow Express timetables and costs
Will the customer require overnight accommodation?	One night in Glasgow and one in Edinburgh	Directories and gazetteers for accommodation or Internet accommodation sites
What grade of accommodation?	Four- or five-star hotel	
How will the customer want to travel around Scotland to his appointments?	Hire car	Hire car companies and prices, detailed from Internet or directories

Figure 6.20 What your enquiry form might contain

25 Aug 2005	0930	Heathrow Express, London Paddington Station
	0953	Arrive Terminal 4, Heathrow Airport
	1000	Check-in Terminal 4 Heathrow for flight BA1478 to Glasgow International
	1125	Departure flight BA1478
	1245	Arrive Glasgow International
	1300	Collect hire car (Hertz) – Ford Focus 1.6LX
	1530	Meeting at ZXY Co., Fleet St, Glasgow
	1700	Depart Fleet Street, drive to Edinburgh
	1900	Check in Barnton Thistle Hotel for 2 nights Car parking available on site
26 Aug 2005	0930	Depart hotel Drive to meeting with ABC Co., Queensferry Rd
	1030	Meeting at ABC Co.
	1130	Depart ABC Co. Drive to Stirling
	1430	Arrive JJ Brothers, Stirling
	1530	Depart JJ Brothers, Stirling Return to Barnton Thistle Hotel, Edinburgh
	1930	Evening function at Barnton Thistle Hotel, Edinburgh
27 Aug 2005	0830	Check out of hotel Drive to Glasgow International Airport
	1030	Arrive Glasgow International Airport Return car to Hertz
	1040	Check-in British Airways, flight BA1483 to London Heathrow
	1140	Departure Flight BA1482 to London Heathrow
	1300	Arrive London Heathrow, Terminal 4
	1330	Heathrow Express to Paddington Station
	1353	Arrive Paddington Station Taxi or tube to office

Figure 6.21 An itinerary ready for approval by the customer

Assessment guidance

To meet the requirements for Assessment Objective 4, you have to prepare and present two itineraries that are fully costed. These must be for two different customer types (e.g. a group and a couple or individual), and must have complexity within them. The P&O example given earlier is fairly straightforward as it is for a couple, on a cruise for a week, with no extras involved. If this couple had booked car hire at one of the ports, taxi transfers to Southampton, or pre-booked excursions at other ports, this would have made it more complex.

If you were planning a ski trip for a group of students, for example, you would have to consider equipment hire, methods of transport which would keep the group together (coach or flight), discounts for groups, and accommodation types. This would make a complex itinerary suitable to meet the requirements for assessment.

When you are planning your own itineraries, it is important to keep records of your information sources whilst you are searching for the detail of the itinerary, as well as notes to form your explanation of why specific types of travel have been chosen to meet the specific needs of the customers.

You will also need to make some reference in your explanation as to how you met the legal requirements of travel organisers, in terms of consumer protection. Did you choose an agency that has an ATOL licence, or ABTA licence? Have you complied with all the relevant consumer protection laws?

Test your knowledge

1 Explain *three* benefits of obtaining advice and booking through an independent travel agency.
2 Indicate the place in the chain of distribution of a miniple travel agency.
3 Explain why the market share of the multiple travel agencies is greater overall than that of independent agencies.
4 How does a hypermarket set targets and measure its performance?
5 Identify and describe *four* products and services provided by retail travel agencies.
6 Explain the difference between a flight ticket and a flight voucher.
7 Describe the benefits of hiring a car at a destination for a couple travelling with young children.
8 Explain, using a named example, how global distribution systems aid the work of travel agents.
9 'The use of the Internet has affected the way customers arrange travel.' Analyse this statement and the effect it has on the marketing strategies of agencies.
10 Describe three types of promotional techniques used by holiday hypermarkets.
11 What are the main features of a guidebook?
12 Identify the types of information needed from a customer before undertaking a search for a suitable travel package.

Resources

* *Trade Travel Gazette*
* *Travel Weekly*
* Travel agency managers and websites

UNIT 7

Hospitality

Introduction

Hospitality can be described as the *provision of accommodation, food and drink services away from home*. The hospitality industry provides customers with this.

People are the main focus of the travel and tourism industry. Whether someone visits a destination for leisure or for business, and stays a day or several nights, the welcome given on arrival and the quality of service experienced during the stay will strongly influence the memories that person takes away. Therefore, good customer service matters to everyone and is the heart of business operations within the hospitality industry.

You will study the practices and procedures used by major hospitality providers in order to improve or develop their customer service provision. This will be linked to developments in information technology (IT), which is often used to provide more effective and responsive customer service.

In order to complete the required portfolio work, you will need to visit a variety of hospitality outlets to gain details about accommodation, accommodation services, food and drink services, corporate hospitality provision and customer service in hospitality.

How you will be assessed

This unit is assessed through your portfolio work. It will comprise an investigation into the provision of hospitality in travel and tourism, as follows:

* sectors delivering hospitality and the effects of seasonality, tangibility and perishability
* types of corporate hospitality
* types of food and drink services
* customer service issues and the importance of information technology.

Sectors delivering hospitality

Hospitality is the provision of food, drink and accommodation. For the most part the recipients of hospitality will be away from home, so the term can be expanded to include *all* the products and services offered – including travel, entertainment, recreation and leisure activities.

Hospitality consists of a mixture of *tangible and intangible* elements of both products and services.

* The product consists of the food, drink and accommodation.

* The service consists of the atmosphere and image that surrounds the participants.

THE HOSPITALITY INDUSTRY

Hotels

Restaurants

Leisure and sport

Gaming

Pubs and clubs

Self-catering

Other accommodation

Caterers

Meetings and facilities

Education and training

Figure 7.1 Providers in the hospitality industry

Characteristics of the hospitality industry

The hospitality industry displays many of the characteristics of service industries in general, but with great fluctuations in demand. Demand will fluctuate over time – the impact of seasonality – as well as by the type of customer. Hospitality cannot be delivered without the presence of the customer. The customer is the final judge of satisfaction with both the service and product provided in hospitality. This means that quality assurance is very important, so it will be examined later in this unit.

Achieving a balance between demand patterns, resources and operational capacity is a difficult task facing managers in hospitality. Too few customers overall will lead to financial ruin for the organisation, and too many customers can reduce the quality of the experience and leave customers dissatisfied.

There is a great variety of providers of hospitality. The industry is vast and ranges from huge multinational companies, which own chains of hotels or restaurants across the globe, to small local businesses managed by one or two people.

Accommodation types

A wide range of accommodation types is available in the UK. An important distinguishing feature is between *serviced* and *non-serviced* types.

Customers staying in serviced accommodation will expect things to be done for them. The availability of such services, even if they are not used by the customer, is included in the price charged. With non-serviced accomodation, services for the provision of meals, bars, shops and cleaning may be available on a separate

Think it over ...

Figure 7.2 is a summary of the types of accommodation available in the UK.

COMMERCIAL		NON-COMMERCIAL	
Serviced	*Self-catering*	*Serviced*	*Self-catering*
Hotels	Caravanning	Youth hostels	Private caravans
Motels	Camping	YMCAs	Private camping
Guest houses	Villas	YWCAs	Home exchange
Bed and breakfast	Apartments		Private motor home
Farmhouses	Holiday cottages		Second home
Activity centres			VFR
Holiday camps		Educational institutions	
Holiday centres			
Holiday villages			

Figure 7.2 Types of accommodation available in the UK

1 Discuss the main differences between commercial and non-commercial accommodation providers.

2 Can you think of any other accommodation providers to add to the diagram?

commercial basis, as in a holiday centre, but they are not included in the price charged for the accommodation.

Hotels

A hotel can be defined as an accommodation outlet with a minimum of six letting bedrooms, of which at least half must have en-suite or private bathroom facilities. A hotel will usually have a licence to sell and serve alcoholic drinks, and will serve breakfasts and evening meals.

There is a huge range of types of hotel, from first-class and luxury hotels which provide full service on a 24-hour basis at a relatively high cost, to small family-run establishments.

International hotels

These are owned by large chain companies operating around the world. Services are offered to exactly the same high standard in each hotel, to reflect the *corporate image*. Customers therefore receive consistency, security and dependability. There are usually many additional services such as secretarial support, high-speed communications networks, and bedrooms that provide working facilities such as a desk and Internet connection.

Theory into practice

Either collect brochures of the major international hotel chains, or use a search engine to locate their websites (e.g. www.radissonedwardian.com and www.mill-cop.com). Find out:

- the locations of their hotels in the UK
- the services and facilities offered
- the price ranges.

Commercial and leisure hotels

These are sited in large towns and cities. They are used predominantly by business customers from Monday to Thursday and by the short-break market from Friday to Sunday.

These hotels offer a wide range of facilities to accommodate the needs of both types of customer. They will try to achieve a reputation for high standards and efficient service, combined with a relaxed atmosphere and customer-orientated staff. In-house facilities often include some form of leisure facilities, limited room services, tea- and coffee-making facilities in bedrooms, plus trouser-press, iron and ironing board, hairdryer, toiletries etc.

Swallow Hotels

Swallow Hotels (www.swallowhotels.com) now operates under the ownership of London and Edinburgh Inns (www.londonandedinburghinns.com). It is one of the UK's leading and fastest growing hotel chains, with 29 hotels in England and Scotland and 28 individually styled inns.

Swallow Hotels produces a Breakaway brochure that offers savings on normal hotel rates. All Breakaways include:

- no minimum stay
- continental or full English breakfast served in the restaurant
- free accommodation/breakfast for children under 16 sharing their parents' room
- free car parking.

These features are aimed at leisure customers. There are many locations to choose from and different types of hotel.

Meetings and events are catered for too. Two conference packages are offered – an 8-hour one (for a day conference or meeting) and a 24-hour one (with overnight accommodation).

Each room has an en-suite bathroom, direct-dial telephone, satellite TV, radio, tea- and coffee-making facilities, hairdryer and iron, ironing board and trouser-press. All the hotels have restaurants and lounge bars.

Many of the hotels also have leisure facilities – a heated indoor swimming pool, spa bath, steam room, sauna, gymnasium and relaxation area. Some hotels also offer health and beauty treatments.

What would be the appeal of Swallow Hotels to (a) leisure travellers, and (b) business travellers?

Resort hotels

Resort hotels are aimed mainly at customers for pleasure on a medium-stay basis (four nights or more). The accommodation ranges from simple unlicensed bed and breakfast establishments to licensed premises offering food and drink throughout the day.

These hotels aim to give customers the intangible aspects of hospitality, rather than a wide range of products and facilities. The emphasis is therefore on the friendly atmosphere. Repeat business – the same customers returning year after year – is an aim of these hotels.

Theory into practice

The traditional British seaside holiday is often in a resort hotel. Select a major seaside destination and research the resort hotels available there.

Transient hotels and motels

These are often budget establishments. These may be found at motorway service areas, near motorway junctions and on major road routes. All offer a basic standard of accommodation with few facilities, to provide for the needs of business travellers.

Ibis, Sofitel and Novotel are all brands belonging to the same budget chain, Accor (www.accor.com). These hotels all provide budget accommodation.

Theory into practice

Find out how the facilities and services of budget accommodation differ from other types of hotels.

Inns

Inns provide bed and breakfast accommodation within a traditional public house environment. A restaurant and bar will be open to non-residents and will provide food at lunchtime and/or during the evening.

The Sycamore Inn on the edge of the Peak District is a freehouse with a restaurant and accommodation (Figure 7.3). The inn's owners developed a website (www.sycamoreinn.co.uk) that allows regular customers to e-mail restaurant bookings and visitors to book accommodation. The inn has five full-time staff, with the owners living on the premises.

Figure 7.3 The Sycamore Inn

1 **Find out what 'freehouse' means.**
2 **What type of customer do you think would use inns such as the Sycamore?**

Guesthouse and bed-and-breakfast accommodation

There are over 30 000 privately owned and managed guesthouses, including about 11 700 bed-and-breakfast (B&B) establishments in the UK. Most B&Bs are open all year round, but are fullest from June to September. Usually they are entirely financed by their owners and run by only two or three people, who are sole traders. Most have fewer than three bookable rooms, and although 30 per cent of B&B occupiers are business travellers, most B&Bs aim at tourists. Breakfast will be available and an evening meal may be provided as an extra.

Feorag House is a 5-star guesthouse in Glenborrowdale, Argyll, Scotland, with three letting rooms (Figure 7.4). The 5-star status means that it is of exceptional world-class standard.

Peter and Helen are the live-in proprietors and have gained the award Investor in People, as well as other awards for their customer service provision.

Feorag House is open to guests at all times who can come and go as they wish. Due to the isolated nature of the property the guesthouse is never locked.

Services

There are no TVs in the guest bedrooms, but the owners will put one in if requested. Facilities for washing, drying, ironing and shoe-cleaning are

Figure 7.4 The view from the grounds of Feorag House

all available on request, as is the loan of bathrobes. Peter and Helen will make tea or coffee for their guests at any time of the day, but if guests wish to have the facility to make their own a kettle and other items needed will be brought to their room.

Maps and guidebooks are available for guests to look at in the sitting room. There is also a folder in each bedroom which contains headed writing paper and envelopes. There is also a local guidebook, local information and information about Feorag House. Peter and Helen will advise guests on the activities available and assist in making arrangements for fishing, sailing and stalking.

There is no mobile phone reception, so a landline telephone is provided for guests' use, along with a small notebook for recording the time taken to make a call. Guests are asked to fill this in and are charged 20p a minute for UK calls and 50p a minute for long-distance calls.

Meals

Afternoon tea is available in the sitting room between 4.30 p.m. and 5.00 p.m. A full four-course dinner is served at 8.00 p.m., followed by tea or coffee and a selection of homemade chocolates. Guests are invited to gather in the sitting room for a complimentary pre-dinner drink at 7.30 p.m. The guesthouse is not licensed to sell alcohol, but guests are encouraged to bring their own wine for the evening meal.

Guests are asked the previous evening at what time they would like breakfast and whether they will want porridge. Early-morning tea can be provided in the guest's room. Breakfast consists of freshly squeezed juices, toasted homemade bread and marmalade and a choice of cereal or fruit options. This is followed by a full cooked breakfast.

Health and safety

If there is an emergency during the night, Peter and Helen can be reached on the top floor of the guesthouse. Fire extinguishers are at the bottom of the stairs and by the front door. Guests are asked to raise the alarm if there is a fire and ensure that everyone congregates in the car park. Smoking is not permitted in the bedrooms and dining room, and guests are asked to consider others before smoking in the sitting room. Dogs should not be fed in the bedrooms or left unattended at any time.

1 What aspects of Feorag House are unique?
2 What type of customer do you think would wish to stay at Feorag House?

Hostels

One of the main providers of hostel accommodation is the Youth Hostel Association. More information can be found on the organisation's website at www.yha.org.uk.

Holiday camps

Holiday camps offer entertainment as part of the package, besides accommodation and catering. Billy Butlin set up the first British holiday camp at Skegness on the Lincolnshire coast in 1936. Now there are three parks. Entertainment includes a line-up of well-known bands and themed weekends.

Butlin's (www.butlins.co.uk) is popular with families with older children, with breaks classified as U, PG or 18. Food outlets such as Harry Ramsdens, Pizza Hut and Burger King are featured. The Skegness site has the capacity for more than 8500 guests. Each park has a Skyline Pavilion where all the entertainment is provided. Accommodation is classified as Deluxe, Gold, Silver and Standard. Deluxe and Gold come with a widescreen TV and DVD player.

Pontin's (www.pontins.com) has eight parks. The average capacity of each park is 3000 and they are popular with families with young children. They also offer Gold Breaks for the over-50s. Day visitors are not allowed on to the sites. Tribute bands and themed weekends provide a packed calendar of entertainment. Accommodation is in Club, Classic and Budget apartments, with Club apartments in prime locations and including digital TV.

Holiday villages

Holiday villages are different from holiday camps as there is limited arranged entertainment. People who choose holiday villages are more likely to want to explore the local area. Traditional holiday villages are offered by Park Resorts (www.park-resorts.com), Haven Holidays (www.havenholidays.com), British Holidays (www.british-holidays.co.uk), Hoseasons (www.hoseasons.co.uk) and Blakes (www.blakes.co.uk).

CASE STUDY

Center Parcs

Center Parcs (www.centerparcs.co.uk) developed in the late 1980s, with a slogan 'We wouldn't dream of organising you'. The first village was opened at Sherwood Forest in July 1987.

Center Parcs offers high-quality accommodation in fully equipped villas, apartments and lodges, set amongst trees and streams, and each with its own private patio. These villages successfully integrate conservation into a commercial development by ensuring that an attractive natural environment is created, so that a customer's first impression is one of peace and tranquillity and a sense of being at one with nature. The concept is to cater for a year-round market, including short breaks and winter holidays, which appeal to the growing interest in healthy lifestyles.

The short breaks are either midweek breaks from Monday to Friday or weekends from Friday to Monday. Longer stays take place during traditional holiday periods.

A resort in a woodland setting is offered, a couple of hours drive from large population centres. The centre of the village is covered with a transparent all-weather dome which encloses a tropical atmosphere around an extensive leisure pool – the Subtropical

Swimming Paradise with a constant temperature of 85 degrees Fahrenheit. The pool has wild-water rapids, water slides, spa pool, wave pool, solaria and children's play pools, surrounded by luxuriant tropical plants and trees. Additional features may include racquet sports, bowls, miniature golf, a bowling alley, lake fishing, water sports, walking, cycling and horse-riding, as well as a number of beauty treatments – all of which are based around the lodges, shops, restaurants and bars.

The success of the Center Parcs idea can be seen in the occupancy figures of over 90 per cent at all villages and repeat bookings of more than 60 per cent within a year.

1 **What types of customer do you think would visit Center Parcs?**

2 **In what ways do Center Parcs differ from holiday camps?**

Health and fitness resorts

These are actually hotels with extensive leisure and exercise facilities. They are likely to feature a pool, sauna, solarium and fitness room, along with a selection of other activities such as golf, tennis and squash.

Figure 7.5 Looking after 'body and soul'

At The Belfry hotel, for example, in the AquaSpa you can 'experience the unique 2-hour Fire and Ice Bio-thermal Treatment'. The owners promise that 'you'll find it invigorating, relaxing and fun'.

Classifying and grading accommodation

It is no simple matter to differentiate between accommodation units of varying types and standards.

Provision was made under the Development of Tourism Act 1969 for the compulsory classification and grading of hotel accommodation in Britain, but this was widely resisted by the industry itself and the BTA made no attempt to enforce it. A voluntary registration system was first introduced in 1975. The separate National Tourist Boards of England, Scotland and Wales were left to devise their own individual schemes.

The system remains a voluntary one, but hotels taking part receive regular checks from inspectors, and can display the grading or advertise in regional tourist board publications only once they have been approved. Because it remains voluntary, only a very small proportion of the total accommodation sector in the United Kingdom is registered.

There have been attempts – as a result of harmonisation within the European Union – to introduce legislation for a common grading scheme for hotels within the member countries.

At present some countries impose compulsory registration within their own borders, but different grading schemes are used throughout the EU, each involving different criteria. It is considered that comparison between hotels of similar status in different countries is virtually impossible to make.

Tour operators have devised their own systems of assessing properties used in package holidays abroad to meet the needs of their own clients. Thomson Holidays, for example, uses a 'T rating', based in part on their own customers' assessments of the accommodation. Panorama Holidays (www.panoramaholidays.co.uk) allocate 'Q ratings'. This is based on a scale of 1 to 5 (5 being the highest) and reflects Panorama's overall opinion of the facilities, service, food, comfort and location of each property.

Accommodation ratings in England

In response to consumer demand, the Automobile Association (AA), VisitBritain and the RAC joined forces to create one overall rating scheme for serviced accommodation, using stars to represent hotels and diamonds for guest accommodation (guesthouses, inns, farmhouses, B&Bs). This scheme places emphasis on quality provided, especially in areas of cleanliness and guest care.

Serviced accommodation: stars for hotels

Star ratings symbolise the level of service, range of facilities and quality of guest care customers can expect. Hotels are required to meet progressively higher standards as they move up the scale from one to five stars. The gradings are:

* *One star* – practical accommodation with a limited range of facilities and services including food and beverage. Service may be informal. There is a high standard of cleanliness throughout, but decor, furnishings,

fixtures and fittings may have a domestic quality. Three-quarters of bedrooms must have en-suite or private facilities comprising either bath or shower and WC.

* *Two stars* – small or medium-sized hotels, perhaps with limited public areas, better equipped bedrooms, all with en-suite/private bathroom and a colour TV. There is often an element of personal service and management and staff are smartly and professionally dressed. A lift is normally available.

* *Three stars* – higher standards of service and facilities, including larger public areas and bedrooms, a receptionist, room service and laundry. Management and staff are smartly and professionally presented and usually uniformed.

* *Four stars* – accommodation offering superior comfort and quality; all bedrooms with en-suite bath, fitted overhead shower and WC. There are spacious and well-appointed public areas. There is more emphasis on food and drink and a serious approach to cuisine. Room service is available for all meals, plus 24-hour drinks, refreshments and snacks. A dry-cleaning service is available. Excellent customer service is expected, with a formal professional service structure with smartly presented uniformed staff. There will be extra facilities depending on location and style of operation, such as conference and banqueting, business centre, health and leisure suites.

* *Five stars* – a spacious, luxurious establishment offering the highest international quality of accommodation, facilities, services and highest quality cuisine. There will be a range of extra facilities such as suites, health spas, gyms and conference and banqueting facilities. Rooms usually cater for both leisure and business stays. You will feel very well cared for by professional, attentive staff providing flawless service. Guests will notice the attention to detail compared with four-star properties, and these hotels set the highest international standard for the industry.

Theory into practice

Research the different accommodation grading systems available in:

* Northern Ireland (www.discovernorthernireland.com)

* Wales (www.visitwales.com)

* Scotland (www.visitscotland.com)

* Channel Islands (www.jersey.com and www.visitguernsey.com)

* Isle of Man (www.visitisleofman.com).

Theory into practice

As a group, collect together leaflets and advertisements for hotels in England that show their star ratings. Group together hotels of the same rating. Discuss the similarities in the facilities and services offered in each group.

Serviced accommodation: diamonds for guesthouses

Diamond ratings for guest accommodation reflect visitor expectations of this sector, where quality is seen as more important than facilities and services. Guest accommodation is required to meet progressively higher standards of quality and guest care as they move up the scale from one to five diamonds. The gradings are:

* *One diamond* – clean and comfortable accommodation, providing breakfast and helpful service.

* *Two diamonds* – an increased level of quality and comfort, with greater emphasis on guest care.

* *Three diamonds* – well maintained, practical decor, a good choice of breakfast dishes, a higher degree of customer care. At least 40 per cent of the bedrooms will have private or en-suite bathrooms.

* *Four diamonds* – an even higher level of quality and comfort, with a good level of customer care.

* *Five diamonds* – excellent quality in furnishing and rooms. At least 80 per cent of bedrooms will have en-suite/private bathrooms. Excellent levels of customer care are expected.

Theory into practice

1 Other accommodation types are graded. Find out more about:
- grading for self-catering
- grading for holiday, caravan and camping parks
- grading for narrowboats.

2 Accommodation can also be thoroughly inspected against demanding criteria in relation to its accessibility. Research the National Accessibility Schemes for:
- mobility
- hearing impairment
- visual impairment.

Special awards

* VisitBritain also provides Gold and Silver Awards. These are awarded to establishments that not only achieve the overall quality required for their rating, but also reach the highest levels of quality in those specific areas which guests identify as being really important to them.

* RAC Gold Ribbon is awarded to hotels that consistently demonstrate a commitment to superlative customer care, service and accommodation.

* RAC Blue Ribbon is awarded to hotels that consistently demonstrate a commitment to high standards.

* RAC Sparking Diamond Award is made to guest accommodation that achieves excellent standards of cleanliness, hygiene and attention to detail.

* AA Red Diamonds are awarded to the AA's top 10 per cent of four- and five-diamond rated guest accommodation that have achieved quality in their business, bathrooms and public areas.

* RAC Warm Welcome Award is made to guest accommodation that makes the guests feel 'at home' from the minute they arrive to the time they depart. The hospitality of the host is the key to winning this award.

* AA Rosettes are made to hotels serving food of exceptionally high quality. One to five rosettes can be awarded, acknowledging fresh home-cooked food right through to international level cuisine.

* AA Breakfast/Dinner Awards are for guest accommodation that exceeds quality requirements at the respective diamond level.

* RAC Dining Awards are awarded on a scale of one to five to serviced guest accommodation that demonstrates good food and dining atmosphere.

Think it over ...

What are the benefits of special awards to (a) the accommodation provider, and (b) the prospective guests?

Provision of food and drink

Catering is the part of the hospitality industry that is concerned with the preparation, distribution and serving of food and drinks. It includes cafés, fast-food outlets, restaurants, motorway service areas and pubs.

Public houses (pubs)

There are many types of pub, meeting the needs of different types of customer. The traditional 'local' is a community pub and caters for those who live or work within walking distance of its location. A destination or venue pub would attract people from a distance who travel there on a predetermined basis because of the entertainment or facilities offered. It may also serve as a 'local' for the neighbourhood, such as the Queen Adelaide in Kingsthorpe, Northamptonshire (Figure 7.6). Another important category is the food and family pub, which most pub retailers see as the pub of the future.

The British pub has been at the centre of many social and sporting activities over the centuries – the modern game of cricket was conceived at a Hampshire pub called the Bat and Ball. Many societies hold meetings in pubs – which, unlike other leisure venues, charge no entrance fee.

The appeal of the British pub lies in its uniqueness. Different types of pub satisfy varying needs in different people. Even though the big brewers have branded pubs, no two pubs are the

Figure 7.6 The Queen Adelaide pub, which has a traditional game of Northamptonshire skittles

same – each has its own character and atmosphere, shaped by the local environment, the licensee and the customers.

Café bars

There is a new generation of 'chameleon' bars developing – cafés by day and bars by night. One example is 'A Bar 2 Far' which sells coffee and pastries in the day and is a pre-club bar in the evening. During the early part of the day the lighting is bright and as the day progresses the lights go down and more coloured ones are introduced. A music system allows different music to be played at different times of the day, from mellow to slightly upbeat to very clubby.

Restaurants

There are many different types of establishment which sell food for consumption on or off the premises. Restaurants may provide a waiter/waitress table service, and/or a takeaway service.

Figure 7.7 A typical fast-food takeaway

Fast-food outlets

The concept of these hospitality providers is based on the speed of preparation, service and consumption. Fast-food outlets and takeaways offer menus with limited choice, no reservation systems, fast service of the entire meal at a low cost, and a level of service suited to a customer who wishes to eat off the premises. The product is standardised, so wherever you go in the country the product will be practically the same. The types of outlet include:

- fish and chip shops
- burger bars
- fried chicken restaurants
- ethnic takeaways (Indian, Thai, Mexican, Chinese etc. – see Figure 7.7)
- sandwich bars
- pizza and pasta parlours.

The location of fast-food outlets is important. Few customers will travel far for this meal experience, so most are sited in urban centres or on busy main roads where there are facilities to park or drive through. The price to the customer is of paramount importance, and it is a highly competitive market.

Contract catering at event venues

Contract catering, also known as the food service management industry, services that sector of the industry where the provision of food and drink is not the main activity. As part of the travel and tourism industry, contract catering is therefore provided at events that can be considered tourist attractions – such as major sporting activities like the Olympic Games and Royal Ascot.

CASE STUDY

Millennium Stadium, Cardiff

All kinds of events take place in this 74 600-capacity venue (Figure 7.8). It was the home of the 1999 Rugby World Cup and, since 2001, has hosted the FA Cup Final while Wembley Stadium is out of action for redevelopment. It hosts other events such as fashion shows, the British speedway grand prix, opera, rock concerts, drive-in movies and product launches. Catering at the multipurpose venue is operated by Letheny & Christopher, a firm owned by Compass (www.compass-group.co.uk), which has a 10-year concession-based contract which turns over £3.5 million a year.

The food on offer varies. For the football fans attending the Cup Final, hotdogs and pies at £2.50 each were sold from 41 retail units. In contrast, 3500 corporate hospitality guests enjoyed a choice of five sit-down menus in executive boxes. A typical menu would have included crab and prawn terrine, braised shank of Welsh lamb, and white chocolate and Baileys torte.

Catering at the Cup Final requires 900 staff to be employed, including 15 chefs.

Figure 7.8 The Millennium Stadium in Cardiff

1 List at least ten events of national and local significance.
2 Try to think of all the food and drink that should be provided at these events.
3 Is there likely to be any difference between the national and local events?

Leisure outlets

Many leisure outlets, from sports centres to golf courses and theme parks, offer hospitality.

CASE STUDY

Alton Towers

Within the Alton Towers theme park (www.altontowers.com) there are a variety of outlets providing food and drink, including Pizza Hut and KFC, as well as snacks and drinks vending machines.

There are also two hotels – the Alton Towers Hotel and Splash Landings Hotel. They offer different styles of break. As hotel guests, customers are entitled to unlimited theme park access and exclusive access to Cariba Creek Waterpark. Guests benefit from priority show seats, early rides on Nemesis and Air, and priority access on selected rides.

Cariba Creek Waterpark is a huge indoor complex covered by a domed roof, plus heated outdoor pools. It is a warm family friendly environment with water-based entertainment.

The Alton Towers Hotel has themed rooms such as the Chocolate Factory, sponsored by Cadbury. The dressing room is a box of Milk Tray, a box of Roses is the TV stand, luggage is on a rack of Cadbury's fingers, and the wallpaper design is a torn wrapper of a chocolate bar. The Fizz Factory room is sponsored by Coca Cola and sleeps six. It has Coca Cola on tap all the time.

There is also a spa at the hotel, which includes saunas, steam room, tepidarium, foot reflexology baths, pool, jacuzzi, whirlpool and multi-sensory showers. There are also personalised treatments available such as steam and purifying clay treatment, facials and body treatments.

The Splash Landings Hotel is Caribbean themed with rich, bright colours and exotic fabrics. The Beachcomber rooms have driftwood style furniture, traditional Caribbean lanterns and window shutters.

There are two restaurants available in Splash Landings. The Secret Garden provides meals flame-cooked on a wood-burning stove. Flambo's Exotic Feast has authentic Caribbean cuisine and family classic dishes, with great views over the waterpark. Snacks can be picked up from Quenchers in Cariba Creek. There are also a number of bars available such as Ma Garrita's tropical terrace, the Captain's Bar and the Dragon Bar.

There is also the Alton Towers Conference Centre (Figure 7.9). It is uniquely themed and has state-of-the-art facilities with a variety of rooms to suit any size of event, with up to a maximum of 550 delegates.

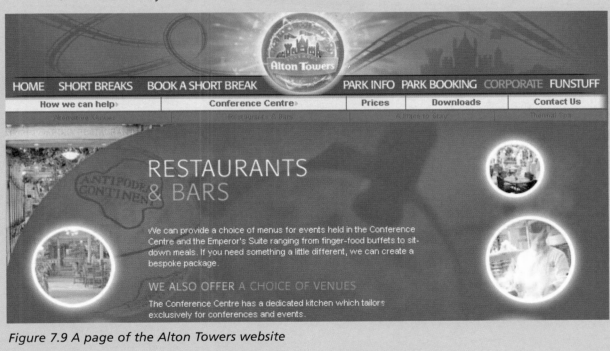

Figure 7.9 A page of the Alton Towers website

Research the hospitality provided in leisure outlets in your local area.

En-route and on-board services

Travel hospitality incorporates rail and roadside catering outlets as well as those on board different methods of transport.

CASE STUDY

Tebay Service Area

Tebay Service Area, also known as Westmorland Motorway Services, is an award-winning service station on the M6 motorway in Cumbria. The services are unique as it is the only one in the UK to be built and run by local people who came together solely to run the service area. Much of the food offered is produced and prepared locally in Cumbria, and the buildings reflect the style of Cumbrian houses and farmsteads. Other services on the motorway system are part of large corporate organisations that provide uniform service throughout the country. Tebay offers something unique and special. The service area includes Westmorland Farm Shops which sell local and speciality foods.

Adjacent to the services, and accessed from them, are other hospitality providers. The Tebay Park Touring and Static Caravan Site (www.tebaycaravanpark.co.uk) can be used as a base for a touring holiday or a convenient stopover for those travelling north or south on the M6 (Figure 7.10).

The Westmorland Hotel (www.westmorlandhotel.com) is also accessed from the Tebay Services (Figure 7.11).

Compare and contrast the types of travellers who will use Tebay Caravan Site and the Westmorland Hotel.

Figure 7.10 A leaflet for Tebay Park

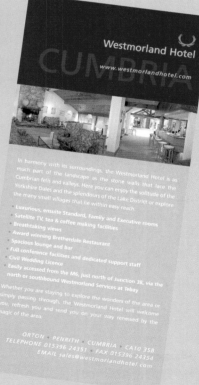

Figure 7.11 Information on Westmorland Hotel

Virgin Trains on-board menu

Virgin Trains (www.virgin.com/trains) provides a menu in its *hotline* magazine which is provided free to passengers on the trains.

'Whether it's a coffee and a snack, a tasty hot Aberdeen Angus cheeseburger or our continental-style roast ham and provolone cheese on red pepper roll, we've got it all on board. And with our range of soft drinks, beers, wines and spirits, you're bound to find something to quench your thirst. ... Please be aware that the menu can vary by route and train type.

- *Drink like a fish* – includes hot drinks, cold drinks and alcoholic beverages
- *The best thing since sliced bread* – a range of tasty rolls and sandwiches
- *Food, glorious food* – tempting hot meals or tasty pasta and salads
- *Watch the crumbs!* – a selection of mouth-watering treats'

Research food and drink provided on-board on air and sea transport.

Scale of the hospitality industry

The hospitality industry is one of the main areas of growth in the UK economy. It has reported year-on-year growth since 1996 and contributes some £21.5 billion annually to the treasury through direct and indirect taxation.

In total, the industry employs over 1.8 million people in the UK working in around 300 000 establishments. Forecasts over the next couple of years are for sustained growth, and it is predicted that a further 170 000 jobs will be needed in the industry by the end of 2005. Total catering and accommodation expenditure by domestic and overseas tourists in the UK amounts to 59 per cent of total tourist spending.

Think it over ...

Why do you think the hospitality industry is growing so fast in the UK?

Employment in hospitality

Think it over ...

In Unit 1, a report was given of employment within the industry (see Figure 1.4 on page 10). The statistics relating to the hospitality industry are:

- hotels and other tourist accommodation
- restaurants, cafés etc.
- bars, public houses and nightclubs.

As a group, analyse the patterns of employment in hospitality using these statistics.

A major problem in hospitality is the recruitment and retention of staff, and a shortage of skilled people. In the UK, the trend is towards increasing numbers of unfilled vacancies in hospitality, for two reasons.

First, the hospitality industry is not considered appealing by prospective employees. Second, many applicants are considered under-qualified by the industry.

The hospitality industry is considered by many prospective employees to be low-paid, with long hours of work and poor conditions. Because of this negative image, fewer people are seeking hospitality qualifications. In fact, government statistics show that the hospitality industry has four of the top ten lowest paid occupations – kitchen porters, bar staff, catering assistants and waiting staff. Labour turnover is high, with many employed in hospitality seeing it as a stop-gap job until they find another one.

The hospitality sector is not for those seeking a nine-to-five, Monday-to-Friday work pattern. It is an environment that doesn't suit all. However, it may be appropriate for those who want to work in a customer-focused business environment where there are a wide range of specialist opportunities. For those who are flexible there is the opportunity for rapid career progression. It is not uncommon for successful management trainees to reach general manager positions in large hotels within five to seven years of commencing their training. The skills shortage already referred to provides an environment for rapid career progression.

The range of jobs in hospitality

A recent edition of a local newspaper carried the following hospitality jobs in travel and tourism:

- Marriott Hotel Northampton requires Head Housekeeper, Breakfast Chef and Chef de Partie – Great salary along with excellent benefits
- Overstone Manor requires full-time Grill Chef – £13 500 per annum
- Barretts Club requires full-time and part-time Bar and Waiting Staff – Excellent rates of pay and working conditions
- Ibis Hotel Northampton requires Room Attendants – 4 hours per day, including weekends
- The Quays, Billing, requires Head Chef – £18 000 per annum
- The Hunting Lodge Hotel, Cottingham, requires full-time Hotel Receptionist – 40 hours a week on shifts over 5 days

Hotel manager/general manager (GM)

GMs are responsible for every aspect of the hotel. They ensure that guests enjoy their stay, staff work together as an effective team, and the business runs at a profit. In a small hotel, the GM is involved in the day-to-day activities, including reservations, receiving guests etc. In large hotels there will be department managers to ensure the smooth running of the kitchen, restaurant, bars, housekeeping, banqueting, sales and marketing, personnel and training. As the person in charge, the GM is ultimately responsible for the health and safety of everyone on the premises, for food safety, for upholding the licensing laws, for consumer protection and employment legislation.

Reception manager

Reception managers are in charge of the reception and reservation staff – the 'front office'. The team might be based at the front desk and their responsibilities include the switchboard and portering. In a large hotel, reservations are usually taken in a back office.

Besides the usual duties of a departmental manager (recruiting and training staff, organising staff rotas, controlling budgets, health and safety and attending meetings), a reception manager is likely to have regular guest contact, welcoming and registering arrivals, answering queries, taking bookings, preparing bills and taking payments.

Reception staff are at the hub of the hotel, telling guests about the facilities available and encouraging them to use these. Achieving maximum occupancy and maximum revenue are constant challenges, requiring a keen eye to be kept on all business issues, negotiating skills, and often some risk-taking (such as over-booking on the assumption that a percentage of arrivals typically fail to turn up). Security of the hotel and guests is a major part of the job.

Reservation manager

The reservations office plays a major role in filling the hotels' bedrooms at the best prices. The manager and team will handle reservations by telephone, letter, email and fax, promptly and efficiently. Computers, faxes, photocopiers, various filing systems, the telephone and the franking machine are likely to be the main tools. Skills include negotiating the best terms for the hotel with tour operators, travel agents, reservation agencies, corporate customers and the individual guest in search of a bargain.

A courteous, helpful attitude is necessary. Regular meeting with other heads of department and the front-of-house team will be held, and regular updating is necessary on promotions and special activities, group bookings, VIPs and other special guests etc.

Receptionist

The receptionist greets guests on arrival. A good first impression – the welcome, personal appearance and the appearance of the reception area – is very important. Administrative skills are important to deal with reservations accurately and efficiently, prepare guest bills correctly, and ensure that the necessary information goes to housekeeping and other hotel departments.

Many guests make queries at reception, as well as complaints and other problems that are less easy to deal with.

Receptionists are responsible for taking payments, exchanging foreign currency and, in some hotels, working the switchboard. Selling is a key skill – a timely suggestion can persuade a guest to upgrade his or her room, to stay longer, or to eat in the restaurant.

Receptionists may have to respond to reservation enquiries by telephone, in person and by letter, fax and email. Most hotels use computers for reservations and word processing, so receptionists need to be competent in this area.

In an emergency, receptionists need to know what their responsibilities are, which may include assisting guests to evacuate the building, calling the emergency services, and checking that all guests have reached safety.

Head housekeeper

Head housekeepers are in charge of the cleanliness of all the guest rooms and the public areas of a hotel. Much time will be taken up in supervising and training staff, planning staff rotas, dealing with the suppliers of linen, cleaning materials and guest supplies (sachets of tea, coffee, soap, shampoo etc.), stock-taking, budgets and other paperwork (maintenance reports, room checksheets, safety audits etc.). A key area is controlling the costs of cleaning materials, linen, laundry, maintenance and wages.

Head housekeepers will liaise closely with other heads of department and the general manager, and attend the regular heads of department meetings. Head housekeepers also need to meet regularly with housekeeping staff. Good relations with reception staff are crucial, so that they know when rooms are ready to relet, and housekeepers know when rooms can be serviced or guests have asked for special requirements.

Maintenance is another key area. Problems need to be reported quickly so that repairs can be carried out promptly and rooms kept in good order. It is important also that the equipment used (vacuum cleaners, polishers, trolleys etc.) are in sound order and used safely. A regular part of the head housekeeper's routine will be checking that high standards of cleanliness are maintained, that rooms are correctly serviced and that all equipment is in a safe condition.

Room attendant

Job titles vary (room maid and chambermaid are common terms) and the work depends on the type of hotel.

High standards of cleanliness are greatly valued by guests. A methodical approach is essential to achieve this to avoid spreading bacteria from dirty surfaces to those just cleaned. Hygiene is important to prevent risks to own health, as are safe working methods when using cleaning materials, equipment and when lifting and moving items. When finished, the room must look exactly right and welcoming to the guest, with everything in place, and with supplies of soap, drink-making items etc. replenished. Guests will be expecting to see room attendants looking well presented, to greet them pleasantly and deal with enquiries helpfully.

There are procedures to follow for lost property, for making beds and every other cleaning and servicing task. Another concern is security, of yourself, the guest, the property of the guest and the hotel. Room attendants will have a key or key card to all the guest rooms.

Duties may also extend to cleaning the public areas of the hotel. Usually this is done in the early morning, when there are few people about. At regular intervals, special cleaning tasks have to be done, such as shampooing furnishings, or damp-dusting high surfaces. In some hotels, the room attendants work in teams.

Restaurant manager

Restaurant managers need to liaise effectively with other heads of department, and good relations with the kitchen are a top priority. Restaurant managers will take meal reservations, greet guests as they arrive and show them to their tables. Some restaurant managers also hand guests the menu, and return to take the order, advising on the choice of dishes, wines and other drinks. The job is to keep an eye on all tables, guests and staff, so that you can spot and deal quickly with anything that is going wrong.

It is courteous to check that the guests are enjoying their meals. Complaints will happen, even when nothing has gone wrong, so diplomatic skills are essential.

The restaurant manager recruits and trains restaurant staff, plans staff rotas, ensures that routine duties such as cleaning the silver are attended to, and that licensing and health and safety legal requirements are complied with. Before service, staff will be briefed on the day's menu, any large bookings and VIP guests. Stocks of cutlery, glassware, china and other restaurant equipment are the responsibility of the restaurant manager.

Waiting staff

Waiters have a key role in the enjoyment of a guest's meal, complementing the efforts of the kitchen. Skills of timing are needed to ensure there is no delay in bringing the food from the kitchen, and that it is served attractively.

Waiting staff advise guests on the food and drink available (selling skills are an important aspect of this), serve the food and drink without unnecessarily disturbing the guests, keep the table clear of unwanted items, replenish drink and wine glasses, and generally keep the restaurant looking pleasant. In some hotels waiting staff are also responsible for greeting guests, showing them to their tables and taking orders. At the end of the meal waiting staff may be responsible for collecting payment.

High standards of personal presentation and hygiene are expected. Food, or the surfaces of the china, cutlery or glassware that will come into contact with a guest's mouth must not be touched. Working safely so that accidents are avoided is another essential. Waiting staff help prepare the restaurant for service and clear away when the guests are gone.

Waiting staff may be called upon to serve at banquets, cocktail parties, special dinners, weddings and other functions, and to serve meals in guests' rooms if that is the hotel's policy. Waiting staff must be knowledgeable on the laws relating to the serving of alcohol.

Head chef

The head chef is in charge of the kitchen, planning menus, developing new dishes, ordering and storing food, organising staff rotas, supervising the work, and recruiting and training new members of the team. A head chef must inspire and motivate the whole *brigade* (as kitchen teams are called), demonstrate culinary flair, and be an excellent business manager.

In the smaller kitchens, head chefs normally have hands-on involvement in the cooking. In bigger establishments the head chef is normally at the hot-plate during meal service, shouting out the orders to the different sections of the kitchen, making sure the presentation of the food is right and the order correct before it is taken out by the waiting staff.

Food hygiene and health and safety are major concerns, and head chefs will deal with visits from the environmental health officer to check standards and discuss the food management system. Close liaison with the general manager is needed.

Other kitchen staff

* *Chef de partie.* This is a senior position in the kitchen, a hands-on role with responsibility for preparing, cooking and presenting a range of dishes.

* *Commis chef.* This is the starting point for a career in hotel and restaurant kitchens. It involves a lot of the preparation work and basic cooking, under the supervision of more experienced chefs.

* *Kitchen porters.* They do the operative jobs in the kitchen, such as washing-up and peeling vegetables if necessary.

Banqueting manager

For many hotels the conference and banqueting business is a major source of revenue. A banqueting manager will ensure that facilities relating to these areas operate profitably, and will be involved in every aspect from marketing and selling to ensuring that the events run smoothly and that bills are paid. Attention to detail is crucial, along with excellent organisational and administrative skills.

Events manager

This is a truly hands-on position with a specialist event catering company or as part of the management team of a conference centre. Events managers liaise with clients and suppliers, produce pre- and post-event costings, train and direct a team of casual staff, arrange transportation, and sometimes also make the tea!

An events manager needs to be a clear communicator, a skilled planner and administrator, as well as a strong team leader. Events managers take the ideas, aspirations and concept of the client through to the smooth and efficient operational running of the event. In developing and negotiating the details of the event with the client they will demonstrate a grasp for detail and essential business acumen, yet have the flexibility and imagination to deliver a memorable and successful occasion for all of those concerned.

An events manager must also have the ability to respond rapidly to changing situations, be it the weather, traffic congestion preventing the team getting on site, or late modifications to the client's requirements. Backing this up must be a sound knowledge of health and safety legislation, employment practices, sales and marketing techniques, and financial control systems.

Publican

A publican both owns and runs a pub and can put his or her own individual style on the business – for example, the type of customers it attracts, the range of food and drinks served, the people employed, the decor, available activities and suppliers used. A public house that is run independently of a brewery is known as a 'freehouse', because the publican is free to select the suppliers.

Other pubs are owned by a brewery or retailing chain and are run by tenant landlords, who have leased the premises, or by managers who are employees of the company.

Even in a large pub with a team of managers, a lot of time will be spent during the hours of service circulating among customers, always keeping an eye on what is going on. Time needs to be spent on dealing with suppliers, planning staff rotas, recruiting new staff, helping staff to improve their performance, arranging advertising

Figure 7.12 Bar staff: a popular part-time job for students

and other promotional activities, paying bills, working out and paying wages, preparing tax and VAT returns, checking takings, banking, health and safety checks and countless other tasks.

Bar staff

Bar staff are employed to help set up the bar area, stock the shelves and refrigerators so that drinks are available and at the correct temperature, serve drinks, take payment, clear tables, wash glasses (usually in a machine) and clear up after service (Figure 7.12). Good customer service skills are important, as is working in a safe, hygienic manner. High standards of personal presentation are needed to give the right impression.

Theory into practice

For each of the jobs outlined above, explain what the following skills entail and how they can be put to good use in hospitality:

- practical skills (e.g. serving, menu knowledge, clearing, area maintenance)
- personal skills (e.g. communication, IT, social skills)
- organisational skills (e.g. ordering, planning , teamwork).

Qualifications required

Not only are there many different roles and areas of work in the hospitality industry, there are also numerous routes into them. Figure 7.13 presents an overview.

> **Theory into practice**
>
> Select a job in hospitality you are interested in. Find out the qualifications and experience that are needed to enter the job at operative, supervisory and management levels.

Trends in sectors of hospitality

Hotel trends

Budget hotels are the fastest growing segment of the industry. Although hotels have the highest percentage of full-time workers (60 per cent), this proportion has been falling over recent years and the number of part-timers is therefore expected to increase.

The hotel market is divided into two main sectors, corporate (business) and consumer (leisure). The corporate sector is the most

SCHOOL

Any GCSEs and A level qualifications will be useful, particularly English, Maths and a language.

WORK EXPERIENCE

Most work experience in hospitality is of benefit, whether it be casual work in the evenings or at weekends, or a formal work placement as part of your education.

COLLEGE

A wide range of hospitality-related courses offer practical preparation and training for work in hospitality.

WORK

Full-time work can be gained at operative level in hospitality straight from school. Alternatively there are combinations of work and study with a variety of professional training schemes.

These apprenticeships are work-based training programmes aimed at equipping young people with communication and teamwork skills, in addition to key business or craft skills relating to specific roles. Training is provided by the employer, a local college or training provider. Larger companies often have in-house training schemes.

UNIVERSITY

Academic and vocational qualifications are numerous:

- Hospitality courses focus on management and business skills and give the opportunity to gain practical skill through work experience.
- Conversion courses are taken by those who have a degree not related to the hospitality industry yet wish to develop degree-level skills in hospitality-related areas.
- Postgraduate study is for those who have spent some time in the industry and wish to expand their business skills

PROFESSIONAL QUALIFICATIONS

These can be worked for at any point in your career. Different qualifications require different levels of formal education and practical experience, so these can be gained at any level from operative, to supervisory to managerial.

Figure 7.13 There are various routes into work in the hospitality industry

significant in terms of size, with revenue being generated not only from bedrooms and meals but also from the use of facilities like conference and meeting rooms. The corporate sector was adversely affected by international events, such as the terrorist attacks on the USA on 11 September 2001, the SARS outbreak, the war in Iraq and a downturn in some global economies. Many hotel groups have therefore moved their focus to the leisure market in order to compensate for the shortfall in business.

There has been a rise in the percentage of the UK population staying in hotels for both leisure and business purposes. Three in ten Britons used this type of accommodation in 2003, with the largest increase being in weekend leisure breaks and midweek stays for business travellers. Figure 7.14 shows statistics for a recent one-year period.

	AUGUST 2004	AUGUST 2003
All UK hotels:		
Occupancy (%)	76.5	76.3
Average rack rate (£)	64.47	62.24
London hotels:		
Occupancy (%)	84.8	83.7
Average rack rate (£)	76.06	74.76
Provincial hotels:		
Occupancy (%)	73.7	73.5
Average rack rate (£)	59.82	57.01

Source: Horizons for Success

Figure 7.14 Data for hotel occupancy

Key terms

Occupancy rate is the measure of how successful a hotel or other accommodation provider is in filling available bedspaces over a given period. **Rack rate** refers to the full, published price at which a hotel room is sold.

Depending on the current level of demand, it is likely that the rack rate will be discounted for particular customers, at specific times of the week or year, and for special events. Many hotels offer high discounts for room occupancy at the weekend when they are not being used by business travellers. This clearly illustrates seasonality and perishability in hospitality.

Think it over ...

Where has there been the largest increase in occupancy and rack rate between 2003 and 2004?

Restaurant trends

The range of restaurants includes takeaway food outlets, fine dining, ethnic restaurants and coffee bars. The latter is the fastest growing type. There has also been significant growth in branded restaurants. More people are employed in restaurants than in any other sub-sector of the industry, with employment forecast to grow by 21 per cent. Restaurants also account for the largest percentage of establishments in the UK. The vast majority are small and micro businesses with owner operators.

Figure 7.15 shows some statistics for the quick service (fast-food) sector over an 8-year period from 1996.

YEAR	NUMBER OF OUTLETS	MILLIONS OF MEALS	FOOD SALES (£M)
1996	29 677	1930	6178
1997	29 244	1908	6164
1998	28 253	1924	6254
1999	28 527	1908	6256
2000	28 694	1909	6126
2001	29 050	1874	6324
2002	29 384	1946	6393
2003	29 451	1959	6381

Source: Horizons for Success

Figure 7.15 Fast food trends

Theory into practice

1. Describe the trends in the number of fast-food outlets, meals sold and their value, as shown in Figure 7.15. What impact do you think the trend in healthy eating will have in the future on this type of restaurant?
2. Research figures for different types of restaurant. Describe and explain any trends observed.

Pub, club and bar trends

This group is the second largest sub-sector in terms of total numbers of establishments and workforce. It employs 15.5 per cent of all employees in the industry. However, labour turnover is high, mainly due to the large number of students employed.

Figure 7.16 shows some statistics for the public house trade over an 8-year period from 1996. These are outlets where food accounts for less than 50 per cent of turnover.

YEAR	NUMBER OF OUTLETS	MILLIONS OF MEALS	FOOD SALES (£M)
1996	57 404	1036	3112
1997	55 874	1053	3282
1998	54 450	1085	3357
1999	53 261	1139	3434
2000	52 356	1107	3337
2001	51 565	1062	3186
2002	51 506	1070	3327
2003	51 352	1081	3355

Source: Horizons for Success

Figure 7.16 Public house trends

Theory into practice

1. Describe the trend in the number of pubs, meals sold and their value, as shown in Figure 7.16.
2. Discuss the likely future trend in pubs and pub meals.

Types of customer

Customers may be regarded as *regular, occasional* or *chance.* All types must be treated with respect and courtesy if you wish them to return with more business. The hospitality industry provides a service to its customers. Every customer is special and will require some slightly different service and have a different perceived need.

* *Individual customers* are generally fairly easy to look after. Their needs do not put strain on the resources of the organisation and they are often well satisfied with the service they receive.
* *Groups* bring substantial income to many hospitality providers, and therefore should be given special consideration regarding their requirements. Special arrangements are generally made to greet groups on arrival.
* *Business customers* are usually travelling at their company's expense and out of necessity rather than for pleasure. Time will be of the essence, so quick, efficient service is especially important.

Theory into practice

As a group, brainstorm other types of customer using hospitality. What are their specific needs? How should different types of hospitality outlet cater for these needs?

For example, inbound tourists in a city centre hotel may need a member of staff who speaks their language, information as to what there is locally to do and see, and possibly facilities to exchange currency.

Assessment guidance

For Assessment Objective 1 you have to investigate the *scale* of the hospitality industry, as well as the *types* of hospitality providers (including official grading systems). You must also describe employment characteristics within the industry. You must illustrate this topic with examples at both national and local levels.

For Assessment Objective 2 you have to investigate *two* organisations in the sector, one that provides hospitality services and one that provides a corporate hospitality package. Corporate hospitality is descibed in the next section.

Corporate hospitality

Corporate hospitality falls broadly into two categories:

✳ Organisations invite existing clients or potential new customers to attend a prestigious event (usually sporting or cultural). Others organise events, exhibitions and conferences for existing or new customers (to stimulate new business, inform on current/new developments, training of personnel etc.). This aspect of corporate hospitality is explored in the Huntingdon racecourse in-depth case study in this section.

✳ Services and/or facilities are provided for business people – for example, a hotel room with work space, modem point, 24-hour room service, corporate room rate, express checkout and conference rooms. Other examples are on-board transport services such as executive lounges, business-class cabin on an aircraft, or first-class provision on trains. Information on the provision for business people in hotels is included later in the Huntingdon Marriott Hotel in-depth case study starting on page 275.

What is corporate hospitality?

Corporate hospitality at event venues is concerned with any event for the benefit of an organisation entertaining clients or staff at the organisation's expense. It gives the opportunity for an organisation's staff to bond with clients, partners, suppliers or the press in a relaxed environment. This shared experience is expected to result in more business, greater efficiency from the workforce, or simply a better working relationship. The benefits of corporate hospitality are intangible, and it is very difficult to measure any return on investment. This is a growth market.

The main products for corporate hospitality are spectator sports, participant activities and sports, the arts and culture. Spectator sports like football, rugby and cricket dominate the corporate hospitality market, accounting for nearly two-thirds of all corporate hospitality revenues. The main sport for corporate hospitality is football, with 5 per cent of the major league clubs' seating capacity devoted to corporate hospitality offers.

A study of Huntingdon racecourse

This extensive case study provides details of particular packages that were available at Huntingdon racecourse at the time of writing. Visit www.huntingdon-racecourse.co.uk to get up-to-date information about the corporate hospitality packages on offer.

Huntingdon racecourse (Figure 7.17) holds eighteen National Hunt (jumps) race meetings a year. Situated in the east of England, it is owned and operated by the Racecourse Holdings Trust (www.rht.net) which operates seven large and six small racecourses in the UK (Huntingdon is one of the small courses). RHT is committed to maximising the revenue-generating potential of each racecourse, and takes every opportunity to develop the courses as attractive leisure venues as well as centres of excellence in racing.

Facilities at the racecourse

Corporate hospitality packages are available for groups as small as ten or as large as 200 at Huntingdon racecourse. Organisations wishing to use the racecourse for corporate hospitality are sent a booking form along with terms and conditions. The booking form needs to be completed and returned to the racecourse. A deposit invoice is sent by the racecourse and once this is paid by the organisation the booking is

Figure 7.17 Huntingdon racecourse

confirmed. The client is then guaranteed that they have the facility requested in the booking form. The client is then contacted three to four weeks prior to the event to clarify any special requirements.

There are six corporate boxes that provide excellent views of the racecourse from their private balconies within the grandstand; these cater for 10–30 guests. They are situated in close proximity to the betting ring facilities and the parade ring.

For larger groups there are trackside chalets with excellent racecourse viewing on two levels. These accommodate up to 70 people on each floor and are an ideal venue for hosting larger corporate events.

Corporate packages available

There are currently two packages:

* The Classic package includes a private box, day member badge, Classic buffet or three-course luncheon and racecard. The price is £72 plus VAT per person – this does not include drinks.

* The Thoroughbred package is priced at £78 plus VAT per person. This includes a private box facility, day member badge, coffee/tea and Danish pastry on arrival, Thoroughbred buffet or four-course luncheon and racecard. Again, the price does not include drinks.

Additional extras offered as part of the corporate hospitality package include the option of booking a 'tipster' for the day, who can take the guests through the racecard, giving tips on what and what not to back. Tote betting vouchers can be ordered in advance, starting at £5 per person. These vouchers can be personalised with a company name.

The Peterborough Chase Restaurant caters for up to 150 people. It has glass-fronted viewing of both the course and the parade ring. This offers organisations a private viewing balcony, Tote betting facilities, television and a licensed bar. A Raceday package in the Peterborough Chase Restaurant includes day member's badge, table for the day, racecard, coffee/tea on arrival, three-course meal and light afternoon tea. The price for this is £60 per person, excluding drinks.

There are also Weekend Racegoers packages. These include an afternoon of racing and a night at a local hotel. Two packages are available:

* The Winning Post package includes day membership badge and racecard, a pint of beer or a glass of house wine, Newmarket sausage & mash lunch voucher, £2 Tote betting voucher and one night's accommodation at the Brampton Travel Inn. This is priced at £55 per person.

* The Champions package includes day member's enclosure badge, private box or trackside suite and a racecard, a pint of beer or a glass of house wine, lasagne served with salad at lunch, £5 Tote betting voucher, and one night's accommodation at the Huntingdon Marriott Hotel. The price of this package is £100 per person.

All corporate hospitality guests receive passes to use the car park closest to the entrance. Guests are directed to their box on arrival by attendants. The hospitality is well signed, and the name of the organisation hosting the corporate hospitality is on the door of each box. Once guests arrive at the box they are greeted by their host who will be looking after them for the day.

Conferences and meetings at the racecourse

On days when there is no horseracing the facilities can be used for corporate hospitality activities such as conferences, exhibitions, meetings and company activity days. The facilities include two conference rooms catering for up to 120 guests theatre style and 150 guests banqueting style. The larger conference room has blackout facilities. Six syndicate rooms are also available which can be used for smaller meetings or as breakout rooms. Three of the rooms are adjoining and can be opened to cater for larger meetings or small conferences.

Two-storey trackside suites with racecourse viewing balconies are an ideal venue for small or large parties. Each floor houses up to 75 people. The racecourse covers 175 acres, of which 45 acres are car parking. These grass areas can be hired for special events, countryside sports days or activity days.

There are a variety of conference day delegate packages available:

* The Premier Day Delegate is priced at £32 per person, for a minimum of 30 delegates. This includes the main room hire, three servings of tea/coffee and biscuits during the day, two-course premier finger buffet lunch or a two-course fork buffet lunch, orange juice and mineral water with lunch, mints and table refreshments, OHP, screen, flipchart and car parking.

* The Classic Day Delegate is £27.50 per person for a minimum of 30 delegates. This includes main room hire, two servings of tea/coffee and biscuits during the day, a finger buffet lunch, afternoon tea and cake, OHP, screen, flipchart, table refreshments and car parking.

* The Half Day Delegate is £24.35 per person for a minimum of 50 delegates. This is similar to the Premier Day Delegate, but with only one serving of tea/coffee and biscuits. Room access for this package is available either in the mornings from 8.30 a.m. to 1.00 p.m. or afternoons from 1.00 p.m. to 5.30 p.m.

Further rooms are available for hire as luncheon rooms or breakout suites. Smaller meetings can be accommodated in the syndicate rooms – these cater for up to 12 delegates. Rates are £85 per room, with catering extra.

On non racedays all rooms are available for hire, with a range of banqueting menus available. The seating configuration best suited to the needs of individual organisations can be selected (Figure 7.18). Figure 7.19 shows the tariffs for the rooms and configurations.

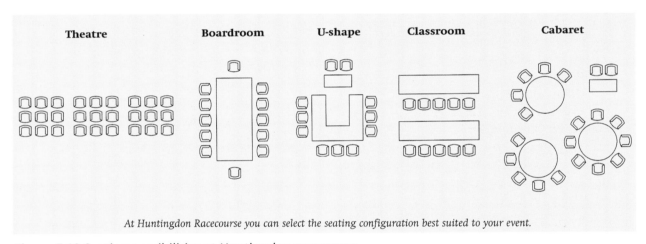

At Huntingdon Racecourse you can select the seating configuration best suited to your event.

Figure 7.18 Seating possibilities at Huntingdon racecourse

	BANQUETING	THEATRE	BOARDROOM	U-SHAPE	CLASSROOM	CABARET	COST
Peterborough Chase Room	150	120	46	34	42	54	£450
Bevan Suite	80	50	24	22	28	32	£350
Lenton Suite	60	30	20	18	20	–	£350
Trackside Chalet	–	30	16	14	20	24	
Racecall Room	–	36	18	14	24	24	
Syndicate Room	–	20	12	11	10	–	£85

Figure 7.19 Room capacities, seating plans and room-only prices (excluding VAT) at Huntingdon racecourse

Marketing of Huntingdon racecourse

Huntingdon markets its corporate hospitality packages and facilities in various ways. It holds open days to which representatives from organisations that may wish to use the facilities are invited. Food and drink are provided, and staff show the facilities available. A lot of business is repeat bookings, so organisations that have used the racecourse previously are contacted directly to encourage them to re-book. Huntingdon also advertises on local radio and in the local press, but this is more to promote the racedays rather than the hospitality packages.

Types of accommodation and accommodation services

Traveller accommodation can have a variety of *component parts*. These are depicted in Figure 7.20.

Each accommodation outlet will provide accommodation *services* to ensure that each component part functions properly and provides a high level of customer service. Figure 7.21 provides a summary of what is required.

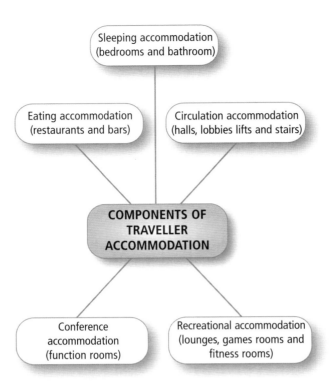

Figure 7.20 The components of traveller accommodation

Figure 7.21 Accommodation services

A study of Huntingdon Marriott Hotel

This extensive case study provides details of what the Marriott Hotel at Huntingdon had to offer at the time of writing. Visit www.marriott.co.uk/cbghd to get up-to-date information about the organisation's tariffs and offers. Figure 7.22 depicts an extract from the hotel's brochure.

Huntingdon Marriott Hotel
Kingfisher Way, Hinchingbrooke Business Park, Huntingdon, Cambridgeshire PE29 6FL

tel 0870 400 7257
fax 0870 400 7357
web www.marriott.co.uk/cbghd

Marriott Central Reservations
UK 0800 221 222 USA & Canada 800 228 9290

Restaurant and Lounges
Brooke's Restaurant and Lounge Bar.

Conference Facilities
Seven conference rooms accommodating up to 260 delegates.

Parking
Car parking available.

Leisure Facilities
Complimentary: indoor heated swimming pool, fully equipped gymnasium, steam room, spa bath

Local attractions
Huntingdon is Cromwell's birth town and is steeped in history. Cambridge is only 18 miles away, horse racing at Newmarket and Brampton, Grafham Water, Nene Valley Railway, Duxford Imperial War Museum are all nearby.

Directions
From the South (A1) follow A14 East to Cambridge, Huntingdon and M11. Pass Brampton Racecourse and at the next roundabout the hotel is on the right.

From the North (A1) take the A14 East to Cambridge, Huntingdon and M11. Exit the A14 towards Huntingdon. At the roundabout turn right on to the A14 West. The hotel will be on your left.

From the Midlands J19 (M1) M6 follow A14 to Huntingdon. Pass Brampton Racecourse. Continue as from the South. From Cambridge M11 follow A14 North, turn off for Brampton racecourse and M1/M6. At the roundabout the hotel will be on the left.

Reservations and Payment
Reservations are held for guest arrival by 4pm. You can guarantee your booking simply by advising us of your credit card number when you book. Mastercard, American Express, Diners Club and Visa are accepted. Cheques are also accepted when supported by a current cheque card issued by a major UK bank.

Check In and Check Out
Check in is available from 2pm
Check out is by 12 noon on the morning of departure.

Accommodation
150 air conditioned bedrooms all with ensuite bathroom, trouser press, iron and ironing board, satellite channels, hairdryer, mini bar, modem/fax link, voice mail and tea and coffee making facilities.

Figure 7.22 Part of a brochure for Huntingdon Marriott Hotel

INVESTOR IN PEOPLE

© Marriott Hotels 2003

The hotel accommodation tariff

Marriott Leisure Breaks are a range of packages that include (Figure 7.23):

* no minimum stay
* complimentary use of leisure facilities
* extensive continental and full English breakfast buffets served through to 11 a.m. at weekends
* free accommodation for up to two children under 16 sharing with parents, and free breakfast for children under 5.

Huntingdon Marriott Hotel

Kingfisher Way,
Hinchingbrooke Bus. Pk.,
Huntingdon,
Camb. PE29 6FL
Tel: 0870 400 7257
Fax: 0870 400 7357
www.marriott.co.uk/cbghd

Accommodation Tariff
Valid from March 2004– March 2005

Midweek Rates
Sunday to Thursday

March 2004 – March 2005

Deluxe bedrooms	£123.00
Executive bedrooms	£143.00
Luxury Suites	£173.00

Our Executive bedrooms & Luxury Suites entitle you to a Complimentary Full English Breakfast.

Weekend Rates
Friday to Saturday

Deluxe bedrooms	£104.00
Executive bedrooms	£124.00
Luxury Suites	£154.00

* * Marriott Leisure Breaks * *
Available Friday and Saturday nights

	Bed & Breakfast From	Dinner, Bed & Breakfast from
From 1st March 2004	£52.00	£72.00

Prices are per person, per night based on two people sharing a deluxe bedroom.
A supplement of £20.00 per night is applicable for single rooms.
All leisure breaks are subject to availability, please contact our reservations department for further details on **0870 4007257**

Please refer to our brochure for detailed terms & conditions.

INVESTOR IN PEOPLE   Whitbread Group PLC. Registered in England No 29423. Registered Office: CityPoint, One Ropemaker Street, London EC2Y 9HX

Figure 7.23 The tariff at Huntingdon Marriott Hotel

Circulation accommodation

The ground-floor plan of the Huntingdon Marriott Hotel shows the reception lobby area. This has soft furnishings and a front desk and leads to lifts and stairs (Figure 7.24).

Sleeping accommodation

The Huntingdon Marriott Hotel has 150 guestrooms, all of which are air-conditioned. All the rooms include private en-suite bathroom with complimentary toiletries, remote control television with free satellite channels, direct-dial telephone with voicemail, fax/modem connections, STSN broadband Internet access, personal minibar, tea- and coffee-making facilities, hairdryer, iron, ironing board and trouser-press.

Access to the rooms is via a keycard. These are inserted into a reader in the lobby area of each guestroom, which controls the lighting and the air-conditioning and temperature control for each room.

A courtesy tray is provided, which has all the equipment and commodities needed for guests to prepare their own hot drinks such as tea, coffee and chocolate. The equipment includes a kettle, teapot, cups, sachets of beverages, sugar and milk. Biscuits are also provided.

The minibar is a small refrigerator containing miniature bottles of spirits and appropriate mixers (tonic, ginger, soda), quarter bottles of wine, bottles of beer and small bottles of fruit juice. Minibars also contain vacuum packs of cocktail

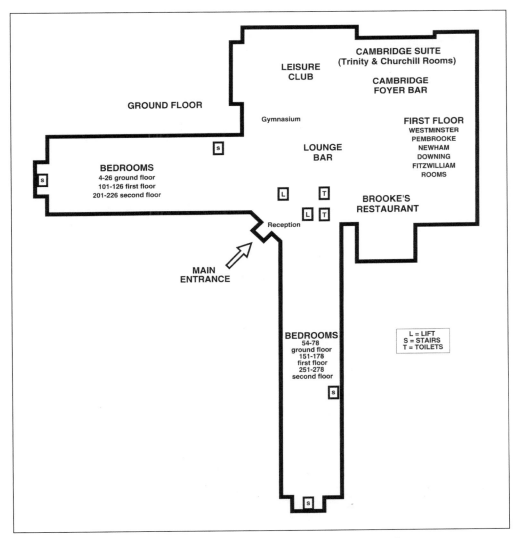

Figure 7.24 The ground-floor plan of Huntingdon Marriott Hotel

nuts or crisps. Guests help themselves from the minibar, which is electronically tagged, so that guests are charged for any items consumed.

The hotel directory

In each guestroom is a hotel directory giving information on the services and facilities available for residents. This information includes:

* *Account.* The account should be settled on departure unless credit facilities have been agreed in writing. All major credit cards are accepted, as are cheques when supported by a valid banker's card.

* *Alarm calls.* Alarm calls can be set via the telephone or television in each room. Wake-up calls can also be booked with the front desk in reception.

* *Car parking.* Free parking is available. Guests are asked to ensure that their car is locked and that all valuables are removed, as the hotel cannot accept any responsibility for any damage to the car or property stolen from it whilst it is parked.

* *Car rental.* Self-drive car hire and limousine service may be arranged through the front desk.

* *Cashier and currency exchange.* The front desk can be contacted for assistance in cashing cheques. Foreign currency and travellers' cheques may be exchanged at the desk.

* *Child-minding.* Arrangements can be made through local agencies, if 24-hour notice is given. Baby changing facilities are located in the Leisure Club changing room.

* *Fire safety.* Fire precautions are vital. All guests are asked to read the fire notice behind the door of their room which gives evacuation details, and the location of the assembly point which is near the front entrance of the hotel. If a fire is suspected, guests are asked to dial '9999', and if the fire bell rings continuously guests are asked to exit the hotel as quickly as possible following the fire exit signs and not to use the lifts. Fire extinguishers and alarms are located in the corridors.

* *Personal safety.* Personal safety and security can be ensured by securing the room at all times

and by depositing valuables for safe custody at the front desk. Guests are asked to report anyone or anything suspicious.

* *First aid.* The front desk should be contacted for first aid supplies or assistance. The desk will also contact a doctor or dentist (on 24-hour call) if needed. There will be a charge if a visit is made.

* *Housekeeping services.* Bed-boards (a flat board which slides between the mattress and the bed base to make the bed firmer), cots, rollaway beds, blankets, pillows and toiletries can be provided. A turn-down service is offered in the evening, when housekeeping will fold back bedspreads and bedding is turned back to make it easier for the guest to get into bed. Any night clothes may be laid out neatly on the bed. The bedroom and bathroom will be tidied and the curtains closed.

* *Laundry.* The housekeeper needs to be contacted by 8.30 a.m. for the collection of any items requiring laundering or dry-cleaning, or items should be handed in to the front desk before 9 a.m. for return by 6 p.m. on the same day. The service is available Monday to Friday. A daily pressing service is available. Laundry bags and lists are stored in the wardrobe of each room.

* *Modem/Internet access.* All guestrooms have Internet access by plugging a laptop into the modem jack located in the telephone. Use of the STSN box when connecting to the Internet will provide high-speed access.

* *Animals.* With the exception of Guide Dogs, pets are allowed only at the discretion of the hotel manager, and there may be a small additional charge. Advance notice is required, and pets are not permitted in any area where food and drink are served.

* *Shoeshine.* A shoeshine is located on the ground floor and the second floor near the lifts. In each room there is a shoeshine cloth.

* *Telephone.* For direct calls, including international and national calls where the code is known, dial 9 and the number required. All calls will be charged at a unit price. For any

assistance dial 0 for the hotel's operator. To dial from room to room, enter the room number only after dialling 3. The telephone provides a private voice mailbox. Automatic transfer of all incoming calls to voicemail and a Do Not Disturb feature are available.

Recreation accommodation

Residents of the hotel qualify for free membership of the Leisure Club for the duration of their stay. The Leisure Club has its own reception, which will take bookings and provide assistance, including the loan of towels. This can be reached by a dedicated telephone extension number. Pre-booking is advised at peak times. Residents are required to show their keycard as proof of 'membership' and to enable charging to an account where necessary. It may also be required as a deposit against equipment hire.

There is an extensively equipped gymnasium with weight-training and cardiovascular equipment (expert instructors are available). The indoor swimming pool is 13 metres and heated. There is also a sauna, steam room and spa. Changing rooms have hairdryers, and towels are provided free of charge.

Children under 15 years of age are not permitted into the Leisure Club unless accompanied by an adult, and supervision is required when children use the facilities within the club. Children under 16 are not allowed to use the fitness equipment, and those under 8 should not use the steam room or sauna. The purpose of these restrictions is to ensure the well-being and enjoyment of all users. Guests aged between 16 and 18 can use the fitness equipment under the supervision of a gym instructor. Children under 15 are not allowed to use the swimming pool unless supervised by an adult.

Conference accommodation

The Huntingdon Marriott Hotel has a range of dedicated rooms and facilities to meet the needs of business and conference customers (Figure 7.25). The facilities are flexible to allow a variety of different layouts to suit all events, from press conferences, product launches and incentives, to sales seminars or training courses.

Event management

The Marriott 8-Hour Package provides a range of services that can be readily adapted to meet individual requirements. From the moment of arrival to the moment of departure, the hotel can take care of every aspect of the meeting or event.

The services on offer are: a dedicated contact on the day who will respond to the client's needs; comprehensive business support services including fax, photocopying, email and secretarial facilities; a range of secure, private meeting and conference rooms; extensive dining facilities for

	BANQUET	CLASSROOM	RECEPTION	THEATRE
Cambridge Suite	260	160	240	260
Trinity Room	90	64	120	120
Churchill Room	90	64	120	120
Downing Room	80	40	100	100
Westminster Room	40	24		40
Pembroke Room	30	20		30
Newnham Room	20	12		25
Fitzwilliam Room				15
Syndicate A				10
Syndicate Rooms	8 boardroom			

Figure 7.25 The capacity of meeting rooms at Huntingdon Marriott

private lunches and dinners; refreshments with themed breaks tailored to specific needs; team-building activities and programmes; notepads and pens, stationery kit, and an overhead projector and screen. There is follow-up after the event to ensure continual improvements by responding to client's needs.

The Marriott 24-Hour Package includes all the above plus accommodation, dinner and breakfast, with complimentary use of leisure facilities

Communications

State-of-the-art communications include high-speed Internet connections and complete data security, web-casting, video-conferencing, technical support, email kiosks, Internet cafés and mini offices.

Business services

Secretarial support includes typing and word-processing, transcription/dictation, and laser printing from a laptop. Use of a photocopier for small quantities is free to residents, while non-residents are charged per sheet. There is no charge for incoming faxes. Outgoing faxes are charged at £1.50 for UK numbers and at £2.50 for international numbers.

Equipment can be rented. A £15 refundable deposit is required for such items as adaptors and phone chargers. Other equipment, which needs to be booked in advance, includes computers, printers, scanners, VCR with monitor, slide projectors and other office equipment.

Other available services include a courier, tabulation of figures, translation, notary, travel/tour arrangements, general secretarial services and a temporary/private secretary. Advance notice is required for these services.

Eating accommodation

The Brookes Restaurant offers modern and traditional dishes. It is open for breakfast (buffet style), lunch and dinner each day. The restaurant is very popular and the hotel cannot guarantee the availability of tables for dinner for guests staying on a bed and breakfast basis.

Brookes Café is available within the main restaurant and provides a variety of light meals and snacks in an informal and no-smoking environment. The Lounge Bar is a more relaxed dining area, with a selection of wines, beers and spirits as well as snacks and light meals.

Vending machines for drinks and snacks are located on all floors of the hotel. Ice vending machines are located next to them. Each guestroom has an ice-bucket.

Room service is extensive. In-room dining has many dishes that are available 24 hours a day. If an item is not on the menu the hotel will try to satisfy the guest's request. The hotel guarantees to serve any meal within 30 minutes, or no charge will be made. Children's menus are also available from room service.

Breakfast as part of room service is served from 6.30 a.m. to 11 a.m. This can be ordered by using an order card placed on the door handle outside the room. The Marriott Breakfast consists of a plate of scrambled eggs, bacon, sausage, grilled tomato, mushrooms and rosti potatoes with croissant, bread roll and muffin with preserves, butter and margarine. Drinks include freshly squeezed orange or grapefruit juice, apple or tomato juice, plus choice of tea, coffee or hot chocolate. This is charged at £14.95.

For all room service, £2.50 is added to the final bill.

Theory into practice

1 Fully explain the corporate hospitality provision available at the Huntingdon Marriott Hotel.

2 Investigate the hospitality services available at the Huntingdon Marriott Hotel. Make sure you look at the types of accommodation and accommodation services and the types of food and drink services. Show that you understand the values and attitudes of the Huntingdon Mariott Hotel in respect of its provision and hospitality services.

Types of food and drink services

Food and drink services are provided for travel and tourism customers in a variety of locations and under a variety of conditions.

A note on customer service

Generally, the higher the cost of a meal, the more service the customer expects to receive. At a motorway service station where customers are spending under £10 for a two-course meal, the level of service is relatively low. Customers might have to collect their own food and carry it to a table to consume it, and may be expected to clear dishes from the table at the end of the meal. At the top end of the catering market where customers might be paying over £50 per head for a meal, a full waiting service is more likely to be provided.

When it comes to customer satisfaction in providing food and drink, attention to detail counts. Watch and anticipate the needs of the customer. If the customer's wine or water glass is approaching empty, fill it up again. If the butter dish is empty, get a fresh one. If the customer is near to finishing a course, advise the waiting staff that the table will need the main course very shortly, so ensuring minimum delay, without rushing the customer.

Food service staff are expected to provide more than simply food. Customers expect to find a warm welcome with a smile and to be greeted and dealt with courteously at all times. A sense of humour is also important, as is knowing how much conversation is appropriate. Good waiting staff will know when to say nothing and when to give advice. These are social skills and are extremely important in ensuring customer satisfaction.

Types of service

This section presents brief notes on the main approaches to serving food and drink. The actual names given to the types of service may vary between providers.

Silver service

Food is sent from the kitchen on large dishes, or 'flats', and is then served by waiting staff using a spoon and fork. Silver service is found in good-quality hotels and restaurants. The food is well presented, and customers have control over the portions they receive. Silver service is, however, very labour-intensive and requires much training of staff. It is therefore more costly but a customer does experience full and attentive service.

Silver/plate service

The main item, such as the meat or fish, is plated in the kitchen and served by the waiting staff. The rest of the meal, such as vegetables, are 'silver served'. This approach is commonly found in department store restaurants and medium-quality restaurants. The service is quicker than silver service and so there is a faster turnover of customers. Fewer fully trained staff are required to serve than with full silver service.

French service

All the items of the meal are offered in dishes by waiting staff so that individual customers can take the portion they want. This approach is found at small functions, and obviously in French restaurants. It allows high-quality presentation of the food in the dishes and a very personal service, but it is difficult to control portion sizes.

Gueridon service

Dishes are prepared, cooked or flamed at the table in front of the customer (Figure 7.26). It is found in top-class restaurants. Customers are given a highly personal service by staff with the appropriate skills. This approach is expensive owing to high labour costs, but it produces a relaxed dining environment for the customer.

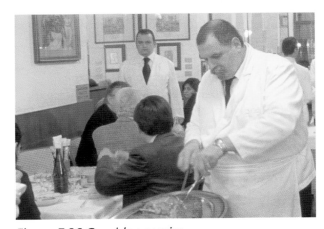

Figure 7.26 Gueridon service

Nouvelle cuisine

The items of the meal are decoratively arranged on a plate and served to the customer. Nouvelle cuisine is found in high-quality hotels and restaurants and offers excellent visual presentation of the food. It is very labour-intensive in the kitchen, and so can be expensive.

Plate service

The complete meal is presented on a plate to the customer. This approach is used in set-price restaurants, cafés, pubs and guesthouses as it allows a fast turnover of customers, saves on labour, ensures that all food is presented to the same standard, and allows portion control. It does mean that more work needs to be done in the kitchen.

Family service

Dishes containing the meal items are placed in the centre of the table for customers to help themselves. This approach is often found in banqueting suites, pubs and guesthouses. It is a faster service than other methods and the customers control the portions they take. It is a very sociable form of dining and suits families with children.

Counter cafeteria service

Customers queue to select their meals from a counter or servery. This is found in pubs, canteens and motorway service stations. It is a speedy service and hence reduces labour costs.

Carvery service

The main course is collected by the customer from a central station and taken back to a table to be eaten (Figure 7.27). This is popular for Sunday lunches in pubs and restaurants. It has the advantage of looking good and allows choice for individual customers. It allows portion control to be kept tight and the food is kept hot at the carvery.

Fast-food service

The customer is served quickly from a counter. This is common in takeaways and burger bars. There is a very fast turnover.

Figure 7.27 Carvery service

Types of food
Full meals

A full meal usually consists of a starter, a main course, a dessert (sweet), and coffee. Special occasions might be celebrated with extra courses (e.g. at a banquet with VIPs). Figure 7.28 shows a sample *à la carte* menu with a very wide range of choice. Obviously this would not be possible in a modest restaurant.

Buffet meal

A buffet meal may have on offer hot or cold food. A cold ('finger') buffet might have the following choices, at a typical price of around £15 per person:
- selection of sandwiches (cheese and pickle, North Atlantic prawns and Rose Marie sauce, honey-roast ham, roast beef and horseradish)

STARTERS

Sorbet (vegetarian) – a refreshing scoop of chilled water ice £2.75

Home made soup (vegetarian) – a piping hot bowl of freshly prepared soup served with cream £3.75

Chicken Caesar salad – strips of chicken with a cream Caesar dressing on a bed of seasonal leaves £5.25

Fan of melon (vegetarian) – served with a wild berry compote £4.25

Chicken liver parfait – a smooth blend of chicken livers £5.00

Marbled salmon terrine – served with a lemon vinaigrette £5.50

North Atlantic prawns – served on a bed of baby leaf salad with Marie Rose sauce £5.50

Roasted Mediterranean vegetable tartlet (vegetarian) £4.95

MAIN COURSE

Roast stuffed rib eye – served with herb stuffing and a thyme jus £13.95

Oven baked supreme of salmon - served with Hollandaise sauce £12.95

Roast leg of lamb £12.75

Roulade of pork – served with an apricot stuffing £13.25

Pan seared supreme of duck – served with a port and cranberry sauce £14.25

Oven baked stuffed supreme of chicken – with a sun-dried tomato and mozzarella stuffing £13.00

Roasted vegetable, honey and grain mustard en croute (vegetarian) £9.95

Spinach and feta filo parcel (vegetarian) £9.95

All main courses are served with a selection of seasonal vegetables and potatoes

DESSERTS

Bread and butter pudding £4.50

Chocolate truffle £4.50

Lemon tart £4.50

Profiteroles – served with hot chocolate sauce £4.50

Selection of cheese and biscuits – served with celery and grapes £5.25

White chocolate teardrop – served with a fruit coulis £4.50

Selection of ice creams £3.25

Figure 7.28 An extensive à la carte menu

- buffalo wings served with barbeque (BBQ) sauce
- cod goujons served with tartare sauce
- cajun chicken served with a salsa dip
- breaded jalapenos
- jacket potato filled with cheese
- stuffed tomatoes (possibly filled with cream cheese)
- quiches (cheese and tomato, onion and cheese, mushroom and ham)
- finger éclairs.

Snack meals and fast food

Snack meals are available from some vending machines, canteens and leisure providers.

Types of drink

Alcoholic drinks

The range of alcoholic drinks is huge. It includes beer and cider, spirits and liqueurs, and wines.

Beers are of two types: cask-conditioned ('real ale') and brewery-conditioned ('keg', which includes lagers). All beers are a filtered brew of malt, hops and sugar to which yeast is added. This is then fermented to produce the alcohol content. Ales and lagers differ in terms of strength, which is measured by 'original gravity' – the higher the original gravity the stronger the beer. The stronger beers often have names like Special, Best or Export. Bottled and canned ales and lagers are widely available. *Cider*, which is produced by fermenting apples, tends to have a high alcohol content.

Spirits include whisky, gin, vodka, brandy and rum. Whisky is distilled from grain (barley, rye or maize). The two main styles are malt whisky (produced from malted barley in a pot still) and grain whisky (produced in a continuous still). Blended whisky has various balances of these two types. Brandy is distilled from grape wine. The white spirits include gin (flavoured by juniper), vodka (a base of grain or molasses) and rum (distilled from sugar cane – different production methods produce white or dark rum).

Liqueurs are spirits to which other ingredients have been added (e.g. Archers and Malibu). These, along with 'alco pops', are particularly aimed at the under-30 age group.

Wines are red, white or rosé (pink, slightly sparkling). The latter two should be served chilled. Many hospitality outlets offer 'house wines' in red and white. Vermouths and fortified wines have spirits or other ingredients added. For example, brandy is added to port; vermouths are wines with added alcohol and herbs; and sherry is a fortified white wine from the Jerez region of Spain – the main types are 'fino' (dry), 'amontillado' (medium) and 'cream' (sweet).

Non-alcoholic drinks

These are mainly minerals and 'soft' drinks. Many customers appreciate soft drinks as a healthy alternative, or if they are driving or are too young to drink alcohol. There are many types of non-alcoholic drinks. *Mixers* (e.g. ginger ale, bitter lemon or other carbonated drinks) are so called because traditionally they were associated with mixing with spirits. Today they are just as commonly drunk on their own. *Cordials* (e.g. lime or blackcurrant juice) may similarly be drunk alone or mixed with a spirit). Other *fruit juices*, such as orange, pineapple and grapefruit, are very popular.

Minerals are in cans or sealed with a screw top or crown cork, which is removed in the same way as from a beer bottle. Carbonated drinks should be handled very carefully without shaking, but fruit juices should be shaken gently to distribute the fruit particles. *Squashes* are concentrated fruit juices and need to be diluted with water.

Hot drinks

Tea and coffee are the most common hot drinks, but there are many others. Tea is traditionally served with milk or lemon, and sometimes it is deliberately served cold ('iced tea'). Coffee may be 'white' (with milk or cream), black, or as a cappuccino.

Customer service issues

All staff within hospitality outlets either work in direct contact with the guests or provide an important contribution that will influence the final product or service. All these people need to have a full awareness of customer service issues.

Customer service is a major training and cultural effort in most companies in the hospitality sector. It plays a big part in attaining a competitive edge over companies offering a similar product, with the difference being the human element. Better customer service gives the customer added value.

The entire training programme of any hospitality enterprise must prominently feature customer service as an issue of utmost significance to every member of staff. Customer service training should be part of the induction process, and it should be reinforced in staff notices, staff meetings, management meetings and at every possible opportunity.

A smile on the face of a member of staff can work wonders in the hospitality industry. When a cheery disposition is the result of the employee being genuinely contented, rather than being told to look happy, customer, employer and employee will benefit. It was this ethos that inspired Forte Hotel Group to launch the Commitment to Excellence scheme. The three-year programme has helped to improve employee practices and customer service. The impetus for the scheme was an attempt to halt the high labour turnover. A series of workshops and seminars was developed for employees at every level of the organisation. On completion of the course, staff attend follow-up seminars in which they look at guest satisfaction and identify areas for improvement. Over three years there was a 15 per cent drop in complaints and a 24 per cent rise in the number of compliments expressed by grateful customers and an increase in employee satisfaction.

Assessment guidance

The aim of the next section is to help you prepare for the assessment of customer service provision of your chosen hospitality provider. Consequently the content of the section will be looked at in general terms, with elements from many different hospitality providers.

Skills needed by staff working in hospitality

Practical skills

Practical skills required will vary considerably, depending on the hospitality outlet and the job role. We shall consider the example of working in a public house as one of the bar staff.

In a pub, the bar staff handle financial transactions, usually with cash but sometimes also with credit and debit cards. Modern tills show the total to be charged to the customer, and perhaps the change required, so the burden of mental arithmetic is removed. However, customers still expect efficient use of the till, and to be given the correct change.

Dispensing beer correctly is a skill that has to be learned. The technique for serving keg beer through a free-flow tap is as follows. Select a glass or mug of the appropriate size and check that it is clean, unchipped and unmarked. Holding the base of the glass or the handle of the mug, place it under the dispensing spout at an angle of 45 degrees. Opening the tap with your hand, let the beer run down the inside of the glass furthest away from you. Keeping the tap out of the beer at all times, continue filling, straightening the glass as it fills. The glass may be full or filled to the line, but you must control the flow by turning the tap off before the beer spills down the outside of the glass, which is messy and wasteful. Finally, serve the beer by placing the glass carefully in front of the customer. Ideally the handle of a mug should be to the customer's right.

The technique for serving beer from a hand pump is entirely different and is something of an art. The 'three pulls' rule usually applies. The first pull of the pump handle should be full and smooth. The second pull should be about two-thirds and more gradual. The final pull should be very gradual – just enough to fill the glass, which should now be held vertically.

Other practical skills involved in working in a pub are: metered dispensing, opening and pouring bottled beers, changing a keg of pasteurised beer, changing a carbon dioxide cylinder, using an optic (for spirits), changing a standard optic, serving wine by the glass, and mixing cocktails.

Think it over ...

As a group, discuss other practical skills that anyone working in a pub should possess. Then consider how these skills would be different from those of someone working (a) in a fast-food outlet, and (b) as a hotel receptionist.

Knowledge and application of health and safety requirements

Of particular importance under this heading is interpretation of the many regulations relating to food safety. Anyone who handles food, or articles or equipment that come into contact with food, as part of their duties needs to follow certain essential points of food hygiene (Figure 7.29). In this context drink is also classified as food.

Think it over ...

As a group, discuss the importance of food safety to the outlet and to its customers.

Personal skills

The impression given by staff to customers is crucial. Every point of contact with the customers involves personal communication skills. Staff working in the hospitality industry need to:

* have a positive attitude
* enjoy working with people
* tune in to what the customer expects
* have a desire to please
* get things right the first time
* act responsibly
* truly value the customer.

Body language

Body language is all-important in effective interaction with other staff and customers. What people say to you or what you say to them are often different from what you or they feel or think. The body language you use allows others to

1. Keep yourself clean and wear clean clothing.
2. Always wash your hands thoroughly before handling food and after using the toilet or handling raw foods or waste or smoking. Never use a food preparation or glass washing sink to wash your hands.
3. Tell your supervisor, before commencing work, of any serious skin, nose, throat, vomiting and or diarrhoea trouble.
4. Ensure that cuts, grazes and sores are covered with a blue waterproof dressing.
5. Avoid unnecessary handling of food. Use tongs when appropriate and never cough or sneeze over food.
6. Do not smoke or drink in a food room. A food room is any room in which food or equipment that may come into contact with food is stored or handled. This will include kitchens, cold rooms, dry goods stores, cellars, bars, room service and stills areas. It does not include designated smoking areas.
7. If you see something wrong tell your supervisor. If you think that any of these rules are being broken, or are unsure about it, inform your supervisor. Breaches of these rules could mean that the outlet is breaking the law.
8. Do not prepare food too far in advance of service.
9. Keep food covered.
10. Keep perishable food either refrigerated or piping hot. This rule applies equally to food on display in restaurant or bar areas.
11. Keep the preparation of raw and cooked food strictly separate.
12. When reheating food, ensure it becomes piping hot.
13. Sanitise as you go. Keep all equipment and surfaces clean.
14. Follow any food safety instructions either on food packaging or from your supervisor.

Figure 7.29 Basics of food hygiene

interpret your thoughts by your gestures. If you shrug your shoulders you imply either that you do not care much about what has been said to you, or that you have not understood. A neck scratch can in some circumstances indicate that you are not in agreement. You must be aware of your own non-verbal signals and the effects they could have on your customers.

Eye contact is vitally important as it can give clues to a person's thoughts. As a person's attitude and mood change from positive to negative thoughts the pupils of the eyes will dilate or contract. The different ways in which you direct your gaze could have a powerful effect in face-to-face contact with a customer.

Your tone of voice relays a signal to the customer and evokes different responses depending on your manner and the emphasis placed on the spoken word. It is important to say something in the right way, as well as saying the right thing. More information on this was provided in unit 2 (see pages 65–7) and you are advised to look back to remind yourself of what was said.

It is often necessary to deal with customers on the telephone. When answering the phone be polite, smile with your voice, introduce your organisation and identify yourself. A phone call should be answered within three or four rings.

Active listening skills are important too. Customers want to feel welcome, important and understood. Hearing what a customer says is not sufficient. Active listening involves trying to understand the true meaning of the words used – the unspoken message behind what is said. The tone of voice, emotion and the context of the situation as well as evaluation of the facts contribute to active listening. Simple gestures such as nodding the head, smiling and verbal reinforcement can show that you have 'got the message'.

Summary of essential personal skills

* Try to establish a rapport with the customer.

* Use the customer's name and correct title.

* Avoid jargon that the customer does not understand, and be ready to explain the meaning of terms if asked.

* Use appropriate body language and eye contact whenever possible.

* Be confident *and* competent – customers like to know that you are in control of the situation.

* If unsure about anything, offer to check with someone else and respond quickly.

Handling complaints

The information presented here is based on the 'Spirit of Hilton' training programme. That organisation has created a so-called 'A' team for managing complaints from customers.

* APOLOGISE at once, whether it is your fault or not. You are not taking the blame, but on behalf of the hotel simply regretting what has happened. If you apologise immediately, the customer is more likely to stay calm. Don't try to justify the complaint or blame others – that will imply that the organisation is unprofessional, not really interested and not working as a team.

* ACCEPT the customer's point of view. Get his or her story about what happened, and try not to interrupt. Empathise and show you understand the problem. Ask questions to get all the information and facts, while listening carefully with all your senses. Thank the customer for bringing the problem to your attention. Tell the customer what you intend to do and when you will get back with a considered response.

* TAKE PROMPT ACTION to satisfy the customer. If this is beyond your immediate control, pass the complaint on to your supervisor. Make sure, however, that you give your supervisor the full story. He or she will then be able to get back to the customer with a satisfactory solution. Think about what can be done to stop this kind of problem happening in the future. If appropriate, make contact with the customer again to ask about his or her current experience with your service.

* REMEMBER that, while customers who are dissatisfied with the service are encouraged to tell you about it, 'prevention is better than cure'.

In pairs, discuss each of the complaints below and decide which ones could have been prevented.

- 'My toast is burnt.'

- 'It took ten minutes to be seated in the restaurant – this doesn't give a good first impression.'

- 'The fire alarm woke us at 4 a.m.'

- 'I didn't like the taste of the squid in the salad, I've never had it before.'

- 'The telephone charges are outrageous.'

- 'The electricity went off in the middle of my favourite programme.'

- 'Three of my favourite dishes on the menu were not available.'

- 'I suggest you do some training – the waitress was downright rude to my colleague.'

- 'It took twenty minutes to check-out at reception and there were two mistakes on my bill.'

- 'I had to hold my baby in my arms all through lunch because you didn't have a second baby chair available.'

Organisational skills

Everyone working in the hospitality industry must have excellent organisational skills. These have already been covered in depth in the section on types of jobs in hospitality.

The skills required include *team-working*. Working teams may be made up of individuals with specialised skills that all contribute to the overall outcome. In a small restaurant there may be a chef, a kitchen assistant, a waiter and a manager. Their roles will remain much the same, though in such a small team the manager might on occasions need to fill in for the waiter or even for one of the kitchen staff.

Most tasks in hospitality are carried out by teams rather than individuals. Good products, services and facilities don't just happen – they are the result of concerted effort by groups of people seeking to achieve their common goal.

Welcome Host

*Figure 7.30
The Welcome to
Excellence logo*

Welcome Host is a one-day training programme which concentrates on improving customer care skills (Figure 7.30). Aimed at reception and front-line staff, the course covers:

- welcoming customers – the value of excellent customer service

- understanding your customers – the customer experience

- delivering service excellence – key elements of customer service, customer service trends, setting and maintaining standards and first impressions

- communicating successfully – the communication process, types of communication, techniques in listening, questioning and for the telephone

- providing information and advice – presenting information to customers, knowing the local area and giving directions

- meeting specific needs – providing an accessible service, language and cultural diversity and welcoming customers of all ages

- dealing with difficult situations – the causes of dissatisfaction, handling complaints and resolving conflicts

- boosting business – using customer service to boost business and improve quality.

Find out more about Welcome Host from www.welcometoexcellence.co.uk.

The hotel guest cycle

This cycle can be summarised as follows (Figure 7.31). A potential guest makes an enquiry and, if satisfied with the terms and conditions, makes a reservation. On arrival, he or she registers and is checked in. After the period of residency, the guest checks out. The hotel management will wish there to be follow-up to try to get repeat business.

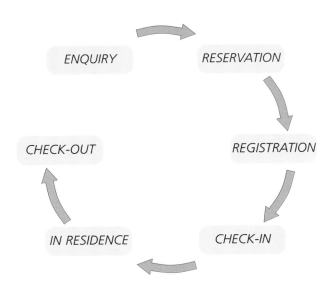

Figure 7.31 The hotel guest cycle

Before arrival: enquiries

During the pre-arrival stage of the cycle the guest chooses a hotel to patronise. The choice can be affected by a variety of factors, including previous experience with the hotel, advertising, recommendation, location etc. The guest's choice may also be influenced by the ease of making a reservation and the reservation clerk's description of the hotel and its facilities, room rates and amenities. The attitude, efficiency and knowledge of the front-office staff may influence the potential guest's decision to stay at a particular hotel.

Proper handling of reservation information is important. If a reservation can be accepted as requested, the reservation clerk creates a reservation record. An effective reservation system helps maximise room sales by accurately monitoring room availability.

Reservation systems

There are a variety of ways in which a guest can make a reservation: in person, by telephone, by letter, by fax or by email.

Reservations may be handled in many ways and depend on the size of the establishment and its location. Many hotels and restaurants now use computerised reservation systems, but some small establishments still use a traditional bookings diary. This records reservation details and basic guest information and is completed on a daily basis (Figure 7.32). Diary entries are made in the order in which they are received on a particular day. Some of the reservation details may also be recorded on a separate bookings chart.

This is a very labour-intensive method for recording reservations and is really only suitable for very small hotels and guesthouses, where there are relatively few bookings at any one time.

With a computerised system, when a reservation is made the advance bookings module of the reservations program is accessed and the display for the relevant night(s) is requested. The computer will display the number of rooms of each type available on a particular night. If the reservation request is for several consecutive nights, the reservations clerk will check the availability on these future dates. Once the booking has been entered and the guest details completed, the computer will then be instructed to accept the booking. The computer will

DATE OF ARRIVAL: 3RD MAY 2005					
Date booked	Guest name	Stay	Room	Terms	Other details
07/04/05	Mr & Mrs Smith	2 nights	24	B&B	Arriving late
08/04/05	Mr Begum	1 night	16	Room only	-
10/04/05	Ms Chan	3 nights	12	Full board	-

Figure 7.32 Example of a traditional booking diary

automatically deduct the requested room from the overall total of remaining rooms available. The screen display will then reset itself ready to accept another reservation.

On arrival

The arrival stage of the guest cycle includes registration and the allocation of a room or rooms. Registration can cover method of payment and any special requirements. When the guest arrives, a relationship can be established with the hotel through the front-office staff. A positive impression needs to be created.

There are legal aspects to the procedures that must be completed by reception staff. The purpose of guest registration is to ensure that everyone using sleeping accommodation is recorded.

The front-office desk must learn of changes in the housekeeping status of each room as soon as possible, to allow maximisation of room sales.

In small guest houses a registration book is used, but this means that guest details – such as addresses – can be read by other guests.

In residence

Throughout the occupancy stage, front-office staff represent the hotel to the guest. The front desk is responsible for coordinating guest services and may include providing the guest with information, equipment, supplies or services. A major front-office objective is to satisfy guests' needs in a way that will encourage a return visit. Another objective during occupancy is the issue of security.

Checking-out and follow-up

During departure both the guest services and guest accounting aspects are completed. The last but one aspect is checking the guest out of the

hotel and creating a guest history record. The final element of guest accounting is settling the account. Once the guest has checked out, the room status is updated and the housekeeping department is told.

One major concern at checking-out should be to find out whether the guest was satisfied with the stay. In terms of sales and marketing, the more information the hotel has about its guests the better it can anticipate and serve their future needs.

New technology at the front office

Integral to the development of the front office has been the introduction of technology. Many hotels are now fully automated with front-office computerised record-keeping.

Computer systems designed for use in the hospitality industry were first introduced in the early 1970s. Those early systems tended to be expensive and used only by the largest hotel properties. Over the next 10 years computer equipment became less expensive, more compact and easier to operate. The development of versatile PCs provided the opportunity for systems to be introduced into smaller hospitality units.

At each stage of the hotel guest cycle the influence of computerisation can be seen. The reservations module of an in-house computer system may directly interface with a central reservations network and automatically block rooms according to a preset pattern. The reservations module may also generate letters of confirmation and pre-registration activities. Lists of expected arrivals, occupancy and revenue forecasts and a variety of informative reports may also be produced.

At the arrival stage, guest information is copied directly from the computer reservation record, and late arrival guests will be entered by front-desk staff. The guest may then be presented with a computer-prepared registration card for verification and signature. The installation of on-line credit card authorisation enables front-desk staff to receive payments by this method.

Throughout the occupancy stage, information on any items consumed by a guest can be transferred electronically to the front desk and automatically allocated to the appropriate account. On departure, the guest is presented with a neatly printed and itemised account. Once the account has been settled this information is used to create a guest history record.

In-house services

Room service

Room service is provided by hotels for guests who prefer to eat and drink in their room instead of using the public restaurants and lounges. VIPs will often use this service to avoid publicity or attention. Guests often use this service for snacks or drinks during the night when the bars and restaurants are closed. Even though it may be more expensive, many guests find the prospect of a room-service breakfast preferable to eating breakfast in public first thing in the morning.

Customer relations

Projecting a positive impression to existing and future customers is vital. The importance of customer service has been discussed in this unit, and in unit 2.

Portering services

Portering services are also known as 'the uniformed service'. They can include parking attendants, limousine drivers and bell persons. Uniformed service personnel have a great degree of contact with guests. They greet and help guests to the front desk and to their rooms. At the end of the stay they take guests to the cashier, out of the front door and to their transport.

Valeting is a very specialised in-house service provided by high-class establishments. A valet may act as a personal attendant to a guest looking after clothing, shoes and serving meals in the room.

Housekeeping services

An effectively managed housekeeping department ensures the cleanliness, maintenance and aesthetic appeal of a hotel property. The tasks performed by the housekeeping department are critical to the smooth running and daily operation of the establishment. The range of duties and responsibilities of housekeepers varies enormously between hotels.

Inventory lists of all items within each area that will need the head housekeeper's attention need to be made. These lists are the basis for developing cleaning procedures, training plans and inspection checklists. Frequency schedules indicate how often items in the inventory lists are to be cleaned or maintained. Items that must be cleaned daily or weekly become part of a routine cleaning cycle and are incorporated into regular work procedures. Other items are inspected daily or weekly but they become part of the general deep-cleaning programme and are scheduled as special cleaning projects.

Health and leisure services

Many hotels consider a basic level of provision for health and leisure services important – such as a swimming pool, an exercise room and possibly a solarium. A swimming pool is the most requested facility in hotels by leisure guests – 90 per cent ask for them (but only 10 per cent use those that are available!).

A wide range of health and leisure facilities can be identified: fitness centre (exercise room), indoor swimming pool, whirlpool, sauna, steam baths, solarium, massage facilities, racket sports, outdoor exercise and jogging trails, and golf. Other facilities are for watersports, such as fishing, sailing, windsurfing, for cycling and horseriding, and for croquet, crazy golf and bowls.

Message services and information services

Hotel receptions are a great resource for information. There are usually leaflets available of local tourist attractions and excursions. Many hotels also have PCs which can be accessed using 'tokens' purchased from reception, and televisions that are set to news channels. Reception staff will also receive messages for guests.

Theory into practice

Visit a local hotel and note what information is provided in the public areas.

Assessment guidance

For Assessment Objective 3 you have to research *one* hospitality provider to assess its customer service practices and procedures. You will be expected to recommend improvements and possible developments in its customer service provision.

For Assessment Objective 4 you have to:

- analyse the current provision of hospitality *in a chosen locality*

- make recommendations for future improvements/developments in provision to meet the needs and trends in hospitality provision *in that locality*.

Knowledge check

1 Provide a summary of the scale of the hospitality industry, locally and nationally.

2 Produce a summary of employment characteristics in the hospitality industry, locally and nationally.

3 Summarise the providers of accommodation nationally and locally, with reference to official accommodation grading systems.

4 Summarise the providers of food and drink, nationally and locally.

5 Explain fully the effects of seasonality in hospitality.

6 What is meant by corporate hospitality?

7 Analyse the current provision of hospitality in a chosen locality.

8 Explain the needs of customers for hospitality in a chosen locality.

9 Analyse the trends in hospitality in a chosen locality.

10 Summarise customer service practices and procedures in hospitality.

11 Analyse customer service practices and procedures in a large accommodation outlet.

12 Describe customer service training available for staff in a large accommodation outlet.

Resources

Besides those mentioned in the chapter, you will also find the following of use:

* British Hospitality Association (BHA) – www.bha-online.org.uk

* Beer and Pub Association – www.beerandpub.com

* Hospitality Training Foundation (HtF) – www.hft.org.uk

* International Hotel and Restaurant Association – www.ih-ra.com

* The Restaurant Association – www.ragb.co.uk

* Hotel and Catering International Management Association (HCIMA) – www.hcima.org.uk

* www.lesiureandhospitalityjobs.com

The following are websites of a selection of hospitality companies:

* www.gleneagles.com

* www.jurysdoyle.com

* www.jarvis.co.uk

* www.costa.co.uk

* www.firstleisure.com

* www.odeon.co.uk

* www.galagroup.co.uk

* www.bass.com

* www.granada.com

* www.whitbread.com

UNIT 8

Working overseas

Introduction

Many students studying travel and tourism dream of working in a challenging and exciting environment. Working overseas for a tour operator as a resort representative or visiting exotic destinations as part of your job often fulfils these dreams – in fact working overseas is often perceived as glamorous and exciting. In truth, these jobs are like many others with routine tasks carried out during unsociable hours. Nevertheless, if you enjoy meeting people, are prepared to learn a language and be paid to travel and work abroad, working overseas is for you.

This unit has strong links to unit 2, where you will have learned how to deal with different types of customers in a variety of situations.

How you will be assessed

Your assessment will be in two parts, one practical and one theoretical. For your practical you will host a *welcoming party* in either a live or simulated situation. Your theoretical work will be in the form of a report, which should show critical analysis, evaluation and understanding of your own role and of the personal qualities required by someone hoping to work overseas.

What you need to learn

* types of job opportunities and companies that offer them
* personal qualities, values and attitudes required to work overseas
* implications of the law and regulations when working overseas
* administrative working practices necessary to maintain success
* operational working practices necessary to satisfy customer needs.

Job opportunities and companies that offer them

Travel agents and tour operators support outbound travel in the UK. Tour operators organise and operate tours, packages and programmes that they then market to customers through a variety of channels, such as travel agents, web pages on the Internet and call centres which respond to media advertising (TV, radio, newspapers).

There are various types of tour operators requiring overseas staff. The most common categories are:

* mass market (appealing to large numbers of the population)

* specialist (e.g. cookery, adventure tours)

* summer sun (destinations available during the summer period)

* winter sun (destinations that entice visitors with their warm climates during the British winter)

* activity (e.g. skiing, canoeing and sailing)

* cruises (e.g. Mediterranean, Caribbean).

Large and small tour operators

The four largest outbound tour operators in the UK are Thomas Cook, MyTravel, Thomson (marketed as TUI) and First Choice. The large tour operators provide employment for thousands of people working in a wide variety of functions such as marketing, sales, reservations, operations, administration, IT, contracts, product development, accounting, and personnel (HR). They also have resort representatives, couriers and tour guides. These large operators are all vertically integrated – Figure 8.1 shows how.

Key term

Vertically integrated companies not only organise holidays, they also sell them through their own travel agencies and provide their own air travel.

Thomson Holidays (TUI UK Ltd)
* Travel agency: Lunn Poly, with over 750 shops
* Team Lincoln – the UK's leading teletext and Internet selling specialists
* Travel House Group – leading regional retailer and teletext business
* Manchester Flights – fastest growing teletext and Internet specialist
* Glasgow call centre, selling Thomson Direct, Portland Direct, Founders Club and Lunn Poly and Web sales
* Airline: Britannia, Britain's second largest airline and the world's largest charter airline

JMC (part of Thomas Cook)
* Product ranges include Neilson, Sunset, Club 18–30, JMC and Thomas Cook
* Airline: JMC

MyTravel
* MyTravel currently have over 100 brands and 2000 travel agencies
* They fly to 65 destinations and have recently expanded into the cruise ship market
* Companies under the umbrella of MyTravel include Airtours, Cresta, Direct Holidays, Tradewinds, JetSet
* Airtours is one of the biggest tour operators in the UK, employing nearly 1400 people in the UK

First Choice
* Airline: Air 2000
* First Choice has an alliance with Royal Caribbean Cruises Ltd
* First Choice brands include Unijet, Falcon, Ski, Lakes and Mountains, Sunstart
* They also have specialist companies such as Citalia, Hayes & Jarvis, Sovereign and Longshot Gold Holidays

Figure 8.1 Vertically integrated companies

There are also many small and medium-sized tour operators. Some of these operators are aimed at the 'specialist' market. You may have seen tours advertised for specialist groups such as painting, cookery, wine tasting or photography tours. They may also offer holidays for single people and sometimes provide travel to far-flung destinations

– some of those more unusual destinations not covered by the mass market operators, such as riding camels in Mongolia and sightseeing trips to Siberia.

Types of overseas representative

You may already be familiar with the role of an overseas representative. There has been plenty of TV and newspaper coverage of the life and work of a rep. However, it is a mistake to see the job as an avenue for glamorous parties with free time to sunbathe or ski! Being a representative can be extremely demanding and tiring, but it can be very rewarding. Most overseas reps work only on a seasonal basis, must live away from home, work long and irregular hours and be able to deal with the pressures as well as the pleasures of working with a public wishing to enjoy their hard earned holiday.

Working as an overseas rep naturally requires excellent customer service skills. It is also important to have an ability to speak a foreign language (or a desire to learn) and a reasonably sound ability with numeracy. It may also help to have a basic knowledge of book-keeping as a good deal of time is spent keeping account of cash and credit card transactions or changing or calculating currency.

The ability to get on with people is vital. A representative comes into contact with a variety of people of all ages and backgrounds. It is essential to have a good sense of humour and the ability to listen and to work under pressure.

Good health is definitely required. A representative will need plenty of stamina as the working hours can be long and irregular and there may be occasions where a rep will need to take charge of an emergency or an accident.

There are a variety of overseas representative roles available, the actual roles depending on the tour operator.

Entertainment representative

The role of an entertainment rep is a demanding one. Usually the person must be able to dance, sing and entertain holidaymakers. This may involve anything from putting on a musical to singing and telling jokes. Organising and hosting games and parties both indoors and outdoors may also be required. The idea is to ensure that guests enjoy their holiday as much as possible. You should have an outgoing personality for this type of employment along with a skill in some form of entertainment.

Resort representative

The resort rep's role is a very responsible one. It may involve:

* checking accommodation for health and safety standards

* meeting and greeting new guests at different times of the day and night at their arrival points and ensuring that they are delivered to the correct accommodation

* organising a welcome meeting

* dealing with complaints

* dealing with public relations issues

* promotional work on displays and posters

* selling excursions and organising entertainment

* a variety of office duties, which involves planning, organising meetings, form filling and report writing.

There are many pressures involved, so being able to deal with problems effectively and without panicking is essential.

Every holidaymaker will expect his or her local representative to have a good knowledge of local information. Reps must know details of local buses and trains, doctors' surgeries and chemists' opening times, directions to the post office, along with opening times of shops and banks. A good knowledge of local restaurants, bars and attractions is required. It will be the rep's job to recommend places of interest to visit and places to eat. It is also important that a rep can provide local information on a variety of topics such as the nearest cycling centre, suitable safe routes for walks and tours, and the local electricity voltage (visitors may need to purchase or borrow adaptors for their electrical appliances).

It may also be useful if a rep has a good knowledge of current affairs. This helps with keeping up to date with world issues and sustaining a good knowledge of both the travel industry and the working world. It is therefore useful to read a quality newspaper as often as possible.

Transfer representative

Some of the larger tour operators may employ a transfer rep. Transfer reps are used only where a large number of passengers continually arrive and depart from the airport. It is vital that a transfer rep has a good idea of the layout of the airport so as to be able to deal with a variety of queries and general problems. As a general rule a rep should be aware of the locations of trolleys, wheelchairs, check-in desks, bureaux de change, taxi ranks, coach parks, the lost luggage desk, toilets and shops.

Ski representative

The role of a ski rep obviously often appeals to people who ski. However, excellent communication skills and tact are required for all ski reps, particularly when the snow conditions are poor!

Think it over ...

As a group, discuss what should go into training packs for (a) a transfer rep, and (b) a ski rep.

Children's representatives

Naturally, if you enjoy being with children this role will appeal. It involves organising activities, games and events for groups of children – often between the ages of three and twelve years. The role also involves checking that the play and activity environment is safe in order that children are free from hazards. The supervising of children at mealtimes along with bedtime storytelling may all be part of the role.

Tour operators ask prospective children's representatives to be qualified with an NNEB or equivalent qualification. Being able to enjoy and understand children is a must. Patience, imagination and masses of stamina are generally good attributes.

Figure 8.2 shows part of an advertisement for a children's representative with First Choice. Read the advert and then draw up a ten-point list of all the attributes and qualities you believe are essential for being a children's representative.

Could you rise to the challenge of entertaining children on holiday?

If you combine a flair for inventing and delivering fun-filled activities with a responsible attitude, we'll give you the support to succeed.

About Us ...

First Choice has teamed up with Warner Brothers to bring the superb Looney Tunes™ Kids Clubs to our resorts.

Tweetys crèche is for 15–35 months and is run by trained crèche staff. Then there's the Bugs Bunny Club for 3- to 8-year-olds, which is split where possible into the Sylvester group for 3- to 5-year-olds and the Taz group for 6- to 8-year-olds. We also run the Wavelength programme for those aged nine and above.

About You ...

- You should be over 19, have up to two years' practical experience with groups or children or a relevant childcare qualification.
- You'll also need to be willing to learn new skills and have boundless enthusiasm.

Figure 8.2 A typical job advertisement from First Choice

CASE STUDY

A life in the day of a holiday rep

The Times headline, 4 August 2001

The following is based on part of the *Times* article:

It was 10.30 a.m. and the sangria being doled out to the wan holidaymakers at the 'welcome meeting' was failing to lift their spirits. As I took to the stage in the hotel bar, a sea of 60 tired faces betrayed few signs that they were in Majorca to enjoy themselves. It was going to be a struggle to elicit a smile, let alone laughs.

But, after adjusting my camel-coloured rep's skirt, I launched into my spiel. I kept to the script, avoided gags and didn't fall to pieces.

It wasn't until the 'if you have any questions ...' part of the talk that I caught sight of the same deadpan faces and realised something was wrong. I'd been holding my microphone at waist height.

No one had heard a word. The only people applauding as I left the stage were my sympathetic colleagues.

Holiday reps are at the front line of the battle between what holidaymakers want from package holidays and what they get. This week, hundreds of thousands of British tourists will be relying on their resort reps to provide information about local attractions, and – more than tour operators would like to admit – to listen to complaints about the standard of the holidays.

My tasks were to run a welcome meeting, oversee an airport transfer, and take part in a cabaret. Within two hours of landing at Palma airport, I was practising my dance routine to the dance song Funky Cold Medina – without the aid of music! Half an hour later I was up on stage for the cabaret with 20 other reps strutting my stuff. OK, I was waving my arms while everyone was stamping their feet, but who cares? I was buzzing.

Next morning I was kitted out in my regulation skirt and blouse. Presentation is very important for a rep. Hair has to be pulled back and girls are expected to wear some, but not too much, make-up. Jewellery is also severely restricted – one pair of stud earrings, one ring on each finger and one bracelet or watch on each wrist. Tattoos have to be covered up.

Drinking heavily on duty or even getting drunk off duty (because guests could see you) is forbidden. Smoking in uniform and swearing are also big no-nos. Maintaining eye contact when talking to guests is so important that wearing sunglasses is forbidden. You are not even allowed to rest them on the top of your head.

After finishing the welcome meeting, my task was to deal with queries from guests, and book excursions.

I was approached by a couple who were unhappy with their room at the back of the hotel and showed me their booking form, which indicated their request for a sea view. Oh dear – this could turn nasty. After checking with reception, however, I was pleased to break the news that I could transfer them to a room overlooking the bay. This may not have taken international diplomacy skills, but the problem was resolved in minutes. The result: one happy couple.

Being a rep is certainly no holiday, the hours are long and the pay is low. Most reps work about 88 hours a week, with one day off. Accommodation and travel expenses are covered.

With a partner, check out some websites of tour operators and write an account entitled 'A day in the life of a resort rep'. Select a different tour operator from that of your partner. Swap details and see whether there are any differences between the two operators.

Application forms

Application forms for the post of overseas rep vary between the different companies. However, they do tend to ask similar questions. As with most jobs, it is important not to rush when filling in the application form. Read it through completely before even attempting to answer the questions.

Figure 8.3 shows an application form issued by First Choice. Note that, to save space on these pages, some of the boxes for applicants' responses have been reduced in size. Normally there would be adequate space provided for a reasonable length of response.

FOR HR USE ONLY

Discover
a career with First Choice

(APPLICATIONS WILL NOT BE PROCESSED UNLESS ALL RELEVANT SECTIONS ARE COMPLETE. PLEASE USE BLOCK CAPITAL LETTERS)

POSITION APPLIED FOR

PERSONAL DETAILS

Surname

Forenames

Known as (if different from forenames)

Contact Address

Postcode

Daytime Tel. No. (include area code)

Evening Tel No.

Mobile

Email address

Address of parents or guardian (if different)

Contact telephone number (if different)

N.I / P.R.S.I No

Date of Birth

Age

Place of Birth

Nationality

Do you hold a valid EC Passport?   Yes   No   Expiry Date

Do you hold a full driving licence?   Yes   No

Please state any endorsements

Distinguishing marks (eg tattoos)

Have you ever been convicted of a criminal offence?

(Declaration subject to the Rehabilitation of Offenders Act)   YES   NO

If yes, please give brief details

If you are applying for a Children's representative you will be subject to the Criminal Record Bureau disclosure service

Are you able to work either or both of the following periods without any visits home?

Summer season: April to October   YES   NO

Winter season: November to March   YES   NO

If no, please specify available dates

If you have had an interview with us before, please indicate date and position applied for

Would you be prepared to work anywhere in our programme?   YES   NO

If no, please state areas not prepared to work and why

Please give any dates you will not be available for interview

Where did you hear about First Choice?

Holiday brochures   TV Advertising   Website   In-flight magazine   Newspapers

Personal contacts   Other (please specify)   Recruitment advert (please specify)

Have you worked for First Choice or an associated company before?   YES   NO

If yes, please give details of position, reason for and date of leaving

Figure 8.3 An application form

Have you worked as a Holiday Representative before? YES [ ] NO [ ] Dates [ ]

If yes, please give details of the company, your position and briefly outline your duties

[ ]

Employment History Please give details of your current or most recent employment

Name and address of employer [ ]

[ ]

Position held	[ ]	Reason for leaving	[ ]
Start date	[ ]	Date left (if applicable)	[ ]
Current salary	[ ]	Notice required	[ ]

Please give details of your previous two positions

Name and address of employer [ ]

[ ]

| Position held | [ ] | Reason for leaving | [ ] |
| Start date | [ ] | Date left (if applicable) | [ ] |

Name and address of employer [ ]

[ ]

| Position held | [ ] | Reason for leaving | [ ] |
| Start date | [ ] | Date left (if applicable) | [ ] |

Education & Qualifications

(Most recent first, include academic and vocational qualifications, e.g. Catering, First Aid).

Please list language qualifications separately as indicated below.

Place of Education	From	To	Subject	Level	Grade

Languages

Detail below any foreign language proficiency, which may be tested at interview: Proficiency: F=Fluent / C=Conversational / B=Basic

Language	Qualifications	Date	How often/when language used	Indicate proficiency

Hobbies/Interests please list

[ ]

Skills

Please indicate experience gained or training received in the skills listed below and provide an example of how you have used the experience or training.

Administration

Entertainment

Caring for adults or children (e.g. child care, nursing, social work)

Please give an example of when you have provided excellent customer service

Please describe an occasion when you have met and exceeded sales targets

What does teamwork mean to you?

Please give an example of when you have successfully worked in a team and the role you played

Please tell us how you manage your time and what systems do you use

(Please continue on separate sheet if necessary)

GENERAL

Is there any period in your life when you lived away from home to work overseas? Please give details

Why would you like to work on our overseas programme?

Health Please give details of any diagnosed medical conditions (e.g. Epilepsy, Diabetes, Asthma, back trouble, long-term medication, etc)

Number of days illness in last 2 years (and reason)

If you would like your application to be passed onto different departments within our organisation, please tick here.   YES [   ]   NO [   ]

References Please give two work references including current or most recent employer.

IF SELF EMPLOYED GIVE CUSTOMER/SUPPLIER CONTACT. PLEASE PROVIDE FULL ADDRESS INCLUDING POSTCODE. (CONTACT WITH CURRENT EMPLOYER WILL NOT TAKE PLACE UNTIL AN OFFER IS MADE)

Name   Job Title

Company Name
Company address

Company Telephone No

Name   Job Title

Company Name
Company address

Company Telephone No

I certify that the information given in this application is accurate and I understand that if any of the above information is subsequently found to be incorrect, my application may be rejected, or my employment may be terminated forthwith.

Signature   Date

Please ensure that you have answered all questions that relate to the position(s) for which you have applied.

This application form, which will be treated in confidence can be returned by e-mail to overseas.recruitment@firstchoice.co.uk **or by post to: Overseas Recruitment Team, First Choice Holidays PLC, First Choice House, 1st Floor, London Road, Crawley, West Sussex RH10 9GX. Telephone us on 01293 588528.**

Working overseas for other travel service providers

Winter employment

The opportunities for winter employment will be illustrated with the example of the Thomson Travel Group, which has over 2000 staff working in overseas positions. The brands currently available from Thomson include Crystal Holidays, which runs award-winning programmes in over a hundred resorts worldwide; Thomson Ski and Snowboarding, employing highly trained staff for short break and long holidays; and Simply Ski, offering chalet holidays of the highest quality in many of the most sought-after resorts. These three brands offer positions as described below.

* *Chalet host/cook.* The role involves keeping things running smoothly and efficiently – cooking, daily cleaning and housekeeping duties, shopping, stock control, budgeting and hosting. There is a need to be friendly, outgoing and enthusiastic.

* *Chalet chefs.* They work in the larger chalets and as part of a team. The role involves running an organised and efficient kitchen – cooking meals, organising the menus, stock control, budgeting and maintaining the highest standards of hygiene. Employees must be flexible and adaptable with good customer-facing skills.

* *Chalet/club hotel assistant.* Hotel Hosts fulfil a variety of roles within the club hotels, from keeping bedrooms and communal areas clean and tidy to serving meals and in some properties running the in-house bar. The job is very demanding and requires applicants to be flexible and team players. Good leadership qualities are also required.

* *Hotel manager.* Managers are required for both winter and summer positions in the club hotels. Applicants for these posts must have had prior experience of working in a hospitality background. They will need to be responsible, approachable and diplomatic with plenty of initiative. Managers are also responsible for motivating their own staff. The day-to-day running of a hotel requires dealing with stock control, administration and accounts. Good knowledge of the local language along with sound IT skills are required.

* *Maintenance person.* Qualified trades people and competent DIY enthusiasts are required to work on the refurbishment of chalets and club hotels during the summer months. Work involves painting, electrics, carpentry and plumbing.

* *Nanny and family nannies.* All nannies need an NNEB, BTEC or NVQ level 3 in Childcare, a diploma in nursery nursing or an equivalent UK qualification. Nannies work in well-equipped resort crèches and clubs, looking after children aged from 6 months to 12 years. A varied programme of activities is organised six days a week along with one night's free babysitting. Family nannies work with families staying in private villas for a specified period. These positions are ideal for nannies wishing to go overseas for a short period only.

* *Children's leaders.* These roles involve looking after children between the ages of 4 and 10 years. The programmes include activities with pick-up and drop-off times from the ski school.

Activities are also arranged three evenings a week. Leaders are required to have had experience of working with children before. Plenty of energy, a great imagination and creativity are required. These are very demanding roles and require sensitivity towards children and their environment. All the roles that involve working with children require a check for a criminal record.

✱ *Office staff*. Occasionally, vacancies occur for general administrative and accounts-based staff to work overseas. Qualified accountants and people with financial or accounting backgrounds with good IT skills are best suited. Language skills and knowledge of database packages are always an advantage.

Other overseas employment

Jobs in hotels and catering

There are many opportunities to work in hotels, restaurants and bars. Roles in hotels can vary from being a kitchen porter to being one of the front-of-house staff. Generally, the work is quite hard and the hours long and unsociable. However, there are some perks involved in working in the hospitality and catering industry overseas, as it is usual that accommodation and some meals are free.

Learning the language and having the opportunity to live and work in a busy and dynamic environment can be quite exciting.

Ski chalet staff

Many ski operators provide ski chalet staff. Their role is to cook meals for the group of people who have booked into the accommodation. This involves preparing breakfast, making packed lunches, baking cakes for afternoon tea and cooking a three- or four-course evening meal. The chalet must also be cleaned inside and out. Snow clearing also falls into the duties of ski staff, because it is important to keep footpaths and access routes to the chalets clear. Although hard work, the main perks of this job are some free time to ski, along with free accommodation and food.

Ski and snowboard instructors

There are many excellent opportunities to work in Europe and America for fully qualified ski and snowboard instructors (Figure 8.4). However, competition for jobs is high and only fully qualified instructors are considered.

Car hire operators

There are hundreds of car hire operators, among which you may have heard of Avis, Hertz, Alamo, EasyCar and Holiday Autos. Jobs with car hire operators call on a range of talents and skills, such as customer service representatives, drivers,

Figure 8.4 Competition for jobs as instructors is high

administration, marketing and cleaners. Most operators provide job opportunities in all parts of the world.

Employment on the move

Adventure travel leaders

Many adventure travel companies use expedition leaders. Tours can vary according to the size of the group and the type of trip. Destinations can range from the Sahara Desert to the Amazonian rainforest.

Proficiency in a foreign language is useful for this. It is also usually necessary to be able to drive groups of people or heavy goods, so both a Passenger Carrying Vehicle (PCV) licence and a Heavy Goods Vehicle (HGV) licence are appropriate.

Cruise ship employees

Cruise ships are often likened to floating resorts, or housing a complete city at sea! The biggest three cruise companies are Royal Caribbean International, Princess, and Carnival. There are also many smaller cruise lines, some of which specialise in particular geographical regions or themes. Figure 8.5 shows the new cruise ships launched in 2003.

There are more than 300 types of job on cruise ships. The majority are involved with catering – such as working in bars and restaurants. However, several cruise companies offer more unusual employment opportunities, such as working in spas, hairdressing, fitness or aromatherapy. Some cruises are organised around a theme, so that lecturers, musicians, dancers or comedians might be required. Roles also exist for cabin stewards and assistant pursers.

There is a clear definition or hierarchy of employees on cruise ships. The officers on board enjoy a superior class of both accommodation and leisure time.

OPERATOR	SHIP'S NAME	PASSENGER CAPACITY
Princess Cruises	Coral Princess	1950
MSC	Lirica	760
Radisson Seven Seas Cruises	Seven Seas Voyager	700
Princess Cruises	Island Princess	1950
Princess Cruises	Diamond Princess	3000
Carnival Cruise Lines	Carnival Glory	3850
Holland America Line	Oosterdam	1800
Royal Caribbean International	Serenade of the Seas	2500
Costa Cruises	Costa Mediterranea	1057
Norwegian Coastal Voyages	MS Midnastol	Small
Orient Lines	Ocean Voyager	2300
Crystal Cruises	Serenity	1080
Star Cruises	SuperStar Sagittarius II	4000
Royal Caribbean International	Mariner of the Seas	3000
Costa Cruises	Costa Fortuna	2720

Figure 8.5 Cruise ships launched in 2003

Ferry employees

There are many ferry routes travelling to and from the UK. Employment opportunities include stewards, service staff (shop workers and cleaners) and child carers. Some of these roles are seasonal because the busy holiday periods call for additional staff.

Airline employees

Cabin crew jobs remain a popular choice for many travel and tourism students. The thought of travelling extensively with free time in exotic locations is often the main motivation for prospective employees. Each airline has its own training policies and clear candidate requirements for cabin crew – such as (for obvious practical reasons) specific height and weight proportions.

Flight crew jobs are much sought after. Some airlines train their own pilots, but there are other options to train, either privately or in the armed forces.

Independence, though, is just one of many qualities we look for in our cabin crew. You'll combine it with a real flair for service, a genuine interest in people, and have broad responsible shoulders. In short, you'll be the kind of person who knows how to make passengers feel like they have star quality.

To work with us, you'll be:
- 19–33 years old
- a minimum 158 cm (5 ft 2 in) in height
- educated to GCSE standard or equivalent
- fluent in both spoken and written English
- a holder of an EU (EEA) passport
- in good physical health
- a confident swimmer.

You'll also need:
- a strong customer service ethic
- a positive, approachable personality
- a supportive approach to teamwork
- a passion for living life to the full.

The company offers good pay and benefits, including a generous concessionary travel scheme.

1 Decide which are the most important qualities required by Virgin to become a cabin crew member. Are there any extra points you think should be added?
2 Why is there a height requirement?
3 Did you know that Virgin Atlantic also employs in-flight beauty therapists? What other in-flight jobs do you think might become desirable in the future?

Jobs on coaches

There are thousands of coach companies in Europe alone. Drivers must adhere to the law and not drive for more than a certain number of hours without having a break. It is also their responsibility to keep coaches clean both inside and out. Some coach companies also employ couriers, tour managers and guides.

The role of a coach courier is very similar to that of a resort representative (see page 296),

except you are constantly travelling! The duties include looking after all the passengers, giving a commentary on the route and of all the sites along the way, meeting and organising with the relevant contacts for services and facilities throughout the trip (such as hoteliers, visitor attractions and restaurants), and possibly organising extra excursions or trips.

Couriers need to be great problem-solvers. They need to be confident and able to deal with emergencies that can occur at any time.

CASE STUDY

The Guild of British Coach Operators

The Guild of British Coach Operators (www.coach-tours.co.uk) is an association of top-quality operators dedicated to providing customers with a first-class service. They provide:

• luxury coaches for charter throughout Britain and Europe

• a comprehensive travel management service.

At the same time they offer:

• guaranteed commitment to the highest standards from all the guild's members

• a wide geographic spread of members across the UK

• 24-hour back-up from all member operators.

1 Using the guild's website, find *three* coach companies that operate from your area.
2 Make a list of where they travel to.
3 Do they use couriers or guides on board?

Jobs on trains

The European train routes with Eurostar are perceived as the glamour routes and therefore much sought after. Eurostar travels through the Channel Tunnel at speeds approaching 186 mph.

The tunnel actually consists of three interconnected tubes – one rail track each way and a service tunnel. It is about 51 kilometres (32 miles) long, and 37 of those kilometres are under water to an average depth of 45 metres (150 ft)! The crossing time from London to Paris is 2 hours and 35 minutes, while London to Brussels is 2 hours and 20 minutes. It is now also possible to take the train from Waterloo International in London or Ashford in Kent to Marne-la-Vallee which is in the heart of Disneyland Paris.

Eurostar is well known for its quality and service. Each train has up to fifteen attendants who are hired and trained in catering and must speak fluent English. All attendants must wear the Eurostar uniform which was created by a French designer called Balmain (Figure 8.6).

Figure 8.6 An advertisement by Eurostar

Sport and leisure organisations

Plenty of overseas work opportunities exist for individuals with specific talents, such as working as a DJ or entertainer. Similarly, coaching sports activities such as football, rugby and cricket can be called upon by many organisations. This section will describe three possibilities for overseas employment: PGL, Camp America and Holidaybreak.

PGL

PGL takes its name from the initials of the man who started the company in the 1950s – Peter Gordon Lawrence. He began activities from the Wye Valley and later expanded into the Brecon Beacons National Park. Activity holidays were organised for 6- to 18-year-olds. During the 1960s and 1970s the business grew and PGL became one of the first UK organisers of canoeing holidays in the Ardeche Gorge in the South of France. Today there is a permanently staffed headquarters at this site.

After continuing expansion during the 1980s, the work of PGL now involves both multi-activity and specialist holidays. The organisation's market has also expanded from the child/youth market to include PGL family holidays. Some of the courses now available are: educational tours for schools, IT, field study, sailing, canoeing, windsurfing, mountain walking, skiing, cultural tours. PGL is recognised by all the major activity organisations (e.g. the Royal Yachting Association and the British Canoe Union).

There are fifteen centres in the UK and nine in France. Employment opportunities include: drivers, coaches for sports and other activities, administration, nurses/first-aiders, site assistants. The following is an example of a tuckshop/domestic role available in France:

'Positions are available to work at our centres in Northern France from February until November and from April to September in Southern France. The positions include a range of domestic duties associated with the cleanliness and upkeep of a PGL centre. In addition you will be involved in the day-to-day operation of the tuckshop facility including the recording of stock and balancing the financial accounts. Full training will be provided for this position, including health and safety training in COSHH and manual handling. You will have the opportunity to participate in your centre's activities during your free time.'

Camp America

Camp America is a cultural exchange founded in 1969. It is part of the American Institute for Foreign Study that organises and arranges programmes all over the world. In 2003, nine thousand people travelled from various countries to work for Camp America.

The summer camps involve working for nine weeks. Camps can have between 100 and 400 campers and each one is themed (e.g. Religious, Girl Scouts, Learning Disabled, Day Camps, Speciality Sports). The job roles available vary according to the camp, examples being sports coaching, language teaching, and camp counsellors. However, a great deal of enthusiasm and a desire to work with 6- to 16-year-olds is essential. In return, workers are given free food and accommodation and the opportunity to travel around America after the camp.

Holidaybreak

A popular and cheap holiday experience for many families is a self-drive camping trip. Those provided by Eurocamp and Keycamp are particularly popular as tents are already erected and all facilities are provided. Opportunities also exist for staying in caravans and lodges.

Today, both Eurocamp and Keycamp are part of Holidaybreak plc which is the market leader in self-drive, self-catering holidays in over 200 of the biggest campsites in France, Italy, Spain, Germany, Holland, Croatia, Luxembourg, Switzerland and Austria.

Holidaybreak recruits for the two brands Eurocamp and Keycamp in a variety of job opportunities, both in the UK and overseas. The following are typical of the roles that have to be filled: area assistants, couriers, children's couriers, montage/demontage assistants (tent erecting and dismantling), repair and maintenance assistants, warehouse administrators, overseas trainers, team leaders, accommodation couriers and resort representatives. Figure 8.7 shows the requirements for a resort rep.

Holidaybreak requires Representative for Regaldive Resort

- To provide assistance and information to resort guests.
- To ensure the smooth running of all aspects of the resort in co-operation with local agents, hotels and dive centres.

Your duties will include:

- producing vouchers for hotels, transfers and dive centres and welcome information for guests, notice boards, resort books and excursion information
- meeting guests in a timely and courteous manner
- working closely with the local agent to train and monitor transfer staff and other representatives in the resort
- to be responsible for accounts issues
- to ensure timely credit card authorisation
- liquidation of excursions booked with local agents
- ensuring payment for dive bookings
- monitoring resort expenditure and income for resort accounts
- to be responsible for health and safety checks, including general maintenance checks for building works or other factors that may affect guests in the resort
- handling all problems in the resort including medical emergencies.

Attitude/skills required

- Excellent communication/interpersonal skills
- Excellent organisational skills
- Ability to adapt and work in another country
- Ability to work on own initiative
- Good team player
- Computer literate

Figure 8.7 A job advertisement from Holidaybreak

Theory into practice

1 Using a search engine, locate the PGL website and find details of all the types of job opportunities with the company in France.

2 Using a search engine, locate the Camp America website and research what other countries Camp America operates in.

3 Visit www.holidaybreakjobs.com to find further information on employment roles.

4 Compile two lists: (a) all your current skills and abilities, and (b) the skills and abilities you would need to *acquire* in order to carry out the role of a resort rep for Holidaybreak.

✳ REMEMBER!

From the Holidaybreak case you can see that the role and duties of a resort representative cover a wide and often demanding remit. You must remember that even if you are working in a beautiful part of the world there may still be detailed operational practices and administrative tasks to be completed. The next section looks at such tasks.

Personal qualities, values and attitudes

The purpose of a rep is, as the name suggests, to represent his or her company. Reps are the 'front line' in the liaison process. They become the public face for a tour operator and the main focus of attention for holidaymakers. It is therefore essential that a rep acts in a thoroughly professional manner *at all times*.

Basic matters

Representatives are typically given a uniform, which they must keep clean and wear when on duty (Figure 8.8). Whenever they visit specific cultural or religious sites they must also adhere to any dress code in force, such as when entering shrines or temples. Maintaining a 'corporate image' in both attitude and appearance is vital. Loyalty to the company must be displayed.

Figure 8.8 Crystal reps in their working uniforms

Staying out late at night or drinking alcohol at inappropriate times is definitely uprofessional behaviour for a company rep. All reps must remember that they remain in the public eye whenever they are in a resort, even when they are not on duty.

Reps must display good common sense and a sense of humour in a variety of unusual situations. These can range from a holidaymaker's antisocial behaviour to adverse weather conditions preventing normal leisure pursuits.

Adapting to a foreign environment

Living and working overseas can be very exciting. However, as with any new job there are associated pressures and stresses involved with acclimatising to the new environment.

You may find yourself in a country where there are seasonal differences. For example, summertime in the UK runs between June and August, but in Australia it is from December to February! Reps may also experience challenges whilst coming to terms with cultural differences. This may involve language, dress, religious practices, gestures, superstitions, and mannerisms.

Theory into practice

We often take our cultural background for granted and assume that everyone else does the same as us. They don't! Read the following examples and then find five more examples from around the world.

Superstitions

In the UK
- number 13 is unlucky
- breaking a mirror brings seven years' bad luck
- walking underneath a ladder brings bad luck.

In Holland
- it is lucky if your nose itches (good news is expected).

In China
- the number 4 is unlucky.

Expressions

In Holland, an insult might be
- 'fat as a toad'.

In Spain, it might be
- 'fat as a whale'.

In Germany, it might be
- 'as ugly as the night'.

Developing independence and confidence

Living and working in an overseas country can sometimes be quite a lonely experience. Leaving friends and family behind can be quite difficult, particularly if you don't speak the language fluently.

Some of the larger tour operators try to place new representatives in the major resorts where there will be bigger teams. There is also the opportunity to make contact with local suppliers such as hoteliers, restaurant owners and the coach drivers. Essentially, confidence and independence will grow as a rep becomes more familiar with his or her surroundings. Having a network of contacts and friends to assist you whilst working overseas is useful. These contacts will grow gradually as time progresses.

Think it over ...

As a group, discuss the pros and cons of working as an overseas representative.

Health issues

Tour operators will inform reps of any vaccination requirements. They will also advise new reps on whether it is safe to drink the local tap water and of anything to avoid whilst working in the foreign country. There will be written procedures on what to do if you become ill, with a register of contacts for local hospitals and doctors or clinics. All reps will have contact telephone numbers of their line managers and head office.

Group dynamics

To be able to work as part of a team is vital. Each rep must know who their line manager is and discuss issues with that person. Good teamwork brings a more efficient working environment and can reduce conflicts with holidaymakers and other staff members.

Dealing with large groups of people requires good coping mechanisms and clear organisational practices. Reps will usually want to support each other, and this can be made easier when everyone knows exactly what their job entails and what is expected of them. A good sense of humour is very useful, as is being able to display common sense when dealing with unusual or demanding situations.

It is advisable to learn as much of the language as possible in order to ease work pressure and to foster good working relations within the working environment.

Stress management

Meeting, greeting and remaining smiling and polite all day, every day, can in itself be exhausting. Constantly dealing with holidaymakers (complaining or happy), tiredness, and having to complete a large amount of paperwork each week can lead to a very stressful environment.

Reps therefore need to adopt a flexible approach to life. Getting as much rest when convenient is advisable, as is talking to other reps and being able to contact and liaise with line managers when situations become difficult. Being able to unwind and relax also helps to alleviate the stresses and problems throughout the day. It can sometimes help to talk through problems or difficult situations with other reps. Nevertheless, reps may need to contact head office when issues arise that they find impossible to solve in the resort.

Assessment guidance

For Assessment Objective 1 you must give a detailed description of the overseas employment opportunities that exist, the range of companies offering them, and the personal qualities necessary for working overseas. Your marks will reflect the amount of detail given and your understanding of the range of opportunities available.

Implications of the law for working overseas

With millions of passengers leaving the UK each year to spend their holidays overseas, their safety and satisfaction are of paramount importance for tour operators. Problems can arise at any time and for many reasons. Here are some of the more obvious situations:

* The holidaymaker has an accident and sustains an injury.
* The holidaymaker misses the coach.
* The flight time is changed.
* There is no room on the flight.
* Luggage goes missing.
* The holidaymaker is unhappy with the service.
* The accommodation is unhygienic.
* Building works are continuing on the accommodation.
* There is a lack of expected facilities.
* There are problems between the passengers.
* There are problems with weather conditions.

You can probably think of many more problems that could occur during a holiday.

Naturally, some of the problems that can occur are not the fault of the tour operator, or indeed any of the suppliers in the resort. If a family travels to a ski resort and there is no snow, that is hardly the fault of the resort rep or company. This only becomes an issue if the ski operator guaranteed snow conditions.

If a holidaymaker is on a package holiday and there is a problem with the holiday the first person to contact is the holiday rep. The rep has a 'duty of care' towards the holidaymakers and should be able to deal with most difficulties. However, from time to time problems may not become apparent to the rep immediately. Some holidaymakers who feel unhappy will wait until they get home before complaining.

Dream holiday became Disney disaster

Daily Mail, 6 August 2001

The following is adapted from the *Daily Mail* article.

The flight to Paris would take a little less than 50 minutes. Or so the Woodward family thought as they boarded their British Midland aircraft for a two-day trip to Disneyland. In fact, their exhausting journey lasted more than 12 hours.

A farce beyond even the bungling Donald Duck saw the Woodwards having to board five different planes before they even left England. By the time they arrived at their destination, one of their days was all but used up and they were too exhausted to enjoy the second.

'We could have swum the Channel quicker. It ruined our holiday,' said Diane Woodward last night.'

She and her niece Samantha Hales spent £1,350 on the trip to Disneyland Paris for themselves, her nephew Rhys, seven, and great nieces, four-year-old twins Jessica and Megan. Mrs Woodward is now fighting for compensation after mechanical faults

meant they were turned off four aircraft.

They were planning a full day around the theme park as they boarded a 6.45am British Midland flight at East Midlands Airport, near Derby, on 18 July. But then, as the plane taxied towards the runway the captain announced there was a problem and headed back to the terminal. Passsengers were told to board another plane for the flight.

'We sat there for a while, but then they said someone had left a door open and rain had got into the electrics,' said Mrs Woodward. 'We couldn't believe what we were being told – it seemed so stupid.'

They were told a third plane was being summoned. It took off, but 15 minutes later the pilot gave out a familiar message. 'He said we would have to return to the airport,' said Mrs Woodward. 'People on board started laughing and shaking their heads. Some were quite angry.'

Airline staff next offered passengers the choice of a 3pm service or taking a taxi to Birmingham to catch another flight. She and Ms Hales decided to go for the 1.30pm Air France flight from Birmingham. But after a lengthy taxi journey the family was asked to disembark a fourth aircraft because of fuel problems.

It was only when they boarded a fifth plane at 4pm that they were taken to Paris, finally arriving at the theme park at around 7pm English time.

The family has had an apology from the tour company Pioneer Travel but is now seeking compensation.

A British Midland spokesman said the first two flights suffered 'technical problems'. The third returned as a 'standard precautionary measure' after a warning light was seen on the flight deck. A spokesman for travel agent Ilkeston Co-op Travel said the company was in talks with British Midland about compensation.

Divide your class into two groups, one to represent the Woodward family and one to represent the tour company, Pioneer Travel. Debate this holiday misfortune and try to come to an amicable solution.

CASE STUDY

Representative inaction

This case was reported in *Holiday Which?*

When Hilary Francis and her daughter Carla booked a 14-night Kuoni package to Egypt, they were looking forward to an exotic combination of sightseeing, cruising and relaxing and snorkelling at a Red Sea resort. The total cost of the holiday was £1950. This charge included one night in Luxor, a seven-night cruise, four nights in Hurghada and two nights in Cairo.

The day before Hilary and Carla were due to leave the cruise ship, 58 tourists were massacred at Luxor. When Hilary and Carla arrived in Hurghada, their room at the Three Corners Village Hotel turned out to be shabby, smelt of sewage and had a shower that flooded the bathroom every time it was used. More worryingly, the Kuoni rep that met them at the hotel the day after their arrival was unable to brief them about possible repatriation and said that the holiday was to continue as planned.

They later discovered the Kuoni guests in other Red Sea resorts were being given the option to fly home. Concerned about the tense situation, Hilary repeatedly tried to contact the rep to ascertain the current position, without success. When the rep eventually came to the hotel, Hilary and Carla, trying to make the best of their holiday, booked an excursion to a local island for snorkelling. But although they waited at their hotel for an additional 45 minutes after the scheduled collection time, no transportation arrived.

The rep telephoned the hotel later to say that the bus driver had forgotten to collect them. He promised to come to the hotel during the day to refund the money, eventually arriving at 9.30 p.m. when he confirmed that they would be collected at 7.30 a.m. the next morning to be taken to the airport for their transfer to Cairo. On arrival at reception in the morning, they discovered that no transport had been arranged and that the rep was nowhere to be found.

Having little alternative, Hilary asked the hotel to call them a street taxi. This arrived in a dreadful condition and was filthy both inside and out. As two women journeying alone, they were understandably terrified about travelling unaccompanied in an unapproved vehicle, especially in light of the recent Luxor shootings.

Back in the UK, Kuoni responded to their catalogue of complaints with a basket of flowers and an offer of £100 (later increased to £200) in compensation.

1 Write a letter to the tour operator complaining about the holiday from the holidaymakers' point of view.
2 Itemise how you as a company representative would have dealt with all the negative issues highlighted in the *Holiday Which?* report.
3 With the help of *Which?*, the two holidaymakers notified Kuoni that they had provided an inadequate service and an inadequate hotel, which meant they were in breach of contract. Eventually, after some disagreement, Kuoni was taken to the Small Claims Court, where the judge agreed that Kuoni had not provided appropriate service and accommodation and the holidaymakers were awarded £1686.76 in damages and £104.90 costs. Discuss the approach taken by Kuoni. Why was it necessary to go to the Small Claims Court? What effect might this action have on the tour operator?
4 Try to find other cases that have been settled in the Small Claims Court.

Fortunately, for all travellers leaving the UK there are many laws and regulations in force to protect them. A resort rep needs to be aware of these laws and regulations and of any contractual obligations of the tour operating company.

Trade organisations

In the UK there are several travel trade organisations that exist to aid their members through promotion and financial protection. These organisations include the Association of British Travel Agents (ABTA) and the Association of Independent Tour Operators (AITO). Both ABTA and AITO have codes of conduct for their members. These codes are broadly a list of minimum standards for operating a travel business.

Association of British Travel Agents

In 2004, ABTA had 1800 members, made up of both travel agents and tour operators. There is a code of conduct for each type of business. The codes aim to ensure that customers receive the best possible service from the time of booking through to after-sales service. This covers the information clients are given and the way complaints are dealt with.

ABTA deals with around 60 000 enquiries per year on all travel-related subjects. There is a useful website giving details of the work of ABTA, its code and a full listing of its members. All ABTA members are given an ABTA number, so a holidaymaker can easily check to see whether a company is a member by logging on to the website – www.abta.com.

The following information is extracted from 'ABTA Building Confidence in Travel'.

Complaints

ABTA provides assistance to clients having complaints against companies that carry the logo. The quality of the holidays and services provided by ABTA companies is crucial to the reputation of the industry, as ABTA tour operators and travel agents are responsible for the sale of the vast majority of package holidays.

Financial protection

ABTA-regulated travel agents and tour operators must comply with strict financial rules. These rules are to protect customers' money and allow the companies to make sure that claims are paid in the event of the failure of a member company.

You can book your holiday knowing that if an ABTA-regulated tour operator or travel agent has financial difficulties while you are on holiday, you should be able to continue as originally planned – and in any event, ABTA will ensure you get back home. If you haven't already started your holiday, you'll get your money back or be given help to make alternative arrangements for the holiday to proceed. Many ABTA tour operators also provide bonds to the Civil Aviation Authority under the ATOL scheme (see page 159).

> **Key term**
>
> A **bond** is a formal undertaking with a bank, insurance company or other official body to pay money in the event of a company failing.

Advertising

ABTA members must not mislead with their advertising and must include all compulsory charges in their prices.

Booking procedures

Before a booking is finalised, an ABTA member must:

* give you accurate information to help you choose the travel arrangements that are right for you
* follow all the necessary legal requirements such as the ATOL regulations and must make you

aware of the terms and conditions that apply

* give you guidance about any health, passport and visa requirements
* ensure all special requests are dealt with properly and confidentially, such as for a disability or medical condition
* notify you if the Foreign and Commonwealth Office has issued advice about the intended destination.

Once a booking has been made, an ABTA member must notify you as soon as possible of any changes or cancellations to the travel arrangements. If the ABTA member makes a significant change, you must be offered the choice of accepting the changed travel arrangements or having all your money back.

If an ABTA member does cancel your booking or makes a significant change to the travel arrangements after the date for payment of the full price, you must be offered compensation – unless the reason for the cancellation or change was outside the control of the organisation.

An ABTA member must notify you as soon as possible of any serious building works at your destination. If you wish, you can transfer to another holiday or cancel and have your money back.

Complaints

If you have a complaint about your travel arrangements you should write to the ABTA member concerned, who will provide you with a full reply within 28 days. If you remain dissatisfied you should write again pointing out the areas of dispute. Again the ABTA member must respond within 28 days.

If you fail to reach a mutually satisfactory position, you can have the matter resolved through the ABTA arbitration scheme. ABTA takes the issue of code breaches very seriously and may take disciplinary action against a member found to have breached the code. There is a Code of Conduct Committee, which has independent representation to consider cases.

> **Key term**
>
> **Arbitration** is a process to resolve disputes.

Figure 8.9 The ABTA website is well worth a visit

Spend some time examining the ABTA website, which is an excellent resource for students of travel and tourism (Figure 8.9).

Association of Independent Tour Operators

AITO is an organisation that represents approximately 160 of Britain's specialist tour operators. Most of these are owner-managed. All members of AITO must provide the highest level of customer satisfaction by adhering to the Quality Charter. All companies admitted to AITO have been checked and must be fully bonded. The AITO code of business practice makes provision for:

✳ ensuring clear holiday descriptions

✳ the use of customer questionnaires for monitoring standards

✳ raising awareness of the importance of responsible tourism.

Locate the AITO website and find out more details of the association's Quality Charter.

Acts and regulations

Trades Description Act

The Trade Descriptions Act 1968 is a law in England and Wales which prevents companies from misleading consumers as to what they are spending their money on. Holiday reps will need to check hotels and other types of accommodation for accuracy against the description in the company's brochure. Obviously if there are any discrepancies then the company must be informed in order that it can print an amendment. If the company does not act it may be in breach of the Trades Descriptions Act.

Consumer Protection Act

The Consumer Protection Act 1987 aims to protect consumers against misleading prices on goods, services, accommodation or facilities available. Therefore, if a holiday is promoted at a certain price in a holiday brochure and the company then tries to increase the price by adding surcharges, the Consumer Protection Act is breached.

The Act applies to all goods and services except some that are specifically exempted. It covers all sectors, whether private, public or co-operative. The provisions of the Act are compensatory in nature. It gives the following rights to consumers:

✳ the right to be protected against the marketing of goods and services that are hazardous to life and property

CASE STUDY

Two holiday disasters and what to do

Tour operator or airline goes bust while you are on holiday

If it is a package holiday and involves air travel, check that the operator holds an ATOL (Air Travel Organiser's Licence) – a scheme that is run by the Civil Aviation Authority. ATOL was set up in 1972 to protect travellers from losing money or being stranded abroad.

Airline loses your luggage

Before leaving the baggage claiming area, a visit to the baggage handlers' desk or office must be made to complete a Property Irregularity Report (PIR). Keeping copies and records of the PIR and the baggage tags will help with locating the luggage. It should be remembered that luggage should always be labelled clearly, carefully and securely.

Devise a holidaymakers' checklist. Identify as many contacts as you can (with their websites) that would help a holidaymaker should something go wrong before, during or after the booked holiday.

* the right to be informed about the quality, quantity, potency, purity, standard and price of goods or services so as to protect the consumer against unfair trade practices
* the right to be assured, wherever possible, access to a variety of goods and services at competitive prices
* the right to be heard and to be assured that consumers' interests will receive due consideration at appropriate forums
* the right to seek redress against unfair trade practices amounting to unscrupulous exploitation of consumers
* the right to consumer education.

Sales of Goods and Services Act

The main acts which cover your rights when shopping or buying a service are the Sale of Goods Act 1979 and the Supply of Goods and Services Act 1982 (amended by the Sale and Supply of Goods Act 1994). Goods must be of 'satisfactory quality' – this means that they must not have any defects (unless the defects are brought to the attention of the buyer). Goods and services must be 'fit for their purpose' and they must be 'as described'. For example, holiday accommodation cannot be described as 'beside the sea' unless it actually is very near to the seashore.

EC Package Holiday Regulations

The Package Travel, Package Holidays and Package Tours Regulations came into force in 1992 (Figure 8.10). The regulations are available from the Department of Trade and Industry (DTI). They are aimed at giving people who buy package holidays protection when things go wrong – allowing them the opportunity to seek compensation. The regulations do not apply just to big companies or professional organisers, but also to anyone who organises packages (whether or not they make a profit – this can include clubs, business or holidays). The regulations add to the protection already in place for consumers – namely the Trades Description and Consumer Protection Acts.

The regulations are quite complicated. The actual term 'package' is defined as something that must:

* be sold or offered for sale
* be sold at an inclusive price
* be pre-arranged
* include a minimum of two of the three elements of (a) transport, (b) accommodation, and/or (c) other tourist services (not ancillary to transport or accommodation) accounting for a significant proportion of the package.

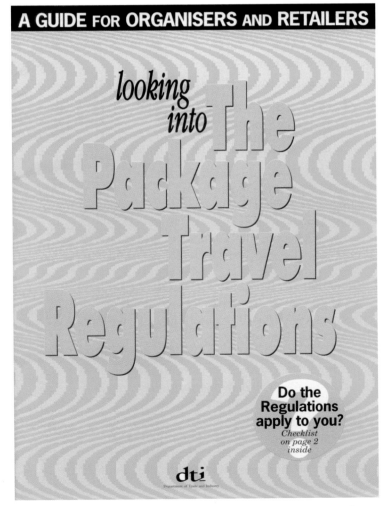

Figure 8.10 One guide available from the Department of Trade and Industry

The regulations cover these aspects:

* Brochures and advertising must be accurate and not misleading.

* The name of the organisation or individual putting together the package must be made known to the customer. The organisation or individual then becomes responsible for any failure of the package or for any part that is not delivered.

* Contracts must be clear and (if in form format) complete.

* If prices are changed the customer must be informed immediately.

* If cancellations occur or terms are changed, such as itineraries altered, the customer must be informed immediately.

* Financial security must be proved.

Think it over ...

1 Mr Smith organises day trips to gardens and charges a single price for the transport and entry fee. Is this a package?

2 Mrs Jones organises fly/drive holidays. Is this a package?

Theory into practice

Obtain a copy of *A Guide for Organisers and Retailers* (pictured in Figure 8.10) from the DTI or your library. Read the sections that cover the definition of a package. With a partner, design a leaflet that is entitled 'Package Travel Regulations'. The aim of the leaflet is to educate tour operators who put together package holidays.

CASE STUDY

Holiday woes

This case was reported in *Holiday Which?*

When Anthony and Pauline Barrett's son decided to get married in Barbados, they saw it as a chance to take a once-in-a-lifetime holiday to coincide with the wedding. They booked a two-week package for themselves and their three teenage daughters at a cost of £2500.

Their choice of holiday was influenced by the fact that their apartments were said by the brochure to feature air-conditioning. However, on arrival at the holiday complex they discovered that the air-conditioning unit in the apartment their daughters were to share didn't work. As a result, the temperature rose, making sleep impossible. Although the fault was reported to the Airtours rep on six separate occasions, the unit could not be repaired. The only option was for all five members of the family to sleep in one room, which they did for 12 of the 14 days. This unacceptable arrangement resulted in a great deal of inconvenience and lack of privacy for everyone. To make matters worse, Anthony and Pauline had to move their daughters' beds to and from the apartments every day to allow cleaning to take place.

To add to the problems, for most of the holiday there was extensive building work in progress in the immediate vicinity of the apartments and by the swimming pool. The constant noise and intrusion made it unpleasant to use the apartments or the swimming pool during the day.

The holiday that the family had looked forward to so much had turned into a complete disaster, although fortunately their son's wedding ceremony – which was held in a different complex – lived up to all their expectations.

The Barretts lodged a complaint with Airtours on returning to the UK and were offered compensation of £160, which they refused. They contacted *Which?*, and the organisation

wrote to Airtours. The offer was increased to £500, but *Which?* still felt that this was an inadequate sum and negotiated with Airtours to increase the figure to £750, which the Barretts agreed to accept.

The issue is that the Package Travel Regulations of 1992 make it clear that facilities advertised in a tour operator's brochure form part of the holiday contract. If advertised facilities are not in fact available, or are not up to scratch, for whatever reason, then you are entitled to recover compensation from the tour operator for breach of contract.

Either visit your library or look up details on the Internet for the *Holiday Which?* site. Try to find other case study examples where holidaymakers have not received the holiday they expected, and find out which Acts and Regulations are relevant to those cases.

Unfair Contract Terms Act

The Unfair Contract Terms Act came into force in 1977. It makes provision for a consumer to be able to dispute any contract that is felt to be unfair or unreasonable. In some instances contracts can be difficult to read (with plenty of small print) and may even be quite ambiguous.

The Act places a number of restrictions on the contract terms businesses can agree to. It lays down rules for the ways in which businesses can use certain terms:

* Excluding liability for death or injury is not permitted in any circumstances.

* Excluding liability for losses caused by negligence is permitted only if it is reasonable.

* Excluding liability for defective or poor-quality goods is permitted only if it is reasonable.

The Act does not give a precise definition of 'reasonableness', but a court would usually consider:

* the information available to both parties when the contract is being drawn up

* whether the contract was negotiated or in standard form

* whether the purchaser had the bargaining power to negotiate better terms.

Generally, businesses will not have the same protection as individual customers. For example, a consumer contract excluding liability for defective goods or services would be automatically invalid. As a general rule, people buying a holiday should always check their contract, and the operator putting together the contract should be equally as careful. The Office of Fair Trading (OFT) has the power to assess a complaint made about the fairness of any contract term drawn up.

Theory into practice

Using a search engine, find the website of the Office of Fair Trading. Visit the site and read more about the Unfair Contract Terms Act 1977.

Assessment guidance

To meet Assessment Objective 2, you will have to write an account of travel legislation, which shows that you are able to apply your knowledge to the interpretation of legal requirements. There are many useful contacts for sources of information on the Acts and Regulations relating to travel and tourism. You are advised to collect as much information on this as possible, using some of the following sources: ABTA, AITO, Citizens Advice Bureaux, the Trading Standards Department, the Office of Fair Trading, the Department of Trade and Industry, BBC's 'Watchdog' programme, and *Holiday Which?*

Administrative working practices

This section looks at the administrative working practices of an overseas representative. A methodical approach to work is essential by keeping notes and files in order, retaining copies of reports and full details of lost or stolen property.

Pre-season tasks

Before the season starts, it will be the job of the representative to check hotels or self-catering apartments for health and safety problems.

Representatives will need to complete a form if there are any problems, such as dangerous fire escapes, dirty kitchens or broken tiles in the swimming pool.

Before guests arrive, it is the role of a rep to meet the local suppliers. It is imperative that a rep gains a good working relationship with these local people, as they will become the rep's contacts during the whole holiday period. These local contacts will include hotel managers and staff, tourist information centre staff, coach companies and drivers, doctors/hospital contacts/clinic contacts, and local agents.

A rep must be able to prepare a noticeboard for holidaymakers, and it is essential that this be kept up to date as the season progresses. The board should display the rep's contact details. The brochures and leaflets used on the board must be altered according to the day and time of the activity and must be clear. It should contain details of excursions and entertainment on offer in the resort, as well as departure and flight details for guests. The noticeboard should never be just a dumping ground for silly pictures. It is a PR opportunity for the company and the rep can create a positive visual communication source by keeping it colourful and informative.

Theory into practice

1 With a partner, choose an overseas destination and then try to collect appropriate brochures and information from the Internet or from a travel agent.

2 Design a colourful noticeboard at least A3 in size, with all the information you can find from the resort. If you have recently been on holiday you can also use personal photos or memorabilia to enhance the display.

Reports

There are a variety of reports an overseas representative must become familiar with. Here are some examples:

* transfer check report form – completed at the end of each transfer

* weekly hotel report – completed for each hotel

* excursion returns – competed weekly
* representative's report form – completed when there has been a complaint, and forwarded to head office
* customer service report form – completed by the client wanting to register a complaint
* compensation in resort – completed by a rep and signed by the client when compensation is given actually in the resort (e.g. for over-bookings or delays)
* medical assistance forms.

Other documentation includes:

* authorisations for debit/credit cards (when a client wishes to pay by credit or debit card for an excursion)
* the rep's expenses – completed each week.

Representatives may also have to administer questionnaires and surveys in order to monitor quality control in the resort. Questions might cover the accommodation, food and overall service (including that from the representative). These comments are fed back to head office, where they are analysed so that the company can continue to offer a good product and service. Should there be a problem with a hotel/apartment or its services, then the company can investigate and act accordingly. It is in the interests of both the rep and the company to ensure that all holidaymakers receive the products and services they have paid for. A customer who has had an unsatisfactory experience is likely to complain, ask for a refund, and will probably never re-book with that company.

Theory into practice

Design a brief questionnaire suitable for a resort representative to hand out to holidaymakers. The questions should aim to find out whether they are happy with the resort and with the rep's services. Keep the questions simple and short, because a long-winded questionnaire stands little chance of being completed by holidaymakers (with the exception of complaints!).

Operational working practices

This section looks at the operational working practices of an overseas representative. This is one of the most rewarding and challenging jobs in the travel and tourism industry. There will be the opportunity to meet many new and interesting people and deal with exciting and challenging situations. The main purpose of the job is to ensure that all holidaymakers in the resort are looked after and given every assistance during their holiday. The main functions involved are: brochure descriptions, hotel information sheets, rooming lists and passenger manifests.

Reps must visit the appropriate accommodation (hotel, apartment, villa etc.) to ensure that everything is in order, and then meet the new holidaymakers and accompany them to their correct accommodation. They should check that coach signs are clearly visible and clean.

The representative's welcoming meeting

Tour operators train all representatives in the art of preparing for and conducting a welcoming meeting for holidaymakers. During the meeting the rep will give out vital resort information and notify the holidaymakers of the details of excursions they have booked.

A rep may have to conduct more than one welcoming meeting in a day, depending on how many new clients have arrived in the resort. Sometimes a welcoming meeting is hosted by more than one rep – they might take it in turns to explain about the different aspects of the resort and accommodation. They can also draw the holidaymakers' attention to the noticeboard and explain any procedures for emergencies.

Assessment guidance

To satisfy Assessment Objective 4 you will be asked to perform a welcoming meeting (real or simulated). The following text covers some of the issues you should consider.

What you will need

The meeting room

The rep must liaise with the hotel manager to arrange the use of a suitable room or venue to hold the meeting. It is important that there be no distractions whilst conducting the meeting, so it is preferable that there isn't any untoward noise from outside.

Equipment

If a PowerPoint or slide presentation is to be made, the rep must check that the equipment is working, particularly if it is hired from the hotel. The rep must also check that there is a reliable socket and ensure that it is at a safe and sensible distance to function successfully. There must also be enough chairs for all guests to be able to sit comfortably.

Posters can be used to draw attention to particular aspects of the resort, along with brochures and leaflets from local visitor attractions and restaurants.

Some reps like to use a flip-chart or overhead projector (OHP) whilst talking. These may be provided by the accommodation venue. Reps may decide to give handouts to the holidaymakers – excursion details, posters, photos or general resort leaflets.

Some tour operators arrange for holidaymakers to receive a 'welcome drink'. Once again it is the rep's job to organise these drinks, and provide non-alcoholic alternatives.

Time-keeping

It is important to keep to time. A rep should be enthusiastic and lively but not take too long so as to bore the audience. There may also be a time limit on the availability of the room, as well as the rep having to move on to other duties.

Meeting content

Here is a typical 'agenda' for a welcoming meeting:

* *Introduction*. Each rep should introduce himself or herself, also giving a brief explanation of his or her role and outlining details about the tour operator.

* *Purpose of the meeting*. Explain what is going to be covered over the next 15 minutes or so.

* *Details of the accommodation*. This will cover facilities available, such as the swimming pool, bar and restaurant. It is also necessary to cover issues of health and safety, such as what to do in an emergency or if an accident occurs. An explanation of emergency evacuation details

and where to find extra information and refuge points must be given clearly.

* *Country information*. Some general country information can be followed by resort information. The general information might cover the resort's local history, health precautions, details of local chemists, water safety, electrical voltage, food, facilities for children, banking hours, post office hours, etc. Here handouts/leaflets can be incorporated.

* *The noticeboard*. Draw attention to the noticeboard, explaining the contents and how often it is updated. Some tour operators ask reps to compile a company file that gives details on the resort and tries to cover all aspects of the holiday and resort.

* *Excursions*. Clear explanations should be given of the types of excursion, where and when they will happen, the cost, and why they might be worth doing.

* *Questionnaires*. Hand out the tour operator's customer satisfaction questionnaire.

* *Question and answer session*.

* *Closing statement of welcome*.

Figure 8.11 gives additional advice on points to remember.

Theory into practice

1 Make notes for your welcoming meeting. Put the main points on index cards to help aid your memory.

2 Design an eye-catching poster for an excursion. This can be used during your own welcoming meeting.

Communication skills

It is essential for an overseas rep to develop excellent communication skills. Other than face-to-face communication, there are three methods that reps have to master: communicating on the telephone, in writing and over a public address system of some kind.

Telephone communication

Being confident in making telephone calls and taking clear messages is essential. Making bookings and confirming details is often done quickly via the telephone. The correct use of telephone communications helps to relay information in an emergency and keep both up to date and in touch with head office.

Written communication

Written communications are an essential part of a rep's role. Legible handwriting is required

---

- Look smart – wear your uniform and name badge
- Don't rush, and stick to your plan.
- Try to make the meeting as interesting and lively as possible.
- Try to look around the room whilst talking.
- Speak clearly and not too quickly.
- Don't talk for too long when selling excursions. Outline clearly the main benefits.
- Make sure all the points are covered. It sometimes helps to make notes on small postcards that can act as prompts.
- Explain how to fill in booking forms for excursions.
- Ensure clients know that assistance will be given to them if required.
- Always leave time for a question and answer session. If you are asked a difficult question don't make up the answer. Explain that you will find out as soon as possible.
- Ensure guests know where to find you.
- Round up the session with a few closing points covering the meeting.

Figure 8.11 Points to remember whilst conducting a welcoming meeting

particularly when dealing with compensation issues and bookings. Attention to detail is vital. The Internet is also a quick and useful method of keeping in touch with other accommodation sites, head office and suppliers. Many reps are given a laptop computer in order to help speed and standardise reports, so good computer skills will be required.

Public address

Most reps will at some time have to use a microphone, so training will be given in good technique. The three golden rules of using a microphone are:

* do not shout

* do not speak too quickly

* use a good clear tone of voice.

Figure 8.12 offers extra advice for making an announcement to a group using either a microphone on a coach or a public address system.

---

1 Plan what you are going to say.
2 When ready, alert the group that you are ready to speak.
3 Give a clear and concise message.
4 Repeat the main points.
5 Thank the group for listening.
6 Pause, allowing time for any questions.

Figure 8.12 Tips for using a microphone

Selling excursions

Selling excursions authorised by the company through a local approved agent is one of the main tasks of a rep. This is where valuable commission can be earned on every sale made.

> **Key term**
>
> **Commission** is the percentage of income made from the sale of a good or service.

Before the season starts, it is essential that reps experience these excursions themselves in order to be able to advise clients precisely on what will be provided. It is useful to know if there is a steep climb along the way, or where exactly the toilets

are en route. Passing on this type of information helps clients to gain a better picture of the excursion and prevents complaints when they return.

The tour operator will give training on selling excursions, and the holidaymakers' welcoming meeting is an ideal opportunity to do the selling. However, if a rep has never sold anything before there are a few golden rules to remember:

* Always make the excursions sound interesting. The rep should try out each excursion so as to be able to speak from experience and explain many of the extra sights and sounds of a trip.

* Give details on when the excursion is happening, where is it going, what can be seen and why someone should visit.

* Be clear about how much it will cost.

These points should be covered for each excursion. Reps should always allow time for questions and give assistance if a booking form needs to be completed.

Finally, a rep will need to collect any monies required for the excursion. Attention should always be paid to the correct details required for taking and securing of money.

Customer service skills

As with all travel and tourism businesses, there are many types of customer a rep will need to deal with. These customers are (a) internal and (b) external. Examples of each are:

* *internal customers* – other representatives, supervisors, head representatives, resort manager and office manager

* *external customers* – hoteliers, apartment owners, local agents, coach companies and drivers, guides and tourist information staff, and so on.

Problem-solving

Dealing with the general public on a daily basis inevitably means dealing with some problems. Most holidaymakers simply want to enjoy their trip. Of course, some things will from time to time go wrong. Occasionally a rep will come across someone who makes a habit of complaining (known as a 'professional' complainer).

There will be many genuine problems, such as a client losing a passport or a serious medical emergency. Whatever the situation, a rep must be able to remain calm and deal confidently with the issue. Sometimes there is more than one solution to a problem. Each tour operator will endeavour to train its reps to deal effectively with any problems that arise.

Problems that have to be dealt with fall broadly into two categories – those concerning the holidaymakers, and those related to the rep's employment and relationships with management and other company employees.

Here are some typical problem situations concerning the holidaymakers:

* flight delay, coach late or breakdown
* missing luggage
* one of the party missing
* medical problems
* personal property stolen
* drunkenness and/or rowdiness
* irate holidaymakers
* a holidaymaker arrested by local police
* a holidaymaker with specific requirements – diet, or needing special access to buildings.

Here are some typical issues concerning the rep's situation:

* relationships with other reps
* time off from duty
* length of time working – expected hours and the actual number worked
* pay
* contractual issues
* accommodation problems/sharing and space issues
* poor supervision and lack of contact with the line manager.

As you can see there are plenty of opportunities for problems to occur. However, as with most jobs in the travel and tourism industry, good training and a confident manner will always help in every situation.

Be prepared!

There are many ways to help prepare for certain situations. Figure 8.13 presents a useful checklist.

1. Always check all information carefully. If there is anything that does not make sense, check with a senior rep, suppliers or head office.
2. Anticipate situations, keep alert to everything.
3. Double-check arrangements – contacts with hotels, coach companies, flight times and numbers.
4. Always keep all contact telephone numbers with you.
5. Be punctual.
6. Never leave things to the last minute – always be prepared!

Figure 8.13 Tips on being prepared

Dealing with complaints

All representatives will from time to time have to deal with customer complaints. These might be made directly to the rep or indirectly to a hotel manager or supplier. Sometimes complaints are made instantly in the resort, while others are made in writing or by telephone to the company after the holiday is over.

Dealing with and rectifying complaints is dealt with in detail in unit 2. However, Figure 8.14 presents a basic guide for reps.

1. Listen carefully to the holidaymaker. Sometimes it is a good idea to write down the problem.
2. Make an apology for the holidaymaker's inconvenience.
3. Empathise with the holidaymaker. It is important not to simply sympathise with the person until the situation has been completely investigated.
4. Be clear on the specific problem. This may involve asking questions.
5. Investigate the problem.
6. Find a solution.
7. Agree a solution with the holidaymaker.
8. Follow up the complaint. Ensure that procedures have been put in place as promised by you. Monitor the situation to prevent further complaints.

Figure 8.14 Tips for dealing with complaints

Role-play with a partner, one person taking the part of holidaymaker, the other the rep. Take it in turns to deal with the complaint.

Scenario one
A customer has just arrived at the hotel and has gone to her room to unpack. She returns immediately to confront you. The room has not been cleaned. The beds are unchanged, and it looks as though someone else is still using the room.

Scenario two
The flight from Manchester has just arrived. You are meeting and greeting three groups and forwarding them to their coaches for onward transfer to their hotels. One couple arrive with a surfboard. Unfortunately, the coach driver will not allow the board to be taken on to the coach, and there is insufficient space for the board to fit in with the suitcases.

To gain good marks for Assessment Objective 3, you will need to use research from a broad range of sources to produce a thorough account of working practices, both administrative and operational, including dealing with complex situations when working overseas. Your evidence must convey an understanding of real industrial practice in this area of travel and tourism.

1 Name the four largest outbound tour operators.

2 List five employment functions available at outbound tour operators.

3 Explain the term 'vertical integration'.

4 List the different type of overseas representative roles.

5 What is the role of the Guild of British Coach Operators?

6 Explain the term 'ancillary tourist services'.

7 How did PGL get its name?

8 List the contacts a rep will make whilst in a resort.

9 Detail the points to remember whilst conducting a welcoming meeting.

10 Outline the procedures for dealing with a complaint within a resort.

11 Explain the meanings of AITO and ABTA.

12 Write brief summaries of the following: Trades Description Act, Consumer Protection Act, Sales of Goods and Services Act, EU Package Holiday Regulations, Unfair Contract Terms Act.

13 List useful sources for finding extra information on the above Acts and Regulations.

14 What do the initials OFT stand for?

15 List the attributes required to be a successful children's rep.

Resources

You will find the following useful:

* ABTA – www.abta.com

* AITO – www.aito.co.uk

* Trading Standards – www.tradingstandards.gov.uk

* Air Transport Users Council – www.auc.org.uk

* Holiday Travel Watch – www.holidaytravelwatch.com

* Civil Aviation Authority – www.caa..co.uk

* Confederation of Passenger Transport – www.cpt-uk.org

* Food Standards Agency – www.food.gov.uk/news/newsarchive/food

* Travel health issues – www.masta.org

* World Health Organisation – www.who.int

* Office of Fair Trading – www.oft.gov.uk

* Foreign and Commonwealth Office – www.fco.gov

Index

Page numbers in *italics* refer to illustrations, those in **bold** refer to definitions